Edwin John Ellis, William Blake

The Works of William Blake

Poetic, symbolic, and critical.

Edwin John Ellis, William Blake

The Works of William Blake
Poetic, symbolic, and critical.

ISBN/EAN: 9783337036591

Printed in Europe, USA, Canada, Australia, Japan

Cover: Foto ©Thomas Meinert / pixelio.de

More available books at **www.hansebooks.com**

THE WORKS

WILLIAM BLAKE

Poetic, Symbolic, and Critical

EDITED WITH LITHOGRAPHS OF THE ILLUSTRATED
" PROPHETIC BOOKS," AND A MEMOIR
AND INTERPRETATION

BY

EDWIN JOHN ELLIS

Author of "Fate in Arcadia," &c.

AND

WILLIAM BUTLER YEATS

Author of " The Wanderings of Oisin," " The Countess Kathleen," &c.

" Bring me to the test
And I the matter will re-word, which madness
Would gambol from "

Hamlet

—

IN THREE VOLS.

VOL. II

LONDON
BERNARD QUARITCH, 15 PICCADILLY
1893

INTERPRETATION

AND

PARAPHRASED COMMENTARY.

THE SYMBOLIC STRUCTURE OF THE MYSTICAL WRITINGS.

BEFORE reading the paraphrase, a glance may be given at the chart facing page 8, which shows the way in which the division of the various poems into books and chapters follows the division of their contents into various classes of fable and symbols corresponding to Head, Heart, and Loins, and the fourfold symbolism of the Zoas. It cannot properly be understood until the reader has mastered the poems themselves, but a partial understanding will help him to feel their coherence of structure and to see them as a whole instead of as a succession of unrelated fragments. One or more typical incidents are taken from each chapter of the poems, and placed in compartments by themselves in such a way as to show in each poem a continuous story running through the gamut of Head, Heart, Loins, four times repeated, or through as much of that gamut as the story requires. In many of the poems there are several such stories. We have been content in most cases to choose the more important. In " Milton," and occasionally elsewhere, more than one are given.

In the first chapter of " Milton," Milton, the masculine, spiritual potency, descends into corporeal life. In the second chapter (which is under the emotional feminine Heart, Ololon), the feminine spiritual potency follows him, that he may not lose altogether the world of emotional beauty, and she, too, grows corporeal. In the Head division of the Head, Palamabron, the imaginative mind, tries to do the work of Satan, the external reason, and brings about in the Heart

division of the Head, a mournful inactivity, for this great
mistake shuts the mind out from emotional joy. In the Loins
division of the Head, external reason, taking upon itself the
separated life of vegetative things, wars upon the paradisiacal
emotions. In the Head division of the Heart, the falling
light, Lucifer, the intellectual or formative portion of the
emotional life descends to organize the external reason into a
personality—into an image of that unity or self-consciousness
of God, whose abode is in the heart, that it may be saved
finally from the indefinite. This personality is itself shaped
in six stages, which correspond to the first six eyes of God,
already described in the chapter on the Covering Cherub. The
giving of personality to the reason takes place also in the
fourth chapter of "Vala" and of "Urizen." The fourth
stage of all things is constructive. The corporeal life is
completed in three stages, but when the fourth comes "the
form of the Fourth" begins to be imprinted on the clay.
The same story is revealed in the incidents tabulated from
"Jerusalem." In the first chapter, which is under the head,
the winter of materialism and corporeal life covers man, and
Divine love, or Jerusalem, is absorbed in Vala or corporeal
love. In the second chapter, tabulated under the Heart, the
Divine Family, or the passive imaginative moods and affections
descend, like Ololon in "Milton," and try to draw humanity
back into the world of imagination, but in vain, for they are
not masculine-inspired energy, and can only soothe, not change,
the will of man. They are a pleasant rest, but man must
wait the fire of God before he becomes regenerate. In the
incident taken from the third chapter, "Affection," Luvah
becomes generate in turn, and threefold fallen man is completed. But now in the fourth chapter the Divine personality
descends into him and he arises into imagination. This story
is identical with that of the fourfold story described in
"Milton," but it stretches further and carries mankind to the
personality of God instead of to the mere semblance of that
personality forced by God upon the reason. The first of the

nine divisions of Vala begins with the entrance of Los and Enitharmon into corporeal life, and the arising out of that life of the spectral reason.

In the second night corresponding to the Heart of the Head, this reason builds round them the beautiful external and feminine or passive world. In the third night the spectral reason wars with its emotional nature, as we have seen Satan in "Milton" war with heaven. The third stage tends always to be a combination of the first and second. Its great symbol is Virgo-Scorpio, the hermaphroditic monster who expresses vegetative life. In the fourth night the reason is forced to take on a personal shape. In the fifth night, or in the Heart of the Heart, Orc, or the love of that beautiful external world built in the second night, is born from Los and Enitharmon. Time and space and all outer things begin to live and move. Reason is awakened by this new energy and begins to explore his kingdom of outer nature. He wanders with a globe of fire—the personal energy, and goes through a series of strange circles from east to west, which symbolizes, among much else, the ever recurring incarnations of man's personal mind. The result of his explorations, or reasoning about outer things, is the creation of restrictive law (a net). In the seventh night (the Head of the Loins), the tree of knowledge or of external nature overshadows all, the mortal body or corporeal personality follows in the fourth stage from the maturing of the mental personality. In the eighth night, corresponding to the Heart and the Loins, a human or imaginative personality is given to mortal love on the fourth night, after its birth from the Heart of Enitharmon. On the ninth night the merely mortal life is completed and ended. Europe, America, and the Song of Los follow, and are tabulated in one line, for they make practically one poem. In Africa (Head) the religions are made, and the emotions are brought under the sway of abstract thought. In Asia (Heart) emotional life gains dominion. In America (the third stage) England, the reason, contends with America its emanation, as

the spectres do with their emanations in the third night of
"Vala." In Europe we get the North (the womb) in its evil
aspect of restrictive external reason and necessity confining
human energy until it breaks away at dawn. Had the chart
permitted, the four poems might have been tabulated under
the cardinal points as follows :—

S.	W.	N.	E.
Africa	America	Europe	Asia
Head	Loins	Womb	Heart

They give when arranged as above a more coherent story,
and repeat the history of the Churches given in the chapters on
the Cherub. In Africa the reason makes laws and religions.
In America the reason is in turn conquered by the emotions and
bodily life (America), a conquest corresponding to the flood,
the closing of the Western gate, and the sinking of the Atlantic
continent. In Europe the mind travels through the Northern
darkness of matter. In Asia it arises into the Eastern dawn,
and the bodily life itself grows joyous or imaginative, and the
dead bones of reason are clothed with emotion. Each poem
is, however, complete in itself. In "Urizen" the first chapter
describes Urizen becoming spectral. In the second he hides
himself with the opaque passive or feminine nature (compare
Second Night of "Vala"), and in the third chapter he tosses
about in this opaque nature. In the fourth chapter he is fixed
into a personality by Los, or, to take the symbol from another
point of view, fallen mind is divided into states or moods
by Time. In the fifth chapter Enitharmon or ideal space
emanates from Los, and the chaos, which in the second chapter
surrounded Urizen, is made mental by being associated with
purely ideal life. In the sixth chapter Orc is born of Time and
space. In "Vala" he is conceived in Night V. Had "Vala"
been divided into "Days" his birth would presumably have
been given on the sixth. It is foretold in Night V., l. 63, and an
account of his youth is then given as though he were already
born, as the poem requires his presence as an understood and

developed personality for Nights VI., etc. He corresponds on the chart to the energy that enables Urizen to explore his world in the Sixth Night of "Vala." In the seventh chapter of "Urizen"—the first of the vegetative triad of chapters—the succession of moods or states made in the fourth chapter becomes restrictive and is symbolized as a chain of days and nights. In the eighth chapter the community of mental spaces summed up under the name Enitharmon grow restrictive also, and are symbolized as a net, and Urizen's sons, the children of vegetative space, as those of Los are of ideal Time, are born; and in the ninth chapter—Loins of the Loins—become wholly corporeal, or in other words, become the multitudes of unimaginative people, who make up the mass of the world's inhabitants. "Thel," a fourfold book, begins not as the other books do for the most part with the chaos of fallen reason. In its first chapter "Thel" talks with the spiritual personality of beauty typified by the lily; in its second—the Heart of the Heart—she talks with the cloud, the fleeting and formless emotions; and in the third—the Loins of the Heart—with the worm, the vegetative instinct in its weakest and most innocent form. In the fourth chapter—the Head of the Loins—she explores for a moment the purely vegetative world of mortality and bodily completion typified by his own grave.

In "The Book of Los," also a fourfold book, Los begins his personality in the first chapter by separating it from the selfhoods or spectres about him. In the second he organizes the void or feminine into elements, a like action to the division of chaos into spaces, in the corresponding chapter—the fifth—of "The Book of Urizen." In the third—the vegetative stage—he sleeps in the world of Tharmas. In the fourth he begins his great contest with the now completed feminine or external world by fixing the reason into the midst of passion, an action which is the other aspect of his chaining Orc in the corresponding chapter of "The Book of Urizen." This action is another instance of that symbolism which makes the third stage always a bringing together of the first and second. Urizen enters external life in the first, Orc enters it in the second, not in his own form, but feminine, so considered in relation to Urizen,—and not here only so perceived (compare "Vala," Night VIII., l. 82), and in the third they are fastened together, that the more living may vitalize the less.

In the first chapter of "Tiriel," Tiriel loses his emanation and so grows spectral; in the second he comes into contact with the emotional life; and in the third he rests in a gentle vegetative forgetfulness for a while. In the fourth chapter he is sustained by Ijim, who fulfils for him an office like that of Los when Los makes Urizen personal, and then, reinforced by the personal fire of Ijim, Tiriel curses or casts the restrictions of space upon his sons in the fifth chapter. In the sixth chapter he curses his daughter Hela—sight—the only sense left to him, and his sight ceasing to be imaginative becomes vegetative. He is now wholly cut off from the spiritual world and stumbles on his way to the caves of Zazel—corporeal life in its absolute unredeemed form. He passes on in the next chapter, &c., to the same emotional life he had approved in the second, but now that he has ceased to be imaginative it drags him into that sleep of outer things from which he can only wake when a last judgment has passed over him.

"Ahania" is a threefold book. In the first chapter Urizen wars with Fuzon, his more passionate side, compacting himself into a spectre. In the second he slays Fuzon with outer necessity, feminine nature, symbolized by a great stone—Sinai. In the third, Fuzon is nailed to that Tree of Mystery whose growth is described also in the last three nights of "Vala."

"The Death of Abel," "The Visions of the Daughters of Albion," and "The Mental Traveller," not being divided into chapters are excluded from the chart, but they, like the various chapters of the foregoing books, could be divided and again divided according to the symbolism of Head, Heart, and Loins.

CONTENTS OF VOL. II.

THE "Songs of Innocence," like the book of "Vala," begin with Tharmas. But it is the innocent Tharmas whose face Vala blesses, whose flocks give her companionship and whose rivers grow reeds well fitted for the pen that should write what "every child may joy to hear." He is now quite different from the "false tongue" or "sense of touch" to whom the spirit of Forgiveness and Imagination was sacrificed. The portion of "Vala" which begins with Night IX., l. 384, shows the return of nature, now the "sinless soul," to the state of innocence.

The symbolic element in the songs is slight, delicate, evanescent. Here, more even than elsewhere, the heavy tread of the interpreter is oppressive. Even the "Little Black Boy," however, cannot be understood, unless it be taken as part of the general mystical manifesto that runs through all the work. In this poem Man's heart and imagination need, we are told, to be exercised for a while on the dark things of the five senses with their seemingly solid and opaque world around. Man is then the little black boy, taught by mother Nature underneath the tree that is the Vine in its good aspect, and becomes Mystery when Priesthood perverts this teaching. The mother, who is the "vegetative happy,"—Mnetha herself,—points to the East while she teaches symbolism. The sun is the signal of Love, that paradoxically manifests itself by giving us a cloud, the dark body, to screen us from Himself. By death or by inspiration we shall presently be free of it, and then it will be seen that the white boy is also the inhabitant of a cloud as

much as he who is outwardly dark. Compare "Jerusalem,"
p. 14, l. 34, and "Vala," Night IV., l. 255, where the
daughters of Beulah—the mild emotions of the bodily regions
—speak, and explain in the same manner as this song the
"garments of Luvah," as the "cloud" or mortal blood is
there called.

In the "Little Boy Lost" symbolic vision is again as
evident as in any of the Prophetic Books. Here the "Little
Boy" is lost, for a while, because the movement of the Light,
as the "Father," is too swift for the mind clogged with body
to follow. He does not at best see the Father otherwise than
as a vapour, and even this flies from him, and leaves him in
the darkness of fleshly growth, which becomes increasingly
"opaque,"—to use Blake's later term. The region of the
darkened West, the shadowy Female, is indicated by the signs
night, and *dew,* as the Adamic Red Earth is by the *mire.*

In the "Little Boy Found," the flying vapour is separated
from the Father and shown to be,—when alone,—only the
fen-light, "wandering,"—the "false morning," as it is afterwards called in "Vala." God appears in the Human form,
which, to the little boy, seems that of his father and leads
him to his mother. Mnetha has become Enion, who loses her
own children in her own element. The Father gives back to
her those who are not advanced enough to leave her, for until
the experience of the lower nature, or senses, is completely
matured, the higher should not be permitted to separate, lest
empty abstraction, and the solitude of the Spectre in Entuthon
Benython and Udan Adan, be the result, and not the ultimate
unity only to be reached through experience and brotherhood.

In the next song but one, the "Divine Image," or "Similitude," is described,—that which he "ceases to exist" whe
"ceases to behold" ("Jerusalem," p. 38, l. 12).

It is this Vision against which "Self-Righteousness" harden
itself "conglomerating" ("Jerusalem," p. 13, l. 52).

In the song called "Night," all the terms are used i
symbolic sense, as in the prophetic books. It relates th

power of the passions, whether devouring loves or destructive angers, when mind has gone down into the darkness of experience from the light of imagination, as when " Urizen fell as the midday Sun falls down into the West" ("Vala," Night VI., l. 258). The last verse tells of regeneration. The lion is Rintrah, with the companion symbol "gold," and stands for the re-risen Urizen. The lions and tigers, &c., are "animal forms of wisdom" ("Vala," Night IX., ll. 701, 830).

The "Infant Joy" is the same referred to in "Vala," Night I., l. 48, and "Jerusalem," p. 22, l. 22.

In "A Dream," the next song, a story is told of insects that is evidently the same as that of the "Little Boy Lost." The "human forms" of these insects are referred to, for when they feel, God feels, Humanity, who "suffers with those that suffer" ("Jerusalem," p. 25, l. 7), and "Man looks out in tree and herb and fish and beast," for these contain the "scattered portions of his immortal body" ("Vala," Night VIII.1.553, &c.).

When the dead wake these scattered portions, furious forms of Tharmas, humanize, with joy,—"Vala," Night IX., l. 607, —their description is in the lines immediately preceding— 590-606.

The song, "On another's Sorrow," is practically an explanation of "Night," as the words,

> ". . sit beside the nest,
> Pouring pity in their breast,"

indicate, with their parallel expression,

> " Pour sleep on their head,
> And sit down by the bed."

The former line being the subject of the first illustration to the First Night of Young's "Night Thoughts."

In the last, the "Voice of the Ancient Bard," the symbolic intention of all is made clear. Morn is identified with the Image of Truth. The word Image here explains the use of the term Imagination, as equivalent to Christ as a spiritual body divinely present in each heart. Doubt, Clouds, and

Reason are words used precisely in the same sense as in the Books where the Reasoning Power builds Vala, identified with the Shadowy Female, from whose clouds, which are blood, doubts are not to be suffered to rise up. That is to say, Tharmas, whose evil aspect is that of the sunset, or blood-red spirit of Uncertainty, is not to be permitted again to kill Imagination, the Saviour.

Songs of Experience.

In the Introduction the Bard speaks out more clearly. Many visions had been seen and some prophetic books written between the date when these songs were engraved (1794) and that of the previous collection (1789).

The Bard speaks with the voice of the East, the sunrise, when in a golden cloud it renews, for earth, the golden age; when Luvah walked from the hands of Urizen in the shadow of Vala's garden ("Vala," Night IX., l. 371), and, speaking the holy word among the ancient trees, called the lapsed soul from the evening dew (l. 384), and showed her that she was sinless (l. 450), and was not, as had been supposed, Sin, though she became such when separate from Man (ll. 619, 620).

But Vala answers that while Jealousy has power, the night is not yet over, nor the morning come. In her all the females of the Prophetic Books speak, and the sin of all the males, as well as their own, is evident. The darkness which belongs to the state when "the masculine separates from the feminine, and both from man"—still has power. This is "Experience."

"The Clod and the Pebble" brings out, for the first time in Blake's writings, a principle that must never be lost sight of, for if it escapes notice, the stories of his myths, and the alternately reproving and affectionate language in which he addresses or describes his personages—the "states and spaces"—cannot be understood. This principle is found in the great idea, that everything can be seen in a good or an evil aspect, yet its individuality remain the same.

Holy Thursday pleads that this world be made more like the world of imagination,—that things should be on earth as in heaven,—though Blake has said elsewhere ("Vision of the Last Judgment") that until after the Last Judgment had passed on each of us this could not be.

But in the "Little Girl Lost" we return to symbolic utterance. This and the companion poem are fitting counterparts to those of the little boy. The little girl is that Innocence who from time immemorial has had no need to fear the lion. But the end of the story is new. The parents do not reclaim the child. They make common cause with the lion. Their own lost innocence is found when they cease to be jealous. They go after the girl, as "Milton" went, in "self-annihilation."

The "Chimney-Sweeper" is symbolic too, though it is none the less practical. The expression "clothes of death," reveals the intention. The chimney-sweeper is not merely a sooty child —though he is this also. Blake is not merely indignant at the treatment the child gets—though he is this also. The chimney-sweeper is Oothoon in disguise, shut up in Bromion's caves, till "all from life" the child would be "obliterated and erased," if God were not "within and without; even in the depths of Hell." The parents, meanwhile, go to church to make themselves "drunk with the cup of Religion" that is offered by "Mystery."

The Nurse who sings next is undoubtedly symbolic. She speaks with the voice of Envy. The use of the word "disguise" as connected with "winter and night"—that is to say with Urizen in the North—is technical in the Blake-vocabulary. It appears in "Vala," Night VII., l. 515. In a more literary sense it is used in the half-bitter and half-playful verses quoted here from the MS. book on page

" 'Twas Death in a disguise."

The sick rose and the invisible worm would be understood as meaning love and mortality, whoever had been the author. But in Blake it must be remembered that the howling (or

sexually passionate) storm of night is the whirlwind of the
North,—reverse of that of the South, from which God spoke
to Job,—and the worm is the chain of jealousy.

"The Fly" has always been popular because so easy to
understand, but the lines

> " Art not thou
> A man, like me ? "

have usually been overlooked. The fly also is an "animal
form of wisdom," and is a man, since "every truth is a man.'
That the fly has its rich array, and man his human beauty
from thought, which is life ; but that man may close his inner
gates by error, while the fly may not, are ideas whose recog-
nition is needed to complete our perception of Blake's thought.
He gives them himself in a few impulsive lines that enter suddenly, as though on quick small wings, into a symbolic story
where they would be least looked for (" Milton," p. 18, l. 20)

"The Angel" is no stranger to literature. He is innocence
in the sense of childish ignorance of evil. But Blake's use of
this image is his own. The maiden queen,—the body, the
portion of mind that is female as distinct from the intellect,
whether in man or woman,—hides its heart's delight from
its own simplicity till childhood is over. So the simplicity
flies. Morn, the young imagination, blushes. But jealou
fears take the weapons of Urizen, and in return find that the
have deceived the poor mortal, who is a prisoner in his ow'
armour, till innocence that should have saved him from th
folly of modesty only returns to find him in the helpless purit
of senility.

The "Tiger" is, of course, the tiger of wrath, wiser in his own
way than the horse of instruction, but always, like the roaring
of lions and the destructive sword, so terrible as to be a
" portion of eternity too great for the eye of man."

The " Pretty Rose Tree" explains the worm in the "Sick
Rose."

The "Sunflower" shows love, as the guide to imagination, or
eternity.

The Garden of Love develops Proverb 56 from the
"Marriage of Heaven and Hell."

The little Vagabond comically proclaims what Blake made
his great purpose of mental life,—

> " Therefore, I print ; nor vain my types shall be,
> Heaven, Earth, and Hell, henceforth, shall live in harmony."
>
> " Jerusalem," p. 3.

In " London " we find the purely literary equivalent for the
passage in " Jerusalem," p. 84, ll. 11, 12.

In the "Human Abstract" no reader will now have any difficulty in recognizing Urizen in the North. The myth explains
the connection of ideas which gave rise to the poem. But
the poem helps to explain the myth.

In " Infant Sorrow," the " fiend hid in a cloud " is the
symbol for the natural man, born entirely evil, and needing
continually to be changed into his direct contrary." That this
change is not to come till after the troublous experiences of life
is the truth that makes the helpless child sulky. The expression " sulk upon the breast," being the same as that used in
" Vala," Night I., 1. 178, shows again how often Blake con-
cealed an allusion to the Zoas under the most simple verses.
His great myth was never far from the background of his
mind.

" Christian Forbearance," taken along with the lines on
the same subject in the MS. book, on the errors of friends
and foes, and the sentence in " Milton," extra p. 3, on the
wisdom of expressing anger, is rather of biographical than
mystical interest, recalls the O'Neil descent, and shows the
struggle of " blood and judgment."

" A Little Boy Lost " is suggestive in its title. The poem
is to a certain extent a substitute for that called " The Little
Boy Lost," and is in many ways its counterpart.

The fuller version quoted by Mr. Swinburne from the MS.
book, shows that the central idea of the poem is the binding
of the young imagination by the chain of religious jealousy,

and the demand that the young passions also shall burn in bondage.

"A Little Girl Lost" gives another picture from the same thought. The ferocity only is left out. The little girl's father suffers for her innocent lawlessness, not the child.

"A Divine Image" gives beforehand an explanation of some of the symbols of "Jerusalem." But no single statement covers the richness of the symbolic suggestiveness, whose fulness is not to be recognized till the whole harvest of paradoxes is gathered in and made into "bread of knowledge."

In a "Cradle Song," the use of the word "light" in the last verse is the same as that in the third verse of "A Little Girl Lost." The word "wake" applied to the heart is used exactly as in "Jerusalem,"—in the last verse but two, page 77, the first line of page 97, and in the "Book of Urizen," chap. VII., stanza 2, and elsewhere. Here and in so many other places the technical or symbolic use of a word may be seen gathering firmness, until the whole language had its secondary meaning and each expression looked two ways, like Janus. But as the temple of Janus was only open in war time, so Blake kept his double meaning for the wars of intellect, and did not allow it outside poetry. His private letters, except when they touch on poetic subjects, or contain verses, are to be read exactly as those of anyone else, though unless the effect of mysticism in maturing the mind and giving steadiness to character is understood, they will always be more or less surprising and even incomprehensible.

"The Schoolboy" again pleads for freedom. The distant huntsman who winds his horn in summer time was presumably taking the hounds out for exercise. It is hardly to be supposed that Blake put in this touch out of his own head for literary effect, not remembering what time of year was the hunting season. The note on the horn was probably heard once and remembered with delight as an exhilarating addition to the pleasant warmth of the green lanes, during one of the

ıg country walks in which Blake and his young wife spent
ɔ many hours.

The last verse only brings in the symbolic use of the seasons.
The concluding poem, "To Tirzah," suddenly enters on
ew ground, and the name of a personage of the myth is
dded to general explanatory allusions. The song may be
looked on as an abbreviated form of all the Prophetic Books.
Experience and sense—the female of mind—have closed in
he true intellect, until it seems as though man had a body
istinct from his mind. But Imagination enters the dark
egion,—Jesus dies,—and the chain is broken.

t
t

y
e

ı
s

i
]

It has been suggested that in order to understand the poem "William Bond," we must read the title "William Blake." Then we are to remember that Blake is supposed to have at one time intended to add a concubine to his establishment in imitation of the characters in the Old Testament, but Mrs. Blake cried, and he gave up the plan. There is at least as much to be said against this interpretation as in favour of it.

The fairies and angels are of sufficient importance in the poem to be considered first. In "Jerusalem," p. 13, l. 29, sixty-four thousand fairies guard the southern gate. In p. 36, ll. 34, 37, fairies are named first of the quaternary, and are ravening death-like forms of the elements, and as states permanently fixed by the Divine Power. On p. 63, l. 14, when the giants and witches and ghosts of Albion dance with Thor and Friga, fairies lead the moon along the valley of Cherubim, bleeding in torrents from mountain to mountain, a lonely victim. The fairy that dictates "Europe" is a mocking and cruel little sprite, who demands to be fed of thoughts of love and sparkling poetic fancies.

Fairies need no more explanation. They are small copies of Fuzon. They belong to the South—eyes, marriage. They receive orders from male desire and give it to that of the female. They are true portions of spiritual experience, and have a right to be visible, even when they are "put off" as all states may be, or die and are buried.

Angels of Providence are not necessarily pure, holy, attractive, superior beings. In "Jerusalem," p. 50, ll. 4, 5, there is a Providence mentioned, who is, like the slaughtering commander of the sack of cities and the massacre of innocents in the Old Testament, a "murderous Providence, opposed to the Divine Lord Jesus." But the murdering done is not merely that of the outer spheres of creation where life lives on death, but enters within and destroys the soul with self-righteousness. This "Providence" (for which, perhaps, a more unsuitable name could not be found) is he whom we are told in the New Testament to fear, because after he has destroyed the body he is able to destroy the soul also.

Some attempt may be made now to understand the poem, but it is undoubtedly among the most difficult in the whole of Blake's collected works. William Bond, whom perhaps the girls mean to kill (it is not said how, but may be understood best in a spiritual sense), goes to church and submits his mind to literal dogma, attended by lower spiritual powers of love and vision. But the spiritual strength of the influences of obedience appear in the form of angels, and drive the pretty impulses away. (Urizen's bands of angels and warriors are also bands of influences that can divide and act in groups. "Vala," Night II. l. 21.)

William Bond entered into the darkest of Urizen's clouds, when he is the Primal Priest in the North, and taking to his bed prepared to die—as Urizen himself did more than once. The depressing influences of the obedient spirits stand at his head and feet, and watch his death. He is now in danger of being good for morality's sake, and not for love's sake—and this is death.

On his right hand was Mary Green. But why she is to be identified with Blake's wife if William Bond was Blake it is hard to see. She might at least have been called Mary Bond

—if not Kate at once, if such were the intention. The introduction of the "sister Jane" is also obscure. Blake's sister
formed part of his household at Felpham, but there is no
record of the concubine incident as having to do with his life
there.

Mary, having heard that William loves another, proposes to
be her servant, while this other is to be the wife of William. It
is never supposed that Mrs. Blake made any such impossible
proposition. William accepts this from Mary Green who is
not Mrs. Bond, and explains that the reason is that she is
melancholy and pale. This equally puts Mrs. Blake out of
the *caste*, for she was a bright brunette, and never was known
to be melancholy during Blake's life.

Finding her sacrifice accepted, Mary faints away and
nearly dies. She is laid by William. The fairies go to her.
The angels leave him. William and Mary then love each other
and are happy. William, in the moral of the poem, incidentally hints that Mary was "naked and outcast." Once more,
not Mrs. Blake.

The poem of "William Bond" should be read with the poem
called "Mary." Here is the "Mary Green," though her
surname is not given. Here are lines about Mary—

> " Oh, why was I born with a different face ;
> Why was I not born like this envious race ?"

which occur also in one of Blake's letters from Felpham,
August 16th, 1803, where they are added to and used by
Blake as referring to himself. In the letter the lines run
thus :—

> " Oh, why was I born with a different face ?
> Why was I not born like the rest of my race ?
> When I look, each one starts, when I speak, I offend ;
> Then I'm silent and passive and lose every friend.
>
> Then my verse I dishonour, my pictures despise,
> My person degrade and my temper chastise ;
> And the pen is my terror, the pencil my shame ;
> All my talents I bury, and dead is my fame.
>
> I am either too low or too highly priz'd ;
> When elate I'm envied ; when meek I'm despised.

"This," he adds, "is but too true a picture of my present state. I pray God to keep you from it and to deliver me in his own good time."

Mary, after uttering the lament of the first two lines, says that to be weak and smooth and not raise envy is "called Christian love." But that if you raise envy and plant spite in the tame and weak, "your merit" is to blame. She goes on :—

> "I will humble my beauty, I will not dress fine,
> I will keep from the ball and my eyes shall not shine.
> If any girl's lover forsake her for me,
> I'll refuse him my hand and from envy be free."

Then Mary went out, "plain and neat" in her dress, and people said she had gone mad. She returned at evening bespattered with mire. She sat trembling on her bed, forgetting night and morning, absorbed with the memory of scornful faces. Her own face is a face of sweet, despairing love, mild sorrow and care, wild terror and fear. In this life it shall know no quiet.

This is the "naked and outcast Mary Green," and not Mrs. Blake, but a phase of Blake's own personality that he chastised and cast out in order not to raise envy. He learns from it that not merely art and fame are worthy of love. Then he enlarges the lesson, and loves the spiritually naked and outcast. Here comes the biographical element, for Mrs. Blake's artistic helplessness might perhaps have been among the rejected "states and spaces" who merited love in their humbleness. But "Mary Green" is more than a personage disguised. She is a mood expressed, a State and, as such, of much more universal interest and artistic importance than an individual. "States are combinations of Individuals."

Less quaint than either of these poems is that called the "Crystal Cabinet," with regard to whose meaning the reader of to-day has once again a standard but erroneous interpretation to clear away from the entrance before he can enter in. The "maiden" in the "Crystal Cabinet" has not, it is true, been supposed to be this terrible but nameless female who has

haunted tradition as Blake's bad angel made flesh. If Blake
had only begun "William Bond" more conventionally with
the word "maids" where he has written "girls," even that
poem might have eluded the biographer. The "Crystal
Cabinet" has been the occasion of a yet more unfortunate
suggestion. A foot-note in the Aldine edition explains it as
giving "under a very ideal form the phenomena of gestation
and birth." This is Interpretation at its wit's end, and is
likely to produce more anger than laughter in any real
reader of Blake. It is adopted with amazing gravity in the
last edition of Gilchrist. Mr. Rossetti enforces his idea by
citing the verses from Felpham that tell of Blake's visionary
faculty, as

" Three-fold in soft Beulah's night ;"

and the passage in the "Descriptive Catalogue," telling how
the "Three Men" in his "Ancient Britons," namely, the
Strong, the Beautiful, and the Ugly, "were originally one
man, who was fourfold; he was self-divided, and his real
humanity slain on the stems of generation."

These passages, it is evident, do not support the "gestation"
theory of the "Crystal Cabinet" at all. Some lines in
"Jerusalem," p. 70, l. 18, &c., would have been of more use,
especially as they belong to a date near that when the
"Crystal Cabinet" may be presumed to have been written.
But in spite of the obvious appropriateness none of the early
editors, who had done everything with Blake except (as
charity must needs suppose) read him, have thought it useful
to refer us to the passage.

The whole of p. 70 is appropriate. It begins with the form
of mighty Hand, sitting on Albion's cliffs, threatening Albion.
He has three heads that contradict one another, and it is his
opinion that ideas are nothing, but that all wisdom consists in
the agreement or disagreement of ideas. Bacon, Newton, and
Locke are the presiding spirits of his three heads. Below
these :—

> " Imputing Sin and Righteousness to Individuals, Rahab
> Sat deep within him hid, his Feminine Power unrevealed,
> Brooding abstract philosophy to destroy Imagination the Divine—
> Humanity: a Three-fold Wonder; feminine, most beautiful; Three-fold
> Each within the other. On her white marble and even neck, her heart
> In-orbed and bonified with locks of shadowing modesty, shining
> Beams mild, all love and all perfection, that when the lips
> Receive a kiss from gods or men, a threefold kiss returns
> From the pressed loveliness; so her whole immortal form threefold,
> Threefold embrace returns, consuming lives of gods and men
> In fires of beauty, melting them as gold and silver in the furnace.
> Her brain enlabyrinths the whole heaven of her bosom and loins,
> To put in act what her heart wills. Oh, who can withstand her power?
> Her name is Vala in Eternity. In time her name is Rahab."

She is, in fact, the mass of meanings (most of which are brought together for reference in the chapter on the Symbol of the Worm), that terrible being to whom Job said, "Thou art my mother."

In "Lafayette" the King of France and the Queen are not without points of affinity with the satanic aspects of Luvah and Vala—in which they are doing the work of Urizen-in-North and Rahab. Their positions are not sufficiently developed in these few verses to make it possible to give them their exact place in the great myth, but that they are modern names applied, on a hint given by passing events, to the great groups of the States is evident. They both belong to the destructive. They contain the first elements of the ideas afterwards developed in the part of the "Song of Los" called Asia, where

> " The Kings of Asia stood
> And cried in bitterness of soul,
> Shall not the King call for famine from the heath
> And the priest for pestilence from the fen
> To restrain, to dismay, to thin
> The inhabitants of mountain and plain
> In the day of full feeding prosperity
> And the night of delicious songs?
> * * * *
> To restrain the child from the womb.
> * * * *
> That the pride of the heart may fail,
> That the lust of the eyes may be quenched,
> That the delicate ear in its infancy
> May be dulled, and the nostrils closed up."

Here the "priest" plays the part given to the queen in the poem. The "pestilence" is that same disease of the soul, namely doubt of imagination and belief in nature, equally brought about by fleshly indulgence and fleshly restraint. The "famine" that the kings call for is a famine of spiritual food because they believe that the sword is the supporter of states. Blake held that art supported states because it could be, and should be, used for spiritual advancement on which alone brotherhood could be based. The sword shrunk up the senses of man, and by limiting each individual limited the state.

By looking at all "false starts and variations," which the editor of the Aldine edition says have "complicated" the poem in the MS., we can find in it something more than an "extremely curious" indication of Blake's "conceptions of contemporary history and politics."

Of all history and politics he had only one conception,— that they were visions drawn out in "strong delusive light of time and space," but would yield symbolic significance if looked at through the altering eye that perceives them as though they were of the South and not of the North among mental Regions.

La Fayette is the type of those who are deceived by the tears of Urizen, and who give themselves as agents to tyranny instead of to sympathy, for the tears of Urizen are nets that bind man to his image. The smiles of Rahab have the same effect. Both "restrain" the true man from development into love and life.

The poem began thus—

> " Let the Brothels of Paris be opened
> With many an alluring dance,
> To awake the Pestilence through the city; "
> Said the beautiful Queen of France.

(*Pestilence* was afterwards altered to *physicians*.)

> " The King awoke on his couch of gold
> As soon as he heard these tidings told,
> ' Arise and come, both fife and drum,
> And the famine shall eat both crust and crumb.'

> Then old Nobodaddy aloft
> (*erased*) . . . . and coughed,
> And said, I love hanging and drawing and quartering
> Every bit as well as war and slaughtering.''

The broken line may still be read as containing an indiscreet word or two unfit for poetry as for publication, and the printer may well respect Blake's erasure. Old Nobodaddy has had the pen drawn through him also, but he is here restored because he explains the idea of the King of France by the fact that one name was substituted for the other when the poem was sketched, both having the same meaning, that of the God of Battles and of executions whose attributes of the sword and the gallows were enough to identify him with Satan in Blake's theology. He is " Urizen drawn down into generation by Orc and the shadowy female " in the extra page of " Milton " written many years later.

The poem, as it first formed itself in the author's mind, went on thus—with old Nobodaddy's speech:

> " Damn praying and singing
> Unless they will bring in
> The blood of ten thousand by fighting or surgery,"

and this was hastily crossed out and the verse recommenced.

Or surgery, added to *the physicians*, shows that Blake is not yet far removed from the ideas belonging to the period of the Island in the Moon. His classification of the professions came later. ("Milton," p. 24, l. 60.)

The poem continues:

> " The Queen of France just touched this globe
> And the Pestilence darted from her robe,
> But the bloodthirsty people across the water
> Will not submit to gibbet and halter."

The last two lines crossed out, and the following substituted:

> " But our good Queen quite grows to the ground,
> There is just such a tree in Java found."

The last line crossed out, and the following substituted:

> " And a great many suckers grow all around."

This seems to have been too " curious " as a " view of contemporary history and politics," and though not erased by Blake, has not been published. We see in it a conception of the vegetative world as that into which Ololon could enter in female form, later, but not in a male form without becoming (as Urizen did, under the similar Tree of Mystery) an enemy of the Human (or imaginative) race. (" Milton," p. 36, l. 14.) La Fayette is at last introduced—

> " Fayette beside King Lewis stood,
> He saw him sign his hand,
> And soon he saw the famine rage
> About the fruitful land.
>
> Fayette liked the Queen to smile
> And wink her lovely eye,—
> And soon he saw the pestilence
> From street to street to fly.
>
> Fayette beheld the King and Queen
> In tears of iron bound,
> But mute Fayette wept tear for tear
> And guarded them around.
>
> Fayette, Fayette, thou 'rt bought and sold,
> For I will see thy tears
> Of pity are exchanged for those
> Of selfish slavish fears."

The poem was to end here, but it had not hit the subject in the centre. Blake worried himself to obtain a better rendering for the last verse that should show that he was aiming at something else than rhymed history. He crossed out the last four lines and began—

> " Fayette beside King Lewis stood,
> His captains false around.
> Thou 'rt bought and sold . . . ."

But this brought the lines into too telescopic a compression, and was given up. This was tried—

> " Who will exchange his own fireside
> For the steps of another's door?
> Who will exchange his wheaten loaf
> For the links of a dungeon floor?"

This was re-written with *stone* for *steps*, and it went on—

> "Who will exchange his own heart's blood
> For the drops of a harlot's eye?"

But this was perhaps too historic and not sufficiently joined by symbolic terms to widen meaning. It was crossed out. So were the following:

> "Will the mother exchange her new-born babe
> For the dog at the wintry door?
> Yet thou dost exchange thy pitying tears
> For the links of a dungeon floor.
> Fayette, Fayette, thou 'rt bought and sold,
> And sold is thy happy morrow.
> Thou gavest the tears of pity away
> In exchange for the tears of sorrow."

His dungeon was the net of Urizen, for the next lines are—

> "Fayette beheld the King and Queen
> In tears of iron bound,
> But mute Fayette wept tear for tear
> And guarded them around."

The final intention, to judge by the Nos. 1 and 2 written against these two stanzas, seems to have been that they should be the whole poem, and all the rest should be thrown away as not pointed enough. Unfortunately, the word "tears" was exchanged for "curses," in a doubtful moment, and the symbolic value spoiled.

These verses were written after the "Songs of Innocence," and probably before those of "Experience"; certainly before the "Everlasting Gospel," as their position in the MS. Book shows. The "Songs of Experience" were engraved in 1794, and probably written for the most part in 1793. Lafayette was arrested and imprisoned in the fortress of Olmutz, in Moravia, in 1792. Blake may have written after this incident to give expression to the idea that his real imprisonment dated from his sympathy with the "tears of iron" in which the King was bound. These were "chains of the mind," for "a tear is an intellectual thing."

The expression, "dog at the wintry door," became a permanent symbol for the needs of the flesh. The new-born child was always the spirit of prophecy. The words "bought and sold" enable us to connect these verses with "Vala," Night I., l. 462—written about 1797.

"Every tenth man is bought and sold and in dim night my word shall be their law."

The tears that are chains are necessarily selfish, even where made by delusion from pity. The release is self-annihilation, as taught in "Milton," p. 39, l. 40, contrary of the satanic teaching.

The "Gates of Paradise," soon after the "Lafayette," are of incalculable value as interpreting the Prophetic books. Their "keys" will open the meaning of all the myth, though they will not, of course, explain its story.

The "Songs of Experience" would come in here chronologically, but as they have been placed for convenience with the "Songs of Innocence," some of the shorter pieces may be referred to next that need but few words of comment. The "Chapel of Gold" is not readily placed in the symbolic system because of the swine at the end. From a merely literary point of view it is evidently another form of "William Bond," and of "Mary." The golden chapel is the hot sunshine, in which love was first sought. The pig-stye is the moony night. The pigs are the naked and outcast. The serpent's poison is calumny. Each part of this poem finds its counterpart in the others. It seems to have a second meaning, in an artistic sense. The chapel suggests art, or the Temple of Fame. The serpent must be naturalism, the pig-stye the place to which the visionary artist betakes himself, not because, like the Prodigal Son, he has spent his fortune, but because, having none to start with, he refuses to acquire any in what he thinks, artistically considered, to be bad company.

"Love's Secret" and the "Wild Flower's Song" are laments over the impossibility of perfect unreserve in this world if a quiet life is to be lived. They are counterparts to "Mary," and to the "Visions of the Daughters of Albion," where Oothoon is another name for Mary. The "Golden Net" is the story of "pity seeking dominion" in another form. It belongs, as the "Crystal Cabinet," to the life of Vala who is here seen, not as one virgin three-fold, but as three. The region of the three, it will be noticed, are East, North, West. The Net was disguised in gold to make it seem to be of the South. The idea is,—catch the eye and the man is caught. "What we look on we become."

"Scoffers" belongs to the "Grain of Sand in Lambeth." It explains itself in connection with the symbols in "Jerusalem."

The points of the compass in "Day-break" suggest the journey of Los. He leaves the North, goes through the "terrible East," sees the wars of Urizen and Luvah, and foretells the regeneration of Urizen when he shall arise like the lion in the "Songs of Innocence," whose eyes flowed with golden tears. The Western Path is that towards Eden— outwards every way—in Imagination, and is not here the region of Tharmas, in an evil, dark, vegetative sense.

The "Thames and Ohio" are to be read by their regions only, as East and West, in the sense of Void and Eden, or Urizen and the innocent Tharmas.

"Young Love" naturally precedes "William Bond" and might be put into his mouth at the beginning of his story.

Passing by "Riches," only noting that *world*, *devil* and *earthly kings* are used as equivalents, and passing "Opportunity" as containing no symbolic enigma, and "Seed-sowing" with the reference to the sowing by Urizen in the ninth book of "Vala" —and passing "Barren Blossom," with the note that it must be read with "Milton," extra page 3, we come to "Night and Day," and find ourselves in the presence of the subject of William Bond turned the other way up. Here is no Mary Green, nor Oothoon. Her place is taken by Rahab, the "harlot coy." This is the truth whose contemplation led William Bond into the error of failing to perceive that when seen from another side the same problem would yield a different solution, until Mary's fainting fit at the bedside gave him light. "In a Myrtle shade" is not written merely, as has been supposed, against the chain of marriage and morality, but against that of the flesh itself. Love will not only refuse, when existing in a given lover, to be bound to a woman because this lover is personally united with her in legal marriage. Love refuses to be bound to that other vegetable, the lover's own body, and the mundane shell itself. Love has a right to the "land of dreams beyond the morning star."

"Idolatry" repeats the statement made elsewhere that the classics have the same origin as the Bible, but are perverted as well as stolen from the same sources of inspiration. The "Will and the Way" are the comic equivalent for the sad acknowledgment of the power of reserve in all the romantic poems, which have one single subject wherever found, that it is the nature of bodily tendencies to be frightened at mental enthusiasm, or, as stated in "Jerusalem," the daughters of Albion fly before the Spectre of Los, revealed as undisguised desire, while Los himself dare not approach them openly lest he be vegetated under their looms. ("Jerusalem," p. 17, l. 7.)

Broken Love, the Mental Traveller, and the Everlasting Gospel must be considered more in detail.

THE MENTAL TRAVELLER.

1.

I travelled through a land of men,
  A land of men and women, too,
And saw and heard such dreadful things
  As cold earth-wanderers never knew.

2.

For there the babe is born in joy
  That was begotten in dire woe,
Just as we reap in joy the fruit
  That we in bitter tears did sow.

3.

And if the babe is born a boy
  He's given to a woman old
Who nails him down upon a rock,
  Catches his shrieks in cups of gold.

4.

She binds iron thorns about his head,
  She pierces both his hands and feet,
She cuts his heart out at his side
  To make it feel both cold and heat.

5.

Her fingers number every nerve,
  Just as a miser counts his gold;
She lives upon his shrieks and cries,
  And she grows young as he grows old.

6.

Till he becomes a bleeding youth,
  And she becomes a virgin bright;
Then he rends up his manacles
  And binds her down for his delight.

7.

He plants himself in all her nerves,
  Just as a husbandman his mould,
And she becomes his dwelling-place
  And garden fruitful seventyfold.

8.

An aged shadow, soon he fades,
  Wandering round an earthly cot,
Full filled all with gems and gold
  Which he by industry has got.

9.

And these are the gems of the human soul,
The rubies and pearls of a lovesick eye,
The countless gold of the aching heart,
The martyr's groan and the lover's sigh.

10.

They are his meat, they are his drink,
He feeds the beggar and the poor ;
To the wayfaring traveller
Forever opens his door.

11.

His grief is their eternal joy,
They make the roofs and walls to ring,
Till from the fire upon the hearth
A little female babe doth spring.

12.

And she is all of solid fire,
And gems and gold, that none his hand
Dares stretch to touch her baby form,
Or wrap her in his swaddling band.

13.

But she comes to the man she loves,
If young or old, or rich or poor ;
They soon drive out the aged host
A beggar at another's door.

14.

He wanders weeping far away,
Until some other take him in ;
Oft blind and aged-bent, sore distressed,
Until he can a maiden win.

15.

And to allay his freezing age
The poor man takes her in his arms ;
The cottage fades before his sight,
The garden, and its lovely charms.

16.

The guests are scattered through the land
For the eye altering, alters all,
The senses roll themselves in fear,
And the flat earth becomes a ball.

17.

Stars, moon and sun all shrink away,
A desert vast without a bound :
And nothing left to eat or drink,
And a dark desert all around.

18.

The honey of her infant lips,
 The bread and wine of her sweet smile,
The wild game of her roving eye
 Do him to infancy beguile,

19.

For as he eats and drinks he grows
 Younger and younger every day,
And on the desert wild they both
 Wander in terror and dismay.

20.

Like the wild stag, she flees away,
 Her fear plants many a thicket wild;
While he pursues her, night and day,
 By various arts of love beguiled.

21.

By various arts of love and hate,
 Till the wild desert's planted o'er
With labyrinths of wayward love,
 Where roam the lion, wolf, and boar.

22.

Till he becomes a wayward babe,
 And she a weeping woman old;
Then many a lover wanders here,
 The sun and stars are nearer rolled.

23.

The trees bring forth sweet ecstacy
 To all who in the desert roam,
Till many a city there is built,
 And many a pleasant shepherd's home.

24.

But when they find the frowning babe,
 Terror strikes through the region wild;
They cry: " The babe ! the babe is born ! "
 And flee away on every side.

25.

For who dare touch the frowning form
 His arm is withered to the root ;
Bears, lions, wolves, all howling fly,
 And every tree doth shed its fruit.

26.

And none can touch that frowning form,
 Except it be a woman old ;
She nails him down upon a rock,
 And all is done as I have told.

The Mental Traveller is at the same time a sun-myth and a
story of the Incarnation. It is also a vision of Time and
Space, Love and morality, Imagination and materialism.
Like all the sexual symbols it covers three meanings and
implies the "form" of a fourth. It will bear a separate
interpretation from the point of view of each Zoa, a Urizen
interpretation, an interpretation for Luvah, for Tharmas, and
for Urthona.

It will not be difficult for the reader to whom Blake's
symbolism is no longer a mystery and a confusion, to trace
these meanings. As in most other obscure passages, Blake
in this poem gives us many a hint where to look for the
pages of parallel narrative in the Prophetic Books that throw
light on its meaning. The hints are to be found sometimes
in the picture suggested, and sometimes in catch-words or
technical symbolic terms whose idea is not elaborated here,
but elsewhere.

The land where the Mental Traveller journeys is within us.
The men and women are "affections, children of our thoughts,
walking within our blood-vessels." ("Jerusalem," p. 38,
l. 33.) One of the numerous water-colour illustrations to
Young's "Night Thoughts" in Mr. Bain's volume represents
Luvah and Vala in the act of "going down the Human
Heart." The male and female persons of this poem are,
among others, Luvah and Vala.

In this land are "breeding women, walking in pride,
bringing forth under green trees, with pleasure, without pain,
for their food is blood of the captive" ("Jerusalem," p. 68,
l. 37).

If the babe is a mental emotion, an infant joy showing the
Human Form, he is given to the Nameless Shadowy Female
who, in her ancient form, unites the attributes of Rahab,
Tirzah, Guendolen, Enion, Vala, and all the others. She is,
in fact, the Mundane Shell, Love, being "brought into
light of day in pride of chaste beauty" ("Jerusalem," p. 22,
l. 17).

He is bound on a rock which is a rock of blood ("Jerusalem," p. 83, l. 56) that becomes opaque hardness, covering all vegetated things ("Jerusalem," p. 67, l. 5). The feminine nature drinks up the affections, symbolized as sons of Jerusalem, Dan and Gad (*ibid.* l. 22). These affections are, indeed, the Human Form, Mercy, Pity, Peace and Love being its Regions, now bound, or nailed, down to the rock ("Jerusalem" p. 67, l. 44), or stems of vegetation ("Jerusalem," p. 67, l. 44, to p. 68, l. 9).

This catching of the shrieks in cups is one of the sports of amorous play among those in the wine-press of Luvah who are the human forms of weeds,—so identified are the Rock, Blood, Female, Vegetable ("Vala," Night IX., l. 768, and "Milton," p. 24, l. 38). All this belongs also to war (name of the wine-press), enemy of art, and therefore of Man. It belongs to the separation of the Masculine from the Feminine, and both from Man ("Jerusalem," p. 90, l. 14). When the knife cuts the head it is denial ("Jerusalem," p. 67, l. 24). It cuts off eternity in those who submit to it under the Epicurean Philosophy of Albion's Tree ("Jerusalem," p. 67, l. 13). When it cuts the heart it is love refused in cruelties of holiness that takes the flesh from the victim and examines the infant's limbs ("Jerusalem," p. 68, l. 57). Thus the Woman Old acts to the Infant Joy, as Albion and as Tharmas when in the moral state of morbidity and error ("Jerusalem," p. 22, l. 20, and "Vala," Night I., l. 46).

These show who the child on the rock is. But the woman becomes young, and the child old, by the law that a punisher mingles with his victim's spectre ("Jerusalem," l. 14).

When the result is that both are. of one age, then they change parts, and he turns to Orc at the moment when Orc set himself free and conquered the Nameless Shadowy Female.

As he grows old the wealth of his soul consists of the accumulation of his own smiles and tears. But he is male, and mental, and these things make the joy of others, when he "teaches in song"—as the overworked phrase has it—what he "learned in suffering."

From his mental fire a form of beauty springs that becomes another man's delight. He, like Tiriel, is driven out, having exhausted his masculine—that is to say, mental—potency. It was a part of Blake's belief in the reality of mental creations that they could eject their creator from his own world.

It is now the business of the mind who has done its own work to enjoy another's, as another enjoys his. ("In seed-time, learn ; in harvest, teach ; in winter, enjoy "—" Marriage of Heaven and Hell," first proverb.)

His mental guests, no longer thought of by him, become scattered. His mind alone concentrated them. His cottage vanishes. (Was this written at Felpham ? Compare the expression about the Flat Earth becoming a ball, and the phrase in Mr. Butt's letter, September, 1801.)

What has happened is this. The man has entered a state of mortality, and vegetation drawn down to it by physical love, when mental had fatigued him as the shadowy and other females drew down Zoas and spectres into generation.

Presently a new mental birth takes place. A babe is born. It must be given up to the old laws of the Mundane Shell. Golgonooza is built on rocks ("Jerusalem," p. 53, l. 17), and if the idea is to enter into consummate bliss, it must enter into a mortal. (Truth must be a man.) ("Jerusalem," p. 69, l. 31, and p. 86, l. 42.)

Thus the thoughts and the thinker melt into one another, the labours of art and the experience of love being the gates through which the mental passes to the personal, and the personal to the mental.

BROKEN LOVE.

1.

My Spectre before me night and day
Like a wild beast guards my way.
My Emanation far within
Weeps incessantly for my sin.

2.

A deep winter, dark and cold,
Within my heart thou didst unfold ;
A fathomless and boundless deep ;
There we wander, there we weep.

3.

He scents thy footsteps in the snow,
Wheresoever thou dost go,
Through the wintry hail and rain.
When wilt thou return again ?

4.

Dost thou not in pride and scorn
Fill with tempests all my morn,
And with jealousies and fears,
Fill my pleasant nights with tears ?

5.

Seven of thy sweet loves thy knife
Has bereaved of their life.
Their marble tombs I build with fears
And with cold and shadowy tears.

6.

Seven more loves weep night and day
Round the tombs where my loves lay,
And seven more loves attend at night
Around my couch with torches bright.

7.

And seven more loves in my bed
Crown with vine my mournful head,
Pitying and forgiving all
Thy transgressions, great and small.

8.

When wilt thou return and view
My loves, and them to life renew ?
When wilt thou return and live ?
When wilt thou pity as I forgive ?

9.

Never, never I return.
Still for victory I burn.
Living, thee alone I'll have,
And when dead I'll be thy grave.

10.

Through the Heaven and Earth and Hell
Thou shalt never, never quell,
I will fly and thou pursue,
Night and morn the flight renew.

11.

Till I turn from female love
And root up the infernal grove
I shall never worthy be
To step into Eternity.

12.

And I to end thy cruel mocks
Annihilate thee on the rocks,
And another form create
To be subservient to my fate.

13.

Let us agree to give up love
And root up the infernal grove.
Then shall we return and see
The worlds of happy Eternity.

14.

And throughout all Eternity
I forgive you, you forgive me.
As I, dear Redeemer, said :—
This the wine and this the bread.

The above is the true text of this poem with the numbering
of the verses as finally arranged after three re-considerations
by Blake. Not a word is altered from the original. The
poem as printed in the Aldine Edition and elsewhere is
erroneously arranged, partly from numberings of verses put
experimentally and then erased by Blake.

Before looking for the meaning of this we must once more
remind ourselves that sin and righteousness should always be
attributed to States, or moods; never to Individuals.

The essential sign and unfailing indication of sin is to be
found in the denial by one human mood of another human

mood's right to exist, if existence be a joy. This is to be taken as the root-doctrine, without which the poem mistakenly called "Broken Love" cannot be read at all.

1. The story is of the condition of man when in Error. His foresight unaccompanied by imagination, his mere expectation of memory, that which is an "unformed chaos" when seen in front of a man, guards his way from the freedom of imagination. In doing so it restrains him, and in restraining him it sins. Far within him, his emanation, the affectionate side, not the creative power of imagination, weeps for his sin.

2. But since joys are holy, not griefs, her weeping only leads to another sin. She adopts the convictions of the unformed memory. She believes that experience is life, and deepens the winter, the mortality, of the fleshly region of the five senses, unfolding its fathomless abyss in his bosom. In this boundless deep,—for truth has bounds; error, none,—the two wander and weep.

3. Wherever the affections wander in the world of experience the reason pursues them, for he is now the personal consciousness, the man himself. When will she return from wandering in the wintry places where he can follow at all? When will love belong, that is, once more to mental, not to the wilderness of bodily life? (Compare "Milton," *extra page* 32, l. 5.)

4. For love in the region of experience is in the region of selfishness. Like a spectre, like personality of Reason or Memory, the emanation or affection takes to itself pride and scorn, adds jealousy, and becomes the worse tyrant of the two, growing to be the more convincing and restrictive, unmystic, unvisionary form of consciousness.

5. Seven of the Reason's Loves, which should become by joy, Creative and Imaginative, she bereaves of life by cutting them apart from their own affectionateness. Thus the mind that should live, or create and love, is kept in its deadness, its separateness from inspiration and slavery to its own tendency

to become memory. The number seven signifies that of
spiritual, not corporeal manifestation. With fears and tears
the selfhood of the man builds tombs for these loves, the
tombs being dogmas. If alive they would have needed no
tomb. The higher mysticism is not communicated by dogma,
but by interchange of unspoken but keenly vital thought.

6. Two more groups of seven loves perform by night and by
day the function of the seven eyes of God in "Milton," and
give the man consciousness of his sleeping body.

7. A third seven crowning the head with vine, indicate to
the mind the great symbol of growing nature as a mute
sacrament of brotherhood (Christ, the "vine of eternity").
Thus they teach the thought to forgive the bodily, or wintry
Affections for their sinful attempt to deceive him into a
belief in material experience, and for restricting the freedom
of mental creation; such being the transgression of the natural
affections, the weeping, hidden Emanation.

8. These affections are only right when they are the places
of pity and the impulses of forgiveness. They have no
business to wander (or transgress) as "female will" into the
place of production of mental convictions. When will they
return from this, in which they are dead; and once more live?

9. The affections in error answer that they will never leave
the region of experience. They will drag the mind there
living, and when dead to creative power, they will be its
grave, for the body with its dark, non-mental, unforgiving
female, jealous, domineering love, is the grave.

10. The tenth verse has two readings. At first Blake
wrote, "Thou shalt fly, and I pursue," but perceiving that
the natural pursuer is the Spectre or essence of experience,
and that the Emanation has now adopted that essence, they
change parts. She becomes the pursuer. He, by right of
contemplative thought, has (like Los when his fall changes
oblique and at last his head rises) made the elements pliant,
to rise or fall in at will. So he flies through the regions—the
Head, Heart, Loins, now called Heaven, Earth, and Hell, that

the domineering love can never destroy, or quell. She still pursues the now changed mind. She has taken its sin, as a disease is caught by infection. The mind returns to health, for contraries cannot both be ill at once. It has ceased to be spectrous or tyrannic.

11. Till the man turns from placing his affections on things of this world,—called in the aggregate female love,—and roots up the infernal grove of vegetative attraction, he can never be worthy to step into the happiness of mental love and creativeness.

12. But error to be put off must have a body,—it only ceases to be an infection when it becomes a dogma. So he gives her to the rocks, and dogmatizes her into the region of corporeally conceived and analyzed fact away from the dangerous and infectious form of spiritual unspoken attractiveness. He creates another form, a truly spiritually female, the Imagination's bride,—and she, as love should be, is subservient to inspiration, and does not seek to master it. (Compare "Jerusalem," p. 43, l. 7.)

13. Yet with a last clinging to the bodily attractiveness that was once so sweet, he suggests that they shall live together by giving up "love"—in the sense of exclusiveness and jealousy—and that they together root up the infernal grove—the growth of the tyrannic element in each. Then should they both see the eternal portions of mind where are no such qualities.

14. Thus the only personal act left is that annihilation of personal tendency, the act of forgiveness, and when it is performed this is found to be the bread (of sweet joy, as elsewhere called), and the wine (of delight).

Note.—The text of the poem here is reprinted from the Aldine edition, the present editors not having seen the MS.

The above interpretation does not exhaust the ideas symbolized in the poem. It only selects one thread of meaning and indicates it slightly with the object of enabling the reader to obtain a coherent view of the work.

OF this poem we have no finally arranged text which Blake can be supposed to have prepared for publication. It lies before us, a litter of helpless fragments at the mercy of an editor.

Mr. Rossetti, in the Aldine edition, has put these into moderately good order, but has cut paragraphs up and transposed lines in an arbitrary manner. He has selected the most readable passages, avoiding repetitions that occur with only slight variations in the MS. book. But he has taken liberties difficult to justify, making suppressions, and unnecessarily cutting asunder connected sentences. When he tells us in a foot-note that the poem is published *in full*, we cannot quite look upon this as a serious utterance.

To understand the poem we must consider the time of Blake's life, when it was written, and the circumstances which gave rise to it, as well as the artistic and religious theories which dictated its form. These points have not yet been touched on at all in any edition.

As in the poem "Jerusalem," "Christ" means here the Human Imagination, the junction of the four regions of Humanity. The poem takes the New Testament to be a story that was first lived, then written for its symbolic purpose. The poem does more. It colours the story deliberately and consciously with the personality of the writer. Each of us sees the "Last Judgment" in a different way, as Blake had observed in the essay written in the MS. book just before the composition of this poem. He was now about to show, claiming the same right of individual imaginative vision, how he saw the Gospel. He wrote the poem not earlier than the latter part of

1810, and portions of it may belong to 1812. This is shown by the way in which the lines fit any chance space in the MS. book left by the "Vision of the Last Judgment," which bears for title,—"For the year 1810, Additions to Blake's Catalogue of Pictures, &c.," and by a phrase repeated in the "Screwmuch" lines of 1812. In this prose story of the Vision, "The Saviour, the true vine of eternity, the Human Imagination," had already appeared as "coming to Judgment, and throwing off the temporal that the Eternal might be established." Blake's mind was making its great struggle to rise above the wretched angers and troubles of his life, while recognizing the symbolic purpose of these. He was burning with indignation and sick with disappointment. Stothard had reaped the crop that he had sown. The *Examiner* had endeavoured to drive him off the field of art, as though he were a trespasser, because he tried to harvest some of his own corn. Poverty sat by his chair; the wolf howled at his door. Old friendships were failing. New enmities were growing. He recoiled from all outside influence and resolved to make what he could of his body as symbol, and his mind as life, looking in these for so much of form, and of mind Divine, as might be fitted for his understanding, and for his usage and duty.

The words which in the Aldine edition begin the poem, were written, probably, with no intention that they should form part of it. They are more probably a preface or dedication which expressed the private origin of the work. They are evidently addressed to Stothard, when read in connection with the phrase "Friend of all Mankind," in the Screwmuch lines of two years later,—a brief overboiling and return to quarrelsome life. The "long, hooked nose" also points to Stothard. The "Vision of Christ" is necessarily personal. Each looks in a glass, and, seeing himself, worships. This is the doctrine for which the "little boy" in the "Song of Experience" was bound in an iron chain.

Mr. Rossetti's sense of propriety, guided by his entire lack of mental companionship with Blake, has led him to sup-

press two lines about the nose in the dedication of the poem
he professes to publish in full for the first time. It should
run :—

> "The Vision of Christ that thou dost see,
> Is my vision's greatest enemy.
> Thine has a long, hook nose like thine,
> Mine has a snub nose like mine.
> Thine is the Friend of all Mankind,
> Mine speaks in Parables to the blind.
> Thine loves the same world that mine hates,
> Thy heaven-doors are my hell-gates.
> Socrates taught what Melitus
> Loathed as a nation's bitterest curse.
> And Caiaphas was, in his own mind,
> A benefactor to mankind.
> Doth read the Bible day and night,
> But thou readest black where I read white."

Blake's nose—short, stumpy, fist-like, compressed, but
strong, was not of the hollow-bridged turned-up character,
but he always called it "snub." He used to like to think he
personally resembled Socrates. In the same MS. book there
is a scrap by itself evidently of this date :—

"I always thought that Jesus Christ was a snubby, or I should not have
worshipped Him if I thought He had been one of those long spindled-nosed
rascals."

As a matter of fact, his designs show that he adopted the
conventional profile when representing Christ for other than
emphatically personal symbolic purposes. This phrase belongs
to a period only, not to the whole of his artistic life.

Another fragment of the same date, as is seen by its handwriting and its place—it being wedged in after what was
intended as a completed paragraph in the "Last Judgment"
—sheds more light on the mood of the moment.

"Thinking as I do that the Creator of this world is a very cruel Being, and
being a worshipper of Christ, I cannot help saying to the Son,—Oh, how unlike
the Father! First God Almighty comes with a thump on the head, and then
Jesus Christ comes with a balm to heal it."

Of the theological views scattered through the larger poems,
some few must be summarized and contrasted for this particular

work. In reading it one must remember that Jehovah, in the
persons of the Elohim, and by the agency of the Angel of the
Divine Presence, created this dark world as an act of mercy
and of cruelty. It is of mercy because it enables the weak
emotions to look through symbols upon prophecy, and also
because it passes away, being under Time. It is of cruelty
because it cuts off joys of mind and adds on pains of mind—of
that lower and shrunken part called body. It is also Satanic,
because it is the region where the Accuser triumphs by means
of the law which is "the strength of sin," as the lesson in
the Anglican burial service reminds us. Satan is the Accuser.
Accusation is the great mental sin. Other sin is merely
physical, and belongs to the things of Time that pass. Accusation is not the only mental sin. Denial is equally deadly.
Satan is not only the moral accuser but the denier of Imaginative
truth, for he would have Reason and Memory only considered
to be intellectual attributes. With these he builds the dark
fiction of error—a belief in that delusive Goddess Nature, who
is the mother of physical morality, and of mental immorality.
She is Mary, the pure, and Rahab the Harlot. She is Rahab
because she binds the red cord of blood in the eyes, the
windows of the soul. She is Mary, because it is of that cord
the red robe of flesh is made that was put on by Christ at
the incarnation. Thus Mary is the greater Rahab. Rahab's
harlotry is typical of mental mixture of convictions. It may
be found in the physically pure. She is therefore called the
Harlot-Virgin.

The Image of God in which man was made is the form of
the Imagination. This is common to all men and will end by
becoming One Form. It will unite all. It will survive all. It
will redeem all, saving them from violation or experience and
the slavery of belief in nature, in accusation, and in the mental
permanence of sin. In a word it saves them from Satan, God
of this world. Reason and memory tend also to unite men's
personalities into one great Temporary Delusion. This is the
great Satan, opposite of the great Saviour. It is negative,

imagination only being positive. It is not the final Humanity and Union of all, but the final Limit of Opacity, the aggregate of separateness massed. It is piled-up dust, not the water of life. It coheres by the water of death; fleshly instinct. It is bound by the fire of vegetation; fleshly growth and decay.

At the incarnation Christ put on this water and this fire. The one burned the other. He ended by putting them both off. His mother was Law and Nature. His body was Satan. When crucified he was his own destroyer, destroying the Serpent in Himself. This Serpent, Satan, was what was nailed to the tree. This body was destroyed or devoured in three days. This devouring is the meaning of the serpent with his tail in his mouth. Christ's self-sacrifice (or suicide) was the thrusting into death of Satan, and who had become Himself as a result of the Incarnation. It was the eternal putting-off of Reason and Memory and Morality as delusions, that Imagination, Eternal Present, and Forgiveness might survive.

The cross was the tree of vegetation, since it was the burning stake at which Satan was consumed. It was Moloch, the Wicker Man of Scandinavia. It was also sensuality. Sex in the body is the cross because it is vegetative division and vegetative transfixture. Lust is fire. It is also the basis of our human imagination which develops from it. Thus lust, seeking to destroy mind and make body everything, unites the sexes bodily, consumes their separateness, and is the basis of that union which is the entrance of mankind into the state called Man. In other words, it is the destruction of the dust, type of separateness, and the release of the Image of God from that dust by the Breath Divine that moved on the waters and made them the source of Unity in the infinitely divided. Thus it made dust water, and water fire, for the waters burned up the divisibility of the Divided, and the Divided ceased to exist as Dust.

Thus, to this hour, Satan also, himself the type of Christ by being Christ's mental opposite, tempts man to lust that he may accuse him, restrain him, make him take morality for religion,

and so absorb him in the delusions of Nature and live in his
absorption. But the Divine element in man does not leave
him when he enters into lust, but accompanies his three regions
of Head, Heart, and Loins, as the Form of the Fourth accompanied the three men in the furnace. It takes Man in all men
into this vegetable fire, and comes out of it with him. Satan
also sacrifices himself in the vain attempt to sacrifice others
to himself. So he also becomes a Redeemer while still the
contrary of the great Self-Sacrificer, and his suicide, with its
evil intent, complements the good suicide of the crucifixion.

This latter suicide began when God allowed his Image to be
of two sexes, and when " Male and Female created he them,"
whose name was called " Adam "—red earth.

Thus as the final unity results from a thousand divisions, so
paradox and contradiction create truth.

The paradox of the Two Redeemers lies deep and is
difficult to disentangle. Still deeper is that of the two
Creators. As there is a mortal body and a spiritual body, and
they are not the same, and as neither was First Cause of the
other, so also there is the Creator who is the Lamb's Father,
and is the ultimate Eternity, and the Creator who is the Dust's
Father, and is the ultimate death. Both are the Father of
Christ. One is the father of his Satanic body; one of himself.
He is the Son of Man, son of the Image of the Eternal, on the
spiritual side. This is the meaning of the phrase, " Thou art
a Man. God is no more." The word *is* can only be applied
to Man, for Man is a word meaning Mind or that which
Exists. *Is* applies only to existence. There can be " no
more " in God, for more than Mind, or than that which Exists,
must be inconceivable as an existence. That " more " would
be a portion of Nonentity or of outer Nature, that is to say,
delusion, and finally therefore Satan, and not God. Humanity,
the abstract noun containing the same idea, is thus mentality.
The lines—

> " Thou art a Man: God is no more.
> Thine own Humanity learn to endure,"

when stripped of all that makes them lovable and poetic, and with nothing left in them but the naked incontrovertibility of their skeleton of truth, might read :—

"Thou art a Mind. Eternal is Mind : Eternal Mind is no more than Mind. Thine own Mentality learn to know as the region of religion and adoration, while all else is that of negation merely."

In the "Everlasting Gospel" the plane of utterance constantly changes. As Los rose and fell when element became pliant, so Blake speaks now from the higher, now the lower. At one moment a word is used in its mystical, at another in its popular sense.

Blake is seen in this poem thinking aloud to himself. His intention develops in spite of him. Begun at the time of his Felpham troubles as an artistic protest—art being the ritual of his religion—it escaped the bonds of the impulse that called it into being. It takes the form at one moment of a question addressed by the poet to his imagination, then it becomes an answer—even more, a manifesto.

Such as it is, the value is so great as helping to the interpretation of all the rest of the symbolic writings, and it so fitly supplements the prose essays, the Songs, the "Jerusalem," the "Milton," and "Vala," that while it cannot be finally read without them, it is not a mere piece of decorative literature. The making a text, the choosing a final version of it, is not yet the most important, or even the most justifiable task that can be undertaken. The first thing is to put on record all the scraps, versions, or repetitions we possess. They will be found here to the uttermost word.

Beginning with one of the last segments—because it is that over which Blake has written the title of the poem, probably intending it to supersede other versions—here are the lines as Blake left them.

The Everlasting Gospel.

FINAL VERSION.

Was Jesus humble, or did He
Give any proofs of humility ;
Boast of high things with a humble
    tone,
And give with charity a stone ?
When but a child He ran away,
And left His parents in dismay.
When they had wandered three days
    long
This was the word upon His tongue :
" No, earthly parents, I confess
I am doing My Father's business."
When the rich learned Pharisee
Came to consult Him secretly,
Upon his heart with iron pen
He wrote, " Ye must be born again."
He was too proud to take a bribe ;
He spoke with authority, not like a
    scribe.
He says, with most consummate art,
" Follow me : I am meek and lowly of
    heart,"
As that is the only way to escape
The miser's net and the glutton's
    trap.
He who loves his enemies hates his
    friends.
This surely was not what Jesus
    intends,
But the sneaking pride of heroic
    schools,
And the scribes and Pharisees' virtuous
    rules ;
But He acts with honest triumphant
    pride,
And this is the cause that Jesus died.
He did not die with Christian ease,
Asking pardon of His enemies.
If He had, Caiaphas would forgive :
Sneaking submission can always live.
He had only to say that God was the
    Devil,
And the Devil was God, like a Christian
    civil.

PREVIOUS VERSION.

Was Jesus humble, or did He
Give any proofs of humility ?
When but a child he ran away,
And left His parents in dismay.
When they had wandered all day long,
These were the words upon His tongue :
" No, earthly parents, I confess
I am doing My Father's business."
When the rich learned Pharisee
Came to consult him secretly,
He was too proud to take a bribe ;
He spoke with authority, not like a
    scribe.
Upon his heart with iron pen
He wrote, " Ye must be born again."
He who loves his enemies hates his
    friends.
This surely is not what Jesus intends.
He must mean the mere love of
    civility,
And so He must mean concerning
    humility.
He says, with most consummate art,
" Follow me, I am meek and lowly of
    heart,"
As that is the only way to escape
The miser's net and the glutton's trap !
But He acts with triumphant, honest
    pride,
And this is the reason Jesus died.
If He had been Antichrist—creeping
    Jesus—
He'd have done anything to please us :
Gone sneaking into synagogues,
And not used the elders and priests
    like dogs.
Humble toward God, haughty toward
    man,
This is the race that Jesus ran.
But when He humbled Himself to
    God,
Then descended the cruel rod.
If thou humblest thyself thou humblest
    Me ;

Mild Christian regrets to the Devil
    confess
For affronting him thrice in the
    wilderness.
Like to Priestley, and Bacon, and
    Newton,
Poor spiritual knowledge is not worth
    a button.
But thus the Gospel of St. Isaac
    confutes,
"God can only be known by His
    attributes."
He had soon been bloody Cæsar's elf,
And at last he would have been Cæsar
    himself.
And as for the indwelling of the Holy
    Ghost,
Or Christ and His Father, it's all a
    boast,
Or pride and fallacy of the imagination,
That disdains to follow this world's
    fashion.
To teach doubt and experiment,
Certainly was not what Christ meant.

What was He doing all that time,
From ten years old to manly prime?
Was He then idle, or the less,
About His father's business?
Or was His wisdom held in scorn,
Before His wrath began to burn,
In miracles throughout the land,
That quite unnerved the (?) seraph
    hand?
If He had been Antichrist—creeping
    Jesus—
He'd have done anything to please us:
Gone sneaking into synagogues,
And not used the elders and priests
    like dogs,
But humble as a lamb or ass,
Obeyed Himself to Caiaphas.
God wants not man to humble himself.
That is the trick of the ancient elf.
This is the race that Jesus ran:
Humble to God, haughty to man.
Cursing the rulers before the people,
Even to the temple's highest steeple.

Thou also dwellest in eternity.
Thou art a man. God is no more;
Thine own humanity learn to adore,
And thy revenge abroad display,
In terrors at the last judgment day.

ANOTHER VERSION.

(Apparently earlier.)

Was Jesus gentle, or did He
Give any marks of gentility?
When twelve years old He ran away,
And left His parents in dismay.
When after three days' sorrow found,
Loud as Sinai's trumpet's sound.
"No, earthly parents, I confess
My heavenly Father's business.
Ye understand not what I say,
And, angry, force me to obey.
Obedience is a duty, then,
And favour gains with God and men."
John from the wilderness loud cried;
Satan gloried in his pride.
"Come," said Satan, "come away;
I'll soon see if you obey.
John for disobedience bled,
But you can turn the stones to bread.
God's high king and God's high
    priest
Shall plant their glories in your breast,
If Caiaphas you will obey.
If Herod you with bloody prey
Feed with the sacrifice, and be
Obedient; fall down, worship me."
Thunders and lightnings broke around,
And Jesus' voice in the thunders
    sound.
Thus I seize the spiritual prey.
Ye smiters with disease make way.
I come, your King and God, to seize.
Is God a smiter with disease?
The God of this world raged in vain,
He bound old Satan in His chain,
And, bursting forth His furious ire,
Became a chariot of fire.
Throughout the land He took His
    course,
And traced diseases to their source.

And when He humbled Himself to
God,
Then descended the cruel rod.
If thou humblest thyself thou humblest
Me.
Thou also dwellest in eternity.
Thou art a man. God is no more.
Thy own humanity learn to adore;
For that is my spirit of life.
Awake, arise to spiritual strife,
And thy revenge abroad display,
In terrors at the last judgment day.
God's mercy and long suffering
Are but the sinner to justice to bring.
Thou on the cross for them shall pray,
And take revenge at the last day.
Jesus replied in thunders hurled,
" I never will pray for the world ;
Once I did so when I prayed in the
garden.
I wished to take with me a bodily
pardon.
Can that which was of women born,
In the absence of the morn,
When the soul fell into sleep,
And archangels round it weep,
Shooting out against the light,
Fibres of a deadly night,
Reasoning upon its own dark fiction,
In doubt, which is self-contradiction ?
Humility is only doubt,
And does the sun and moon blot out,
Roofing over with thorns and stems
The buried soul and all its gems.
This life's five windows of the soul
Distort the heavens from pole to pole,
And leads you to believe a lie,
When you see *with* not *through* the
eye,
Which was born in a night to perish
in a night,
When the soul slept in beams of
light."

He cursed the scribe and Pharisee,
Trampling down hypocrisy,
Where'er His chariot took its way,
The gates of Death let in the day,
Broke down from every chain a bar,
And Satan in his spiritual war
Dragged at His chariot-wheels. Loud
howl'd
The God of this world. Louder rolled
The chariot-wheels, and louder still
His voice was heard from Zion's hill,
And in His hand the scourge shone
bright.
He scourged the merchant Canaanite
From out the temple of his mind,
And in his body tight does bind
Satan and all his hellish crew ;
And thus with wrath He did subdue
The serpent bulk of Nature's dross,
Till He had nailed it to the cross.
He took on sin in the virgin's womb,
And put it off on the cross and tomb,
To be worshipped by the Church of
Rome.

There is nothing in this poem on its personal side so
difficult to unravel at a first reading as the allusions to Pride
and Humility. They seem to overlap and contradict each

other till they become a moral tangle impossible to straighten out into any thread of meaning, or weave into any garment for thought. Blake, however, knew what he intended to convey, and in his mind there was no confusion on the subject. By looking into the different expressions and comparing them with others of the same class in his different writings we notice that pride and humility may be tabulated in their good and bad aspects thus :—

Good Pride.

Elation of joy and delight in Vision.
Adoration of the Divine in Adoption, by sympathy with the Divine, of its Self-approval.

In a lower plane :

Healthy Satanic pride in the energy of that lower part of mind called body, which has also a right to its elation because "everything that lives is Holy."

"Honest, triumphant pride," in "act," as when the merchant Canaanite is scourged out of the mind.— ("Thought is act.")

Bad Pride.

"Sneaking pride of heroic schools," the Homeric or chivalrous pride that is self-satisfied equally for killing and for sparing the vanquished. This is the Serpentine pride.

In true mental warfare, the vanquished ought either not to be vanquished, or not spared. Error is the enemy, and though Sin is to be forgiven, Error is not. Thus war, in Eternity, is a "fountain of life," for it is directed against error, death ; not against love, life, for the propagation of death.

Death and Error are Reason when confined to the experience of the five senses, proud of its humility, its limits and arguments. This is the "yea-nay creeping Jesus,"—the lower imagination pretending to brotherhood without the true material of brotherhood,—common inspiration.

Humility—always bad.

"The most sublime act is to set another before you." ("Proverb of Hell.") The sublimity consists in perception and adoption of his well-founded elation and annihilation of your own envy : not in Humility which is forbidden and sinful as modesty is (which blasphemes the Symbol of God,—the naked body). Humility is forbidden because it is doubt, not faith, and doubts the Godhead in ourselves, His chosen Temple.

The last version of the poem given above hardly overlaps the others in more than a few places, so far as verbal

similarity is concerned. It is uncertain what Blake intended
finally to do with it. Was all to have been left out? Had he
considered his work too long? Was there loss of interest,
and change of mind? The MS. book gives no answer.
The version on the left, here printed, seems to have been
the last. It is written in the smallest hand, crushed into
places only just left for it, and has the look of being an
amended copy.

It concludes, after the words "slept in beams of light,"
with the marginal note "78 lines." It will be noticed that it
contains a greater number, but a study of the MS. shows that
the lines from "He did not die with Christian ease" to
"certainly was not what Christ meant," were written later
and marked for insertion at the place in the poem where they
are here printed. The lines of the segment are seventy-eight
without them. They are the afterthought of an afterthought.
At their close a mark occurs that the next passage is to be
that beginning "Was Jesus chaste?" &c., which contains
ninety-four lines, and was numbered to avoid mistakes and
the reading in of other passages, the lines being somewhat
scattered among other MS. There are actually ninety-six, the
last couplet having been added after enumeration. A pencil
note on the first page of this long passage must be reproduced. "This was spoken by my spectre to Bacon, Newton,
and Locke," &c., and four lines also in pencil on the
margin,—

> "Did Jesus teach doubt, or did he
> Give any lessons in Philosophy;
> Charge visionaries with deceiving,
> And call men wise for not believing?"

These have no place assigned to them in the poem,
and would bring the ninety-six lines of the segment to
a hundred. It sheds light, however, on the symbolic
meaning of chastity. Bacon, Newton, and Locke, when
seen as one man, are in the state called Rahab (as

"Jerusalem" tells us). Rahab,—the Earth,—Mary,—are
three states of the woman taken in adultery. All have
female names because they are states of the earth, of the
body, that is of the dark and temporary part of mind.
This poem is dictated by Blake's spectre to them, but it is the
spectre Los,—spectre of the living, not Satan, the ultimate
of the spectres of the dead ;—a difference explained in Vala.

After "when the soul slept in beams of light" the
following was, therefore, all that remained in the MS. of the
poem, as Blake intended to print it.

> Was Jesus chaste, or did he
> Give any lessons in chastity ?
> The Morning blushed fiery red.
> Mary was found in adulterous bed.
> Earth groaned beneath, and Heaven above
> Trembled at discovery of love.
> Jesus was sitting in Moses' chair.
> They brought the trembling woman there.
> Moses commands she be stoned to death.
> What was the sound of Jesus' breath ?
> He laid his hand on Moses' law.
> The ancient heavens in silent awe,
> Writ with curses from pole to pole,
> All away began to roll.
> The Earth trembling and naked lay
> In secret bed of mortal clay.
> On Sinai fell the hand Divine,
> Putting back the bloody shrine,
> And she heard the breath of God
> As she heard by Eden's flood.
> " Good and evil are no more ; '
> Sinai's trumpets cease to roar.
> Cease, finger of God, to write ;
> The heavens are not clean in thy sight.
> Thou art good, and thou alone ;
> Nor may the sinner cast one stone.
> To be good only, is to be
> As God or else a Pharisee.
> Thou Angel of the Presence Divine,
> That didst create this body of mine,
> Wherefore hast thou writ these laws
> And created Hell's dark jaws?
> My presence I will take from thee.
> A cold leper thou shalt be,

Though thou wast so pure and bright
That Heaven was not clean in thy sight;
Though thy oath turned Heaven pale,
Though thy covenant built Hell's jail,
Though thou dost all to chaos roll
With the serpent for its soul.
Still the breath Divine does move,
And the breath Divine is love.
Mary, fear not. Let me see
The seven devils that torment thee.
Hide not from my sight thy sin,
That forgiveness thou mayst win.
Has no man condemned thee?"
"No man, Lord." "Then what is he
Who shall accuse thee? Come ye forth,
Fallen fiends of Heavenly birth
That have forgot your ancient love
And driven away my trembling dove.
You shall bow before her feet;
You shall lick the dust for meet,
And though you cannot love, but hate,
You shall be beggars at love's gate.
What was thy love? Let me see it.
Was it love, or dark deceit?"
"Love too long from me has fled.
'Twas dark deceit to earn my bread.
'Twas covet, or 'twas custom, or
Some trifle not worth caring for
That they may call a shame and sin;
Love's temple that God dwelleth in,
And hide in secret hidden shrine
The naked human form divine
And render that a lawless thing
On which the soul expands her wing.
But this, O Lord, this was my sin,
When first I let the devils in,
In dark pretence to chastity,
Blaspheming love, blaspheming Thee.
Thence rose secret adulteries,
And thence did covet also rise.
My sin thou hast forgiven me.
Canst thou forgive my blasphemy?
Canst thou return to this dark hell,
And in my burning bosom dwell?
And canst thou die that I may live
And canst thou pity and forgive?"
Then rolled the shadowy Man away
From the limbs of Jesus to make them his prey,
An ever-devouring appetite

> Glistering with festering venoms bright,
> Saying,—" Crucify this cause of distress,
> Who don't keep the secret of holiness !
> The mental powers by disease we bind,
> But he heals the deaf, the dumb, the blind,
> Whom God hath afflicted for secret ends.
> He comforts and heals and calls them friends,
> But when Jesus was crucified
> Then was perfected his galling pride.
> In three days he devoured his prey,
> And still devours this body of clay.
> For dust and clay is the serpent's meat
> That never was meant for man to eat."

In this Christ is seen telling His mother to show her sin. This is not confusion but symbolism. He stands for the masculine, she for the feminine ; he for mind, imagination, truth, forgiveness, and light; she for earth, the five senses, deluded mind, morality, repentance, secrecy, deceit, and all that is dark. She is the West and North, He is East and South.

So ends the only other completed portion of this poem.

A few words follow the note " 94 lines."

If they were intended to close the poem, then they should be followed by its concluding couplet, marked elsewhere as to follow the portion beginning,—" Was Jesus chaste ? " &c.

> " I am sure this Jesus will not do
> Either for Englishman or Jew."

But in looking at the end of the segment, Blake seems to have forgotten this trivial climax which was not under his eye at the moment. On what is left blank of the page where the portion is which ended first with—" still devours this body of clay,"—which received the couplet " For dust and clay," &c., as an afterthought, Blake is seized with consciousness of his own mission and duty in the matter, and starts afresh.

> " Seeing this false Christ, in fury and passion,
> I made my voice heard all over the Nation.
> What are those ——— ? " &c.

And so the MS. of the Everlasting Gospel terminates for us

with a loose end. What was the rest? We are entirely in the dark. One suggestion presents itself at once.

In "Jerusalem," p. 27, the poem, "To the Jews," the seventh stanza begins—

"What are those golden builders doing?"

Can it have been intended to follow here? There is no particular reason to think that it should do so. But no other line that commences with the same words is known to us. Should one be found in an MS., not now at hand, it will require consideration on its merits.

One of the few dates given in the whole MS. book is in the following note on the edge of a page, seemingly written just after the essay on the Vision of the Last Judgment, and therefore not far from the time of "Everlasting Gospel."

"23rd May, 1810. Found the word golden."

This means probably that opening some book at hazard to see on what word his finger would fall, Blake discovered that the word "golden" was so thrust upon his intention. A similar incident is recorded under date several years previously—August, 1807. "Jerusalem"—begun, as to its engraving, in 1804—was still in process of transference to metal. But the most that can be offered in the absence of Blake's complete MS. is that material for a surmise exists, not for a certainty, and the "golden builders" and the "golden string," in "Jerusalem," may or may not have been Blake's intended sequel to the "Everlasting Gospel."

After "What are those ——— ?" &c., a few more lines are found, a scrap never woven into any place, probably superseded by portions of the long passage already given.

Another couplet is to be found for which no place can be assigned. It is interesting as an additional proof that when seen in this light Satan, the serpent, is crucified.

"Nail his neck to the cross: nail it with a nail.
Nail his neck to the cross: ye all have power over his tail."

This is coherent with the following, also a scrap, for
" pride " is satanic.

> " What can be done with those desperate fools
> Who follow after the heathen schools?
> I was standing by when Jesus died.
> What they called humility I called pride."

It accounts for the expression—" seeing this false Christ,"
&c. Both the true and the false are to be found indicated in
different parts of the poem. But here, again, we are pulled
up short at the edge of a cliff.

As for the meaning, glancing back at the table of good and
bad pride we gather as doctrine that Christ's two natures
impelled Him to crucifixion. He went to " humble Himself to
God," and also to proudly destroy the serpent in himself; his
own spectre, or Satan. This Satan is the false (view of)
Christ worshipped still. The pride that led to Satan's
destruction by his Owner, Who was incarnated in him, was
Satan's pride. It was the emotion of adoration rightly
applied by Christ to His Humanity, wrongly to His personality,
just as His humility was wrong when it humbled His Humanity
to His personality when supposing itself to do the reverse.
The paradox is of the richest. Truth flies both ways along
the course of one figure of speech, as messages and answers
in the mysterious action of electricity go in opposite directions
at one moment along one wire.

There remains a section of forty-eight lines, printed in the
Aldine edition, which are still to be found on a separate
piece of paper stuck into the end of the MS. book. It is not
certain what position Blake intended to give them. Mr.
Rossetti has placed them nearly at the beginning, and in this
seems to follow the sense of the lines. They appear to have
been written later than the rest by the handwriting. Perhaps
they were an afterthought intended to supersede much of the
rest of the poems, but rejected by the author before he made
up his mind how to fix them in.

Was Jesus born of a virgin pure
With narrow soul and looks demure ?
If He intended to take on sin
His mother should an harlot have been,
Just such a one as Magdalen
With seven devils in her pen.
Or were Jew virgins still more cursed,
And with more sucking devils nursed ?
Or what was it that He took on
That He might bring salvation ?
A body subject to be tempted,
From neither pain nor grief exempted,—
Or such a body as might not feel
The passions that with sinners deal ?
Yes, but they say He never fell.
Ask Caiaphas, for he can tell.
" He mocked the Sabbath, and he mocked
The Sabbath's God, and he unlocked
The evil spirits from their shrines,
And turned fishermen to divines,
O'erturned the tent of secret sins,
And all its golden cords and pins ;
'Tis the bloody shrine of war,
Poured around from star to star,—
Halls of justice, hating vice,
Where the devil combs his lice.
He turned the devils into swine
That he might tempt the Jews to dine :
Since when a pig has got a look
That for a Jew may be mistook.
' Obey your parents.'   What says he ?
' Woman, what have I to do with thee ?
No earthly parents I confess,
I am doing my father's business.'
He scorned earth's parents, scorned earth's God
And mocked the one and the other rod ;
His seventy disciples sent
Against religion and government,
They by the sword of Justice fell,
And him their cruel murderer tell.
He left his father's trade to roam
A wandering vagrant without home,
And thus he others' labours stole
That he might live above control.
The publicans and harlots he
Selected for his company,
And from the adultress turned away
God's righteous law that lost its prey."

This closes the available matter from which to select a text for the " Everlasting Gospel" that shall include the literary beauties of all these morsels. The task is above the powers of any editor. The simple method is to take the only piece to which Blake has given the title himself, seventy-eight lines, and add the ninety-four, and the concluding couplet, " for dust and clay," &c., which he has indicated as intended to follow.

The result would give us the text as finally selected by the author. But the rejected portions, even the earliest and least satisfactory, that which is printed last here, contain so much scattered interest that Mr. Rossetti, it seems, had not the heart to exclude them. The result is that the Aldine text is fancifully arranged, and sometimes is unnecessarily weak in effect, wanting both continuity and cadence. It is guilty, as has been seen, of deliberate suppression of lines from the midst of paragraphs without the shadow of an excuse, even where no repetition of such lines in another portion is to be found. Much may be pardoned on account of the difficulty of the task of selection. The only editorial sin that calls for distinct notice being the unsupported and incorrect statement of the footnote that the text of the poem is given " in full."

THE MARRIAGE OF HEAVEN AND HELL.

RINTRAH,—the wrath that is of the reprobate, or man's amorous fury, rages in the burdened air,—the region of the heart. Hungry clouds, or blood that has its own needs and cravings also, swag on the deep, or region of the loins, and all external nature.

Once, before it was revealed that everything that lived was holy, the just man kept his course through this life, the veil of death, by treading in meekness the perilous path of virtue. But now Freedom shows beauty like roses, and sweetness like that given by the honey of bees, in the road where morality had only revealed a desert or a heath.

Then in every cliff and tomb, in every high and hard law and every dead formula, symbolism showed an unsuspected beauty, and the body of man became prolific of spiritual progeny as his dry law, and matter-of-fact religion of sublime poetry.

Then, it being seen how small a matter is the letter and how great the spirit, and the right of free-love being claimed with free imagination, the villain left the path of conventional dogma and pretended also to be a perceiver of the freedom of truth.

This tends to drive the just man into an asceticism which is by no means otherwise forced upon him.

Now, the tempter puts on soft hypocrisy, and honest anger accompanies the just man into the desert,—the region of conduct, not of imagination.

This is because in man's heart a lion, a conscious hunger

comes from the mind, the south, while in his loins the all-pervading moist maternity of nature awakes and hungers also.

THE BOOK.

When a new imagination begins, a new heaven begins, and this, in a degree, happens at the birth of each man. When Blake was thirty-three the Eternal Hell revived,—that is, the eternal energies of nature, th   globe of blood, as else-where symbolized—or the Eternal Female, whose red dress is seen in the margin of the Argument. This Female is not yet separate. She becomes so at revival, and hence a marriage is possible.

Blake had been long under the influence of Swedenborg's writings when he was thirty-three. He now suddenly sees that these writings have been folded round the enthusiastic energy of his own personal mind like grave clothes round a dead body. But this body—a portion of the eternal hell, or eternal energy—casts off the cerements and sees the author of them as though he were the angel left watching after Christ had risen, a helpless holy presence in the place where a divine deed had been done.

"Now is the dominion of Edom." Edom was where Adam, who was Schofield, was "new created," which thing the spectre of Los saw, indignant, but Los was not moved. ("Jerusalem," p. 7, l. 26.)

When the five senses under the symbols Egypt, Philistia, Moab, Edom, and Aram are spoken of, Edom is the fourth ("Jerusalem," p. 49, l. 43). They are mentioned under the four points in the order—Eye, Ear, Nostrils, Tongue; an unusual sequence, equal to South, North, East, West—instead of South, East, West, North, as is usual. Each form indicates a cross,—that of the Two Contraries. But the symbolic position of Moab is not indicated as that of the loins, so certainly as would be expected. In "Jerusalem," p. 92, l. 23, Edom is mentioned again, taking along with Egypt the position usually assigned to Canaan in the triad Amalek—Canaan—Moab. In the end, Blake entirely puts off the dominion of Edom, "O Lord,

what can I do? My Selfhood cruel marches against thee
deceitful from Sinai and from Edom, into the wilderness of
Judah, to meet thee in his pride!" ("Jerusalem," p. 96, l. 8,
&c.) And this Selfhood is the Serpent into which Man entered
six thousand years ago. (Compare chapter on the Worm.)

Edom, then, is Nature that was re-created when the worm
was seen to be holy because of the Incarnation. It is also
relegated to its place, the place of beauty and seat of judgment,
the loins, the earth, the grave. Its rehabilitation is to be like
that of the palaces broken down when God's sword is bathed
in heaven, and both spiritual and earthly pride are humbled,
until it is shown that happiness and safety belong not to any
form of pride whether of angel or king, but to the simplicity
that thinks no evil,—as told in Isaiah xxxiii. and xxxiv.,
to which Blake bids us to turn.

The Kabalists tell of seven early worlds destroyed before
this world began. They call these seven worlds Edom. Blake
uses the idea contained in this myth without repeating it or
endorsing it.

The plea for evil follows. It is mere energy when rightly
understood, and a necessary portion of the pair of wedded
contraries without whom is no progression.

The voice of the Devil is made to utter the fundamental
doctrine of Blake's philosophy, and of all transcendentalism,
and all pure science,—the doctrine whose negative half is contained in the formula :—Man has no body distinct from his soul.

Body is soul's energy and delight ; Reason is its limit.

Milton in "Paradise Lost" has given to the limiter of
desire the name of the Messiah. The angel of the Divine
Presence is called Satan. But in the Book of Job the limiter
of the higher spiritual joy (symbolized under terms of patri-
archal and pastoral prosperity) is called Satan, and his limits
are poverty and disease, the weakness of mind, and its folly.

The limiter (who is really Satan as Reason) believes the
force of desire that it controls to have been actually cast out.
But the Devil, as the delighter, says that the mobility of God

is distinguished from his eternity, that this mobility is Christ, that it fell, or went out into the void which then became nature, and, on returning, that it formed the joys of heaven from that which it took from the energy, or "eternal hell" outside.

The Holy Ghost is desire,—which must be taken to mean not flesh-hunger, but exuberance—not merely a thirst, but a conflagration. On this exuberance, presently to be identified with the symbol of the genital organs as being Beauty, Reason, or the limiter builds ideas by cutting and shaping the energy into material for building—not by adding anything of his own. The central potency of energy, the dweller in flaming fire, usually miscalled Satan, became Jehovah when the death of Christ had completed the experience and therefore personality of the Godhead.

But Milton only saw in the Father, Destiny; in the son, Reason; in the Holy Ghost nothing vital or personal,—nonentity. Notwithstanding this, being a true poet, Milton did his best work when writing of the expanding forces, not the contracting or boundary-making forces, and was thus of the Devil's party without knowing it.

So ends the utterance of the Voice of the Devil. It expresses Blake's own views, but not at all in the form which his maturer mind gave to them. Urizen in the South is the dweller in Flaming fire. Urizen in the North, the limiter, who is often indistinguishable from the Miltonic view of the Man of Sorrows, and who is Reason among other things, and is a builder also, while Orc, his opposite, is, whether for good or evil, the Devil of this book. The Christ and the Satan of the books of "Jerusalem," "Milton," and "Vala," is distinctly different from the "Messiah" of the Marriage of Heaven and Hell,—different by development, not by change. The Satan of these books also takes a place hardly foreshadowed by the "Devil" of the "Marriage."

Blake was here attempting to write his doctrines without the aid of the myth, using merely popular terms. His difficulty was insuperable. The popular terms would not fit his ideas, and the attempt to employ them in a new sense with parenthetical scraps of explanation has caused such obscurity that anyone who does not know Blake well enough to see what he intends to convey in spite of his method of conveying it, will not see anything here but paradox.

The "contraries" now used may be sorted under their mythical equivalents as given in the later books, in tabular form, thus :—

Jehovah (after Christ's Death).	The Divine Unity.
(before)	Urizen in the South.
Christ.	Los, or Imagination,
The Heaven formed from what was stolen from the Abyss.	Golgonooza, or Art.
The Devil.	Orc.

These are not exact equivalents, but sufficiently nearly so for the tracing of Blake's ideas from one form of expression to another. The ideas themselves changed under the action of the expression as time went on.

The First Memorable Fancy.

"Hell" is used throughout for the double meaning which always belongs to fire,—passion and enthusiasm, the creeping Orc that organized a serpent body, and the fiery Orc that set free the Americans. Buildings mean systems, and garments bodies of the figures who go to make up the systems. The opening might read :—

"When in the heat of enthusiasm and enjoying its delights, which to the merely obedient and reasonable seem to be torment and insanity, thinking that proverbs would show the higher wisdom better than myths or designs, I collected some."

The idea that the enjoyments of genius appear to be torment to those who do not share them, is worked out in the conversation between Urizen and Orc in the first pages of Night VII. of "Vala."

The rock on the abyss of the five senses appears in all the

books. It is the rock of separation, the division of man from man, on which Albion took his seat ("Jerusalem," p. 28, l. 12), which Blake attributed to the divorce of reason and morality from imagination and forgiveness, or love—that is, the rupture of what he now called the marriage of Heaven and Hell, and later on simply the division of the masculine from the feminine. This is the rock of the North, and is the seat of Satan. The rock of the South is the power of Divine Forgiveness and the permanence of imaginative form and of the "true surfaces" of things which appear when the apparent (phenomenal) surfaces are corroded away. It is the Throne of God, beyond which Reason would exalt law by making Mystery the sanction of Morality. ("Jerusalem," p. 78, l. 18). The fine senses are called an abyss here, a flood elsewhere.

The devil's first question hints that a bird has two appearances. One is its true form and includes the shape of its mind and emotions. The other is its apparent form of feathers "closed" by our five senses. This "closing" is what "creates" the outer form by making it seem solid. It is Satan's "world of opaqueness" (called Luvah's when Luvah was Satan. "Jerusalem," p. 73, l. 22), and its creation is the paradoxical act of cruelty and mercy produced by shrinkage of mind, not by miraculous solidification of vacuum into matter.

THE PROVERBS OF HELL.

The first proverb is divided into three parts which correspond to the triad Head, Heart, Loins. But they are placed in reverse order—Loins, Heart, Head—the exterior being the first. The proverb would read, if written in terms of the true Regions :—" Learn from the Loins; teach from the Heart; enjoy from the Head."

Passing by such of these proverbs as are figurative only in an obvious sense, with little reference to the peculiar use of words symbolically which was Blake's second language, we come to the seventh and twelfth which compare wisdom

and folly in a manner that show a peculiar kind of wisdom,—
imagination, vision, the perception of "true surfaces,"—to be
meant; and a peculiar kind of folly,—the subjection of the
mind to outer nature, apparent surfaces, and its own
"narrowed perceptions."

The "food" of the fifteenth proverb is the food of emotion,
wholesome to the soul when coming straight from imagination,
not so when caught by the bodily organs which are nets and
traps designed either by Time (as the Mundane Shell) to be
put off in time, or by the weaker spirits of creation that they
may have a dwelling-place. The veins and blood-vessels of the
body are the typical net. Morality is its mental equivalent
when made of a tissue of laws. Compare "Jerusalem," p. 42,
l. 81; "Vala," Night II., l. 154; "Urizen," chap. III.,
Stanza 4. See also above, chapter on the Symbol of the
Worm.

The proverb also means;—All good virtue is obtained without the threat of punishment—all good morality without law.

Such wholesome food is described in one of the letters from
Felpham as

"The bread of Sweet Thought and the wine of Delight,"

and again in the poem "Broken Love":

"Throughout all eternity
I forgive you; you forgive me;
As our dear Redeemer said,
This is the wine and this the bread."

The next proverb with any obscurity for the reader not
accustomed to Blake is the forty-fourth. As "The plough
follows words, so God rewards prayers." It contains a reading
of the fable of Hercules and the carter, suggesting that when
Hercules had irritated the carter into helping himself, he had
answered the carter's prayer for help and justified it, since until
after the prayer the carter was incapable of the effort. Compare
"Jerusalem," p. 43, l. 12, and Blake's personal statement that
when imagination failed him he prayed.

The forty-fifth proverb explains the symbolic use of the images, *tiger* and *horse*, in all the Books.

The fifty-fourth proverb—"The soul of sweet delight can never be defiled"—anticipates the argument of Oothoon, as this soul is named, in the "Visions of the Daughters of Albion," p. 3.

The sixty-seventh proverb shows Blake in rebellion against the art of his day, and in rebellion also against what he knew to be the art of all days, simply because he had learned to hate the word "improvement." That improvement does not mean merely the straightening of crooked roads, but rather the making of a discordant curve into a harmonious curve by altering it until it can enter its true place in a sequence, he himself knew perfectly well, when he was not angry. But on questions of art-criticism he was generally angry.

The sixty-ninth—"Where man is not, Nature is barren"— sketches the thought afterwards completed when he described nature as "the void outside existence which, when entered into, becomes a womb." ("Milton," p. 44, l. 1.) It is identified with the symbol of the rock, being also called the Satanic Void, and the false Centre, thus connected with the symbol of the blood-vessels, the net, &c. ("Jerusalem," p. 33, l. 19.)

On p. 11, Blake is still seen searching for some word by which to describe the mental personalities to whose influence we owe what is more than the experience which comes from moment to moment. Later on he called them States,— "combinations of Individuals" ("Milton," extra page, 32, l. 10), the highest form of combination beneath the ultimate Unity being that called the Council of God. They are called Zoas, Princes, Angels, Geniuses, and (also in the plural) Gods, as here.

All reside in the Human Breast because all beyond is the "void outside existence." But the time came when Blake grasped the idea of omnipresence in its final paradox by which it includes not only presence in that which exists but

in that which does not. "God is within and without."
(" Jerusalem," p. 12, l. 15.)

The next memorable fancy states the fundamental doctrine
of transcendentalism in its positive form,—" a firm persuasion
that a thing is so, makes it so." This is the root of hypnotic
suggestion and all magic. Incidentally it refutes the negative
side of transcendentalism which is apt to deny nature any
objectivity, for it is evident that objectivity can come into
existence from its opposite by means of a firm persuasion.

All these paradoxes would lead inevitably to insanity if
insanity were merely a mental and not a moral state, but Blake
has defined it as identical with selfishness, that is the contrary
of brotherhood, and declares it to be the "natural" state of
us all.

An important expression of Blake's views is contained in
the Memorable Fancy when the Poetic Genius being considered
to be the same thing as God, each man's conscience is necessarily considered to be the same thing as his genius. This
repeats an explanation given elsewhere of Blake's use of the
word *knave* for a man who was wicked enough to be deficient
in genius or "innate science."

In the Memorable Fancy that begins on p. 15, an indication that we are in Hell is given by the order of the four signs
of the first chambers of the printing-house. The Dragon-
Man of the cave is not said to be Urthona, but we perceive
him to be a nameless form of this Zoa, joined with his
spectre, who divided in the early pages of "Jerusalem."
The caves he clears are the dens that Urizen explores afterwards. He is the porter of the Northern Bar in "Thel."

In the second, the sign of Tharmas, the Serpent,—ancient
symbol of the water-region,—is adorning the cave with gems.
From here come the attractions of "false beauty."

In the third is the eagle, symbol of air,—the heart-region,
or Luvah.

In the fourth the Lion, symbol of Urizen in the south.

The unnamed forms of the fifth chamber are probably akin

to the Gnomes of Palamabron. They are not part of the fourfold humanity, but are rather impulses of expansion than of
origination. They pass forward the inspirations of the four
regions to the sixth, where the highest dark form is reached,—
that of the closed book.

A seventh stage must have been that of manifestation, and
the books would have opened themselves.

Blake was not ready to go so far yet.

That the giants who framed this world live in it in chains is
the next thing told in the story. The great liberation has not
arrived.

That the chains are the work of weak and tame minds
recalls the description in "Vala" already referred to in the
description of the nets which are made when "the weak begin
their work." (Night II., l. 154.)

The Prolific and Devourer here contrasted are also the
Eagle and Serpent. But they are both devourers from the
point of view of one another.

Blake's use of the word Man was universal. It included
God, and did not exclude Nature. Everything had "Human
forms identified, even Tree, Metal, Earth, and Stone"
("Jerusalem," p. 99, l. 1), and "Every Truth is a Man"
(MS. Book).

The Antediluvians lived before the flood of Time and
Space, or as it is also called, of the five senses. This flood is
creation. Of our Energies that belong to the pre-natal eternal
in us, one, now known to us by the form of its impulse that
drives us out from all restraints, is well symbolized by the
figure of that Son of God whom He sent to put a term to His
own Law. Law, according to Blake, being rightly called
Christ's mother. Christ still lives, tempting us to freedom.
Satan, tempting to delusion, acts partly by His means,
and through Him, since in His ultimate form He is known
to us as our Imagination. Satan the Accuser, the wicked
Satan, is practically another being altogether. It is in the
Transgressor, not in the Accuser, that the Saviour shall be

seen, with astonishment. (" Milton," p. 11, l. 31.) *Everything* (including Satan) has two aspects.

An angel attempting to show the poet his eternal lot, takes him through a stable (place of tame instruction), a church (of restraint), its nether vault (of buried passion), to a mill,—type of the grinding of reason in analysis, or argument of law in nature. Mental darkness as of a cave succeeds, and finally the mere blank, such as nature without a spark of humanity is, or as reason without a fragment of poetry. The roots of trees are here, the nether parts of vegetation, the humblest form of blind life. Below this is nothing conceivable to which the mind can lend existence. Here the imagination pauses. Blake proposes to pass to the void in search of God. Six stages of descent have been gone through. What of the seventh ?

The first of the six was a stage of servitude, the next of moral restraint, and so onwards in emphasis of oppression. Blake, who always preached liberty, prepares us for a picture of the vision seen in the void where presently in accordance with the proverb that " standing water breeds reptiles of the mind," between the spider-web rays of the black sun, abhorrent creatures prey on one another. Between the black and white spiders, the poet's lot is cast by his guide. We half see an allusion to the fact that his poetry lies between the black and white lines in which it is written, for we have not forgotten that we but lately heard of men who "took the form of books." If this be the true meaning, there will break out from between the lines a view of diabolic poetry as it appears to a timid angel.

This happens. Cloud and fire burst from the place where the poet's lot is cast. Tempest, and nether deep darken from it. The old serpent, nature and its impulses, swims the mental tempest in a horrible form. Green and purple, not the colours as in ordinary poetry of jealousy and tyranny, are on his forehead as on a tiger's,—the figurative tiger of wrath. They are the hues of instinctive growth and passionate blood.

The angel, like an alarmed conscience, retreats in fear of the lower nature thus revealed, and leaving a fungus, the parasitic blind life of some formula, in which he had found repose, climbs up into the intellectual protection of the analytic will.

Then all vanishes, and a singing voice tells the poet that the horrors he saw were a vision of what his own nature, if he tamed it down under the yoke of the weak, would become. The "alteration of opinions" here hinted is evidently the alteration of growth, like that of stream to sea and seed to tree, not mere variation like that of the weather-cock.

Now, the poet, who is the Lion referred to in the last words of this Book, proposes to take the ox, the angel, who must not have one and the same law with him, lest he be under oppression, and proposes to change the vision and show him in turn his own fate.

First they fly "westerly through the night till elevated above the earth's shadow." The West is the region of vegetative passion. If they go upwards through it they must be journeying from North by West to South, the reverse of the direction of Urizen's movement when he fell. The poet takes the timid angel far enough this way to escape the influence of earthly night. Then he dashes at the centre of the source of vision, the sun of imagination, not the dark sun of the inhuman void. Here, as of right, the poet puts on innocence. Now the angel is evidently a pale inspirer of Swedenborg. It was to supplement and partly refute Swedenborg Blake wrote the present book. So to keep hand in hand with the Angel he takes Swedenborg's volumes, and soon sinks with them from the glorious clime of poetic vision. Let any reader say whether, starting from that clime with that weight of kind, clear, cold commentary, he has not had the same experience.

All the planets, the arbiters of character and the dividers in old time of man's qualities, are passed but the sad Saturn. Even he is too poetic. A mere "space," if space it may be called, is all that the mind dwells in which, originally timid, submits its feebleness to domination by the system of another.

But the angel's lot must be considered more in detail. The space, an intellectual gap—for the stars belong to the pure reason in this symbology—peoples itself when contemplated. It is clearly the seat of religious war. The jarring sectaries who struggle with and consume each other are at the bottom of a pit into which those descend who read the Bible controversially. The bricks of the houses recall the twenty-second Proverb of Hell. They symbolize the dry-baked dogmas. The religious,—(for to Blake religion was a word seldom used as representing reverential emotions in the aggregate, but generally as bondage of non-mystic dogmatism and morality) that is the chained monkeys,—are books like the men were in the sixth chamber of the house of poetry. The skeleton of one is Aristotle's Analytics when brought from the Space to the Mill.

The twenty-first page and the twenty-second and third need no comment, being themselves commentary.

The promise of the Bible of Hell, with which the present book ends, was never redeemed. It has been supposed that this refers to Blake's version which had only reached as far as the book of Genesis, of the Bible itself "as understood by a Christian visionary." This was shown to Mr. Crabb Robinson in 1826 (see "Memoir," p. 146), and was probably the first draft for the chapter-headings which Blake had begun to add to the MS. copy of the Bible in old English letters, left unfinished when death stopped his work the following year. It was begun for Mr. Linnell and only the first chapters were completed. The titles of them are given here (p. 169). The MS. shown to Mr. Robinson presumably was destroyed. (See "Memoir," p. 167.)

After this promise the book of the "Marriage of Heaven and Hell" closes with the definition of what Blake used to call the "indefinite," or the law not altered for each individual, but oppressive because forced on opposites.

THE "Song of Liberty," though issued from Blake's press under the same cover with the "Marriage of Heaven and Hell," is really a separate book.

It begins with birth, whose pang is made known by the groan of the Eternal Female in the first line. She is identical with what is called the Eternal Hell in the first lines of the "Marriage."

1. The Eternal Female groaned. She is Enitharmon in particular, and all the other females in her, not excepting the "Delusive Goddess Nature." Her groan was heard over all the earth—that is to say, it was known in every region of the Natural Man, beginning at the North, the ear, the "Earth of Eden." ("Vala," first lines.)

2. The east and the west, the heart and the loins—Albion and America—centre and circumference,—felt in sickness and silence and faintness that a new birth was near.

3, 4, 5, and 6. Shadows of prophecy—emotions ready to become inspirations if set free—shiver along by the lakes and rivers and mutter across the ocean; for these lakes and rivers are symbols for nerves, in their spiritual, not corporeal form (compare "Jerusalem," p. 98, l. 16), and this ocean is the Atlantic, the symbol for the spiritual reservoir to which all joys go. France, Spain, and Rome mentioned in succession, after Albion, show that Albion is in his Urizen-aspect, and though East, as contrasted with America, is

North for Europe—itself North as a region in the world's divisions. Thus the Zoas are indicated :—

Urizen	Luvah	Tharmas	Urthona
Albion	France	Spain	Rome.
S.	E.	W.	N.

The points of the compass here correspond with " Regions of Humanity," and those of the map, for once, are sacrificed.

This sequence, if it be the correct reading, would be enough to indicate that here we have a different book from the preceding. In the " Marriage," the Zoas were not indicated in this order. Here we come on the name of one of them for the first time.

It may also be noticed that the group—Lakes, Rivers, Sea— is a triad, indicating Head, Heart, Loins, and not, as in the "Marriage" when a triad is presented, Loins, Heart, Head.

We have passed a barrier in going from the last book to this one, and everything reads in its true order now. No longer what is under seems above. Many years later we find in Blake's sketches for Dante the sequence of circles in the " Inferno," given as a diagram with No. 1 at the bottom, and the marginal note, " 'This is upside down, but right when viewed from Purgatory after they had passed the centre," an observation whose kinship with the problems now considered has been already noted here. (See above, " Memoir," p. 138.)

It must be noted that when the Churches were grouped later under the quaternary,

Paul,	Constantine,	Charlemagne,	Luther,
S.	E.	W.	N.

Luther, the enemy of Rome, is made to occupy the position here given to Rome. This has an indication of its own. Urthona being Keeper of the Gates (" Vala," Night IV., l. 41) or Porter of the Northern Bar (" Thel "), is equally well symbolized by the Pope, the ancient key-bearer, or Luther, the rude liberator, although his liberation was so merely material or " Northern," that where his work ended that of

Adam needed to begin again "in eternal circle." ("Jerusalem," p. 75, l. 24.)

France is now bid to rend down her dungeon, that is, to liberate her imaginative genius from imprisonment in blood and anger. For Luvah is cast into these furnaces of affliction and sealed ("Vala," Night II. l. 10), and for this reason, among others, "Luvah is France," victim of the warring self-hoods. ("Jerusalem," p. 66, l. 15.) Spain is bid to burst the barriers of old Rome. Here the "closed western gate" is indicated in the aspect which unites it with the wall of Los, the bar of Urthona, the Mundane Shell, the Veil, &c. (compare "Symbol of the Worm"), and it all means the containing restraints of the flesh that shrink up the mind from eternity. These are both moral and physical. The keys of Rome are double. Rome is bid to cast her keys into the deep—the void —and weep; or enter into it with fructifying water and the pangs of repentance. (Compare "Milton," p. 19, l. 50, and p. 44, l. 1.)

7. The seventh paragraph of the "Song of Liberty," since seven is the number of spiritual manifestation, explains, as would be expected, the first. The birth announced by the groan is perceived. It is that of Orc, though not so named yet. He is simply the "new born terror," or self-hood. The terms are equivalent, just as their opposite "self-annihilation" is equivalent to "inward complacency of soul."

8. On the Atlantic mountains, those heights of mind where intellect was free to sport with its own emanations, now barred out by the lower even if spiritually-formed passions, Orc stood before Urizen, who was not fallen yet.

9. But he is jealous.

10. He therefore seized Orc by the hair, the energy, and threw him down, as he afterwards threw Ahania, his "invisible lust."

11. The fire is falling through the stars, the lights of cold intellect, towards the outer void.

12. It is still time for all men to get advantage from his

spiritual warmth. The Citizen of London is to look up and enlarge his countenance. London here stands for the North, Urthona's place, the shadow of Golgonooza—not for the East, as when England is taken as a whole earth in itself. Let the Jew leave the pleasures of acquiring for those of sympathy, deserting the counting-house of egotism for the table of hospitality in the East—Luvah's land, the heart. Let the African of the South, who is darkened most under the greatest light, since Urizen has gone North, also widen his forehead. More things are to be perceived than can be seen through the narrow chinks of his cavern.

13. The fire fell past them from North, by East and South to West, in the inevitable circle.

14. The west, the water, the hoary element, fled from him. Tharmas fled from Urizen in Vala, and as Orc falls, Urizen falls, attached to him by his jealousy. Tharmas fled northwards. Urizen fell northwards. They fought as they went together. (Night VI., l. 54.) The fire contended with both. ("Vala," IV., l. 156.) Tharmas removes his waters from Los (father of Orc), and reveals the ruins of fallen Urizen. (Night VI., l. 10.) The fires war with both water of Tharmas and snow of Urizen. All these Zoas are one within the other. They are all human regious and energies, and the act of falling, or passing out into the exterior of soul called the World, or the Body, identifies them. They all go with the sun when they do so.

15. Urizen's "army of horrors" are summed up here under symbols explained by their number, that of the warring sons of Albion, of whose deeds we are told in "Jerusalem."

16. When they reach earth their spiritual portion is buried for Orc and Urizen when separated are like the affections rent from the understanding, a separation that roofed Los himself—the "ever apparent Elias"—in Albion's cliffs. ("Jerusalem," p. 74, l. 29.) Urthona is the shadow of Los and his dens are all that part of human mind that is of earth, wherever found.

17. Sullen fires, watery flames emerge round the gloomy King Reason all night, just as Tharmas emerges from Urizen's ruins. His fall with his hosts, is in "Vala," Night III., l. 153. The emerging is seven lines further on. It is caused by Orc passing through their regions.

18. Urizen leads his hosts to the wilderness of Law, where Babylon was built afterwards.

19. But Orc has passed on to the East again.

20. There he loosens the eternal wisdoms of instruction (horses) from the dens of night (also called the rock and the literal interpretation of the Scriptures), and promises through freedom and inspiration an end to the world's lusts and discords, such as neither jealousy nor restraint could give.

Chorus.

The chorus assumes that mental acts are creative, and that the perverted spirit is seen as the restraining material.

While these paraphrasing notes have already exceeded considerably the length of the pages which they partly explain, the reader will hardly need to be told now that they do not exhaust all the relationships between the short "Song of Liberty" and the myth of the prophetic books. Energy passed through, leads to good; if restrained it leads to stagnation; and stagnation leads to corruption. This is the doctrine. Even Tharmas, lowest of energies, to whom the highest was sacrificed ("Milton," p. 3), laid the foundation of the Spiritual City. ("Vala," Night V., l. 79.)

This may be looked on as Blake's first book, and yet his last. His own date for it, at the end, tells us that the pages here reproduced were engraved in 1822, but that the original stereotype was done in 1780.

It is hardly credible that the book as we have it (it is a book of only two pages) is the same in every word as that which was first stereotyped on the long-lost plate.

The handwriting is very irregular, but in general character it resembles the very latest of the pages inserted by after-thought into the body of "Jerusalem," pp. 56 or 61, for example. The larger letters are akin to those that make up such pages as 15, 22, and 80, while there is nothing at all that resembles the general appearance of the first nine pages of "Jerusalem," or those that begin the different chapters.

Page 61 of "Jerusalem" suggests by its allusions that it was written and engraved by Blake with the "Ghost of Abel" on the table before him. He probably intended to incorporate all of this that was not direct drama, but incidental expression of opinion in "Jerusalem," and then found that it could not be done to his own satisfaction, and so re-engraved his lost plate.

What changes were made in it cannot be certainly known. The general tone implies that it was a very early composition. The expression, "Prince of the Air," belongs to the "Marriage of Heaven and Hell," and not to the time when air was more closely related to Luvah.

The preface is probably very late. The question addressed to Byron under the symbolic name of Elijah, or Spirit of Prophecy ("Jerusalem," p. 44, l. 31), cannot have belonged to the year 1780, since Byron was not born till 1788.

In 1820, Byron was in Italy, conspiring against the Papal government with the friends and relatives of Countess Guiccioli. This may have been the wilderness from which Blake would recall him by a name that was to remind him of the duties of a poet. It is equally possible, and more probable, that the descriptions of scenery in "Childe Harold" provoked the reproach. Blake, in his old age, was exceedingly suspicious of any praise of nature, lest it should assume that nature was a reality—this being the sin of atheism.

The "Ghost of Abel" has on it the stamp of visionary realism. No man who pretended to have visions, but did not have them, could conceivably have written it. There is hardly a sentence that does not assist the reader in comprehending the myth of the Prophetic Books, and the tone of mind in which they were written. But there is, perhaps, nothing which in itself requires to have light thrown on it either by parallel quotations or direct explanation. It may be left along with the sibylline leaves and the inscriptions round the Laocoon as forming rather a key to Blake's mythic and symbolic meanings, than as so many additional enigmas.

TIRIEL.

THIS book, supposed by Swinburne to be the first of the "Prophetic" series, is a treatise on Old Age written in the form of a myth, with the purpose of showing the decline of life as it appears in the mirror of symbolic poetry, and of using senility in its turn, as itself a symbol.

The name, the title, the description of Tiriel, both in "Urizen," and the story in the present book, must all be read together, in order that his significance and character may be recognized. He springs from contradictory elements, belongs to two opposite symbolic regions, and the only portion of his story told in detail here shows him as the exact reverse of what had been during the stronger part of his life.

In the book of "Urizen," Chapter VIII., stanza 3, Tiriel's birth is heard of :—"First Tiriel appeared astonished at his own existence like a man from a cloud born." He is there called Thiriel, a more appropriate spelling, especially if in his youth he was a young and bright form of Ithuriel. Those that follow are Utha from the waters, Grodna from the earth, and Fuzon from the fire.

The four have a relation to the elements, Tiriel being especially to be understood by all the meanings which relate to the symbol Air.

But air, when the elements are arranged in reference to the symbolic cardinal points of the compass, belongs to the East. Water belongs to the West.

Tiriel, born of a cloud,—or rather—as astonished at his own

existence as though he were a man so brought to birth—is,
since clouds are watery and airy, related to the two opposites
the East and Western regions.

In his period of strength he was " King of the West," the
story says. That is to say, he is the East ruling the West,—
Air ruling Water.

Under the meanings of the symbolic East, we shall see in
" Jerusalem," for feature, the nostrils, and for region the
" Centre unapproachable for ever," and for tendency
" toward Ulro,"—or the mental error of belief in matter,
by which everything that so enters is "vegetated and born."

The West, on the contrary, has the Tongue, for symbol,
and " toward Eden, outward everyway," for region and for
tendency. It is the dominion of Tharmas, coequal with
Urizen, the " false tongue," the " parent power darkening,"
the " sense of touch." It is the region of growing life in
the ordinary sense. It is " three-fold " in character, and
is trebly full of the delusions of sex, and of nutrition. The
" false tongue " is described in the book of " Milton,"
as consisting of a false brain, false stomach, and false
bowels—compounded together—Sin.

None of this enters into the narrative of the book of " Tiriel,"
but it must be remembered, in order that what is otherwise
confusing or contradictory in appearance here, may be seen
as actually arising out of Blake's symbolic system.

Tiriel, described in " Urizen " as Urizen's first born, whose
brothers are Utha, Grodna, and Fuzon, appears in the book
called after his own name, as having two brothers, Ijim and
Zazel.

These are not his brothers in the sense of being sons of
Urizen, but as secondary regions, or divisions, or companion-
symbols of himself. In " Jerusalem," one of the sons of
Albion is described with similar significance as the " father
of his brothers in the shadowy generation."

Tiriel being son of Urizen—born when Urizen the Prince
of Light, whose region is rightly the South, was temporarily

frozen in the dark North—is thus a paradox, the son of a
paradox. There is a universality about him since his father
had relationship with North and South, and he with East
and West. Urizen is the eternal Restrictive, Constructive,
Reasoning Intellect. From the prohibitive laws he has
invented in the North, he makes in the East the World of
Destiny, though he ought to be in the South, Architect of
Imagination, and sowing the seeds of his imaginative human
states with Western prodigality.

Tiriel being of the air, is Eastern, or central; or egotistic ;
and of the cloud, fructifying and prolific. He is the selfish
tongue, the logical, reasoning, moral, unsympathetic, unloving
tongue. He is the Tongue of the Head,—or Head of the
Tongue. The sense of speech, not of touch.

Ijim is the Heart of the reasoning tongue, the false stomach,
the enthusiasm that can "defend a lie," that is, can nourish
an opaque body of error, built from reasoning based on the
senses, not on inspiration. Zazel, in magic, is called the spirit
or character of Saturn, that is, the heaviness and earthy
melancholy of the loins, prolific only of death. He is the false
bowels, in fact, for *now* in the West the human division is not
Head, Heart, Loins, but Tongue, Stomach, Bowels, or Words,
Heat, Error.

In " Vala " a line occurs—

" The mountain cried to the mountain, where art thou, oh ! brother mountain ? "

and in the manuscript the last word was amended by Blake
into Tiriel, " Vala," Night I., line 357.

In another line of the same poem, Night I., line 37-38,
say :

" Why wilt thou take Jerusalem from my inmost Tir(i)el,
Let her lay secret in the soft recesses of darkness and silence.

Tiriel's earthly, or impersonal symbol, is, then, a mountain,
and his age, his hardness, his blue hair, like the sky on the
summit, and his invocation to Myratana, whom he calls his

Soul, and Fire, all belong to the image. Mountains, the contrary of valleys as masculine, of feminine, and reason of instinct, are used symbolically in all Blake's work in connection with indeas of intellectual energy. They are seldom looked at as the symbol of this quality seen under a good aspect, but, since Urizen fell, rather as connected with mental and moral tyranny. (Compare " Vala," Night V., l. 192.)

The name *Tiriel* in old magic stood for "the intelligence of Mercury." Cunning, an attribute of Mercury, is among the characteristics of Tiriel in old age, as we learn from the speech in which his brother Ijim reproaches him him for this quality. "The weak in courage is strong in cunning." (Marriage of Heaven and Hell," page 9, proverb 50.) In this, as in many other places, a hint is found that Blake was not unacquainted with the symbolism of occultists and students of magic.

Chapter I.

The story begins with a conjunction,—" And aged Tiriel stood before the gates of his beautiful palace." The palace is a man's inner mind, where he lives in the pride of his strength. The story of Tiriel's youth and manhood is not told. This book begins as a sequel. Tiriel is now old, and is already outside the gates of himself.

With his age came the death of Myratana, his wife, for in symbolic story, the wife lives only by derivation from the man's strength. She is his emanative or vivifying passion made visible, and dies when his old age, with its merely distinctive reasoning, begins.

He cursed his sons, the fruit of his strength, for the loss of that which lived only in them now, and not in him, had brought him to this weakness which killed his wife. Therefore he called them murderers of their mother.

They were, in imagery, the streams of the mountain, born of its inner fruitful fire, as opposites to its nature, and

wandering down like serpents, bearing its fruitful or
nourishing power away. Their trees and grass, though
offered by them to the summit above, like clothes and beds
by his sons to Tiriel, could not mount higher than themselves, or cover the high bald peak to which they owed
their life.

Then with the hatred, such as is felt by ungenerous egotism
for the receivers of its gifts, and such as the unspiritual
character in man feel for the posterity that will see the light
after he is in darkness, Tiriel cursed his sons, and hated the
strength that had been his. His son Heuxos,—who as his
name has it must be a fallen star,—called a son of Zazel,
Urizen's mere bodily powers, and who had already cursed
him because enslaved by him and cast out from the pleasures
of mind and made to wander in the rocks, the barren corporeal functions that lay up no treasures in the soul.

Tiriel himself now wandered away from the sight of his sons,
that is from his own memory, for memory had made all his
pleasures become pains. He sought to find comfort in pride
of joyless morality that was now as blind as himself, like a
mountain in darkness.

Chapter II.

As he wandered he knew that he was blind. The eyes in
symbolism are the place of marriage. By them our souls
within wed the beauty of the "visions of Time and Space,"
called mistakenly, Nature. The old and wifeless are, therefore, symbolically, the blind. He felt the sun, for his heart
was still hot, but the moon, that governs the tides, and is
symbol of the yearning of the flesh, was to him as though it
did not exist. On dry deserts the former King of the
watery west has no queen, nor realm.

He that leadeth all, led Tiriel to the dwelling-place of his
own contrary.

This contrary was not solitary as he, had no memory or

angry as he, no pride, no cunning as he, it lived in the persons
of an ancient couple, Har and Heva, who had reached second
childhood. They dwelt in a valley in tents, not in a palace.
They had no egotism. They took the bounties of nature,
such as they could still enjoy, passively, as they had taken
the departure of their sons, the joys of their prime. Filial
love was still possible to them, and they, aged themselves,
lived with their mother who could not come to second childhood any more than Tiriel could, because she was solitary,
and childhood must have its equals or it dies. Mnetha, the
ancient mother, lived, as Tiriel, by the energy of her own
egotism, but it was an egotism of love that attached her to
home, as his was that of hate which drove him abroad.

Opposite to Tiriel in everything, Har and Heva are the
spirits not only of companionship and passive happiness and
sweet forgetfulness, but of kind hospitality. Yet when he
came to their open doors they ran from him at first with
instinctive fright. Foolish as they were they knew he was
a king whose palace was of bones and rottenness now,—
though once of "ivory,"—when it was Myratana's bosom.

But egotism though it curses when it feels strong is very
propitiative when weak. Tiriel kneeled down,—Intellect
humbled itself before instinct. He threw away his staff,—
logic or the "silver rod" of the motto to the Book of Thel.

Then Mother Mnetha, strong in possession of her home,
and not fearing cunning or eloquence in a mere wanderer
shorn of the substantial material and only part of egotism for
which she had any regard, pitied him and encouraged her
children to play with and feed him. He received some little
taste of borrowed passionless pleasure so that he might not
die of anger, envy, and hate.

He hid from them that he had been king of the West, or
master-force of the sense of touch and master-intellect of the
arguing, rebuking and unpoetic tongue. He claimed further
back. Urizen in the North (reasoning from the loins),
intelligence busy with cold laws of material things only,—

had been his father. He pretended to have been Urizen though without daring to take the name. He said he was the father of the northern or earthy race.

Mnetha was troubled and trembled, for this touched her where she could feel. It was terrible to think that there were races of fellow creatures not born of the instinctive domestic loves, not destined to reach the happy domestic old age. Yet she fed Tiriel and denied him no innocent temporary happiness that her dwelling-place provided.

CHAPTER III.

The instinctive old children still will have it that their guest is Tiriel. They know him by the smell of ripe figs still lingering on him (" Urizen," chap. 7, stanza 8). They innocently know of wicked joyous pride by the touch of instinct that once gave it strength, and carelessly recognize care in him who has lost all else.

He, old and wretched, bald, without the flaming hair of the mind's inner fury of youth, still boasts. It is all his pride can do now, except to curse. He vaunts the merriment of his own lost youth of whose strength he pretends, and indeed feels, to have been a guest, now forced to leave the joyous palace and wander.

Har and Heva would have him stay with them, but their simple pleasures that at first saved him from the agony of hunger or envy, now only make him impatient and angry. Madness,—that is to say egotism, which Blake frequently asserts to be the same thing, and dismay, which is egotism weak and afraid, force him to wander and forbid him to enjoy.

He takes his staff, his last strength of personality and determination, and seeks the woods, the place of melancholy.

With what strength he had gathered while resting a little while from anger in the region of instinct, blind old Tiriel wandered forth and presently came to entrance of the forest.

He found that it was the gate of his own heart. For the heart is rightly the cornfield where the harvest springs—the inspired experience of our imaginations with which we should sow the soil (our life of days and hours and space and power) with seed of art and thought and imagery, even with tears without which no growth comes. But its strength being used only for selfish pleasure, no harvest grew in the neglected heart, but only wild dark forests, where a savage giant dwelt.

The savage's name was Ijim; he was the brother, or second self of Tiriel. He was not used up yet. He came out strong and angry and railed at his helpless master. The passion of the selfish heart survives the strength of the loins.

Tiriel, the egotistic intellect of the loins, had been master of Ijim, the egotistic emotions of the heart, though he had never been the stronger of the two. " The weak in courage is strong in cunning." It was still all Ijim could do to come forth and meet him.

Seven years,—a full creative period,—time to make a world and rest,—had passed since Tiriel had seen his own heart.

Now his heart gave him strength enough to carry him in memory to the place where his early joys, his sons, still lived. Ijim bore Tiriel back on his shoulders.

But while doing so, Ijim rebuked him for the debased forms in which he had shown himself. Nine shapes his wit had taken,—a lion, a tiger, a river, a lightning cloud, a serpent, a toad, or newt, a rock, a poisonous shrub, and at last for the ninth, a blind old man, as though by inversion of natural things this were his birth indeed, because it was the revelation of himself, while the nine angers and destructions were the months before birth, during which his body was preparing for the light.

But, though, when borne on the strong shoulders of Ijim, Tiriel faced his own past boldly, he could not return to old days. Tiriel bade Myratana be called, but she could not come.

Tiriel's heart refused to share the bitter realization of this truth and, in the person of Ijim,—its genius,—turned away, flinging a last denial in the face of fact, and departed to its old shadowy, reckless grief,—the melancholy forest.

CHAPTER V.

Then Tiriel stood, heartless and angry, in his own Palace, now the rotten bones of memory and reason where all that he owned was built up. But its inhabitants were joys that no longer delighted him, and as his anger cursed them many died of earthquake and pestilence,—sexual passions, active or indolent. But as the sons died, his five daughters— the five senses—ran and caught him by what was left of his bodily form—his garments.

His youngest daughter, Hela, sight, remained. She was not the sight that gives pleasure, not the sight that weds soul to vision, but the exterior sense that is outside of our true selves though it may guide our footsteps through mortal things. The other four daughters perished. A few ruins of the palace were left, and thirty sons, each the genius of one of the " thirty cities " told of in the book of " Urizen," remained, but only to wither. Later on Fuzon called them away, as the book of " Urizen " also relates.

CHAPTER VI.

And Hela was eyes to her father. Now, relieved of anger with himself in the form of his past, and released from memory of his old pride, his sons being dead, Tiriel thought he could live, like Har and Heva, in happiness with Hela for his innocent companion, and so bid her lead him to their vales.

He commanded her to do so under threat of a curse such as had destroyed her brothers and sisters. But in doing so he rendered obedience impossible to her. No man can scold himself into being placid and instinctive, however much

his angry egotism may desire to put on this pleasant mood.
The reasoning tongue in vain tries to force the unreasoning
pleasures to come and replace the joys of materialistic convictions. Tiriel's last remaining sense, his memory of sight,
for in so far as he lived in the present he was mentally blind,
only mocked him with the view of a world he could no longer
enjoy, and in his fury he bid this solitary gift, this last passive
or feminine perception, become a source of agony to itself and
him. Serpents writhed in the locks of Hela's hair. That is
to say, her energy,—hair,—gave life to nature,—serpents,—
in pain and sorrow,—writhing.

CHAPTER VII.

Led by this living torture, Tiriel wandered to the consciousness of his own loins, as before he had found his way to
where its heart knew its own power. He found the genius of
the region, Zazel, the foolish slavish instinct, who would not
work for him now that he was old, but threw after him like
dirt the undelightful memory of unesteemed delight. Tiriel
went by, beating his breast, humiliated at last, and Hela
only hoped to end her life by the wild-beast stroke of some
wandering destructive chance. But agony frightens accident
away, and death does not come by wishing.

Then Tiriel, broken down in every attribute that estranged
him once from his own contrary, found the abode of that
opposite self, and reached once more, not by reaction, but
going forward, the vales of Har and Heva, which he might
no more leave.

CHAPTER VIII.

Maternal Mnetha, doubting that there must be still some
egotism in him, came to the gate of the lower garden of
lesser pleasures, and threatened to kill the remnant of his
selfishness with an arrow of her motherly beauty.

But Tiriel meekly answered the soft voice that threatened bitter things, named himself frankly without cunning or subterfuge, and asked to be taken to Har and Heva.

Having arrived where they were, Tiriel, grovelling at the feet of Har, took him by the ankles, for there is no part of still upright instinct that fallen reason will not cling to.

Yet with a last flash of his old wit he claimed instinct itself for his father, or the father of the errors that had, by counter-action, driven him to become the barren thing he was, after making him the destructive thing he had been.

For though there be good loves, there are no good laws, once set a law going, and it will roll over the lion and the ox in equal oppression. Even Har, though not wicked, was, as a law-giver and a father, mistaken.

Then Tiriel lamented aloud over the mystery that people are born without enough perception of the infinite to save them from believing in mortal illusion and error. The worst error is that of education, practised by force through slavishness, that is, through mental action aroused under the whip of Grecian mockery, and therefore based on a belief in the five senses,—not in imagination (commentary to page 52 of " Jerusalem "), and leading to the place of cunning and destructiveness, a journey the reverse of that which Tiriel's old age followed : the journey of his youth, past the regions of Zazel and Ijim to the palace that he had angrily ruined and deserted at last.

With this protest, the poor personal, egotistic reason, the hollow eloquence of the tongue, the loveless mental king that lived five years, the number of his senses, with the wife or strength of his youth, waiting daily to see a curse fall on his sons, his joys, felt the weight of his death-sentence on himself, and at the feet of witless, helpless, impulse fell down and died.

CHAPTER I.—THEL QUESTIONS MORTAL NEW-BORN JOY.

THE daughters of inspiration led their flocks of innocent imaginings, all but the youngest, who became fascinated by the fear of incarnation. She, the pure spiritual essence,* ever fleeting because ever incarnating, laments her momentariness (1-5). In her lamentation she numbers over things that express her to man—the life of spring—the rainbow—the passing smiles of infants—the voice of the dove. (She is transient beauty, and above all, the fleeting and pensive charm of youth and virginity) (6-14). The first flowering of innocent organized joy out of earth, typified in the lily, replies and tells how weak and small it is, and yet it is protected by heaven. Why then should Thel lament? (15-25). Thel replies that the lily has many uses, it nourishes innocence —lamb—for instance, but she has none and is as fleeting as a cloud (26-36). The lily bids her ask of the cloud to say for what purpose it shines in the morning. The lily calls down the cloud (36-40). The cloud—a mortal vegetative desire— appears, and the lily, who is a pure undesiring joy, bows its modest head (41, 42).

CHAPTER II.—THEL QUESTIONS MORTAL VEGETATIVE DESIRE.

Thel asks the cloud why it does not complain when it is so fleeting (1-4). The cloud answers that its steeds, the mental powers that bear it on its course, drink of the springs

---

* *The spiritual oil of Boehmen and at times also of Blake.*

where the horses of Love, himself, drink. It knows that it must pass away, but so do all things. And when it passes it goes to greater love and life. It nourishes the flowers or joys by its death, and then rises, being made one with the dew. Its feminine or darker and more shadowy portion, redeemed by its death, thus remounts towards the sun of love (for the desires arouse the otherwise dead portions of the mind into life) (5-16). Thel replies that she is not like the cloud for she feeds neither flowers nor birds, and yet passes away, though useless, to be the food of worms (17-23). The cloud answers that to be the food of worms—of generated life—is a great use and calls up the worm—that she may hear its voice (24-29). The dumb young life sat upon the lily, or showed itself within the innocent spiritual joy. The cloud having fulfilled its purpose and called up the worm, as it had been itself called up by the lily, sails on (30, 31).

Chapter III.—Thel Questions Mortal Vitality.

Thel sees the worm like an infant wrapped in the leaf of the lily and none to love it (the generative life is perceived to be the beginning of regeneration—the destroyer and creator are one) (1-6). The clod of clay hears the voice of the infant and begins to cherish it; the generative life is wrapped in the physical body (7-9). The clod speaks to Thel and tells her that nothing lives for itself. God cares even for her—lowliest of things—and calls her the mother of His children. Thus the clod also lives on and loves (10-18). Thel ceases to lament, because she had not known that God nourished the worm with milk and oil, with the material and spiritual essences—the food of the generated life and the basis of the intellectual fire in the clod as in herself—and therefore she had complained when she found she was to be absorbed into the bodily clay (19-25). The clay bids Thel enter its house and see what awaits her there (26, 29).

CHAPTER IV.—THEL HEARS THE LAMENTS OF THE MORTAL
BODY.

The power who guards the realm of clay, lifts the bar that
shuts spirit out and Thel goes down to see the place where
sleep the dead, those who have died out of pre-natal life into
bodily dwellings. She sees that all the living desires and
affections draw nourishment and find support—are rooted—
in this place of generation (1-5). She wanders along
among vegetated emotions—"clouds"—through places of
emanative or attractive feminine power—"dark valleys."
At last she hears the voice of her own body—her "grave-
plot" (6-10). It laments because of the mysterious sorrows
and limitations of the flesh (15-20). Thel flies back in
terror to the land of un-embodied innocence from which she
came (21, 22).

THE Daughters of Albion are mythical personages, described
in "Jerusalem" as controlling in each of us the vegetative
powers. ("Jerusalem," p. 5, l. 39.) They inhabit the nutri-
tive and procreative organs. They work at the "looms" in
which that garment of our souls, the body, is spun. They are
what used to be called animal spirits, before that phrase
became obsolete as the expression of a metaphysical conception, and survived only to describe that bodily cheerfulness
which used to be attributed to a benign influence of the
spiritual causes of bodily functions. It must never be lost
sight of that "body" is only a name for the visible and outer
portions of mind, figuratively, for the form given by words and
thought.

Nothing that belongs to the region of the loins can be a
secret to the Daughters of Albion. Their visions are the
visions of the Eye of the Loins, not of the Eye of the Head,
or the Eye of the Heart.

In "Jerusalem" (p. 41, l. 15, and following) is a description
of the dwelling-place of Oothoon. In a sense she does inhabit
a region of space, but the material portion of her house and
its mental dimensions are put in playfully emphatic contrast.
She possesses a grain of sand in Lambeth—near the "Parent"
river—that Satan cannot find. That is to say, no accusation—
for Satan is the accuser—can be brought successfully against
that very small portion of material flame which attaches to
her. This grain of sand opens miraculously within and
reveals itself to be a palace. Here both "Jerusalem" and
"Vala," both poetic and natural love, may repose and be
hidden from the terrible action of the mortal created-body,

which is identical with Satan, with Urizen in the North, and with the literal interpretation of the Scriptures.

Oothoon is not always even confined to that palace. In " Jerusalem " (p. 83, l. 27, and following) she is said to hide herself in Oxford—used always as the name typical of a " place of thought," with Antamon, the " Prince of the Pearly Dew," as he is called in " Europe," the artistic spirit to whose hands we owe beauty in form. (" Milton," p. 27.) Here she conceals herself in " chaste appearances," lest Hand, the chief of the Satanic personalities of fallen Man, destroy his affection.

In the poem of the " Visions " she is not hiding at all, but revealing herself in emphatically unchaste appearances, and it is difficult at first to see her through the glamour of her own symbols. The comment of most readers of these pages will be the reproach which Enitharmon in " Europe " addresses to her: " Why wilt thou give up woman's secrecy, my melancholy child ? "

" Woman's," or nature's, " secrecy " is a term for Theotormon. Yet Oothoon is essentially a being of beauty. She equals Thel ; in a physical sense, perhaps, she surpasses Thel. She is certainly more beautiful than Hela, for Hela's hair is filled with serpents, and she is the Gorgon beauty whom thought has turned to pain and poison, for thought changed the " Infinite " itself into a serpent. (" Europe," l. 120.)

Oothoon's beauty being spiritual is able to protect the poor natural beauty of Leutha. She is her " charming guard " when she lives in the tent of Palamabron, the genius of the pen. (" Milton," p. 11, l. 44.)

This idea that beauty was a protection was probably at the root of Blake's decision—so far as it was not decided for him and dictated to him—to adopt the poetic form for his philosophy. " When I tell a truth," he says, " it is not to convince those who do not know it, but to protect those who do." Who these were is indicated in another saying of his, not altogether consistent with it, but giving it light none the less. "I have ignorance to instruct, and innocence to defend." Those who know truth are thus seen to be the Innocent.

As the expression of a truth, the description of spiritual beauty as a defence for natural beauty needs no argument to support it. Under the name of good taste the world has admitted her protection, and the claim that æsthetics, if rightly understood, includes ethics is being loudly urged, though not too loudly, in our own deaf day.

Oothoon's importance is shown by the division of the region of her influence into its own three kingdoms of Head, Heart, Loins. This is indicated by her three lovers. When she hides in places of thought with the formative spirit ("Milton," p. 27, l. 13), she is the Eye of the Loins in the Region of the Head. It is her last position when she is left in Oxford with Antamon. The present poem relates her grief because Theotormon, who is the sadness of the human heart, rejects her for having yielded to Bromion, who represents the violence of fleshly fury. Sorrow refuses to be consoled by beauty; brutality refuses to be converted. With art and thought alone she has her final happiness because her final usefulness.

Oothoon is of the region of the blood, of the cloud of the loins. She belongs to that "Hell" or "Abyss" from which, in the "Marriage of Heaven and Hell," we are told that Messiah stole something of that with which he formed Heaven. This is part of the symbolic suggestion contained also in the phrases about "the divine members" being "ideas," and Christ and his apostles "artists" and Theotormon giving the gospel to Jesus, considered as the Man of Sorrows ("Africa," l. 24).

Antamon, like Oothoon, is a cloud (the blood symbol). He is related to Tiriel, the "man from a cloud born," but his functions are not separated from his origin. Tiriel passed from the province of the life-giving and became a destroyer. Antamon is the "golden cloud" who speaks in the book of "Thel." He is not named there. Of those who converse in

the book of "Thel," only Thel herself is given by name.
The rest are under the descriptive term of their symbols.
Oothoon is able to live with him finally because she also is a
cloud. There is a picture of her as one, raining over a field
of corn, in "Milton," p. 44. But clouds are not only the
kind nourishers with rain. Lightning has access to them, and
they have no defence. Oothoon could not resist Bromion.
After Bromion had rent her, she wept all her tears quickly
away and had no more, but as a cumulous cloud in the high
air showed snowy limbs within which the eagles could find
pure water reflecting the qualities of the river.—(Theotormon.)
Yet from such a cloud new lightning might yet fall, in the
fulness of time (symbolically Bromion's child), thus forming
the link that binds Oothoon evermore to all violence and fury
of fire, whether in the heights or the deeps, therefore she is
chained to to a flame given forth by the earth, when seen in the
"Visions," floating over Theotormon and pleading with him.

Bromion also implies the violence of the Human Reason
destroying imagination. Those come under his power who
pluck the flower of desire in the region of natural and not of
imaginative beauty—the marigold of Leutha's vale.

ARGUMENT.

The "Argument" of the poem might also be called the
prologue. It is spoken by the principal character, and sums
up the story.

"I," says Oothoon, who speaks for the imaginative beauty
in all visible things to which the sense of sight can wed the
soul, "loved Theotormon," who represents the spiritual origin
of those natural sensuous emotions from which spiritual beauty
emanates.

"I was not ashamed," Oothoon declares, and rightly. "I
hid in Leutha's vale," she adds. Leutha's vale is the place
of natural beauty. It is at once in the sky with the moon,
and in the loins of man in which region the moon has her

dwelling. (For Leutha, see "Milton," p. 9, ll. 28, 32; p. 10, ll. 3, 50; p. 11, ll. 7, 12, 36, 43. "Europe," l. 205. "Africa," l. 28.)

"I plucked Leutha's flower," Oothoon goes on. But in this she had placed herself under another spiritual condition. She had attempted to take to herself some of the purely natural and sensuous material. It is as though a statue of a goddess were to endeavour to attract by the device of a temptress. It is even more. A poem written to prove something whose demonstration should be mathematical, would repeat in another form the error of this flower-plucking.

In a moment Oothoon finds her fault. It was that of Eve and Psyche, and Pandora. She passed under the dominion of intellectual powers that are those of coercive reasoning, not of beautiful persuasion. "The terrible thunders" (thoughts; "Jerusalem," p. 3, l. 24) "tore my virgin mantle" (her realm of free, pure, unthinking joy) "in twain."

The Poem.

1, 2. Enslaved to the labour of building the human natural body, or "portion of the soul discerned by the five senses," the Daughters of Albion—the loving tendencies with maternal force in the tissues of the body—weep with the tears that mysticism knows to be creative, and in the mountains and valleys—the male and female bodily and mental regions—they sigh towards America, or the Western region, the procreative powers.

3, 4. Oothoon, the soul of that portion of the soul, its softness and beauty, not its genius or power, wandered in the woe of yearning after more beauty, along the courses of the changing life of nature, and the flowing blood of man, seeking some natural beauty that she could "steal from the Abyss," to satisfy her desire to be ever more and more beautiful, as Thel sought to be more and more useful.

5, 6. She came to the marigold, the generous joy in the

natural heart, like the cloud in the vales of Har. But the
flower was attached to the earth by its stalk, not to the sun
by a ray.

A spirit herself, she saw the spirit of the flower. It seemed
a nymph, a "guardian of the Western gate" ("Jerusalem,"
p. 13, l. 28), a fortress of the closed passage to Eden.

The nymph was its imaginative form. Yet it was so like a
flower (a watery or instinctive emotion) that at first Oothoon
did not dare to pluck it.

Had Oothoon been able to take the nymph and leave the
flower—take the mental and leave the bodily portion of the
great experience of instinct and love—all would have been
well. But if this could be, bliss could be perfected in the
soul, and a chaste body woven over an unchaste mind,
compare "Jerusalem," p. 21, ll. 11, 12; p. 63, l. 26; and
p. 86, l. 42.

7, 10. The nymph gave her fatal advice. To her, the
plucking of the flower, the detachment from earth of one of
its beings of beauty, would be nothing. Earth would grow
another. The soul of sweet delight inhabits"for ever the
kingdom of ugliness and forces it to manifest its powers by
producing beauty.

11, 13. Oothoon, as she tells in the prologue, detached the
natural beauty, and placed it between her breasts, between the
sources where in maternity love nourishes innocence, and
where in virginity, beauty attracts power. There it was in
the central region of feminine grace, where the whole soul of
Oothoon, herself the soul of the loins, sought to exist in
delight. There she turned her face, her eyes, her marriage.

14, 15. In a moment she was free of the sadly laborious in
her life. She was away from the place where Theotormon
wept, and the Daughters of Albion laboured. She left the
tears of flesh and its dark laws of production and flew into its
beauty and joy.

But there is no law so terrible as the law of paradox in
action. Oothoon had plucked the flower, and thus she was

flying through air, over water, bearing earth on her breast, toward fire.

In mystic symbol she was going up the spiral to the higher or inner ("Jerusalem," p. 71, l. 6), having started from the West (Theotormon) touched outer or lower earth, North (the flower-stem—Leutha's vale), passed lower East (the air, the flower detached and placed on the heart) and brought it to lower South—the golden petals on which the eyes dwell—and now flying impetuously over West—"Theotormon's reign," the river of Leutha's vale—she must in a moment reach higher North.

That is, she must reach the intellectual limitations belonging to the world of generation, the ear.

She did so. Bromion, the strong demon of that land, rent her "with his thunders," as a cloud in the air is rent, and as a joy is torn by a thought, when it brings itself under the dominion of Time (who is not mentioned here, but whom we know to be father of Bromion, and called Los or Urthona: labourer at the Furnace of Affliction; Porter of the Northern gate). Oothoon has endeavoured to make her flower of bliss last beyond its proper limit, which, as Enitharmon reminds her in "Europe," is "between two moments."

16, 17. When Bromion had rent Oothoon with his thunders, the "faint maid"—faint as spirits are who approach earthly life —(compare Elohim in "Milton," p. 11, l. 23; "Vala," VIII., l. 395; and Orc, in the Preludium to "America," l. 17)—lay "on his stormy bed," the thundrous air; for in this second voyage to the Northern world Oothoon had passed into the second region where there is a new air and clouds above, just as Thel went, without harm to herself, by permission, into a world where there are clouds below earth. But Thel's "below" was really "above," like Oothoon's, for we are told she "entered" into the "secrets" of the land, and inward is upward. The land is outer, its secrets inner. Soon her woes appalled Bromion's discordant, unpoetic thoughts, his "thunders hoarse."

18, 25. Bromion spoke. He addressed Theotormon. The virgin Oothoon was no longer a virgin. She had plucked a flower. Virginity is passivity. She had committed an act of violence. In that instant Bromion, who is violence, had entered into her. The two were one; an adulterous pair.

Let the life of dark water—the jealous dolphins, lesser equivalents of the whale in symbolism—sport round this pair, he said.

Theotormon's soft American plains, or yearning tendencies, belonged to Bromion now, her north, natural; south, mental passion,—his ear and his eye. In type of this the native races of America, on the earthly globe, rule by the infliction of pain, and their maids find the beautiful in the fearful.

Oothoon—the eye of desire—is condemned, in fact, to find beauty in nature, whose soul is reason, and whose conviction is pain, whose morality is punishment, instead of in pure imagination. She is set to the labour of "forming a heaven" from what is "stolen from the abyss," a work that once more connects this story with the giving of the gospel by Theotormon, in "Asia." And Bromion scornfully bid Theotormon protect (with beauty such as he had given to Oothoon) the child who in fulness of time should have in it some of the hardness of reason as well as the softness of love.

26, 33. Then Theotormon, the ruler of the growing, but not of the desiring loins, father of Beauty but not pardoner, suddenly felt fury. Storms tore his limbs. Anger entered the wound. Bromion mingled with him. He obtained access to Bromion's caves, and there fastened both Bromion and Oothoon back to back. Thus he bound back to back his own fury and his own meekness in his own loins, now become the cave of violence, and yet the cave of restraint, and thus it was that he condemned himself to sterility, for productive contraries are face to face.

Here is seen a counterpart to the myth of the binding of Orc, whose enchainment to the rock, awoke Urizen to creative productivity,—a complete contrast. ("Urizen," chap. VIII., stanza 5.)

He sits by the gate of his own loins, weeping. Below him the waves, whose voice is of slaves and of children, or strong thoughts, and innocent thoughts in the natural and instinctive life, bought from money, or restrained by forces that do not nourish and should not control them. They are beneath the sun, the eyes, and grow cold, or blind, in the religious caves, the unused organs of life.

31, 39. Oothoon's first tears went when her virgin mantle was torn, the remainder are locked up as a result of her enchained state. She had none to repent with when Theotormon reproached her. She had grown wholely eastern, his opposite. And she called the eagles, "portions of genius," in "Proverb of Hell," No. 55, of the air, of the east, of the heart to show how truly she reflected the west, the desire of parenthood, a female impulse even in a male. ("Jerusalem," p. 64, 1. 13.)

These eagles are the same told of in the "Memorable Fancy," who there with "their wings made the sides" of another cavern, infinite. They would do so to Bromion's cave also. Oothoon called with holy incorporeal and intellectual voice. She bid the eagles rend the bosom that she had defiled by placing the plucked flower on it, thus rendering it opaque.

40, 42. They came, rent Oothoon (who was within Theotormon), revealed Theotormon's smile (child) within her, Bromion having been also within Theotormon. The symbolic meaning is as evident as the myth is involved.

43. The daughters of Albion, in the darkness of their bodily labours, hear her woes and echo her sighs, called down to them as to the Matron Clay, who echoed in her voice the sighs of Thel.

44, 61. In Oothoon now is heard the voices of the Daughters of Albion, who in actual England worship purity and sorrow, as the dusky daughters of the aboriginal Americans worship the violent.

Why, she cried, does jealous sorrow sit at the entrance of

life's energies and pleasures and powers, while beauty in vain
persuades him that these things are beautiful? The village
dog—the natural animal body—barks at the breaking day;
rejoicing that mind finds beauty in him? The nightingale—
the sweetness of unseen beauty before the spirit knew that
love and beauty were the same—no longer laments. The lark
—at the moment of whose mounting prophecy breaks through
nature, by whom the inner and outer infinite touch ("Milton,"
p. 15, l. 27; p. 35, l. 61; p. 36, ll. 2, 12; and p. 44, l. 29)—is
ready in the ripe harvest of the senses, in the heart, to mount
in a moment; while the eagle, like genius set free from
experience, shakes the natural and literal in life from his
wings and is ready to arouse the mind in the heart—the sun
in the East—where, when East was the heartless night of
error, man has slept too long. (" Jerusalem," p. 25, last line.)
Arise, pass inward; that is to say, to the higher Man, O
Theotormon, thou sorrowing, growing, secret imprisoner,
and nourisher of nature. Beauty that sprang first from you
is pure.

Then Oothoon—speaking in the name of imaginative vision of
love—spoke in the name of art, and related what happened to
her when she was tied to Bromion, the demon of Earth. Poetic
idealism was denied to her. She was confined to the unimaginative. She was told that morning was the rising of the sun,
not as she saw it (accompanied as elsewhere told by singing
angels), but a mere bright shadow, like an eye in the eastern
sky. Night was confined to its felt horrors, only Bromion,
her fellow-prisoner, the personified fury of the senses, could
hear her lamentation.

62, 73. Are the senses then so important, she asked, that
because she has touched one for beauty's sake, she must be
chained to them and made to suffer their imprisonment? Is it
by sense that the chicken shuns the hawk, the pigeon measures
the sky, the bee builds her cells? It is by the God-given and
inviolable spiritual identity within them, she would imply,
for the mouse and frog have the same senses, yet their

identity drives them to assume different shapes, and rejoice
in different joys.

By the same cause the wild ass is untamable, while the
camel follows man. They know that the tiger and wolf have
regions within them, whose symbols are ear, eye and nostril
(North, South, East), but though the symbols are the same in
their sensuous uses, their spiritual uses are different in each
different identity.

The blind worm (type of the helpless unborn child), loves
to curl round the bones of death (the embryon soul clings to
its mortal house), and the ravenous snake (type of the procreative hunger of man) gets poison (the attractive charm
that makes mortality magnetic), and the winged eagle (genius)
loves the sun (the light of the mind).

Ask where they get these qualities, said Oothoon, and then
tell me where the thoughts of man that have been hidden under
his appearance and experience truly dwell, for such a place
must and does exist, and is the spiritual fount of things,
the everlasting Humanity.

74, 80. I am silent at night, the time when flesh lives and
mind sleeps, she said, and could be silent also by day when
mind wakes if the genius of sorrowful and fruitful love would
but cease to be jealous of joyous and beautiful love and turn
his eyes, his active powers of marriage, towards me. I cannot
be injured by having seen the beauty of joyous passion, she
cried, for I still hold within me the image of the sorrowful
fruitfulness, and even the dark jealousy of love, for this, taken
alone, is also beauty.

But forgiveness is love and is becoming to its sorrowful
side. Though I were like the beauty of woman when child-
bearing has marred it as the worm mars the fruit, or though
I were stained by a touch of the "red earth" (of Adam)
which stains the immortal river of generated life, and that
might stain the white swan herself; or though I were
blackened by the smoke of the river where labour of man, or
household labour, meet, and their darkness and sorrow arising

could smirch the innocent purity of the new-washed lamb, yet earth, water, or fire have no permanent hold on me if jealousy does not give it to them. I bathe in my own beauty and am the pure and mental thing that has in fruitfulness its home.

81, 96. Then the jealousy, the secrecy, the sadness of love, replied, as Theotormon spoke.

What, he asked, is the dark body, or the bright imagination, to one overflowed with woe? Has thought substance? Does joy grow from earth? Do sorrows swim in rivers? Do discontents live in mountain clouds, as people in houses, so wretched that they are refused access even to despair?

He implies that such rooting of the emotional in the sensuous nature, ought, if understood, to bring joy and sorrow under the power of Oothoon, and so under his power. But joys of old and forgotten thoughts escape beyond his reach, and he has no means of knowing where they go, nor whether they will return for good purpose or for evil.

So spoke Theotormon, for the spirit of jealousy never ceases to distrust the spirit of beauty, and cannot share its high flight.

97, 109. Then Bromion, the being of rage and earth, spoke. Dark as he was, he was less buried in mental night than the jealous spirit overflowed with woe.

Is there not a mental world, he said, where the types are eternal of things that are temporary? (This is the doctrine of the Platonic " idea.") Is there not war other than of sword and fire? (Is it not propagative imagination?) Is there not other sorrow than poverty? (Is it not sterile religion?) Are there not other joys than wealth? (Wisdom which the golden bowl cannot hold?) Is it not true that the oppression of one law for the lion of fury and the ox of patient labour is felt and real? Is not mental fire eternal,—not mortal as a lion? and are not chains also mental and everlasting, not passing away like the ox and his yoke? Is it not because of that with which mortal limitations correspond in the mental world that mortal men, the unfortunate phantoms of existence, are bound down from the mental and eternal life?

110, 112. Oothoon was silent. But for a day and a night the sighs of the Daughters of Albion echoed back hers, as their ears received her woes and so made them generated.

113, 116. Then Oothoon cried to Urizen, the origin of sorrow, who took his delight in tears since he had passed into mortality. He was all mental light once, in happy eternity or pure imagination. He became the cold intelligence that teaches man the need of mortal restraints and seeks by his tears to change man into a being all made of reason and all devoid of imagination's joys like himself.

117, 142. But Oothoon showed jealousy the picture of itself as she saw it in a glass where different images appeared. She held up to him the figure of gluttony laughing at generosity and narrow eyes, at beauty of labour that cannot be bought. She showed the ape as his fitting counsellor, type of mischief and lust, and the dog (bodily appetite again) as schoolmaster to his thoughts, his children, teaching them to follow only for personal bodily gratification. Is not spiritual identity above the senses even in men as in animals? Does it not alter the senses themselves? Does the despiser of the poor see as the hater of usury sees? Do they love in the same way, since sight is marriage? Can the generous man ever feel the low delight of the bargainer? Even among equals, does the worker of the city suffer as the worker of the fields? Is the man who pays to make fruitful land waste that the price of food may be raised for his own advantage, like either of them? His very eye (mental) and ear (bodily procreation) are different. The whole world is different for him. When the farmer has worked, is it by one of the five senses that the parson takes a share of his reward and makes him pay for his own mental thraldom, to the profit of a rule that has no pity for love or beauty but makes an iron bond of that horror of horrors, an ill-assorted marriage with all its complexity of heart-wickedness and heart-wretchedness?

Then suddenly breaking from the limits of her catalogue of concrete examples, Oothoon returned to symbolism and finished her argument on the trivial place that sense holds in the vast of life, under symbolic and not less cogent forms.

143, 154. Does the whale, strong in the ocean, or dark fury in instinctive fruitfulness (the western watery region), worship at the parental instinct's footsteps in the mind as the bodily yearning; the hungry dog, who is the northern, the earthly craving? Strong as he is, the whale is confined to his own region, and in the air—the heart—has no power as the birds of that element have, whether the eagle, bird of freedom; the raven, bird of portent; or the vulture, bird of carnage—which among them contain the completeness, or the Head, Heart, Loins of that universe. Even that which is suitable to sense may escape it by simply being too vast. The spider, though she may spread her web on a stone, cannot conceive a cliff; and the fly, feeding on one fruit or one grain, takes no pleasure in the harvest of which his mind has no idea. (The order of symbols —West, North, East—will be noticed under their masks of whale, dog, bird.)

Freedom and genius despise the bodily life of sense—as the eagle, the earth, and the metals beneath it; but the laborious who dwell in it—like the mole—to dig and delve there, know of its treasures; and the worm shall tell thee the worth of earth, for she loves underground, and thus introduces by her joy a palace of eternity in the jaws of the grave, as the babe begins an immortal soul in the mortal womb. Over the porch of her region this is written,—" Since the worm is happy in his love, be you, O Man, happy in yours, and what you enjoy with sense shall be made sweet to you, since mould is sweet to the senses of the worm by the spiritual power of love, and your joys shall renew from earth as infancy from mortal change.

155, 171. Then from lament and pleading, suddenly Oothoon, touched by the magic companionship that beauty finds in beauty, burst into joy at the image of infancy. Its lusts are free and fearless, it is not ashamed of its bodily pleasures. Modesty is the child of mental death, night and sleep, whereas infancy ought to be. Modesty calls innocent joy what innocent joy should call modesty, the false and unclean and deceitful thing. If modesty is to be praised, then beauty, which it hides, is disgrace, and all the joys of life, by the same condemnation, must be branded with harlotry, and Theotormon himself with unhealthiness and unreality combined.

172, 185. But Oothoon told Theotormon that she was not an impure thing. She was the joy of every sight that can be seen. She was the happy marriage of the eye with colours of dawn and sunset. She was the joy even in desire itself, and in the visionary creations of youth cut off from other indulgence. Unable to imagine any other motive for anything but the one central power of her own existence, the desire for beauty and hatred of the unlovely, she asked Theotormon if he jealously sought solitude because acts of love were not beautiful ? Even then he is in error, she cried, for the darkness that he finds instead is horrible.

186, 189. Urizen, father of Jealousy, and none but he must be to blame. He has taught this to Theotormon. He shall be accursed from the earth—from the loins; for taking love and giving sorrow he is the enemy and the destroyer of beauty.

190, 196. Love, cries Oothoon, should be free. Self-love is jealousy. It is envy and the creeping skeleton. Its eyes are not the eyes that give love, but watchful lamps. And the marriage bed they should warm with their life is frozen. It belongs only to the region of generation, the icy North.

197, 203. But Oothoon, the happiness of beauty, knows no such thing. She is not the spirit of earth and ice but of light, air, and soft sweet drops of water. She will catch for Theotormon, since he is after all the genius of " our immortal river," the joys a river needs, girls of silver or gold, white clouds and red, and they shall mingle freely, and Oothoon will not check the propagation of joy by any jealousy that should mix an element of earth, the blighting of the east, the mortality of the individual centre.

204, 209. For where the mortal and base desire of possession and egotism come from, there joy goes. The gold on a miser's secret floor is not the glorious raiment of the sun. He knows neither the love that belongs to the unpossessed, nor that which belongs to the generously given. The beam of pity in the heart, that labours like the ox to help the laborious, expands the eye and blots out the evil shapes of night.

210, 224. What if there be stormy blasts on the water and pestilence in the fen? The seafowl rejoicing in the storm, and the snake in the marsh, render them holy. So does the delight of the soul make holy the tempest and the quagmire of bodily sense.

215, 216. And as she spoke the Daughters—the passions and spirits of the blood—of Albion, the Man who had fallen into mortality—hear her woes, and echo back her sighs.

NOTES.

The reader will see if he turns to the large chart that Theotormon is the third of the sons of Urthona, and Oothoon his emanation. Bromion is the fourth son—that is to say, Theotormon is a form of Mental Feeling, and Bromion, Physical Will. Theotormon is related to water and the vegetative, yet still mental desires. Bromion to earth and the dark fires. Oothoon, the fire of the cloud, is in symbol, lightning; a fire that, falling from water, is buried in earth. Her love is the volcano, " belching incessant from the summits of the earth." But the symbol is not the explanation of the poem, only of the relation of its parts to one another. Next comes the relation of all to ourselves and to universal man.

List of animals, birds, &c., in Oothoon's speeches :—

(a) She addresses the eagle.

(b) She mentions in describing day-break :—

　　(1) The village Dog.   Desire, as hunger, by day,

(2) The Nightingale. Joy ⎫
(3) The Lark. Hope ⎬ in desire.
(4) The Eagle. Faith ⎭

(c) She mentions in her argument about the senses :—

(1) The Chicken and how it shuns the Hawk. Prey and hunger—as in "Thel" and the Worm.
(2) The tame Pigeon. Mild Faith.
(3) The Bee. Industry in love.
(4) The Mouse. Secrecy.
(5) The Frog. Fertility.
(6) The wild Ass. Rebellion.
(7) The meek Camel. Attachment.
(8) The Wolf and Tiger. Hunger and rage, by night.
(9) The blind Worm. Weakness, the ultimate master.
(10) The Snake. Horror, the growth of weakness.
(11) The Eagle. Faith, the opposite of weakness.

She mentions, when seeking comparison for her sorrow-stained nature :—

(1) The Worm that feeds on fruit. Weakness ⎫
(2) The Lamb. Innocence ⎬ The three purities.
(3) The Swan. Virginity ⎭

She mentions in her address to Urizen, when recounting the various kinds of joys :—

(1) ⎧ The man with a great mouth who laughs at a gift. Passion.
(2) ⎨ The narrow eyelids that mock at labour above payment. Calculation.

(3) ⌠ The Ape.   Joyless lust.
(4) ⌡ The Dog.   Hunger by day.
(5) ⌠ He who condemns
        poverty.   The censorious accuser.
(6) ⌡ The hater of usury. The righteous wrathful.
(7) ⌠ The giver of gifts. The generous.
(8) ⌡ The merchant.   The prudent.
(9) ⌠ The citizen.   ⌉ Types of the possessor of
(10) ⌡ The husbandman.   │   substance   and   power,
(11) The fat hireling.   │   who is out of touch with
(12) The parson.   ⌡   hunger.
(13) ⌠ The Whale con-   Satiated passion (ruler of
        trasted with the   watery region).
(14) │ Hungry Dog who   (Unsatiated — youthful
        scents the moun-   hunger.
        tain prey, &c.
(15) │ The Raven.   ⌝ Rulers of the region of
(16) ⌡ The Vulture.   ⌡   air.
(17) ⌠ The Spider.   Creature of a lower element
                                —earth.
(18) ⌡ The Eagle.   Ruler of air.
(19) The Fly.   Lower creature of air.
(20) The Mole.   Lower creature of earth.
(21) The Worm.   Lowest and highest of earth.

All the above are to be considered in connection with
the regions, if not types of men. If men, in relation
to giving or having.

After denouncing modesty she mentions :—

(1) ⌠ The Sun.   Generous gold.
(2) ⌡ The Miser.   Ungenerous.
(3) The Ox.   Faithful labour, herald of
                               day's work.
(4) The Bat.   Faithless attempt to imitate
        faithful joys.   Doubt, herald of incredulity and
    restraint, and literal interpretation of scripture and

of experience, is the Bat that flits at shut of eve,
having left the heart that won't believe.

(5) The Owl.
(6) The Tiger. } Night.
(7) The King of Night.
(8) The Seafowl.   Cold.
(9) The Gnat.   Destruction.

Those that are contrasted or mentioned together in some
obvious way are united with brackets.

1. Since the day of creative thoughts, the thunders of old time, when earth—or the five senses—was begun and made the chariot of Leutha—bodily beauty—Eno, the aged mother, has guided it, for the maternal power rules in the material sphere of thought.

2. Beneath the eternal vegetation—that oak which the mistaken Druids supposed to be imagination—Eno trembled, and, shaking the earth, was delivered of children; that is, of speech.

3. She called aloud on the times that had ceased to be, when the four quarters of humanity—now known as four evils— were, in right of imaginative freedom, four blameless things. When from the masculine—joy, and the feminine—love, came the child, adoration. (The three, as we learn elsewhere, became Selfhood, Pity and Desire.)

She calls to the four regions by their fallen names :—

Envy, Waste, Wantonness, Covet,	they correspond to the old forms of	Luvah. Tharmas. Urthona. Urizen.

4. Who, not being opposed as the limitations of matter oppose the freedom of idea, were harmless.

5. And generous, joy-giving, love-giving, and fruitful.

6. At this outcry of the ancient maternity, living flames of the wrath and desire, the heart and loins of imagination that together make creations possible, ran through the generative region of prophecy. The fires were armed with destruction of freedom and plague of the senses that are open to pain. They were thus creative,

This moment is the same as that told in the eighth stanza of the second "Book of Urizen."

Prophecy was watching the shadow or chaos, the unorganized body of restrictive reason. Los watched Urizen's dark globe.

7. Los manifested himself to eternals as the spirit of freedom. He divided the eternal fires that were beating around him and round Urizen's dark world. They are seen in the seventh stanza of the second chapter of "Urizen." These fires are feminine as compared with the fires of Los, for wrath is masculine compared with desire.

. 8. Los, having caused wrath to enter desire and so destroyed its virginity, caused imagination to enter sense, dividing its materiality, and remained there, the master.

9. He reduced the flames to their own opposites, darkness, trembling, hiding, and coldness.

10. But inactive sense, since the days when Eno guided the chariot, leads to inactive imagination in each individual man, and in Los. The flames turned to black marble of Egypt, to purely corporeal emotion, and so, frozen with lack of divine heat, closed round him.

CHAPTER II.

1, 2 and 3. (As the tomb triumphed on Christ for three days, so) for three stanzas the dark of maternity triumphs on the light paternity, materialism on imagination. At the third the rock is broken, and the spiritual body is free; Los is impotent in the first stanza, rending in the second, utterly liberated in the third.

4. And suddenly finds that he has made an error. He should neither have bound the senses to be only sense, nor have destroyed them for being only sense. He suddenly finds himself in vacuum.

5. And so he falls, for truth has bounds, error none. But . his fall is fructifying even now, for he whirls as he falls,

measuring night and day, and where circles are, there the
void will presently bear fruit.

6. And his fall having done its first work, changes to an
oblique motion, and presently his head that had been downwards (for when the bodily man enters into activity of the
loins, the spiritual man within him is reversed in all its
regions, its head is in the bodily loins, its loins in the bodily
head). This moment corresponds in the story of Los to that
of the third stanza of the fourth chapter of " Urizen," where
the eddies of his wrath settle to a lake.

7. In the ages of sorrow Los expiates his error, giving it
organs, that it may be rightly met and put off in the end.
Such was his action in the region of the loins.

8. In the dark purple air, the region of the heart, he floated
sideways in sorrowful feminine feeling, and gave his emotion
to all that has not up and down but long and wide for its
mystic measurement, even to accident and chance.

9. And in the region of the head, the falling but still
prophetic Mind organized itself, and became that which is
called by mortals Imagination.

(The last three stanzas exactly show the contrast between
the book of " Urizen " and of " Los." Both enter the
feminine darkness. Both organize themselves. Urizen propagates restrictions and a net from the watery region of
tears, from the loins, or pitiful and watery portion, in the head.
Los ends by propagating freedom, the pliant faculty of
entering into all the vacuity called nature, from the fiery,
or mental and wrathful, region of the head *of* (or spiritual
head *in*) the loins.)

Chapter III.

1. The loins are a duplex symbolic region of earth and
water. The earth Los had cast away. The water he must
vivify.

First with lungs he brings air to the water, or heart to the loins.

2. Emotion entered the region of sense, and they both became weary first, struggling after.

3. Struggle leads to fruitfulness in eternity, and the waters became torrents, the lungs became organs.

4. Presently, in the region of material sense compared to which heart is masculine—as head is masculine compared in its turn with heart—a form is born of heart and loins, collected from the spawn of the waters as the burning globe of Urizen from the fires of the air.

5. Then, as in " Urizen " (Chapter V., stanza 4), Los smote the north from the south region (darkness from light, earth from fire, or loins from head), so now he separates the "heavy from the thin," west from the east, water from air, loins from heart.

6. The two loins, or female elements, water and earth, clove together—being the "heavy"—and sank ; that is to say, passed into the outer or lower of human nature, while the " thin " or air, flowing around the fierce fires, coalesced with them and going to the upper or inner, really began uniting the scattered fires into an orb, a self-hood.

CHAPTER IV.

1. At this, light or human imagination first began. The pure fluid conducted the light from the fires. Air, the influence of the heart, being added to fire—passion of the head. Forthwith by this light Los beheld the void's spiritual form. It was a serpent. It was the backbone of Urizen. It was the system of logic or mere coherence without imagination, experience without inspiration, natural tendency without exaltation, the vast "chain of the mind " that "locks up," the head, heart, loins of unimaginativeness in the book of " Urizen " (Chapter VI., stanza 4) into forgetfulness, dumbness, necessity.

2, 3. Los, astonished and terrified at his own experiences,
now made furnaces that there might be a counterpart to the
pipes that drew in the spawn of the waters. He formed the
anvil and hammer. Just as the loins are a duplex region, so
is the heart, a place not only of breathing but of heating,
with a fire as well as an air of its own, otherwise the loins
would overbalance the region above them and the outer control
the inner. Then began the binding of the cold head—of
Urizen. This is the moment of the close of the second and
the whole of the third chapter of " Urizen."

4, 5. And while outwardly he merely enclosed Urizen's
fountain of thought under a roof (" Urizen," IV., 8), he was
really condensing the moods of desire into a self-hood which
should eventually bring them forth again as its own, whether
under the name of Orc, or under any other.

6. Oft the incomplete vitality was quenched in the deeps of
its own material. This is the strange alternation of experience
and imagination whose ultimate symbol is the ever buried and
ever rising Christ.

7. And nine ages completed the fruitful circlings of the fires,
for the whirling that began in void, went on in torrents of
water, after earth was burst, and is now in fire, so that the four
regions are all fructified. Then Los knew that the product
he had made was completed. What is called Orc when seen
from another portion of the visionary world, and is changed to
a rock, and awakens Urizen, is now brought as a glowing rock,
or sun, and to it is chained the backbone of Urizen, his system
of scientific and moral restrictiveness.

8. On this hot and dark rock Urizen lay—head chained
to loins—in torment, as Orc lay in torment on the cold rock
—loins chained to head. For the furnaces with their fires
had joined the regions that the waters had divided when heavy
and thin fell apart, for in this version, pity divides, as elsewhere pity unites, what wrath divides—action and re-action
being eternal.

9. And from this orb of fire, a paradise whose four rivers

spring from the mount of rocky brain and the marsh of vegetative heart, the completed form, the human illusion, the body form in which we see among clouds (in a glass darkly) the spiritual and real human form, was completed.

NOTE.

In the numberings of the stanzas of this book, the main meaning of the 3, 6, 7, 9, 10 are as in "Urizen," creation, preparation, manifestation, separation or birth-completeness.

But the whole is seen from another side. "Los" is, as it were, the second book of "Urizen," and perhaps was intended to have been so called, when in the previous year he called its predecessor the "First book of Urizen." It, however, is better entitled "Book of Los." Where the same subject is touched in both books, it will not always be found that the allusion is invariably from a fifth stanza to a fifth, or from a fourth to a fourth. But that does not in any way destroy the value of what may be called the numerical cypher as used within the limits of each. The sequence of the main story gathers meaning from the numerical hint, no less faithfully in the books taken separately, and each for its own department of the vast myth.

PREFACE.

THIS is the story of one of the eternal states or moods of man, which are from everlasting. The individual enters these Moods and passes on, leaving them in the Universal Bosom, as travellers leave in space the lands through which they go. The name of the Mood is Urizen.

PROLOGUE.

Urizen is seen in vision as the primeval priest, or spiritual father, assuming power among the spirits or imaginative moods of Great Eternity, an unimaginative mood by contrast, or rather he desires to be so in order to be a separate self—self-contemplating—and dominate other moods. The Eternals therefore gave him a place in the region of selfishness, of personality, of experience, the North, the iron land that the senses create in the mind, for the land of the South, from which he first came, is mind-created, not merely mind-analyzed. It is in the bosom of God, and no selfishness is allowed there, no personality that is not merely a means of brotherhood.

CHAPTER I.

1. Separated from the imaginative, Urizen ceased to give light. He became a shadow. (Shadow means cloud or liquid, and has the qualities of blood, the dark region of sensuous action.) He became like a void, a vacuum, like nature that

is not conscious life; that is, not anything except the
potency of unfertilized maternity. (What is not conscious life
is nothing to itself.) He was Urizen, with no other eternal
attributes left than that of potency. And this was hidden.

2. Eternals propagate by division, and by their masculine
portions, or States, acting on their feminine portions, or Spaces.
Division is the first step of paternal action. Urizen divided
and measured, he fertilized, as well as he could, his void.
The void entered into, such is the eternal law, becomes a
womb. Compare "Milton," p. 43, l. 37. It was ninefold,
and the number in itself was a promise of offspring. Change,
but not light, appeared. In dark desire of fatherhood, yet
with no creative imagination, Urizen struggled in desolate
loneliness, for the senses, inhabitants of the North, are not
Human company.

3. He sought to get offspring from the first forms of
experience that came to hand. The dim, half-impersonal
senses supplied him with what they had. His forsaken
sensuous nature (the wilderness which he had deserted when
he gave up joy for power, and imagination for mechanical
contrivance and reason) supplied him with such feelings as
beast, bird and fish may have, earth, air, and water being
their makers, or as serpent, the great sign of Universal Material
Nature, or as mere element, or fire and its opposites, flaming
wind, and cloudy vapour. He strove with all, the strife
that the giver of fertility strives with the receiver. (In
Eternity war and the chase give life, not death. Compare
"Milton," p. 34, l. 50, to p. 35, l. 4.)

4. It was a silent activity, a dark revolving. (Revolving
means conception.) There was neither sound, humanized
passion, nor light,—eternal imaginative passion. There was
only the heat of self-torment. He sought to have ideas
without having joys. His enormous labours were mere
misery, as of maternity, not joy, as of paternity. He was a
self-contemplating shadow.

5. But Imagination with its Eternals saw him by his own

light, though he lay closed in forests, always the type of
dark, melancholy, all absorbing vegetation.

6. But he had a kind of vitality, though it was harsh.   He
prepared thunders (thoughts), wheels (demonstrations and
revenges), and terrible sounds as of sea, silence as of snow,
scourging as of hail, hardness as of ice, and dreadfulness as
of a thunderstorm in harvest time.   Such were the offspring
first begotten by the Primeval Priest, the unimaginative Mind,
the tyrant Reason, alone in his self-hood.

CHAPTER II.

1. At this time Earth was not, for when we contemplate
mind in this portion of the vision that is its history, we
do not yet see Earth, nor globes of attraction, nor any other
personated forms of space.   We do not see either the drop
of water, or the drop of blood; only the first Shadow, the
primal Cloud.

The Shadow (which contains the five senses, and their
attendant of Reason), not having yet solidified is still gifted
with the powers of imagination which it will desert in order
to get power over imagination.   Thus it belonged to the region
of eternal life.   But it had entered into Self-hood by self-
contemplation (under the law, " what we look on we become,"
compare "Jerusalem," p. 34, 1. 50), and was thus already
beginning to be the great Satan, or Error, and receive a
body, that it might be put off by death.   It was for this that
he was given a place in the North.   But much must be seen
before the vision will reveal that this is its meaning.

2. Suddenly, while Urizen was lying as a mere self-
contemplating shadow, the sound of a trumpet was heard.
This means that desire began.   The story in this second
chapter goes back a stage to tell more in detail what has been
broadly hinted.   At the sound of the trumpet the Heaven,
that is to say, Urizen's propagative faculty, and vast clouds of

blood rolled round his dim rock—for so must the hardness of a self-contemplative shadow be called.

3. And the trumpet caused creative imaginations and joys, —myriads of eternity, for these moods are also persons,—to hurry at its shrillness, at the intensity of the craving.

And with a terrible division eternity parted right and left. This eternity was Urizen's shadow. It was feminine, as all shadow must be. Its division was the loss of its virginity. Fragments of life were seen upon it, needing a male counterpart to enter into full existence. Urizen himself should be that counterpart.

4. But his self-begetting had only produced destructive forms. What else does reason and analysis engender? Yet fire ran over his regions and his deserts, for the heat of life abandons unwillingly the least creative part of mind.

5. But the fires gave no light, for they belonged all to the region of the five senses, the void, the womb, the feminine obscurity, experience. They were not the inspired light fires of prophecy.

6. And Urizen rushed into this region to hide himself in the contemplation of temporary mental states of the lower or sensuous plain. He would hide himself as the seed in the earth that he might bring forth harvest. But all he gained was that he fell under the curse of the unprophetic, non-eternal senses, and though eternal himself, tasted the bitterness of age and despair.

7. And his world became manifest to the prophetic eye of eternals outside it, as a black globe, and finally as a dark heart. It had the passion of growth, and its blood ran to quench the prophetic fires that beat on it from without, as in all of us happens to this day.

8. But this called up a spirit who had not yet advanced. Los, the Eternal Prophet, the moving or vehicular form of Urthona, the true regent of the northern land to which Urizen had come to dominate,—Los, labourer at furnaces whose bellows are lungs, and forger on anvils of affliction with a

hammer that is the heart-beat, perceived Urizen's symbolic world to be part of his own machinery, and came forward to watch over it. All else in Eternity stood aloof. Los is Time, and he drew nearer as the other powers stood further off.

9. And Los wept and suffered, for though he is Time as seen by mortals, he is Eternity in himself, and all the self-hoods that are rent from Eternity are rent from his side. Urizen was so rent. He became darkness, blood, experience, mortality, all that is not imagination and inspiration. He became as the Feminine principle, without its lovable emotional symplicity. He became jealousy, which is always female nuinstinctive, unmaternal made for destruction, even when it is the jealousy of God.

10. And when rent away he lay in a stony sleep.

11. This sleep of Urizen was his complete entrance into the unimaginative sphere, the clod of clay. It would have been death but for Los. (Elsewhere we read, Los is Time. Time is the Mercy of Eternity. Mercy changed death into sleep. The word summing up all this is Creation.)

12. Los howled (the howl is the sound-symbol for desire) in sign of his yearning to organize. Urizen was disorganized and rent from Eternity. Eternity is brotherhood and unity. Urizen had become self-hood and isolation. His organs that were lost were imaginative ideas. Without them Urizen had lost all that was distinctively masculine in his eternal or spiritual structure. He had entered into the feminine state. Los howled or desired over him as a male over a female, as he did again over Enitharmon, as Heavens over Hells, mind over energy ; or as the spirit brooding in Genesis on the waters or the Breath on the Dust. But his desire not being for his own sake it healed the wound in him, made by the wrenching of Urizen apart.

13. Urizen having no desires outside himself could not heal. He slept because undesirous, yet was rifted with changes because still propagative by the potency not yet destroyed within him. He was an " Eternal " still.

14. Till Los (seeing that there is no way out of Self-hood but by its own perfection, as there is none out of the circle of the senses but by their expansion till all circles unite in an infinite circle, just as many soap-bubbles coalesce in one) aroused his fires, horrified at the restrictiveness of clay.

CHAPTER III. (*misnumbered* IV. *by Blake as may be seen in the facsimile*).

1. Los, viewing this deathly sleep, was astonished and frightened at the vision of hurting bones, for bones are symbol of sense confined within the narrow nerves, not free to roam the firmament of intuitive inspiration.

2. And he was astonished and frightened at the sulphurous Immortal, perturbed and raging, for Sulphur is symbol of opaque generative bodily disturbance, with no expansion fit for Immortals, and its rage is not their wrathful creativeness.

3. And Urizen raged in pitch—the horror of the dark heart —and nitre, destructive intellect, round the furious limbs of Los, round those ideas that were his prophetic members.

4. Therefore Los began to form nets and gins, that are systems of thought and life, and by correspondence, organs of the body. And he cast these round to catch the troubles of Urizen as our organs catch the perishable pains that, by the law of Merciful Creation, shall die with them.

5. And though Los, being also Time, binds nothing but change the great Unbinder, yet he binds this fast, and so the changes of Urizen in Iron of Experience and Brass of Passion were bound.

6. And these were the changes.

CHAPTER IV.

1. In his perturbed sleep, as the dark ages of torment rolled over Urizen, Los by his beating on the rivets thus divided the night.

2. While the Immortal in sleep became more and more mortal, and his ideas entered more and more into the strange form in which, to this hour, inheritance is passed on from father to son by the sulphurous fluid of transmittable life.

3. But the spiritual side of mortality is the mortal or temporary part of mind called Reason, Religion, Morality, cold, without imaginative fire, and clear, without mixture of blood; it settles at last in the soul, snowy cold, from the spent heats of passion. It settles after rolling. Its waves are billows of eternal death. Compare "Jerusalem," p. 39, l. 8.

4. Then is the head a mere forgetfulness of eternity, the heart a dumbness to love, the loins a necessary law of nature, and man's mind is locked away by the pre-occupation and kept as in fetters of ice from eternity, the free Imagination, while ever still Time beats, and those fetters are as ice of iron and brass,—cold experience, cold emotion.

5. Then is the mind enclosed in brain and skull, for so much of it as works is but a function of an organ.

6. And in the first age of this sort of life the expansive nerves of eternity become, in comparison, the bony chain of Time.

7. In the second age the senses that are of the blood disengage from these, as a darkened Eve from a darkened Adam.

8. In the third, by marriage of these obscure ones, the limited eyesight—for eyes are ever a symbol of marriage—becomes fixed in its narrowness and materialism.

9. In the fourth, by fruitfulness of this marriage, in pangs of child-bearing hope, the ears—symbolic gates of the World of Generation—are created.

10. In the fifth, the nostrils, symbol of outer world breathed into inner heart, are the next visionary forms.

11. And in the sixth, the tongue and throat, whose craving and whose receiving are more material and dark than that of ear or nostril, come to the growing obscurity.

12. Then eye, ear, nostril, throat—all the four gates of the cloudy region of sense being shrunk to the capacity that

they own in this place of night, the completed self-hood arises and with his left hand south and his right north, turns away from the light, the east, towards the vegetative region of the west—place of setting sun and falling dew.

Chapter V.

1 & 2. Still hints of eternity may be gathered, for Vision sends its message even to the mortal eye, but all the rest of the wisdom and joy of eternal life rolls in vain like myriads in a crowd that is an ocean, singing unadmitted round a fast closed wall of rock.

3. And Urizen's true life became obliterated like a dream, for so seems the world of imagination to the world of outer reason, or experience.

4. And with a shudder—symbol of the separation of a child from its mother, of the total isolation of a self-hood—Los smote those two worlds apart in Urizen. Then, since by organizing him Los had mingled with Urizen, entering into his inert by prophetic power, as male mingles with female, they were both found together in one dark silent void.

5. And this void was not fertilized. It had the virginity of primæval night, and the beholding of it struck horror into the soul of Los.

6. Los wept. But tears are fruitful. Pity, a feminine, a child-bearing possibility, began in the void as he saw Urizen in chains.

7. And fertilizing power poured down the cliffs or upright rocks of the intellectual petrification and system he had created, for immortal potency was still within it.

And this Pity, by further separation of nerves and blood, as the sea, in Genesis, divides from the dry land, became more emphatically the feminine red drop of the body.

Such division occurred in Los, through pity of Urizen, before his death-image, and such takes place in the immortal imagination of each man as he weeps over the cold corpse, Reason.

And now, though in so elementary a manner was it manifest that the vision seemed remote, as a far star seems, yet this division was beheld by the eternal brotherhood of ideas that people the imaginative eternity.

8. And by the bodying power of tears and cries, this mere globe, this embryonic pity in the air—for the air is the heart—took presently the female form.

9. At sight of emotion separate from imagination Eternity shuddered, as Los had shuddered at the sight of separated Reason and Self-hood. This shudder delivered that female form, as a born child, as a divided region.

10. And the Eternals gave her her name and fled, for imagination flies from unimaginative reason.

11. And the Eternals demanded a tent, a system of experienced emotion to hide the new couple.

12. And they began to weave it. It is, in the mind science, in the body generativeness. We shall be told in another book that in social life it is architecture. ("Milton," p. 24, 1. 56.) It is construction, a nearer approach to creation than analysis, or reason, though not the same thing.

Chapter VI.

1. Los who had pitied separate Reason, now pitied separate emotion. He saw that she could be fructified and attempted to fructify her. But the sentiments shrink from the exultations,—love trembles before prophecy,—space quivers under the power of Time ; Pity fled.

2. But Los presently succeeded in his object, and the shudder of the Eternals again marked an epoch in the great story of the fructifications.

3. And Enitharmon—as the female now is called—felt herself engendering helplessness, for such is that which vision

beholds as a worm,—and the Eternals began to erect the tent they had woven.

4. But the helplessness lay not instantly organized, as an infant is not born the moment it is conceived.

5. By day, by the light of imagination, it was beheld as an infant. But by night, that is to say, when it was seen in its dark and mortal aspect, it was no more than a worm. Therefore, day revealed it in air, night in earth, day in the bosom, night in the womb.

6. But as a secondary part of the great law that Time, as a portion of eternity, or prophetic creation, is the Mercy of Eternity; yet when time acts through generation on blood, or Imagination on Pity, the offspring enters the region of Pain and Poison called by mortals Life, through the gate of its own helplessness. The worm became a serpent. Its hissings revealed its growth. As hot iron hisses quenched in water, so the prophecy of its father became quenched in the pity of its mother, and joined into nature in itself. Then came a cry. Pain followed the quenching. Then with many throes, or many maternities, this birth passed the lower or animal experiences. It was transmitted through the elements by the vehicles of life in each. The fish bore its pain in the sea, the birds in the air, the beasts in the earth, as the serpent had through quenching fire. Finally it took form as infant, Humanity.

7. And in this shape it manifested itself; a gloomy vision to the eyes of the dwellers in imagination.

8. They shrieked; birth is terror. Their powers were paralyzed, for the shadow of the body is a paralyzing weight on the powers of light in mind.

9. And in the shape so beheld, delving the womb of earth, it issued forth, bringing the flames of its paternity with it, for the child was male.

10. Eternity closed the mental powers in the woven tent of system, that no more prophecy could behold them as before.

CHAPTER VII.

1. The child was named Orc. He is desire personified. He feeds on the milk of pity, turning it to mortal fire.

2. Los aroused Enitharmon, dividing her pitying sleep with the cleaving of passionate wakefulness. In so doing, desire began to threaten to enter into her. This aroused the jealousy of Los. He felt it tighten his bosom like a girdle. By pity he threw it off in the region of generative love. But by day, by imaginative light, he perceived what was happening to Enitharmon, and jealousy bound his breast again.

3. The often broken and still renewing girdle, falling on the rock of memory, grew there to a chain.

4. So they took desire to a high moral place of the masculine activity of mind, and Orc, being led to this mountain, was bound there, though Enitharmon wept. Yet beneath the shadow of deathful analysings, Pity and Prophecy bound Desire to morality by the chain grown on memory.

5. And the deathful shadow, being Urizen, heard the child's voice, and the child's nature began to enter into him. He also wished to have sons. He began to awake to life, and since all mortal things exist in the mortal part of mind, all things began to awake as this awoke.

6. Then the temporal mind began to explore the sensuous capacities which are the dens in which it dwells.

7. And as an immortal, when alone, only propagates by division, he began to prepare means of division suitable to his region.

8. Having prepared these fourfold, like the fourfold forms of life through which Orc went before born into human form, he planted a garden of fruits, for his four stages had been mechanical and earthy, and vegetation, not humanity, was their highest outcome. From this garden came the smell of ripe figs, mentioned in the second chapter of " Tiriel."

9. But Los, calling up his energy, poured round Enitharmon fires of prophecy to defend her from the cold positive of

temporal desire, and the cold negative of analytic and moral reason.

10. And she became the mother of many prophetic or imaginative forms of living thought.

CHAPTER VIII.

1. Urizen explored his dens, in all the three regions, or head, heart, loins, these being seen in his earthy northern place of abode as mountain, moor and wilderness. He took a globe of imagination to see by, and as he went forms of life from his forsaken mountains—for he had left his original southern hills for the northern—struggled so far after him, and annoyed him as dreams annoy reasonable men.

2. They were dread terrors, delighting in blood, not friendly shapes as when in the south. They loomed brokenly in his night, and terrified him.

3. The worst were the most complete, for some were self-hoods as organized as he. Tiriel, Utha, Grodna, and Fuzon, rulers of the sub-division of the northern world, of the air, water, earth, fire of the earth, came to his sight. His daughters too—that is, his instinctive, not his mental sub-divisions—arose from lower animals and herbs, growing by accretion of the lesser divisions, not by division of greater.

4. But no divisions of moral intellect can have the completeness of the whole, no truth can tell all truth, no law enact every restriction, no mortal consent to perfect mortal prudence. So he cursed the sons and daughters of his mind for not being purely mechanical products of experience.

5. For he saw that mind lived by breaking down experience. The ox moaning in the slaughter-house, showed him the strength destroyed to feed strength; and the dog shut from the wintry door, showed desire barred out lest it should satisfy itself at the expense of desire. The door opened to the ox, led it to death; that shut on the dog closed it from life.

The ox is natural strength, the dog is natural craving. So Urizen wept, and called it Pity, and his tears flowed down on the winds; and the air being the region of the heart, tears became to him the Eve within his ribs, as the drop of blood to Los.

6. And his tears fructified the region of air in their way, for they were breathed in by his nostrils that lead to error, the world when everything that enters becomes a self-hood. And the cold shadow so born followed him wherever he went over the three-fold infinite number, or thrice ten abodes, or cities, of his numerous divided offspring.

7. And the shadow took shape as a web of tears, a female thing, not complete, yet recognizable in embryo.

8. And he twisted this net into a system as dogma and theology twist vision and mysticism.

9. And then the female was born, and perceived as the Net of Religion.

Chapter IX.

1. Then the mental sub-divisions of Urizen contracted into organisms of bodily narrowness as he himself had contracted, and as men's intellects do under Religion when Religion is a net, not an inspiration.

2. And these mentally shrunken creatures that should have been infinite, though seven feet high, were dwarfs compared to that giant stature into which they should have grown.

3. For six days earth was made by the shrinkage of these intellectual powers, usually called creation, and on the seventh day they were completely bounded from all visionary life, and they rested in that hope which a literature, more modern than Blake's, has called Agnosticism. This is the story of the creation of the delusion called Nature, not of Creation in the full sense of the term. For Creation produced the means by which that delusion was able to delude, and also our escape by death from its power.

4. And their three-fold infinite organic emotional dwelling-places shrunk to a mortal's heart, and died a mortal's death.

5. And they buried their imaginative emotions in restriction, and the laws of prudence being so formed were called laws of God, Morality having put on the aureole.

6. And the salt floods of bitter passion beat round those dwelling-places of emotion, whose symbolic name is Africa; but this shrunken portion, Egypt.

7. The self-hoods within self-hood, under Urizen's cold mental unimaginativeness, had ever less and less of brotherhood, for the formulæ of intellect do not mingle as those of mysticism, nor the moralities sympathize as the inspirations.

8. So Fuzon, the one fire-like child of this northern universe, called his enthusiasms together and left earth, dropping the contemplation of experience altogether.

9. And religion, the shrinking tendency, the salt, or astringent female of tearful nets, became a globe, a region.

ANALYSIS OF PERSONAL CHANGES.

Urizen, going North, enters into the Personality of Urthona, whose vehicular form is Los, and whose region Earth, and the gate of generation.

Here he solidifies until he becomes a black globe, shaped like a heart.

This solidification sets free from the mingling a portion of Urthona's masculine potency which belongs to him as a vehicle, not as a region. This is Los. (Compare "Jerusalem," p. 53, l. 1.)

The globe is, as compared with Los, feminine. Los, desiring and pitying over it, weeping and howling, organizes it as though engendering on it till it is complete; but, for lack of desire, quite dead and motionless. At this, though himself confined within the same stillness, he pities it. The first female, Pity, or Enitharmon, begins.

While Urizen lies asleep, Los, wedded to Enitharmon, produces desire and binds him to a rock lest he should contaminate Pity. — *Orc*

Bound to the rock he is in touch with Urizen in his moveless Northern state, and, awake with desire, Urizen moves. He sheds tears that become a second and cold female, who produces, by simply shrinking up into moralities, the ideas that divide from Urizen's infinity. Her race all die. Enitharmon, enclosed by Los with inspiration, bears a race that live.

Symbols of the Book of Urizen.

The characteristic of this book is, on a superficial review, its use of some favourite terms which belong to the symbolic vocabulary of Jacob Boehmen. These are, in particular, Sulphur, Pitch and Nitre. But the adaptation of them to the myth is Blake's own, as is his use of Boehmen's Quaternary, or Four Divisions, wherever found.

Reference to the other books and to the chapters on the Zoas, the Elements, and the Contraries will supply detailed explanations of much that will show a more subtle symbolism than can be indicated in a rapid analysis of the story of the poem.

Numbering of the Poem.

There is a secondary, but completely sustained, symbolism in the numbering of the chapters and stanzas.

The number three especially indicates correspondences with hidden things, or ideas overlaid by their symbols as the body of Christ by the rock of Joseph's tomb.

The number is often repeated, that is to say, the three stanzas become six before the darkness is dispelled. This is to indicate the six days of creation, during which God entombed his ideas in that which appeals to the darker, or sense-portion of our imaginations.

It also indicates what Boehmen calls "three dark creations." But the examination of this closely would lead to the study of a mysticism other than Blake's, and not endorsed by him in its absolute completeness. The number seven is the number of manifestation. It will always be found at the head of a stanza in which development reaches a point of characterization or imaginative visibility not arrived at before. The number nine always indicates birth. It is the number of the months of gestation. By comparing the ninth with the seventh stanza of such chapters as contain both the difference between the symbolic use of the idea of generation and that of manifestation will be clear.

The number ten, as in Swedenborg's account of the biblical numbers, always indicates completeness, even the completeness of numberlessness in the case of multitudes.

Twelve is the double six, and emphasizes the cadence by repetition.

Fourteen, the double seven, introduces a second manifestation of some self-hood, some signalized character.

The numbering of the chapters has the same significance as that of the stanzas. The difference in length of the chapters is introduced to enable them to contain the number of stanzas appropriate respectively to the significance of each.

It will be noticed that Blake thought of beginning the third chapter after the tenth stanza of the second, but saw that the second needed fourteen stanzas, and took out the word. He forgot to alter IV. into III. at the beginning of the true Chapter III., and so in his own copies there are always two Chapters IV. The error is an oversight of no consequence when a consideration of the significance of the numbers enables us to be certain of the true reading.

NOTES.

C. 1-12.—The general structure of the book may be seen by the following table of correspondences:—

Head. Darkness.			Heart. Light.			Loins. Fire.		
Head.	Heart.	Loins.	Head.	Heart.	Loins.	Head.	Heart.	Loins.
	Chaos.		Spine.	Heart.	Eyes.	Ears.	Nostrils.	Tongue.
	Chaos.		Earth.	Air.	Fire.	Earth.	Air.	Water.
Self-	Opaque-	Tossing-	Time.	Space.	Ten-	Memory.	Religion.	The
hood.	ness.		(Spirit)	(Essence)	dency.			Sense
								or Body.

Though different in expression and distribution of emphasis the main structures is in agreement with Jacob Boehmen's scheme of creation. The first triad is identical with the alchemical categories, salt, mercury and sulphur; as contraction, motion, and whirling. It must be remembered, too, that the first and second of any triad produce the third, as alchemical salt and mercury produce sulphur.

To recapitulate the abstract of the book: in the first chapter a self-hood arises in eternity; in the second it hides itself in darkness, and so enters the womb of nature; in the third it tosses with agony, and these tossings are fixed into various states of consciousness in the fourth chapter; the fifth sees the creation of an organized outer nature; and the sixth the birth of passion, the product of the states of consciousness and their nature; the seventh and eighth chapter see the rise respectively of memory and moral restraint, and these solidify in the ninth into the mortal body.

Prologue, l. 2.—"Religion" used in its common Blakean sense of restriction.

L. 3.—North is equivalent to matter.

C. 2, v. 2, l. 1.—A trumpet means a creative or unimaginative thought; musical instruments are always generative.

V. 2, l. 2.—The cold clouds of Urizen are changed by the

"fury" into "clouds of blood" to symbolize the making into emotional life of the self-hood through its contest with its opposite universal existence.

ch. 2, V. 3, l. 8.—A harmony of all forms of life had existed in eternity. When the self-hood is separated away from it, he takes with him but fragments of life, being himself a fragment. The mere contractive and repellent forms symbolized by the "frowning cliffs" remain with him.

ch.3 V. 8, l. 1.—The dark globe is, among other things, the globe of the earth; globes are always self-hoods in their most elementary form of centres of attraction, hence Blake considered the world of reality and unimagination to be flat, thus viewed as the mere nether limit for the feet of spirits. When Urizen formed this cave-like opacity about him, he entered the womb of nature, from which he is born as man's reason in the last chapter.

C. 3, v. *verse 11, l. 2.*—"A clod of clay" is the term constantly applied to the beginning of material life in the womb.

: *2, 3*. V. 2, 3.—Pitch, nitre and sulphur are an alchemical first triad referring to earth, air, and fire, respectively. Blake uses them here to express a triple agony of the intellectual, moral and emotional faculties, or of the head, heart and loins.

C. 4, v. 4, l. 7.—"Iron," head; "breast," loins.

V. 6-11.—The order of the states: "bones," "heart," "eyes," "ears," "nostrils," and "tongue," is an epitome of the book from Chapter IV. to the end. The making of bones is analogous to the whole process of fixing the states. The making the heart to birth of Enitharmon, who issues from the breast of Los as a globe of blood in Chapter V. The eyes having a correspondence to the union of Los and Enitharmon to produce Orc in Chapter VI. Eyes being always connected with marriage in the sense of a union of the mental states, and the "spaces" of outer nature. The ears, the first faculty of the last triad, are analogous to the chaining of Orc, the entrance of the logos into the darkness of physical life. The nostrils refer to the air or free spiritual essence entering Ulro or Error, and becoming restrictive and restrictor, *i.e.* to the making of the net of religion. The tongue corresponds to the final product, the vegetative body.

V. 12, 1. 2, 3.—The significance of Urizen casting his left arm to the south and his right to the north, is that he reverses the position of Los, who faces always to the east, like the good spirits in Swedenborg. Urizen, like Swedenborg's spirits of ill, faces westward—or to the vegetative world.

C. 5, v. 4.—Los extinguishes the furnaces in their place in the spiritual south with a blow from their opposite, the north of darkness and matter.

Once more, as often said elsewhere, this account of the book does not exhaust its meanings. The reader who is enabled by these hints to find so much in it as is now described will probably find more for himself, to the increase of his enjoyment of all the rest of Blake's books.

AHANIA.

It has been supposed that this was the poem which Blake intended to call "The Second Book of Urizen." None bearing that title is known. The suggestion is plausible and may be provisionally accepted.

Chapter I.

1. Fuzon, the son of Urizen corresponding to the Eternal Fire, on a chariot—that is on a mood-happiness, or sustaining emotion (compare letter to Hayley, November 20th, 1800, Gilchrist, Vol. I., p. 163), iron-winged, or propelled by attractive and sensuous love,—sparkles of passion shooting from his hair—his energy—down his bosom (region of Emanation) and shoulders (region of the Spectre or egotism), on clouds of smoke (natural blood), rages his chariot,—makes his happiness a fury. He moulds his wrath into a vast globe as the thunderstone is moulded. He, and it, are identical symbols for Urizen's own silent burning mood.

2. Urizen's burning refuses to worship Urizen's darkness.

3. He threw the globe of wrath that lengthened into a beam, just as Urizen's tears lengthen into ropes of a net. The beam is the spear, or arrow, symbol of male potency and desire.

4. Urizen opposed the disk of the sun—the exterior sun—" a black shadow like an eye " ("Visions of the Daughters," p. 2)—which is feminine because it is material and is of the loins. It is the globe of his life-blood. It is in the void, the womb, the heart, and is within the Temple. All the regions are one within the other.

5. It was forged by Los during ten winters—number of multitude—before he caused it to take organic form during seven ages—number of manifestation.

6. But desire tore through the globe of blood and itself turned out to be double,—masculine and feminine, Fuzon and Ahania. (Albion's desire was also double and "was called Luvah and Vala." Night VII., l. 246.)

7. Ahania, invisible because hidden in him like Vala in Satan's loins ("Vala," Night VIII., l. 252), shrieked. Urizen hid her, though invisible, under mountains of jealousy.

8. This caused her to fall outwards towards the "selfish centre." She fell, becoming a division of the Shadowy Female in chaos,—the Spectre or Personal region, circling the loins. She is abhorrent because she is hidden lust.

9. But visible fury and love, frank and masculine, remained as a light of Egypt—as the imaginative and God-like thing in this dark world—till Los beat it in the body of the sun and made it one with the blood, as the Spirit of God and the dark waters were made one in Genesis.

Chapter II.

1. Urizen frowned. The smile is prolific, the frown sterile. His lips took the colour of death, of tears, of contrition.

2. His forests,—his melancholy,—had bred contemplations which were monsters.

3. Of these, the one most typical of the personal in outer nature, a horned or two-sexed serpent, approached Urizen.

4. He struggled with Urizen for mastery. Both used poison of delusion and jealousy. But Urizen was the stronger, and killed the serpent.

5. Then he prepared a bow,—symbol of the sexes,—and having poisoned a rock, or envenomed the flesh of man with a mortal or exterior quality in its desires—(desire is always the Arrow, between the two horns, male and female, of the Bow)—he spoke to the Bow.

6. Oh! Bow,—oh! sexes,—of the cloud of secrecy,—the selfish jealousy of the natural blood—oh! nerve of that monster, —oh! joy of the mortal sexuality,—send this mixture of Reason and law, this materialism—this rock—swift and invisible to the heart of my unmastered enthusiasm, Fuzon.

7. So saying—still suffering from the wounds of his struggle with the serpent—he laid the rock without on the bow-string.

8. At the same time Fuzon unloosed his moods of fury, his tigers, and believed that they had slain Urizen, and that he was God, now, eldest of things. (This is all another vision of the contest of Luvah and Urizen from the book of " Vala." Blake eventually dropped this as less connected with the main visions of the myth.)

9. Sudden sings the rock—(a song of death, a jealousy)— and flew into Fuzon's bosom, "darkening present joy" ("Vala," Night III., l. 11), and deforming him with the spectrous deformity or insanity of egotism, other than that of impulse—the egotism of prohibition. He fell on the edge of the forests,—of the melancholy heart.

10. For the rock, falling to the loins,—the earth,—revealed itself on Sinai as the Table of the Law.

CHAPTER III.

1. The globe shook. Among symbolic motions, that of shaking, like shuddering, always precedes birth. Urizen anointed his wound. The ointment flowed down on the void. The void is the womb of Nature. The snake's poison, made of this ointment, is mortal love.

2. The tree of Mystery is brought forth. (It was afterwards Vala—or rather Vala was made into Mystery by the Serpent. Vala was mother of the babe Urizen, and thus was daughter of the old Urizen. She has two aspects, the attractive beauty of love, and the attractive beauty of morality. Hence she is both mother and daughter of the " Primal Priest.")

3. This tree grew because Urizen shrunk away from immensity. He wrote the book of iron (of mortal love) under its shade. It surrounded him because it takes the place of deserted Eternity as the folding serpent and the winding worm.

4. He with difficulty brought his books, his mental regions, out from under the shade of this tree, all but the book of iron —of love.

5. The tree still grows, the religion which consists in calling the laws of prudence the laws of God, yet triumphs over the region of the outer senses, the eternal, the void.

6. On this tree Fuzon's corpse, the generated body of restrained passion, is nailed.

CHAPTER IV.

1. The arrows of pestilence—the desires of mortal parentage —flew round the living dead-body of spontaneous simple passion.

2. For in Urizen's slumbers of abstraction, a white lake had formed in the air, which is at once the net of religion and the liquid of generation, the catcher of souls in dogma, and of souls in corporeal birth.

3. The body is the mind's excrement, and its darkness is an evil cloud from the disease of the soul. This cloud hardened on the lake, and became the bones of man.

4. Diseases, or tendencies to mortal growth and imaginations, hovered like birds on the cloud.

5. And they were netted and caught by Los around the bones.

6. Till many were organized into the thoughts that seem to us to be fleshly organs, but others remained mere unfulfilled tendencies of nature in the void; horrors because incomplete existences, " ruinous fragments of life." (" Urizen," chap. II., stanza 3.)

7. Round the pale living body of passion, fastened to the

containing flesh, the arrows of pestitential indolent desire flew, and the imprisoned or nailed body was what is understood in the Bible by Israel in the wilderness, a reading indicated by the term " forty years."

8. The ideas of Reason grew more formal, and his fragments of life more hard and less malleable to the will, until the land where the Garden of Eden was to be emerged from the deeps.

9. And the serpent of that garden was composed of the dead passions of Urizen. It was born of them by accretion. Therefore, this is said in the ninth division. In the tenth—number of multitude—Fuzon's groans are heard. They are innumerable.

CHAPTER V.

1. The lamenting voice of Ahania, of Urizen's " indulgent self of weariness," of his " invisible lust," was heard round the Tree of Mystery, where his energy was nailed by religious restraints, weeping. She had no form, for she was an outcast of the mind where form dwells. Her tears from clouds, her fructifying drops from the blood, fell round the tree.

2. And the voice cried that it was far from the mind, and almost wholly non-mentalized into unconsciousness, or body or void.

3. From whence it could see his dark power and dark melancholy.

4. But he had despised her, though jealous, and cast her into the vegetating void of loneliness.

5. She could not even kiss the place where his feet, the nether portions of his imagination, had trod. But when his Head, Heart, Loins, had become Forgetfulness, Dumbness, Necessity, she was sent to the rocks which, with the snow and forests, overgrew them all, and sent to wander there with Necessity.

6. Where, she asked, was his golden palace, the light of

his mind when he was in the South, golden region, where his imaginations rejoiced, his sons of Eternity sang?

7. When his desires sported among eternal and mental mountains and valleys?

8. When his bosom was open, not closed in flesh and bone.

9. When her soul was given to his sons, and his daughters to her chambers; where indulgences and energies could live in harmony and love?

10. And little innocent joys were born from them like innumerable babes?

11. And even the external and female things of the void and of the flesh were happy as fatness, and odours and figs?

12. Eternal science, which in the golden age was mercy, and the architecture of the happy heart, was sown as a seed with generous hand.

13. And the sweat was the symbol of healthy labour.

14. But dark flesh and dark jealousy and dark restraint have ended all the joy.

AFRICA.

IN this book Blake says that he will sing that song, that creative-imaginative impulse—for such is a song—of Los, the prophetic spirit who, in the person of Time, brings division to ultimate unity by re-dividing it; until, by the final law of contraries, it calls up its own opposite.

This creation was achieved by the four forms of idea called elements. In the region of the heart, when created, life began there, for it began everywhere. The instruments of music used for mental productivity are harps. Each of the four points has its own inner four, and in heart-formed Africa, were four of these creative instruments.

Creation is the union of divided things by the power of mind.

In the spiritual world it began when Urizen, the once bright constructive power, made his temple the heart of man. He then faded, though once the "Prince of Light,"—for his power was spent.

Ariston, the power of beauty, shuddered, that is, gave birth.

Then the song, the creation began, and Adam, type of dust, at utmost divisibility, united, stood in the garden of Eden, the place of the "true tongue" who is Antamon, or the "true west."

Noah, the type of male force, surviving the five senses of Man not destroyed by the flood, stood on the mount of Ararat— mount of rescue, and contrasted symbol opposite to Sinai— mount of law.

Urizen (as from this contrasted region) gave laws to the Nations, teaching truth to become imperative in its separated portions, the error of errors, the assuming of will, by what is not the whole.

Just as the writings of the ancients were "stolen and perverted," so Urizen stole the sons of Los and perverted them from inspirers into restrictors.

Adam began to propagate dust, he shuddered with the throes of procreation.

And Noah, the imaginative that never quite dies, faded.

Africa, once place of light, became place of darkness. (This was when thought changed the infinite into a serpent, as told in "Europe.") Then under the influence of this darkness Rintrah gave to Bramah in the East—or region of Luvah and love-philosophy abstracted from union with love. Night spoke to the cloud. The blindness that does not see Eternity when the tent (the eyelid) is closed (as told of Los in "Urizen"), spoke to the cloud, or blood; an eyeless Reason governed Flesh, which in its turn grew dark, as the bright sun-drop of inspiration was quenched in the lightless heart.

So, just as the four Zoas clouded rage ("Jerusalem," p. 36, l. 25; p. 41, l. 26; p. 58, l. 47; p. 74, l. 1; and p. 88, l. 55), so the sons of Los are set against each other when divided, and the universal body of Inspiration is split into the mutually opposing separate religions. At this the masculine fell under the feminine dominion (as during the Night of "Europe"), and thus Noah shrunk beneath the waters. Compare "Jerusalem," p. 7, l. 23; p. 15, l. 26; and p. 75, l. 13. The Noah mentioned in "Jerusalem," p. 67, l. 59, is a daughter of Zelophahad, and one of the sisterhood of heiresses under Mosaic law, symbolizing by their number, five, the senses.

Abram, the new Noah, in whose loins the Divine was concentrated, fled from Chaldea—from the East—for the place was uninhabitable to him since Rintrah had perversedly given abstract law to Bramah there. (Compare, for Chaldea, "Jerusalem," p. 15, l. 28; p. 21, l. 43; p. 36, l. 18; p. 60,

1. 20.) And Moses, upon Sinai, beheld in the clouds of that obscured mountain the dark and delusive forms of prohibition. They were delusive because (compare book of " Urizen ") they were " laws of prudence" that seemed like " laws of God." The true function of Moses is to deliver from Egypt. He should act as Fuzon. Then Palamabron, the great genius of Rejoicing—as Rintrah is of the emotional Pride and Glory and rage of strength—falling in his turn under perversion, and reversing his rightful attributes, gives law, abstracted equally from religion and inspired emotion, to Trismegistus, Pythagoras, Socrates and Plato, under whose names the Four Quarters of the Philosophic Abstract are indicated.

All the sons of Har—all the merely natural men—lived on and propagated as times—creature-divided powers— urged them from generation to generation. All were under law, and rebellious to Har—their natural fatherhood— (compare book of "Tiriel "), and Reason's darkness ruled the region of Warmth. Urizen in his Northern darkness was over Africa, that is to say, for all this story belongs to North (loins) above South (head), or man head downwards.

And Orc was howling in chains, the creative force of desire manifesting itself through the flesh. He was chained on Atlas, mount that divides the heavens from the earth. The chain of jealousy bound him there. Note the triad : Sinai, Ararat, Atlas.

At this the sorrows of Jealousy in the person of its victim Oothoon (see " Visions of the Daughters of Albion ") hovers over and rules and influences the inspired and happy Judah and Jerusalem, and the opposite to what should come does come for this reason from them, as from other quarters. They produce a Man of Sorrows, and wretched Theotormon gives to him the gospel of woe.

Three things have become religious—philosophy, law, and jealousy or grief. The head, heart, loins of the mind.

It remained that the loins of the body should be worshipped.

This came when the human race, withered from the healthy
generative region of joy (joy is the true holiness to which all
this is the opposite), fell into spiritual sterility, and only those
mental forces which suffered from the disease of literalness,
morality, and materialism propagated.

The only thing to do was to proclaim the gospel of sensuous
love as a spiritual code. So Antamon of the morning dew,
and Leutha of the rainbow, types of beauty in water, or the
region of vegetated growth, gave to Mahomet his "loose
Bible."

While this was done in the south, Sotha for the sake of
Diralada (written "Thiralatha" in "Europe"), gave a code of
war to Odin in the north, for war and love are each other's
counterparts, and Sotha and Thiralatha are spirits of the eyes
—region of marriage.

Then the Architect (who is Urizen) built those ideas and
those organs in the four regions that correspond in physical
love to the buildings called churches, hospitals, castles, palaces,
and, that being the limit of his power, the rest of men's minds
and bodies was desert.

And then, in the heart, in Africa, as in Los and Enitharmon,
when the covered tent and curtains were lowered firmly over
them, imagination, in the sense of "Divine Vision," was
obliterated as though it did not exist, and thus brotherhood
became formularized into conventional states of mind and
conventional groups of actions.

But, by the law that "the eye altering alters all" (compare
the "Mental Traveller," stanza 16), Har, and Heva, once
spiritual instincts, having fled from their lawless brethren,
because though weak they loved law, became two doleful
forms, the mortal masculine, the slave of time and of decay,
and its equally pitiable feminine mental counterpart, and all
nature shrunk to the dimensions of the garden where (see
"Book of Tiriel") they were found in a state of imbecile
infancy.

Thus the terrible influences of Time and Space gave laws

and religions to the sons of instinctive life, closing and restraining them from visionary life, till the Reason-worship of the eighteenth century was complete, and the only conception of God they had left—the " mistaken demon of Heaven "— Urizen, who became Satan when drawn down into generation (compare " Milton," extra page), wept his net-making tears and gave this, the worst mental chain of all, as a system of thought to Newton and Locke.

The weight of the flesh grows heavy on the dry mental and moral code—mountains of Lebanon.   It rolls round the " covering cherub "—here symbolized as Rousseau, Voltaire, resting on the Alps, the Atlas hills of Europe or of the North, and on the deceased gods of Asia—the dry-hearted deserts of Africa, and on the Angels; or those who are before all things obedient, and whose morsel of imaginative existence was sacrificed when they obeyed the trumpet of Newton. (Compare " Europe.")

But in the fallen Humanity—Albion—the potency of mind, his guardian Prince, is not quenched though hid by night of experience and the tent of the flesh.

ASIA.

Now in the aggregate, the gods of Asia, also called of Priam, are in their utmost limit of contraction, Adam (See Chapter on " The Covering Cherub "), but the kings are Satan. (Compare " Milton," p. 37, l. 60.)

The gods had been startled into inventing literal interpretations of visions, forcing these on the intellect, calling them religions,—even down to the last system of Reason—and so imprisoning the mind. That was their active life, the result of their entering into the state called Orc, the desire of productivity.

The kings of Asia desire to do some active harm. They wish not merely to restrain by nets, but by punishments,

Famine, poverty, fire, are the engines they would use. That a little happiness has become transferred from the State of Eden to that of generation is unendurable to them. They call it wantonness. They would lead mortal worms from the gates of the grave because these seem to them the gates of feasting and love, and may by joy, even the lowest joy, lead to regeneration. They have nothing else to offer. But they desire to quench the pride of the heart, destroy the desire of the eyes to see vision and to make dull the ear lest it hear an inner voice.

"Can we not do it?" they cried. Urizen heard the cry.

It was a howl of Orc in changed form. It was the desire of opacity. He arose. His wings (the type of that which covers the mercy seat, or creative centre) shuddered.

For the relation between Mercy and Creation, compare "Jerusalem," p. 13, 1. 45; p. 69, 1. 19; p. 73, 1. 39, &c. Creation has its evil, or outer side, as now when the wings, and not that within them, propagated, exteriors became fruitful in their own deadly way.

Urizen's books melted, and their brass, iron, and gold ran down over the regions of heart, loins, and head, as he howled with the passion of sowing his maxims in form of melted metal, and wept, that his net of tears (compare book of "Urizen," chap. VIII., stanzas 7, 8, and 9, and "Visions of the Daughters of Albion," p. 5) might still catch souls and form man to his image, even while the melted pages of bodily and mental suffering fell on them drop by drop. Thus he answered to the cry of the kings, and made it productive.

He clouded Jerusalem and Judea—where Oothoon had hovered—darkening what had been his own bright land. It was the land of Christ (symbol of a Rescuer now, who Redeems Man from drowning in sorrow), an Eastern sign. Adam, symbol of dust, man's limit of materialisation who rescued man from drowning in dust by help of Divine breath, and Noah, his limit of productivity, who rescued the soul from drowning in instinct, thus becoming the second father of the

race. All were gone. The latter two lay visibly dead.
Satan, limit of opacity, whose fiery form of Orc rescues man
by passion from drowning in reason, flamed above the
Northern moralities, Alps. The earth shrunk, and at the last
and lowest redemption, the grave, the flesh, only, rejoiced.
Los could do no more by his song. It ended. Urizen still
wept. When the womb, or Nature, triumphed he always wept,
and in vain. Even then he could not form Man to his image,
though his tears were seminal. Only the Divine Four can
control the true Form.

It was an opinion of Swedenborg that in the Bible the historic books while dealing with facts which occurred, treated them as symbols, as though they had been fable or parable without foundation in fact. Read in this manner these books belonged in their essence to prophecy. Thus the whole of the Scriptures could be classed under the two headings used in the Bible itself,—the Law, and the Prophets.

Blake, weaving historical incidents and names into mystical poetry, did so under the belief that he was following the highest example, and that "prophecy" was the right term for literature so conceived. The book of "America" is, perhaps, the most conspicuous example of this method in his writings.

The preludium tells, under the guise of symbolic myth, that it is the business of the natural rebellion of ordinary fleshly passion to typify the throwing aside of Reason's chilling restraint by imaginative inspiration. The poem points to the American War of Independence as another image under which the same doctrine may be learned.

PRELUDIUM.

Each of our passions has three very distinct forms, or characteristics. Orc is the nobler form of Desire. He is not merely lust, but enthusiasm. The fire of genius in the mind, and the fire of youth in the blood are two kindred energies. The lower is in its way the father of the higher, —they engender each other in fact, as the caress leads to love and love to the caress, while anger brings on the blow and the blow arouses anger.

But while the enthusiasm of a man is still overlaid by the weight of his own youthful strength with its own peculiar cravings, he needs that the vitality in him should be kept alive by concrete emotions and experiences. Till the body is free of earth it must have food grown on the earth.

In the beginning of the Preludium we hear of Orc chained for fourteen years to a rock, while his food is brought to him in iron baskets. This food is experience of corporeal emotion. The iron baskets are the bodily vessels in which such experience is brought to each of us.

Orc, before he begins his active or mature life, is, as it were, a boy bound in chains of time from the exercise of the passions of youth. But Orc is one of the "states" of humanity, and in each individual this part of the myth does not correspond with physical childhood, but with the immaturity of imaginative and poetic vigour. The "food" on which Orc's boyhood is nourished was brought to him by a nameless shadowy female, helmeted, dark haired, armed with arrows and a bow of night, naked, but clothed with clouds round the loins only. She was nameless for the same reason that Orc was powerless. Her time had not yet come. She is, however, practically identical with Vala (Night VII., line 714), and finally, elsewhere, says so. She is shadowy because of the dark, the corporeal; helmeted because devoted to the strife of fructification. Her arms were but the light weapons that fly forward in advance of the great battle, —arrows, desires, or rather provocations. She was invulnerable, and naked, or in-corporeal, for the body is the garment, in Blake's symbolisms. Her loins were clothed, and these were but seen as the formless cloud that when condensed is a drop, not of rain, but of blood. The phrase,—"a bow like that of night, when pestilence is shot from heaven"—in the description of her weapons, further points to the merely instinctive and corporeal functions which she exercised when bringing food to Orc. Pestilence is another symbol for lust, companion to idleness, and source of the "gems and gold" with which the "wild snake" adorns himself—and of the "poison of a smile" (see "Marriage of Heaven and Hell" —"Song of Liberty," and "Thel," Chapter IV.). No effort, because no mental effort, is needed for the exercise of those bodily functions that are one day to be the stepping-stone from which mind, the real vigour, shall rise up.

Orc, speaking to her, told how even while chained by Time, her abhorred and stern father, his spirit still was to be seen in elemental forms. In air, as the eagle that screamed. The scream is the symbol of passion. On mountains, which are the garments of volcanic fire, he was seen as the lion. In water as the whale. In these three regions he was the strongest inhabitant because only in spirit he could go into them. Bodily he is yet bound to earth; and as a worm feebly, because not yet mature, he folds his influence round the pillars,—the limbs,—of Urthona, and in the Canadian wilds, or most Westerly or maternally instinctive region,— that is, on the cloud-covered loins of the shadowy female herself.

But, the time being come, he takes total possession even of the westerly region. The cloud,—the blood-covering,—no longer weighs on enthusiasm. And the offspring of this marriage is a smile. The two forces now see each other as they are. The instinctive cries to the enthusiastic that she will not let him go. Through corporeal means he entered into her nature. This is the symbol of the Incarnation itself. In her dark heart, whence the cloud of blood came, he was thus able to establish the dwelling-place of his image. Africa, "heart shaped," is the symbol. Yet the body shall die. The image of God in descending to the earth descended to his tomb. The eternal consequence of the fact that generation is the gate that leads to regeneration is that when passed through it is eternally destroyed. The Serpent in Canada,—the lotus of the loins,—west of west; the eagle in the heart, of the loins (now Mexico, centre of the western world), the lion in Peru (eyes of the loins, south of the western world); and the whale in the South sea (elsewhere called Erythrean, or of blood red),—the watery or growing liquid region of the loins, or Western world, all drag at the poor shadowy female, and forever she knows that " life feeds on death," as another prophecy reminds us, and that this is the " torment long foretold."

The story of this prelude is told in "Vala," Night VII., line 611, and following lines. In line 622, an identical line from the prelude is repeated. The idea of the symbol of the iron vessels and of the "iron tongue" is explained by the expression " attractive" as applied to steel, line 633 (compare " Jerusalem," p. 82, l. 69). The rending of the cloud is on line 696. In 701, 714, and 782 of the same Night, the Shadowy Female is mentioned, and in Night VIII. also, lines 26, 54, 74, 17, 82, 140, 415, 472, 474. The relationships of the symbol "shadowy female" are there thoroughly wrought out and its connection with length and breadth, the serpent, doubt, cruelty, and all else that is of the body. She, the shadowy female, speaks, and Orc replies at some length in " Milton," extra page 17. " Vala," Night IX., l. 276, adds " the cloud is blood," and mentions its evil or pestilential side as a producer of doubt, Night VII., line 782.

The " caverns " which Orc rends when chained are the " caverns of the grave, the places of human seed," "Vala," Night VII., line 610; and are the " Dens " of Urthona, and of Urizen the great architect, builder of the human heart, and sower of the human harvest, whose "science" in "Vala," tho shadowy female absorbs, Night VIII., line 140. Urizen, forgetful of his own laws, goes to embrace her, and falls into dragon form. "Vala," Night VIII., lines 415, and following.

THE PROPHECY.

The Guardian Prince of Albion, who is Urizen, in his northern and eastern aspect, " Jerusalem," p. 74, line 1, burning in his nightly tent, shot sullen fires across the Atlantic to America, arousing the patriot rebels of that land to meet on the shore, glowing with the blood of that Prince. They were seven in number.

So begins the story. Albion is the Fallen, or incarnate, Humanity,—the darkened Man. Within him are the two regions, England and America, or East and West. All the equivalent symbols for each must be borne in mind every time either is mentioned, or the " prophetic," which means here as always the symbolic, intention of the poem is not to be traced out. They are, as we already know, the following :—

EAST.	WEST.
Male.	*Female.*
Fire and blood.	Water and blood.
The Nostrils.	The Tongue.
Toward Ulro, or the error of matter, the Personal illusion.	Toward Eden, or imaginative love, capable of the error of losing imagination in love.
Inward, to the false centre.	Outward every way, capable of going to the false centre which is within and without.

The story is told from an opposite side of the same image. It is the preludium viewed in a glass,—in fact, in Enitharmon's looking-glass. Thus the Shadowy Female is the rebel, Orc is the Tyrant, or rather his Guardian Prince, seen in spectrous form. The Spectre is a " Guard "—see " Jerusalem."

Now, the " Spectre of Albion," the " warlike fiend " in " clouds of blood and ruin rolled," is " claimed " by Los, the inspirer of the poem " Jerusalem," as his Spectre, his Satan, his self-hood, who is also Urthona,—the fourth Zoa, the Earth elemental in his fallen state.

But page 8 of the extra pages of "Milton" identifies Satan also with "Urizen, drawn down by Orc and the shadowy female into generation."

This, then, is the "dragon Urizen" ("Jerusalem," l. 12) of the "Wars of Urizen" ("Vala," VIII., ll. 410, 422)—who "vibrates" ("Vala," Night VII., l. 609, and "Milton," page 8, line 8)—who is the Prester Serpent, over whose head a cowl of Flesh was drawn, over whom the fleshly Tree of Mystery grew ("Vala," Night VII., line 36, and "Song of Experience," The Human Abstract), and the frozen waters (Night VII., line 64) and who, like every Zoa that falls into a dragon form or serpent, including Orc ("Vala, Night VII., line 152), is identifiable with much that belongs to the Phallic symbol in classic mythology.

After this is considered, the opening line of the "Prophecy of America" has no more enigmatic difficulty. The burning, the blood, are in keeping with the central idea. He is essentially the Male potency.

The story of the Prophecy goes on with a speech from Washington, not in his historic but in his symbolic character as one of the forces of the instinctive imagination, a hero of the "wars of Eden."

He sees a bow bended in heaven,—a reference to that of the Shadowy Female,—and at the same time a chain descending from Albion's cliffs to bind the friends of freedom, that they may be enslaved, tasked, and whipped into forgetfulness.

This climax is to be understood by remembering that the greatest of dangers is lest we should become what we behold, as Los did when he had enslaved Urizen during seven ages, to temporary necessities of physical life, and, like him, we should "forget Eternity."

Albion appeared then on his cliffs in his angry dragon form, as Urizen the Tyrant, masculine energy appears as personality, not Humanity, and instinctive rebellion also shows itself gloomy, as of the cloud.

The Atlantic waves,—waters whose island was the lost Atlantis, abode of beauty,—are between them.

That terrible sickness, the torment long foretold, the mortal illness of generative love, or strife, affects both nations. The Zenith, the place of light and imagination, is angry with them.

The red cloud of blood rose round the orbed heaven that is beneath the bottoms of the graves, the heaven of "Milton," page 17, line 60.

Like a wedge of hot iron,—the attractive metal, the symbol of fleshly passion, yet different from it,—suddenly arose a Vision. It was regeneration arising from generation,— enthusiasm from the mere instinctive rebellion of the flesh. The King of England,—the spectrous Orc,—trembled at the true Orc.

It rose like mars, once the centre when the "planets three," the "regions," as elsewhere called, revolved round it.

The voice shook the temple of the human heart, built by Urizen when he wished to be the universal ruler ("Vala," Night VII., line 110). And the cry that came forth was a proclamation of freedom.

Blake's doctrine of doctrines is here. Enthusiasm and life are the only true morality, and freedom its only atmosphere, imagination its only land. Restraint, even corporeal, is so far an evil that it kills the soul with the body, crushes down the tares with the wheat, and renders the harvest impossible. This doctrine will be recognized as the Christianity of the first, not of the eighteenth, still less of the nineteenth century.

It ended in thunder,—the symbol of Thought. But Albion had an Angel ("Every man," said Blake to Crabb Robinson, "has an Angel and a Devil," and the "Marriage of Heaven and Hell" explains his meaning), and the Angel being a chain-loving spirit of obedience fastened to the Stone of Night, elsewhere the Stone of Trial, the skull in the

Human symbolism, answered like a howling Lion, a desiring but unappeased strength, and identified the voice of freedom as the voice of Orc, the wicked Orc, the dragon Orc, the devourer, or absorber into body of Enitharmon's children, or the joys of life, the drawer down into generation of that which obedient morality would keep at least from the mud, the red earth, the clay, the Adam.

Orc admitted at once that he was the evil Orc, because it was of no consequence so long as he was not prevented by restraints from being the good Orc. He was the harvest all at once,—tares and wheat. He even hit himself harder than the angel hit him by admitting that he was the grovelling, fallen Orc, who climbed, serpent-like, up the tree of Mystery, —the growing body,—and who was thus not only himself, but the Shadowy Female also,—who takes his form in "Vala," VIII., line 82. The active mind, the eternal principle is the life, he proclaimed, not the series of actions, some good, some evil, which were its material manifestations to-day, and are dust to-morrow. The law made to restrain the temporary simply destroys the eternal. He stamps it to dust. It was the mere "law of Prudence" made by Urizen when he dragged the hosts of intellectual lights that should have been starry through the wilderness of mere logic. Notwithstanding fleshly passions, the real humanity walks uninjured amidst their fires. His feet, "the nether regions of the imagination," become like brass—

His knees and thighs, neighbours to the region of the loins and therefore yet nearer to the flames, become like silver.

His head and breast, the place of light, and of emotion, like gold.

But the one Angel voice, the Obedient Tyrant, called on thirteen others to arise in their alarm. The speaker and the thirteen make fourteen, the number of Orc's years of first bondage. He cried that bodily hunger of joy was set free like a wild beast, and that the demons of restraint were losing their power of punishing, or of suppressing the fruitfulness of the earth. For powers figures of imaginative freedom are arising on the edge of the region of instinctive passion,—America,—and in their garments,—innocence in the visionary appearance of children is taking refuge from the lightning of the rage of Fallen Man Albion. But the clouds of blood obscured the vision of the aged obedient angel, so that he saw these things as though far off. Yet the angel knows the red demon, the corporeal dragon, born for imagination, but living on experience, its mother. He is seen on dark America's shore, the lightless, mindless, instinctive region. Through him, rage is made an everlasting state,—an eternal lion of fury, lashing his tail, while a continual cry, a continual craving is heard from Desire,—the ever hungry animal within us,—the eternal wolf.

The trumpet, the invitation to passion, sounds across to the feminine, or instinctive region of fruitfulness. But since the fourteen angels are the years during which Orc was chained, and the shadowy female dumb, no answer comes to their soundings from America.

There is a region to which both forms of passion, the feminine-instinctive, and the masculine-tyrannical, have a common ground. This, called the Atlantean Hills, is the place of beauty. It has been submerged since by the Atlantic sea, symbol of the sensuous feeling springing from the male powers, because of the mistaken and unimaginative reasoning which attends those powers. We hear elsewhere of the error of " reasoning from the loins."

On the Atlantean hills sat the rulers of the thirteen years of obedience, of childhood, and of Orc's chained passivity. The fourteenth, become Albion's Angel, cannot sit with these. The year of change is not an equal brother of the years of waiting for change.

Now they rose fiery, and showed that they had counterparts in the region of instinct, in America, and their leader, Boston's Angel, flew with them as they rose, or passed inward to the air, the heart,—for Man, fallen, is head downwards, and the heart is above the head.

And this Angel threw off his 'obedience, for he said that error must always be; but error and forgiveness, the two joys, bodily and mental, were the contraries that led to life, while restraint and rule cripple life and lead to the only hypocrisy. The very preachers of abstinence did not abstain from what they themselves enjoyed,—namely, feeding on the substance of the innocent,—fat of lambs,—and using the semblance of sympathetic virtues, generosity and pity, for an unrestrained and unvirtuous energizing of their nature, which was the nature of centred personality not of brotherhood; till the really generous, who could not gain access to their energies by hypocrisy, but only by the path of sin, or bodily conscious-ness and forgiveness, with the mental harvest reaped from it, were shut out from the path through the grave to eternity, through experience to thought.

Then they all rent off their garments of dogma and threw down their sceptres of law and went naked but for flames; that is, embodied only in their enthusiasm. Thus these powers passed over America, the West, still symbolic of the region of instinctive life.

In the bodily darkness of that place the divine imaginative powers that had refused the laws of reason, Washington and the leaders of revolt, stood, and the flames enwrapped their region from north, or its bodily sensations to south, or its mental existence.

And not only had the Angels ceased to obey; the demons that Albion sent to restore obedience by punishments ceased to punish. They appear as governors of states in the story, and they join the rebels.

In that region they could not bear their own nature or the chains of the mind that bound them. They rushed to the sea, the western waters, the most instinctive part of the instinctive region, and there fell down before the strongest of those imaginative powers in the folds of whose garment innocence had lately sheltered itself from destruction by the tyranny of reason.

All the arguments sent like soldiers to support the Governors of States, the demons, who are dogmas and rules and maxims;—and all the armed claims of morality to rule— were seized with a new enthusiasm for life and beauty, because Orc, who is the spirit of this fiery joy, showed them visions.

Then the ruler of tyrannic desire in reply showed visions also; from the earthy region to the purely abstract—north to south—he opened out the whole expanse of his mind, and spread the wings of his genius across even the region of beauty, darkening the place where it dwelt. With the diseases of error that doubts imagination he filled the trumpets which should invite to corporeal love (compare again " Vala," VII., line 782).

Then while the imaginative powers that protect instinctive passion stood in enthusiasm and watched and listened, the new demonic armies of error and argument, blighting all dreams with dogma and all life with moral codes, came flying from the angels' trumpet through their region.

But in the four quarters of the instinctive portion of the infinite in Man, which for its western or outward self-abandoning still symbolically America, in New York, Boston, Pensylvania and Virginia, every power and every busy function symbolically—citizens, mariners, scribes, builders—stopped all the usages of life only to defend life from being concentrated by will into individuality and by morality into egotistic denial of sympathy and by reasoning into blind prohibition of beauty. For such was the danger symbolized under the tyranny of Albion. That region was saved from that destruction by its mere red instinct. No more was needed. Its inherent lawlessness resisted power of law to destroy imagination. Its delight of life in life resisted the destructive power of morality, and its enthusiasm resisted the destructive power of reason. So none of the imaginative or infinite part of life was lost to earth, or the corporeal part.

Then on Albion's angels, or reasons, obediences, pestilence, or bodily languorous love, began in streaks of red; and the belief in the corporeal restraint that morality had taught became turned like a plague upon them and infected them into a belief in corporeal licence. The flames of Orc, the imaginative passion, had driven this evil fortune upon them, so that every guardian spirit of every city in the regions of their minds, the true place of nakedness, were in Reason,—and whether of Bristol, or London, or York,—sickened. Bristol as a western town and a port is clearly a loin symbol, London is Urizen in Luvah's place. York is Tharmas and Theotormon, all are of the serpent regions, "length and breadth."

Every division and limb of Albion,—every organ (Ireland, Scotland, Wales),—felt the force of the wild fires. It affected them with an evil influence because they were tyrants and resisters. It tyrannized over them. Flesh grew like a cowl over the head even of the Bard, the Poetic Spirit never yet dead even in Albion's land of egotism and morality. In other words Los became Urizen, the Prester Serpent, Satan (compare "Vala," Night VII., ll. 516, 602 and VIII., l. 458). The Priests become serpents, bodily devourers of dust, rather than take the enthusiasm of the imagination,—for the instinctive or female spirits or instincts even of religion, or restraint, rush up into the blood changed into passionate spirits, and in the long-drawn arches of the arteries feel that their youth is not yet over, though egotism, the one thing that can grow old, has long held them in fetters.

Then followed a short reaction. The "frost" of the nameless shadowy female, the counterpart of Orc's fire mentioned in the Preludium, triumphed over the fire in the torment long foretold. The body grew too strong for the spirit. The laws of prudence overwhelmed the rebellion of enthusiasm. Snow, leprosy, white age, the attributes of Urizen in the north, were the forces that conquered once more for a time. For Urizen is not always manifested as the dragon. He appears as the moral and legal tyrant, for restraint is the left

hand where experience is the right, and both alike belong to
the affairs of the mortal world.   He is mentioned by name
for the first time in the last page of the Prophecy.   The end
of his triumph should come with the French Revolution.
Then the thrones of France, Spain and Italy shook and indeed
fell.   England's throne stood, but it no longer had the power
to shut the five gates of the senses.   Ore entered here in
sensuous flames, his first mode of invasion, and, being once in,
burned on for ever, and consumed the five gates.   That is to
say, enthusiasm and life, even when beginning as mere passion,
end by raising Man above the five senses which no longer
enclose him.   (Compare " Marriage of Heaven and Hell," p. 7,
proverb 19—" If the fool would persist in his folly he would
become wise.")

EUROPE.

In the copy of "Europe" possessed by the brothers Linnell, the
following preface is to be read. It is not in the British
Museum copy. Blake seems to have disused it as out of
keeping with the tone of the rest of the Book.

Five windows light the caverned Man: through one he breathes the air;
Through one hears music of the spheres; through one the eternal Vine
Flourishes that he may receive the grapes; through one can look
And see small portions of the eternal world that ever groweth;
Through one himself pass out, what time he please, but he will not,
For stolen joys are sweet and bread eaten in secret pleasant.

So sang a Fairy, mocking, as he sat on a streaked tulip,
Thinking none saw him. When he ceased I started from the trees
And caught him in my hat, as boys knock down a butterfly.

How know you this, said I, small sir, where did you learn this song?
Seeing himself in my possession thus he answered me,—
My Master, I am yours, command me, for I must obey.

Then tell me, what is the material world, and is it dead?
He, laughing, answered, I will write a book on leaves of flowers,
If you will feed me on love-thoughts, and give me now and then
A cup of sparkling poetic fancies, and when I am tipsy
I will sing you to this soft lute, and show you all alive
This world, where every particle of dust breathes forth its joy.

I took him home in my warm bosom. As we went along
Wild flowers I gathered, and he show'd me each eternal flower.
He laughed aloud to see them whimper because they were plucked,
Then hovered round me like a cloud of incense. When I came
Into my parlour and sat down and took my pen to write,
My Fairy sat upon the table and dictated Europe.

Orc, who was in himself the personified flames of spiritual
desire, had his necessary counterpart, the cloud, that on
which spiritual desire acts, which in its largest conception is
called "matter," and is a maternal element so general as to
be nameless.

This counterpart arising, as emanations do, from Orc's
breast, had, like Hela, snakey hair, for hair symbolizes
the energy of thought, and the serpent is always Nature, the
dust-eater. This hair flourishing in the winds of Enitharmon,
the heart of space, aroused her to speak. (1-3.)

O Mother Enitharmon,—she cried,—wilt thou bring
forth other sons than Orc, for that of which I am made must
make their wives, and I shall be absorbed into their fury,
as a cloud dispersed away by lightning and thunder. (4-7.)
Already my roots are within, in the heavens, the region of
passion, my fruits outside in the cold earth, region of
experience. Destructive experiences that consume imagination are the progeny of marriage with Orc. Why shouldest
thou, the spiritual essence of Space, bring me, by nature
a mere cloud, temporary contrast of the great fire, into life?
(8-11.)

In vain I shrink from them into vegetative instincts of
the region of watery growth. From the sun and moon and
stars, spiritual potencies of red passion, fall the prolific pains
that fertilize me. (12-15.)

Unwillingly, in looking up I find myself married to the
stars by the act of seeing them. These mental forces of
personality have for sons the devouring kings on earth,
and tyrannies of the reason in intellect, when wedded to my
maternal region of experience. (16-19.)

The mountains most desolate; the convictions and
moralities most without imagination; the hearts, or forests,
most dark with the melancholy of mortality; the hollowest
trees, wombs of vegetative maternity, are full of my progeny
—desires that work in experience when experience turns into

mental system. Ah! mother, do not make this mood into an eternal fact. (20-23.)

But thou dost stamp it with the signet of identity, and the flames that are my children make my shadowy nameless-ness darker than ever when they grow definite, and leave me. (24-26.) Can the infinite pass into the temporary? Can flames in truth become infants? Can they be loved and fed with milk and honey, the sweetness of human and the sweet-ness of vegetable nourishment? A smile on an infant's face tells me this can be so, and my complaint is silent.

With this she caused her clouds to enter the region of the loins that experience might become maternal. (26-33.)

The depth of winter came. The loins are essentially, as Winter is, the region of darkness. The north was in its most northern state of identity. Morality and reason triumphed over imagination, flesh over spirit; war ceased. Spiritual propagation ("war gives life in eternity") was suspended. This was caused by the descent of the secret child through the eastern gate, which is the same thing viewed from another point as the arising of the nameless shadowy female from the breast of Orc.

The troops of spiritual contest fled to the places of shadows, the loins, where they make their abode during the winter of man's mortal life. (1-5.)

This night and winter time is the triumph of the instinctive, of the feminine, the activity of Enitharmon. It is the repose of the masculine. Los (or Urthona) who had chained Urizen to the sun (see Books of "Los" and "Urizen") rests from his labour at the furnaces, and Urizen is free of his chain. He is reflected in the north like a meteor. But he is solitary there, he only propagates destruction through grief, and restraint unlike Los, possesses of the moon the loins.

The winds and clouds, during the repose of the fire and light, are invited to awake and sing to the elemental harps. North and South repose, East and West arise and sing. The sons of Urizen, the northern sons, are destructive, and envy the sons of Los who are elemental and joyous. They demand that spiritual life, delight, and not merely intellectual destruction, be attached to experiences, and claim this because joy is among their privileges. (6-24.)

Every son of Enitharmon shall have his temporary, as well as his spiritual joy, and sport by night, the time of experience, as well as war in propagation by day, the time of inspiration.

Orc is bound to earth to become visible by night, and crowned with the vine that he may have the lesser or natural intoxication as well as the spiritual exaltation. (25-29.) The vine is also the symbol of binding, of universal brotherhood by sympathy, especially when used in the highest sense, where it applies to the sympathy through Imagination, and is called Christ, the True Vine.

Orc rose, and manifesting himself as a flaming demon, Enitharmon descended into his light, the feminine puts on desire, experience yearns, earth shares the joy known before to the distant heavens, the male or spiritual potencies. (26-34.)

Enitharmon in her energetic, Orc-like desires, will seek to make this delight of space dominate the delights of time, or state or mood. Then woman must have dominion. "The desire of the man is for the woman ; the desire of the woman is for the desire of the man."

She calls Rintrah and Palamabron, the Southern and Eastern unvegetated sons of Los, the most masculine potencies, and bids them (as Whitfield and Wesley, see "Milton," p. 20, l. 55) tell the world that woman's love (including its fullest indulgence) is sin. They are to preach the resurrection of the mortal, not that of the spiritual, body, into an allegoric heaven, itself a symbol of existence, not an existence. Then joy being forbidden, the male potency may be weakened, the female that rejoices in secrecy may be strengthened. Thus the body's nets will catch and hold the spirit's powers.

Palamabron is bid to bring Elynitria, the arrow-shooting female chastity that repels, until regenerated by sympathy with results not to be analyzed in this part of the story (see "Milton," p. 9, l. 38, to p. 11, l. 36), and Rintrah to bring Ocalthron, the secret jealousy that restricts. These are the two mental powers to triumph in the night, when religion is a literal interpretation of the Scriptures.

Rintrah is bid bring all his troop, all lions, all golden suns in darkness, fury in forests; inspired delight become desire of the jealous, the secondary form of Orc, mere bodily strength. His power helps the dominion of woman. Her net catches nothing more certainly than his fury. (25-54.) Then came the eighteen centuries of Christendom. Woman slept, instinct ceased to have any spiritual energy of her own. Man was a dream, Theotormon the "sick man's dream," of the book of the "Visions of the Daughters of Albion," line 170—and his dream was the Gospel of Sorrows. (Compare the Book of Asia.) And it was a woman's dream, for it was a thing of tears, dark water, natural affliction, not masculine or belonging to eternal spiritual joy that laughs at nature and her grief and her talk of sin, and her tree of good and evil. (55-60.)

Now was seen a mystic sunset and star-light night. Armies divided the peace of the world. Men who lived for the body and reason propagated both. Things were the reverse of what they should be. Instead of the light of heaven as a masculine potency dividing the clouds, shadows, that should be female, came in male form and divided the heavens. These were seen as sunset clouds.

Albion's Angel, who inhabits the sun, fell with the sunset. His own plagues, the mortal-colour, the blood-redness of his clouds, smote him. The cloud, full of fertility—demons of futurity—bears hard on the council house, the feminine hollow into which the setting sun passes, as Albion's angels attempt to gather there in council, in concentrated activity of the Obedient (angels were obedient male potencies). This council or gathering in the tent should have been fruitful, a fertilizing act, as should be every descent of spirit into matter,

or male into female. (61-68.) (Compare "Council of God,"
for contrast, in Vala I., 428; IV., 246; VIII., 1.) But the
angels are overwhelmed. Matter for a while gets the better
of spirit. Then, as the sunset leads to starlight, they arose
in a new form, as intellectual ideas of a purely reasoning
kind, as the "corporeal understanding," as the light of night.
They struggle upward or inward, striving to enter in this
form the imagination, the "bosom of God." In the thoughts
perturbed they tried to follow Albion's angel to his ancient
temple, serpent formed.

This was the great Druid error, the mistaking of spiritual
significance for corporeal command.

The angel went by London to Verulam, which is the English
for saying ("Jerusalem," p. 59, l. 14, and p. 74, l. 3) by
Palamabron to Rintrah.

There, in the golden south, in the eyes, stands the vision
of the temple as it was before it became serpent formed.
Then it was the symbolic temple of Jerusalem (Apocalypse,
.c. 21) of twelve stones, which should be, but is not in the
fallen, or non-mystic state of mind, the number of the
senses, and give light in the opaque region of experience.
But few of them are known on earth. They were left as the
zodiacal symbol when the deluge of the five senses left man
an unvisionary being. Then the eyes only knew perspective,
the ears words of information: the nostrils breathed air, not
spiritual atmosphere. (69-86.)

Thought—the power of Albion's angel at night, of the
stars, the demons of futurity—in fact, the sons of Urizen and
of Albion—changed the infinite into a serpent when the symbol
of productivity seemed nothing but a physical instrument.
The fires of prophecy—of pitying Los—were changed into
the sons of Orc, the devouring and tyrannic passions. Man
attempted to hide from them in sorrows, in instincts, in
forests. These moods gave rise to the pre-occupation of the
mind in scientific study. The heavens were no longer the
plenum of potency, the fatherhood, the life-origin, but by

the sad mood split into the reasoning moods (forests into earths rolling) became the astronomical heavens only, because seen as these only. They became a serpent-temple, image of the infinite shut up in finite revolutions. Then man also, instead of inhabiting the regions of his imagination, was compressed, in angelic obedience, into his own wall of flesh, by the deluge of conviction that overwhelmed him, telling him that all outside the wall was void. God was re-imagined in imitation of an absolute earthly monarch. (87-94.)

But the serpent was the "prester serpent" of the book of "Vala." He now contained in his purple head the head of Man (who is "head downwards"), and this head—the shaggy-roofed human skull, with purple eyes and red lips—became the attractive face that drags the visionary man into the life of the human loins. (95-103.)

Albion's Angel rose on the great stone of night, literal thought, that overhangs London city, the genius of parentage. He saw over it Urizen, the scientific potency on the Atlantic, the ocean of male nerve-power. The brazen book—the book of brass or of the loins—was expanded from North to South, from experience to imagination.

Urizen unclasped his book and began to sow the seed of gloomy literalness on the youth of England, feeding his soul with pity. When he pities he propagates, and in the North his progeny are always unimaginative demonstrations. But Albion's spirit of Obedience and Law, his Angel, compels the youth, as they curse the pained heavens, parental potencies of Urizen, to submit to his ideas. The serpent-temple shadows the island, until Albion's angel in the flames of the desire for a more complete tyranny of literal over spiritual law, howling with a yearning like Orc's fiery passion, seeks the trump, the arousing instrument of the last mood of man, and therefore of the last doom. (104-120.)

He was seen then as a visionary symbol in the form of a judge, flying from the courts to the open land, and the wigs and robes of his office grew to his flesh while he went, as Orc's chain once grew to the rock. (121-127.)

Such was the result of the fury of Orc in the cold northern region of Europe, while Rintrah and his fires swarmed in the deep, and Palamabron shot his lightning down his back— portion whence the spectre, the egotism, the experience, not the emanation exudes. (128-131.)

Enitharmon laughed in her sleep to see that daily life and reason had triumphed over imagination—woman over man— prohibition over inspired freedom, till the spiritual potencies were all weakened. (As elsewhere said, "Genius was forbidden.") (132-139.)

But the flames of Orc still filled Albion's Angel with the mad desire of tyrannizing—still obedience sought to rule ; still restriction desired to create ; three times he tried to blow the trumpet, the productive passion of the last judgment. (139-146.)

But, according to the law, "If a man would persist in his folly he would become wise," from Albion leaped the spirit called Newton, the spirit of sleep ("Newton's sleep" in the poem from Felpham—of "single vision"), and he blew the trumpet. The restrictions of reason cramping spirit overset the restrictions of moral religion and bigotry cramping love and vision. The Angels fell. The dead did not rise. (147-151.)

Then Enitharmon woke—the Spirit of Space arose from the sleep of nature, the watery deluge of the five senses. The incident of her sleep was nothing to the prophetic emanation. She knew not that she had slept, and she called her children to renew the sports of night, the joys of the five senses. (152-155.) Joy is essentially awakening : restraint, sorrow, and reasoning are essentially sleep.

She calls Ethinthus—of whom no more is told than that she is queen of waters, and is to come though the earthworm call. She is a feminine emotion, and that she is a subtle name for the moon in this symbolic connection is left as a suggestion. She may be one of the " Fairies that lead the moon along the valley of Cherubim " (" Jerusalem," page 63, line 14) or conduct feminine emotion in sexual channels. It was part of Blake's original scheme to have published "Europe" always as a book dictated by a fairy, as the preface from Mr. Linnell's copy shows.

She is recognized as a feminine western figure, being the queen of waters, but is northern when viewed in contrast with the next.

Manatha Varcyon should be a sun fairy ; a feminine figure of sunrise clouds.

Leutha, luring bird of Eden, emanation of Palamabron and temptress of Satan (in "Milton," p. 10), is a feminine eastern figure (Palamabron is the Eastern, or Luvah-like, son of Los), symbolized by the perfumes of flowers that open at sunrise (as in " Milton ").

Antamon the figure of the cloud, in the East.

Oothoon, the flame in the West.

Sotha and Tiralatha, fairies of the South—the eyes— whose horses are like black pupils.

And Orc himself—all are called to the " red light " of mortal love.

The cry is that of the Moon calling up her clouds, or Enitharmon her winged figures, or fairies.

The call is heard through the four points.

Urthona hears it through Ethinthus, for Los is "possessor of the moon."

Luvah, through Antamon and Leutha.

Tharmas, through Manatha Varcyon, and Oothoon.

Urizen, through Sotha and Tyralatha, but, it being night and Urizen not shining, these two eye-fairies dwell in " dreamful caves." The dream is that of " Single Vision and Newton's Sleep." (Compare the poem written to Mr. Butts from Felpham, published among the letters in Gilchrist, and in the Aldine edition.)

That is to say, the visionary spirits in the hour of the rule of the five senses (Night), and in their region (North), keep their horses (intellectual activities) in the stable and busy themselves with the poetic dreams of Beulah—"consolation of sleepers—land of shades." (156-193, 198.)

In the joys of the senses, in the sports of night, the stars of Urizen, the watchers of darkened intellect, awake to desire and life as Urizen did when Orc was chained to the rock (see "Urizen"). (194.)

Till imagination—the dawn of the East—suddenly beginning, Red Orc shot from the heights of dream down to the level of fact, and his first performance was the French Revolution. (199-201.) Violence rejoiced, sweet pleasure wept. (202-207.) At this Los, as the spirit of prophecy, called all his powers to strive with blood (268-210), and in strife was Blake's mental warfare all his life long.

TABULAR ABSTRACT TO EUROPE.

Night, the period of material or feminine power, comes.

(1) Head	Enitharmon calls for joy. She will bind all pleasure to the "elemental" forces. She calls for Orc, but will have him bound.
Heart	Enitharmon calls for dominion. Not being satisfied with binding joy to matter, she will have matter rule over it. The clouds of restraint and cold unimaginativeness fall upon Albion's guardian. He withdraws into the limits of physical man—the serpent-temple —and tries to blow the last trumpet or effect the last fructification.
Loins	Head invading region of heart and loins. Reason, as Newton blows the trumpet, and autumn instead of spring results.

The meteorological symbolism of the poem may be pieced together as follows:—Night comes on, darkness; the secret child descends first in the east. The sun, Urizen, sheds a faint light along the northern horizon. "Fleecy clouds" float in the air. Orc rises in the form of the northern lights or of a shooting star. The feminine powers long for dominion and the clouds obscure the moon—Los—and cover the world with cold and with increasing darkness. The meteorological symbolism then leaves us for a time to return when the clouds are dispersed and the trump of doom is sounded by Newton. There is a period of pleasant life before dawn, when the fish sport on the waves by the light of the moon. The sun then rises.

The significance of the Preludium is that it deals with the travail of the feminine principle when about to give birth to the soul or tendency that it has clothed in flesh. In the poem itself the Christian era is a great womb from which the imaginative life comes docked of its immortality and clothed with bodily reason.

For much more about the serpent-temple see "Jerusalem," page 67, l. 34. It is there called "the polypus of generation," and is said to have its head, as in present poem, at Verulam, and its heart at Stonehenge. It is six-fold, and includes six symbolic cities—Verulam, Worcester, Chichester, Salisbury, Exeter and Bristol. Being in the south of England, it is a kind of image of the "serpent coiled in the south" of Jerusalem. (p. 14, l. 3.) It is the Phallic symbol again of the Masculine in its separate and spectrous form. ("Jerusalem," p. 69, ll. 1 to 5.) Thus through the polypus we see that Reason is both feminine as a ratio of the five senses which are, in the aggregate, Nature who is Vala and Rahab; and at the same time masculine as its serpentine symbol shows, because it is a destroyer and a warrior, in the form of a fructifier.

It is the "serpent temple" into which the sun was put. The sun is also the plough. On it, as such, Urizen "laid his hand." As such the bulls of Luvah drags it every morning out of the deep. Its quality of identity with the plough belongs to it as an outward symbol or organ of Time, the ever masculine potency.

THE arrangement of "Jerusalem" is the arrangement of a scrap-book, and its story is the story of a paradox. Many visionary forms, many symbolic scenes, many occult names for human qualities are brought together, and after being engraved, are added to, explained, and interleaved with expanded passages, new visions, fresh systems of names. The story is that Man, called Albion,—for a reason hinted on p. 92,—sleeping, or falling under the delusions known as common sense, becomes the prey of death through seeking virtue in the restrictions of morality, not in the expansion of sympathy, and truth, in the comparisons and recollections of reason, not in the impulses of creative imagination. Thus he imputes righteousness and sin to Individuals and not to States, and distributes approval and disapproval, not forgiveness, which is the foundation of sympathy as sympathy is of love. In the end he awakes. He perceives his error. He loves; he lives; and through him love, which is also called Liberty, and Jerusalem, also enter into eternal life free from the accidents of time and the delusions of approval and disapproval.

The four chapters are divided into Creation, Redemption, Judgment, and Regeneration. They refer to states through which individuals pass.

" Jerusalem " is a name taken in what Blake held to be its true Biblical sense. She is a "city yet a woman," and is described both in the visionary and the poetic manner, the following being the references for the places where the principal descriptive passages occur : "Vala," Night VIII., 185, IX., 220. "Milton," p. 4, l. 19; "Jerusalem," p. 54, l. 5, p. 88, l. 1.

The book was written and printed at different periods. It contains fragments also used in "Vala" and "Milton."

To the first period of its printing belong the pages where the writing is smallest and most even, such as pp. 1 to 9, 11 to 14, 17 to 20, 23 to 25. These probably formed the first chapter as originally prepared for the press.

The following are manifest interpolations, and differ in style and character : Pp. 10, 15 and 16, 21 and 22. Their contents alone has a quality of afterthought.

The second chapter consisted of pp. 27 to 29, 35, 37 to 40. It is almost impossible to place page 40 with certainty. Perhaps page 42 should follow 39 and precede 40. They all belong to the same date. It is an interpolation where it stands, yet bears no sign of being a later contribution. If its right place be where 39 is, then the rest would read : 40, 45, 47, 48, 49, 50.

Page 30 is evidently later, as is 31, its sequel, and 32, 33, 40, that all follow each other, and have evidently not been written originally before 35, but after. Page 36 is distinctly and undoubtedly later, and belongs to the same date as 16. The intrusion of Reuben in both was not part of the original scheme. Page 41 is also later than 42, but not so late as 36. Its proper sequel is page 43, which continues the account of what the Twenty-eight saw. Page 44, which follows 43, is ingeniously made to terminate, so as to come smoothly before 45, but it was almost certainly written later. Page 45 ends with a line added in white, as an afterthought, on purpose to introduce 46, whose matter ends abruptly, and makes no pretence to lead to 47.

Chapter III. belongs to the date of many of the above interpolate pages, but is earlier than pages 16 and 36. It is the most incoherent. Pages 56 and 61 are among the latest in the whole book, and most probably were engraved several years after the commencement. Page 57 probably belonged to the preceding chapter. Page 63, though so small in type as to imitate the style of the early pages, is also very late. It stands with its sequel, 64, in isolation, and might be put anywhere.

Page 65 is an early page, but what should precede it cannot easily be said with certainty. Perhaps a page of the same date was cancelled to admit others. Page 66 follows it; but what should precede page 67? It belongs to another time, as is partly shown by the extract from "Vala," Night VIII., whose line 293 is here 44. Night VIII. of "Vala" was probably not written when page 66 was engraved. Pages 68 and 69 follow, but page 70 is earlier, and does not rightly succeed them. It seems to have been intended to precede the page numbered 19, though it doubtfully follows 18.

Page 71 would perfectly follow page 19 and precede 20. It is certainly out of place where it stands, since it does not begin with the word *His*, indicated as the leader at the end of page 70. Nor is it required to introduce page 72, which is of the date of page 16, and probably was intended to be immediately preceded by it. Page 73 is of the same date; 74 is earlier, and probably precedes those in which Reuben's story separates itself from that of the tribes. Page 75 is an isolated page of not the earliest date, but as early as any in the chapter, except 65 and 66.

In chapter IV. we return in the preface to work of an early date. The prose was composed later than the verse, but printed on the plate at the same time. The chapter consisted of pages 78 to 80, 82 and 83, 97 to end. Were there more pages between 83 and 97? If so, one which began with the word "Awake" has been cancelled. Page 81 is an evident interpolation of later date, and interrupts the flow of 80 to 82. Pages 84 to 89 follow each other, and are all of late date; perhaps 90 and 91 follow them; but 92 does not succeed 91 at all. Page 93 follows it but 94 takes a new departure, and

95 follows and rightly precedes 96. The last four lines should be omitted, as the first two of them are found at the beginning of the next page; or else the last two should be introduced as the third and fourth of page 96.

But not only are the pages in most doubtful order as finally arranged by Blake himself, guided by many after-thoughts; but one authentic copy at least—that in the British Museum—while it takes no account of the interpolations here noticed, has a page-numbering of its own.

JERUSALEM.

THE following account of the book of Jerusalem is intended to serve as a companion and an assistant to readers who are studying the poem, not as a description that pretends to be readable by itself or apart from the text. The frontispiece and title-page being numbered 1 and 2, the book begins at page 3, which is a preface to the first chapter. It is itself an explanation and needs no commentary.

CHAPTER I.

P. 4, l. 2.—Of the imputation of sin and righteousness to individuals and not to states, and of the passage through the belief in personal individualism in mind, morals, and sensations, to the belief in the imaginative freedom with its blending of all in all, and its perfect forgiveness that imputes to individuals no sin—such is the theme. The first of these states belongs to the man whose soul, absorbed in the temporary world, is merged in what is temporary, and is thus in a state of eternal death. The second belongs to him who, averting his mind from experience and its deceptions and turning to imagination, is in a state of eternal life.

P. 4, ll. 3 to 5.—This theme calls me,—says Blake,—night after night, through mood after mood of unimaginative experience, and every time that the mind's true light,—morn, —returns it awakes me as divine warmth begins,—sunrise,— and I see the human imagination,—the Saviour, spreading his beams of love and creating the persons,—(words) of this mild eation,—(song).

P. 4, ll. 6 to 20.—He cries,—Awake,—that is,—perceive the

universality of imaginative light,—oh! man, sleeping in experience, the shadowy land,—and expand,—enter the light and
acquire more senses than the five by its action upon you.
Imagination is God's love in all, and friendship between yourselves shall teach you how to feel towards it. But in all that
should be the region of vision,—in the male nerves—(Atlantic)
and the southern region of your souls,—(Surrey) a black
water,—a sorrowful morality of experience and disapproba-
tion, the reverse of friendship, accumulates. Return, Fallen
Man,—(Albion)—return to forgiveness, family love calls
thee,—and weeps at the disease of doubt, and unforgiving
censoriousness that is on thy soul. Thy power of affection,—thy
Emanation, named Jerusalem,—with all her impulses,—her
daughters,—where hast thou hidden her? Imagination and
forgiveness, the vision and fruition, cannot reach her. I am
not a god afar off, but a brother, your true self. And your
emotions of tenderness learned from the sexes, sleepers because
in the dream of the created and temporary world, yet of Beulah,
because of the part nearest heaven (marriage, type of the
larger Unity) you are my members.

P. 4, ll. 22 to 31.—So says man's imagination, but his reason
drags him away with perturbation and he goes to experience
praising individuality and morality, that lead to war and away
from brotherhood.

P. 5, ll. 33 to 35.—Albion the Fallen Man, thus turned away,
jealously hiding his wider tenderness in its narrower form of
sexuality, the parent-stream (Thames).

P. 5, ll. 1 to 15.—And the banks of the stream clouded and
the senses of Albion, porches through which inspiration and
light should have come to him, darkened, and every attribute
and power of his mind, called by the several names of the
geniuses of cities and lands, hardened and shrunk, and among
them dragged under the laws of experience,—the cruelty of
this world,—all his inspired impulses.

P. 5, ll. 16 to 26.—"Trembling I sit day and night,"—(says
Blake) and prays that his hand may be guided while he opens

the eyes of man to his own inner life, of imagination, and tells
under many names the strife of his various misguided reasonings and moralities with his truer inspirations and impulses.

P. 5, ll. 27 to 33.—Such misguided powers are the sons of
Albion, and they war to destroy enthusiasm and to desolate
the city of the sacred inward loves. Four in especial strive
in the heart,—the Eastern gate,—to devour the sleeping
Humanity of Albion turning Pity, and its Outflowing (or
emanative quality), to Rage and Hunger. They are the parents
of all temporal moods,—the souls within the soul.

P. 5, ll. 34 to 39.—The Male potency burns, the Female weaves.
The names under which they are here divided were known to
ancient vision and control in each of us, those vitalities by
which even our bodies seem to grow and vegetate.

P. 5, ll. 40 to 52.—These powers being named, and their merg-
ing into those that are greatest among them, Jerusalem, we
are told, the great inspired love of Albion was dragged along
in a cloud (the cloud is both of blood and tears), and dragged
away in maternal love toward her children, the lesser affections,
into the great smoke of experience and personality.

P. 5, ll. 52 to 64.—With her goes Vala, the merely natural
affection, and they weep together as they become the victims
of abstract philosophy.

P. 5, ll. 65 to 68.—But the spirit of prophetic fire,—Los,—in
the bosom of man, heard. He wept. His pity,—or Emanation,—divided as his tears fell. It became attracted to the
philosophies (starry wheels) in his heart (east) but in his
instinctive region (west) became mere shadow and horror.

P. 6, ll. 1 to 14.—His Spectre,—his reasoning self, driven by
the same philosophies, divided from him, stood over him, filled
him with censoriousness against fallen humanity (murderous
thoughts) and tried to destroy the Human Perfection, the
Divine Imaginative power, in Los himself.

But though suffering he laboured and sang,—(conceived and
created).

P. 7, ll. 1 to 8.—The Spectre, unable to slay Los, carried on the war of reason against prophecy by tears, arguments, science, fear, standing on the darkening Thames,—the ever more physical parental power.

P. 7, ll. 9 to 50.—Under the names of the sons of Albion, and under figure of their inhabiting certain eastern lands, he pointed out how the forces of unimaginative intellect had taken up their abode in moral laws. He told how the Natural affections torture the natural heart (Vala scaled Luvah in the furnaces). He told how Albion's sons and daughters,—his mental and instinctive forces now that he was given up to belief in experience—had so dealt that they had generated a Law of sin among themselves who should yet punish prophecy in his members, that is to say in his system of thought.

P. 7, ll. 51 to 70.—Los answered that the true method did not lie in destroying the impulses for the sake of the intellect and calling this morality. That was death. It lay in learning to see in physical needs a symbol of the great spiritual need, universal unity, and in the forgiveness of sins that should keep pace with physical needs, the way to learn the spiritual love which utters no accusation. He told him too that when this is learned the Incarnation will have taken place. He prays to be delivered from wrath.

P. 7, ll. 71 to 73.—But man's chief intellectual conviction,— (called Hand, Albion's eldest son), was full of cold self-righteousness, that whirlwind of the north which is the direct opposite of the whirlwind of the south out of which God rebuked Job for this error.

P. 8, ll. 1 to 43.—Then Los threatened his own reasoning self that his enthusiastic self should punish and torture it, if it should dare to do anything but obey him, and with this he forces it to work at his enthusiasms. So the spectre was forced to work in the furnaces.

P. 8, ll. 44 to 45.—But in Albion, his chief power of mental self-hood—(Hand)—had destroyed all that was innocent, lovely and graceful.

P. 9, ll. 1 to 11.—For he had condensed the impulses into

hard inaccessibilities, like cliffs of death, and beauty was despised, and a mental system adapted only to the temporary, a body of death, that is of memory, of the past, was formed round Imagination, the Lamb, so that Albion's impulses might be destroyed and his natural system of thought devoured, and mental contest might use up the growth of his harvest of ideas, as war takes away the labour of the husbandman.

P. 9, ll. 12 to 31.—So that the more foolish side of mind became the more formidable, so that Los had need to expose the secrets of the heart, and to make jewels or permanent beauties of its hidden sorrows, that those who did not value the truth of inspired love might defend the lie of bodily love, —the body, not the love, being itself a lie,—that enthusiasm and life might not cease.

P. 9, ll. 32 to 35.—So laboured prophecy to make the impulses of the spiritual Eden,—(spaces of Erin) compelling his own Reason (harsh spectre) to the work.

P. 10, ll. 1 to 26.—He also explained the nature of contraries and negations and the deadness of a mental power that objects and does not create. Therefore he enslaves his own spectre and therefore Los creates system, lest he himself should be enslaved to the system of another,—that is to say, vision compels reason to aid in systematizing mysticism lest the visionary faculty should be enslaved by dogma or science.

P. 10, ll. 22 to 28.—The spectre curses the children of Los, under figure of the sun, and moon, and divisions of the world (Los is Time as well as the prophetic spirit, and these are the appearances he gives as Time to his ideas).

P. 10, ll. 29 to 36.—But Los forbids his reason to object to the children of his imagination. He makes it invisible to them lest they should see it and become what they behold, for he loves and refuses to be ashamed of them.

P. 10, l. 37.—The spectre reviles his emotions, calls them his sins, and claims to love the chief of them all his Emanation, Enitharmon. He utters a lament of agony over his own death, for he is of the memory and of the personality, and pity itself is for ever flinging the grave-stone over him.

The grave-stone is a symbol for the body, in the ordinary material sense of the word. The spectre is the self-hood, self-righteousness, and morality, as well as the memory. Los, as Mercy, the Creative Motive, flings over the personal part, the mortal part—his grave-stone.

P. 11, ll. 1 to 7.—But prophetic zeal obliges even this portion to share his labours, with systems to deliver individuals from systems; for the practise of systematic mysticism delivers the reason from the systematic dogmatism whose non-mystic form is error, so that when a spectre devours the dead, when self-hood absorbs the reasoning faculties, a man's mind might feel pain as though his teeth, symbols of the cogwheels of logic, bit his nerves, symbols of the region of visionary inspiration.

P. 11, ll. 8 to 12.—Then Erin, in whom all the daughters of Inspiration are seen, as they are in Jerusalem, the elder name, came forth from the furnaces of affliction, and her impulses of imagination extended from the extreme to the extreme of mental passivity and activity,—the spaces reached from starry height to starry depth.

P. 11, ll. 13 to 16.—The joys and the labouring wrath of prophecy met and embraced as daughters meet a father. The joys had feared their origin was for ever enslaved to the hard systems and laws of fallen man.

P. 11, ll. 17 to 25.—Then they consulted what to do for Jerusalem, the true great Aggregate of them all.

(Jerusalem is, in fact, the Feminine Head, as Erin is the Heart, Vala the Loins. But their regions are not the same as those of the Masculine Head, Heart, Loins.)

P. 12, ll. 1 to 4.—Los protests with Jerusalem because her tears have given Vala actuality,—from being a tendency,—in fact she becomes Babylon, as seen later.

P. 12, ll. 5 to 15.—But Los also says that he sees the finger of God in the giving of a body, of moral system, to the mere tendency, Vala, the beauty of natural belief, because only body, that is, only system, can be made mortal and put off.

P. 12, ll. 16 to 24.—And the spaces of Vala, the uninspired or natural portion, and of Jerusalem, the light of which Vala is the shadow, were of the same dimensions as those of Erin. And as those of spiritual manhood's mind,—the city of Golgonooza.

P. 12, ll. 24 to 42.—And Los, wondering, sees that sacrifice promotes pity as morality demands sacrifice, and the dead morality produces living love,—Golgotha became Calvary, both led to Zion, the first and the last. He sees it in the tears of mournful mortal desire and mortal morality (Paddington, West of London, symbol of Vala, opposite and emanation of Luvah).

P. 12, ll. 42 to 44.—Los bids the builders of systems go on in hope, even though the mild fires of inspiration, the light, not wrath, wander far away into cold regions of philosophy.

P. 12, ll. 45 to 65.—The system builded by the builders is described with its fourfold regions.

P. 13, ll. 1 to 55.—And with its surrounding land that stretches away, as error (that has no bounds: see Book of Los), surrounds imagination, reaching away into unsystematic experience, delusion, vacancy.

P. 13, ll. 55 to 66.—And Los sees all things permanent, even all exterior things, in the continuance of the mutable that is not merely ever destroyed, but ever constructed. (This is the philosophic conception of the "ideas" of Plato, mingled with the "astral light" of the Theosophists, and the materialist's "laws" and "energy."

P. 14, ll. 1 to 15.—Los sees also the visionary forms as well as the types, and the pictures of things experienced. All are equal, since all are visible.

P. 14, ll. 16 to 35.—And he beholds his own sons, and the drawing in of Jerusalem, who is drawn towards the East, which is at once the heart and the false centre, thus the visionary movement described at the outset of placing the poem.

P. 15, ll. 1 to 34.—And since what the Inspirer sees, the Inspired sees also, Blake beholds the vision of Los, and beholds Los himself, and from this point of view judges the reasoning systems of man,—the schools of Albion, and the primitive systems,—the valley of Hinnom—in the first winter of cold materialistic philosophy and morality based on unimaginativeness.

P. 16, ll. 1 to 59.—Then some of the labours at the furnace and at the looms,—for the feminine weaves, while the masculine forges,—are described, both under their visionary and Scripture names, and their equivalents in English countries. These, tabulated elsewhere in the present work, belong to a set of anatomical as well as psychological correspondences forming a secret language, an arcanum, to which Blake has not left a complete Key.

P. 16, ll. 60 to 69.—And the permanence of human types and forms and motives is compared to that of sculpture.

P. 17, l. 1, 15.—And Los himself being seen, is also a Reasoning Selfhood or Spectre, that of the living, or imaginative ideas. ("Vala," Night VII., l. 306.) He bends his fury against the spectres of the dead, his natural enemies, but against the sweet beauty and impulse belonging to mortal life he dare not go in his complete nature, lest by sympathy they should draw him down,—the charms of nature thus attempt to draw poetry from an inspired use of symbols to a mere repetition of their beauties, so he shows them his spectre—the spectre of a spectre—and his undisguised desire that they should cast off their mortal opacities, limitations, demonstrations, moralities. At this they fly in fear.

P. 17, ll. 16 to 19.—And then Los sees that his own spectre, now separate, must go under perfect obedience,—Reason must be the servant of Inspiration, lest it devour his love, pity, and repose—Enitharmon.

P. 17, ll. 20 to 47.—For the Reason would make her even as the poor daughters of Albion, who mistake mortal love for immortal, experience for inspiration. All divided portions of mind seek their own permanence and one another's destruction. Therefore the Spectre must obey, or an emanation or counterpart will be given him of hell and despair, the opposite of cold reason and its complacency.

P. 17, ll. 47 to 58.—Los's Spectre and Emanation both divided from him—the spectre from his back, the Emanation from his front, for they are Past and Future, Memory and Hope, as well as Reason and Desire. For Los had entered into the deadly night, region of systems and labour, by the use of his own Reason, and in the night, Desire divides from Prophecy even as from mortality.

P. 17, ll. 59 to 63.—Los bids his spectre go to one of the spectres of Albion—Schofield, who is the Natural Man, in contrast with the Spiritual Man, and ask him whether his love is of the East and West (Bath) or of the North and South (Canterbury) whether it is feminine, given to length and breadth—Nature; or masculine, given to height and depth—Mind. He is to remember that both he, and his brother Hand, the undoubted natural head, or reasoning error, are servants of the prophetic spirit who can use them to wreak his vengeance or break them to pieces.

P. 18, ll. 1 to 10.—The nature of the true and false, inward and outward, is explained, and of Vala and Jerusalem, body-mother and soul-mother.

P. 18, ll. 11 to 35.—Hand and Hyle, eldest of Albion's sons cry out against Jerusalem as immoral, and praise self-righteousness.

P. 18, ll. 36 to 46.—Which brings Albion to the ground, where he lies outstretched in the night,—humanity fallen under bondage to law and experience.

P. 19, ll. 1 to 15.—Albion's imaginations, affections, and impulses,—his children, harvests, and birds and beasts wither, and his ultimate personality, the indestructible principle, the Eon, weeps in the void.

P. 19, ll. 16 to 47.—He composes moral systems and

philosophies, and in these cliffs roofs Los in from imagination
—eternity, and, his way to Eden closed, his expansive loves
cut off, his centre darkens, and in it only is Beulah left, the
unity of sexes to keep him from the ultimate death of
separateness from all unity. Los guards the feminine but
pale imaginativeness of this mental state—derivative poetry,
the moon of this night; he can do him now no other service.
The rocky forms of mathematic system and morality stand
up against the living mind of imagination and heart of
forgiveness, or Divine Humanity. So Albion fled inwards into
his darkened centre along his sensations, the currents of his
rivers, bodily nerves, and there found Jerusalem and Vala,
hidden but not dead. They are joy and pleasure. They seek
to soften his hardness of mind into what affections they may
for love of its beauty.

P. 20, ll. 1 to 10.—Albion, entering his darkened centre and
meditating in his personal heart, discussed with his own
attributes his and their convictions. Vala the bodily impulse,
in the web of despair, in the limitations of the corporeal
understanding, that belongs to despair, the past, was full of
love and repentance. Jerusalem who had been hidden in
Vala's region along with her, pleading and weeping, reproached
Vala with having shut her into the winter, or loins, of human
life, reminding him that while both were yet an idea or an
aspiration in head and heart, they had been happy.

P. 20, ll. 10 to 20.—Vala replied that in mortal life the mind
deals only with the past, with remembrance, and besought her
not to recall grief.

P. 20, ll. 20 to 41.—Jerusalem besought Vala not to deny to
her the region of hope, or prophecy, to which her little ones
should have access, if not slain by such prohibition. One love
had united all. Albion had loved both. His bodily strength
had loved Vala, his heart had held Jerusalem, for the senses
love memory as the aspirations love prophecy. His exaltation
had even rent the veil which makes of the past a regret, not a
possession, and of the future a mystery, not an open experience

(for such is the state called fourfold vision in which the mind of a man can walk up and down in six thousand years, and see the past, present, and future existing at once). Then as Jerusalem—inspired love—leaped from Albion's personal bosom, the divine bosom, also in Albion,—the Lamb received her. Then was a time of love. Why has it passed away?

P. 21, 1. 1.—Then Albion makes his great reproach. He is the fallen man, the man whose intellect is plunged downwards into logic, experience, personality, the Head, Heart, Loins of the corporeal understanding. These are in the sight of the Imagination mere Forgetfulness, Dumbness, Necessity, as their loves, leading to bodily parentage and the weaving of fresh mortalities, Envy, Revenge, Cruelty. It is in this state of his regions that Albion utters his wintry words. He has perceived, notwithstanding his state, that his moods of love and dreams of beauty are not one man's secret, but all men's life, and his personality rebels against this. He reproaches his loves with shamelessness because one egotism could not contain them. He himself is ashamed because imagination blushes before unsympathetic reason. He is a prey to doubt because reason cannot achieve the proof of experiences only known to be sane and true by the sympathies or by revelation—(Vala and Jerusalem in their mental aspect.) He has discovered that they are not only the life of the soul but the mainspring of the body's passions. His argumentative states scourge along barren places of the mind, the tender bodies of his imaginative impulses, even as autumn storms drive underground the seeds that in six months will revive with spring. In one speech he sums up all the contests, moral, mental, personal, natural, with which all that is not of growth makes war upon all that is of growth, wherever found. Then Vala spread over him her scarlet veil, and he was forced to be enfolded in the most simple and instinctive growth-impulse of all, and Reason, after being too self-righteous to dream, was condemned to be veiled in a body too instinctive in its vitality to require even dreams for its vital sustenance, or its love-impulses.

P. 22, ll. 1 to 15.—But Albion's head being downwards, or Envy, his heart, Revenge, his loins Cruelty, of deliberate legal punishment, Jerusalem, in Vala, felt terror the moment the veil was round him, she being the veil's life. She felt terror, moral and physical, she felt that to personality, blood means war and hate, that should mean love, as blood's pre-natal life meant. She shrinks from Albion's eyes, conscious of her bodily tendencies, while in his envious soul her bodily inspiration sees the other sin of unforgivingness.

P. 22, l. 16.—Then beneath the silent moon,—(the moon is the feminine locus, now stricken with the dumbness of Albion's revengeful heart, in which the language of love was silenced). Albion speaks the language of experience. He has brought personal love into the light of mental consciousness—day—and like Adam in Eden after eating the fruit, causes innocence, by fancying that it was dead, to be no more. This is the doctrine that Adam's sin was not the nakedness of which he was ashamed, but the following of beauty's act with misguided opinion,—the belief that the state of innocence—an eternal state—was no more. The shame was then his disease, and the beginning of his punishment.

P. 22, ll. 21 to 24.—Jerusalem continues the doctrine, by describing the error, not under figure of eating a fruit, but under that of anatomizing an infant, whose presence is a joy, while his dissection is a misery, and its very condition a death. Compare the "Mental Traveller." "Her fingers number every nerve." The old woman there has the morbid morality of Albion.

P. 22, ll. 25 to 33.—Then Albion bids Jerusalem hide where she cannot be seen or touched. That is, he will have the inspired sympathies made part of the Unconscious, and hidden in the flesh, whose conscious instincts dwelling in the feminine or bodily blood—Vala's robe—shall live while his masculine blood, ideal passion, is drained away. For Luvah is slain,—love is materialized and made spectral, personal. Thus Albion hopes to escape from analyzing joy or envying love.

P. 22, ll. 34 to 46.—Jerusalem, then blood, asked why blood must needs be the origin of sin, and of punishment and war. Personality may be valued for its capacity to forgive, separateness for its delight in joining,—using the well-known figure that identifies the union of sexes by love, the union of sin and righteousness by forgiveness, and of the union of reason and imagination by inspiration.

P. 23, ll. 1 to 7.—But forgiveness restores the soul to righteousness. It annihilates the past, sin being of the past, and, remembrance and reason being of the past, partake of the annihilation. When Albion committed the sin of breaking into the instinctive with the force of the analytical, he destroyed the virginity of instinct. Inspiration came with forgiveness, and raising him to another level, melted his soul in spite of himself, and the separateness of the past was no more a condition of his mind, and the virginity of instinct was restored, the veil of Vala was made whole and more beautiful than ever.

The passage has a second symbolic intention. The Veil is morality. Rebellion for selfish purposes breaks it. It is not permanently destroyed. It mends from this kind of hurt by its own coherence. Only the "Last Judgment" in each individual, and the death of his "natural man" causes it to be finally "burned up," as all things are which we "cease to behold."

In a third meaning the Veil is the delusion of Nature, broken by philosophic doubt, but unbound finally by addition of the experiences of inspiration to those of the five senses and their Ratio, or Reason.

P. 23, ll. 8 to 12.—Jerusalem tells the secret of inspired love again. Forgiveness, the loins of that love, she had invoked with her hand on the moon. She now invokes Pity, its heart, and demands why she is still to be kept by self-hood from Brotherhood, or Humanity, its head, the meeting-place of all relationships, the annihilation of self-hoods.

P. 23, l. 13, 19.—But Albion is in jealous, dark despair.

Self-hood is still his god—(or Satan, opposite of Humanity, or Imagination, or Jesus). Yet he feels the truth of the unity of the regions in the inward or upper sphere of Jerusalem. He confesses his sin—his personal belief in punishment.

P. 23, ll. 29 to 40.—Then suddenly, with the repulsion of pride from the conviction of error, Albion recoiled from his own perception of truth. He had fled inward to his darkened centre (see above, in the reference to Jerusalem, p. 19, l. 36); and now he goes to his closed circumference, which is itself the veil. He cannot break through it again. He carries it with him. He, by force of self-hood, of Envy, Revenge, Cruelty, turns Virginity into Morality, Innocence to Self-righteousness. The veil of Vala becomes of evil import, and its qualities are embodied in cruel laws, not loving praises. He casts it into the Atlantic, region of male potency to catch the souls, desires, of the dead, the people of unimaginative dogma. From caverns of Derbyshire (see chart of counties under Brereton, West, Tharmas), and Wales, of the same region, and Scotland, the North, the region of iron and experienced love, he spoke. He says that the snows of mortality cover the dying limbs of his humanity or imaginations, and that if this is anything but an illusion he calls on the God of Ulro—the spirit of self-hood—to take vengeance on it, and to draw it down into the abyss of torture, the place of past, present, future, in which he is forced to dwell, where innocence is no delight, as it is in imagination, for it takes the face of legality and wields the rod of punishment. But in spite of his cry—which is a demand for the Incarnation and Re-demption — death and annihilation are not the same to the self-hood—death being error, while self-annihilation is Eternity.

P. 24, l. 12.—Instantly he sees that his words will take effect. They recoil on him in the blood of the Lamb slain, that is of imaginative significance killed by being mistaken for corporeal command. He tells of Druid days—love brought

into light of day—the same error told again. The object was
to make inspiration and sympathy ashamed by showing the
element they had in common with the flesh. But self-hood
only can be ashamed, and inspiration and impulse fled from
its intellect as a result, and the free life of creative-imagination
was no more. This was, in fact, the very slaying of the
Lamb.

P. 24, l. 13.—He exclaims on the mystery of imagination
entering experience, seeming to be no more, but living and
forgiving, even demonstration and morality, for the sake of
truth and innocence. He tells of his death, the result of
educating his inspirations into demonstrations, and his
impulses into moral law. He dies, hopeless, crying out
against God's mercy. But his individuality falls into the arms
of the Saviour—the Universal, not the Personal imagination,
though the Veil, the tissue of law flies thundering—with
Sinai's "thunder of thought" (p. 3) from his hand, and knot
by knot enters the vegetative life of all—as law must needs
do—while both male and female energy—Atlantic and
Erythrean—rage against it.

P. 25, l. 1.—Then the region of Beulah is moved and
speaks, evidently by mouth of daughters of Beulah ("muses
who inspire the poet's song"—see "Milton") and shows the
contrast between Revenge, and the Lamb. When Morality
takes Vengeance, Christ is slain, for every troubled heart
troubles Him, and every joy crucified crucifies Him. But if he
descend he will show to Self-hood that imputation of sinfulness
belongs to the state, not to the individual, and when the
Lamb, the Human Imagination, shows this to the fallen Man,
it is redemption.

With the prayer for this redemption, and the record
that many doubted and did not receive it, the first chapter
ends.

Preface to Chapter II.

P. 27.—The preface to the second chapter is addressed "To the Jews," notwithstanding that Redemption is the chief subject of the chapter.

In the triad,—Head—Heart—Loins,—with its equivalents Creation—Redemption—Judgment, it is evident that Redemption corresponds to Heart. The tribes typify those states that dwell "above" (or more inward than) the states called after the names of the sons of Albion (compare p. 71, l. 3.) These were in the region of Creation, and as fallen Man is head downwards, the heart is over the head. It is more inward, for mere Reason is essentially exterior. The progress of the story is from without inwards.

The Jews are "Sons of Jerusalem," and of Albion in so far as Jerusalem is his Emanation. The first prose paragraph announces that the meaning of this is that through them, all mental states or truths, called "Nations," will be united in one religion, the confession of the mental supremacy of Imagination, or the "Religion of Jesus,"—Jesus being understood always as a symbolic name for organized inspiration applied to human purposes through the Human Form, whose Head, Heart, Loins are Mercy, Pity, Peace,—the opposites of Envy, Revenge, Cruelty, which are the Satanic, or Reasoning Head, Heart, Loins corresponding to Demonstration, Egotism, Law.

Albion and the Druids are spoken of in their pre-natal state, that is to say before Imagination fell under the chaotic, or merely remembering and reasoning state resulting from that attention to the delusions of experience which *is* the creation,—outer nature having only existence though this state of mind.

A poem follows, summing up the mental story about to be told in more extended form.

Verse I. The senses and instincts (north and west of London) were the supports of imagination (builded over with Jerusalem's golden pillars). II. They are regions of mental happiness and love. III. And of rest. IV. And of innocence (boys who bathe, and cattle who browse). The triad Love, Innocence, Repose, completes the earliest stage of a prose Humanity (or London) of these Regions. It is the stage before creation and its delusions have come to change the Head—Heart—Loins. V. Childhood, as the period of Paradise of the Mind, is again emphasized. VI. Innocence is identified with forgiveness : Law with pride, and punishment. VII. In the seventh stanza a manifestation (as the number leads us to expect) occurs of the eternity of the work of the golden builders. They are busy in the moist region of instinct,—the tongue, the west, (Paddington) ever weeping, for growth is sad,—even after Satan's first victory (won by forcing instinct to serve demonstration, not inspiration, as in the story of Genesis when the fruit of the tree of knowledge enters the mouth of woman). VIII. With the consequence that the Druids, once inspired, became deluded and passed from mental to personal sacrifice. IX. In the ninth stanza the birth-groan is heard and the shaking, or throes of birth-giving, are seen on the Atlantic Mountains,—the land between East and West. X. Albion's Spectre is named as the offspring so born. It tears forth from his loins, though it is a delusion,— the memory-in-reason of his head, for he has fallen and his head is in his loins. XI. This Spectre is that described in detail when considered in its various divisions as the Twelve "spectre sons "—and Jerusalem who was in the first book drawn Eastward in Maternal Anguish, is so drawn here. She falls through the East of London to the East of English coast. XII. Three Rivers of Europe and Asia, named in succession, one more Eastern than another, rolled red, for Rivers are happinesses, and when Emanative imagination falls into the East (heart, selfish centre), happiness is sought in the region of blood, in physical passions. XIII. Albion's spectre,—the

Demonstrative in Mind, thus by lodging Intellect in Experience and Happiness in Sensation, withered up Holiness in Emanative Imagination (Zion in Jerusalem) from every place of mental life (nations) and gave it birth in the dark land of outward act, narrow as mortal form. XIV. And withered the true Human form,—the expansive shape of the Imaginative Mind with its Light and Forgiveness, into the restricted Form of the Mind of Experience with its cruel laws. This is seen in the fourteenth stanza,—double seven. XV. But the Divine, the Pure Imagination is even in Moral law and experience,—though it weeps in clay like a new-born Infant. XVI. And every Member of it,—every Idea—(feet and hands) upper or lower, though but made for the little space between the gates of birth and Death, has yet some visible quality of Jesus,—of Humanity. XVII. Then the relation of all this with the slaying of the Lamb is seen. It was the dark self-righteous pride that killed the Innocence that was identical with Forgiveness. But the very perception of this sin is the beginning of regeneration. (While Christ was still on the cross, those who crucified knew not what they did. The world learned from the Resurrection.) The Lamb returns to Albion's shore,—Jerusalem is his bride. XVIII. In the eighteenth stanza—double nine—a new birth is prayed for,—that of the Spirit (or eternal part of mind) created to love while personality (or temporary part) is subdued to its fear. XIX. And the Spectre of Albion, named after born in the stanza after the ninth, so here in that following the double-ninth he is claimed and explained as the egotism of the writer,—as all in him that did not belong to Love—Repose—Innocence, nor to Mercy—Pity—Peace. And this evil self also is armed in gold, for it seizes intellect which should be materials for the pillars of the Temple to make of it the material of weapons. XX. The attributes of the Spectre are told. His love is pride. His kindness dwells amid destruction. His heart is for his family,—his own ideas only. His cruelty for every other conception, however true—

all the world beside. XXI. A man's worst enemies are his own
creations, however high an attribute mental creation may be,
if he makes of these a law to subdue others, or to punish them.
Imagination is of Jesus : Dogma, of Satan.   XXII. Then
Blake utters his manifesto.   He will exchange inspiration with
all, imposing it on none.   Then what would lead only to war
will bring mingling of love and mingling of labour.

A few lines in prose follow, explaining in plain terms the
mental position on which the myth is built.   Incidentally they
use the word "Humility" in a sense as the opposite of
spectrous pride.   This is the Humility which is Emanative
and Christian, and its spectre or opposite is the Humility
which "is only doubt, and doth the Sun and Moon put
out."

Chapter II.

P. 28, ll. 1 to 4.—Imagination is forbidden.   The time of
Envy : Jealousy, Punishment, has come.   Fallen Man is the
Punisher and Judge.

P. 28, l. 5, 12.—His Reasons tell him that poetic ideas are
hybrid, belonging to a mixture of fact and fancy in ill-
assorted union.   There is sin in this.   He will reduce them to
fixed forms.   He will not have one man bathe in another
man's mind.   He will have them separate (so that they may
agree as mere coincidences if at all, and disagree as argument
and contest).

P. 28, ll. 13 to 16.—Cold snows of loveless thought drift
round him.   His creative part is frozen.   At this a conception of God as outside the bosom of Man—even outside his
eternal bosom that is not born and does not die—is set up.
At once from the lower part of his mental system—his heel
—the idea of Virtue as a negative quality, an abstaining, not
an act, springs up.

P. 28, ll. 17 to 19.—This idea, once produced, became bigger

than himself. It over-topped him as a tree may over-top a
man, and bending down it shot up all around the central
conception, making his mind one labyrinth of woe.

P. 28, ll. 20 to 27.—The Druid error—the mistake of sacri-
ficing persons instead of personality—is told, with the consequence that Albion's sons, being self-hoods, would have become
victims. But they were mental and entrenched themselves in
laws and formulæ to make Imagination ashamed of itself, as
they were jealous of it. Yet every one had his own emanation with whom he took delight such as he could not justify
by demonstration. Thus they were the first transgressors.

P. 29, ll. 1 to 5.—The Divine Vision appeared as a sunset
in red clouds : symbol of Incarnation.

P. 29, ll. 6 to 27.—With a promise of redemption following
a detailed account of the mental state from which Albion is to
be redeemed, the Sun of this Sunset enclosed the universal
truths—the Human Family—who also are understood to mean
the four Zoas.

P. 29, ll. 28 to 32.—But as the Incarnation or Sunset proceeds, Albion's locks grow dark, for he is the Manhood of the
Incarnation whose Earth and Sea are the darkness into
which the Sun sets. From his darkening locks (his more
and more creatively-deluded ideas, and personalized intellect)
two forms escape, quitting the Divine Family. They are
later found to be Urthona and Enitharmon. They are the
ideas that underlie experience, and experience itself cannot
entirely destroy them. (Time and Space.)

They flee from Albion's egotistic centre, — his valleys
Eastward. They are ideas common to all, and owned by
none.

Then follows the account of a vision seen by Albion, which
is given in more extended form in " Vala," III. 44, &c.

P. 29, ll. 33 to 37.—The subject is the story of Redemption
as told by the Christians who were not mystics during the
eighteen hundred years when " man was a dream," described
in " Europe." Vala calls the scene a vision of Ahania in the

slumbers of Urizen, and closes the account by calling
Albion a "Vision of Albion,"—though this reads like a
clerical error. Albion and Vala walked together on the steps
of fire before his halls (Symbol: Sunset clouds. Correspondence: desires). He ascended, mourning, into his palace,
into his place of emotion—(the bosom of the female is the
ivory palace of the male). Above—or within him, in his
heart—rose a shadow from his wearied Intellect. He is
therefore head-downwards.

P. 29, ll. 38 to 40.—The symbol of this cloud is evening
mist; the correspondence, the tears of Urizen dragged after
him (compare book of "Urizen") with which he strove to bind
man in a net of religion,—Christianity which deals with
sorrow, dogma, morals, not with joy and imagination and
forgiveness.

In this cloud Luvah hid Himself, Los, and Enitharmon as
the version in "Vala" tells us.

Albion, looking up at the cloud, saw Unizen in his faded
state, veiled with tears.

P. 29, ll. 40 to 57.—He worshipped the vision. Vala fell
down and her locks covered the pavement. She worshipped.

Albion, having forgotten his own eternity through attention
to outer nature (the head-downward state), says that he is
merely a creation of Urizen's faded and sorrowing state. He
is now in a state of humility not proper to Christianity. It is
the humility of doubt.

But the sorrow is not that of Urizen only, but of Albion,—
called Man sometimes in the "Jerusalem" version and always
in the "Vala" version. A false Luvah steps out and manifests
himself, the Spirit of Tears. The female-heart of man in
sorrow.

Albion is terrified. This is not the Redeemer for whom he
looked He starts from his sleep and turns his back on Vala,
who is enclosed in his body,—in the loins. Vala is here
Morality, which is itself the Dominion of Pity, or the female,
now Rahab, Babylon, and the Satanic, and so feminine, Luvah,

all contraries to Forgiveness, the true Spirit of the Redeemer.
(Compare p. 64, l. 6; p. 84, ll. 26, 27.) That is, he relegates
her to the spectral chaos that falls from the back of the
loins. For a moment he rights his position and becomes head-
upwards. Compare pictures, "Jerusalem," p. 95, where
Albion rises young and naked, while old age and robes fall
from his back to which they are still partly growing.

P. 29, ll. 60 to 64.—Then another female element of Luvah
appeared—the love of pride. He strove for dominion over
Albion, though he was originally Pity, Albion's sudden change
of position having wrought a corresponding reversal in Luvah.

(This is the story of the struggles of mystics with dogmatists, and of intellect with priestly tyranny in the Christian
period.)

Luvah then smites Albion with boils—doubt and shame,
diseases of the soul.

P. 29, ll. 50 to 80.—A voice calls Enion. It is Tharmas.
Compare "Vala" and "Milton."

P. 29, ll. 65 to 71.—Then the fallen man put forth Luvah
from his presence,—(compare the "Everlasting Gospel,"—
"My presence I will take from thee.") He bids Luvah die for
Vala,—love die for nature clothed in morality. Compare
p. 65, ll. 5 to 11.

P. 29, ll. 71 to 83.—Luvah left the channel of tears and entered
the channel of blood. He became a portion of the jealousy of
darkness. He ceased to have a place in Vala's bosom. This
Luvah is the spectrous Orc,—or false Christ,—(Yea and Nay
Creeping Jesus) of the "Everlasting Gospel,"—mingles with
Albion's spectre (p. 47, l. 12), and is the same as that which
left Vala,—and is Satan, referred to as tearing from Albion's
loins (Vala) in the poem of the preface (p. 27, stanza 10).
These together are the female or level line of the cross.
They mean the serpent on his belly. He fell to the East and
West, and enters Nature, the serpent made out of the ruins
of outer or of inner love,—(the vision does not say),—then
Los's spectre, his emanation, Enitharmon, fled back to join

the Divine Family, and re-entered the bosom of Los, relating there these things.

The place "where Luvah strives" is explained in "Vala," where the tale is told to Urizen by Ahania's visions which are not said to be the forms of Los and Enitharmon.

It is the feminine region of passive, idle sleep. The Watery Image is congealed from the hair of Ahania (whose symbol is a moving cloud). From this Luvah, Vala shrinks. Then his fall from her bosom is told as a fall of the Sons of Urizen from the North and South, the Energy and Light of Imagination, to the East and West, the personal affections and instincts,—region of Accident and Chance when they disobey the Divine Vision. They fall because petrified by Urizen. They are petrified because he casts out Ahania, seizing her by the hair and flinging her from him. From this moment he is a purely spectrous Urizen, who falls in his turn to the East, and emerges in the West as a spectrous Tharmas. All this belongs to the serpent story, that is now illustrated under Orc, now under Tharmas,—Luvah,—Christ. The "Everlasting Gospel" is full of it.

P. 30, ll. 1 to 15.—In "Jerusalem" it is simply told that the Spectre and Emanation of Los had been in the region of the blood to the affections of Albion on a visit, and had seen the sexual Religion of Chastity; compare p. 69, ll. 38, 44; p. 68, ll. 19, 20; and p. 66, ll. 8, 9; and in its early form, before by circumcision the body of error round the Lamb was put off. They praise the mentally straggling personality of the keeper of the gates of Heaven—Urthona's Spectre, Los, Spectre of the Living—because he kept the Divine Vision, or Human (un-sexual) Religion of brotherhood and non-moralizing self-sacrifice in time of trouble, or of fleshly life. He was Albion's friend through the period of his fall. Compare "Jerusalem" p. 96, ll. 20 to 22. They learned the difference between the two religions by seeing that corporeal friends—obedient to the terms of sexual or corporeal religion—might so act (as Hayley and Blake) as to be the spiritual enemies of

those to whom—with insulting benevolence—they professed
to give their friendship. Los and Enitharmon have here
Blake and Mrs. Blake, not clouds of fires only, for symbol,
and their return to the bosom of the Divine Family is figured
in the return from Felpham and South Molton Street.

P. 30, ll. 15 to 20.—Then—to return to the general history
of Redemption as the leading symbol—Albion shrunk from
Los's bosom, — man became Reason-ridden, and Los and
the living Zoas—the Divine Vision—followed him (as the
Seven Eyes of God in "Milton" p. 14, ll. 1 to 8, accompany
Milton) into his central void, his lightless heart,—among
his oaks,—the vegetative symbols of his Druid-error.

P. 30, ll. 16 to 33.—Los prayed to the true Saviour—(not
the Satanic Luvah who puts on some of his attributes to be
worshipped under his name by the warring Christians of the
East and West,—afterwards summed up under the names
Constantine, Charlemagne)—petitioning him to arise and
restore Albion to that which he had been before, relieving
him from the oppression of the dogmatists who compel his
children—his affectionate ideas—to live on hardly any eternal
food, as the oppressive classes compel the poor of the villages,
to whom they then ostentatiously give a little charity. (Compare line 30 of this page with " Vala," VII., v. 115, &c.)

P. 30, ll. 34 to 37.—Los complains even of Beulah, because
there are sexes in Beulah, because even where there is no
morality to oppress but free-love reigns, self-love condenses the
state into a rocky law.

P. 30, ll. 38 to 40.—Therefore, since Albion has entered into
this state in the bosom of Vala, and the loins,—experience,
—and Luvah, who is at once his feminine heart, his
materialized love, and his spectre,—his self-hood of memory,
—has drawn round him the curtains,—(science of corporeal
mind, the net let down round Los when he entered sexuality;
see Book of "Urizen"), and since the dead,—the memory-made
have become mental progenitors of ideas,—awake to generation,—it only remains that by Redemption, or Christ's rending

of the Veil (Imagination's perception of the nothingness of the material world, Satan's Kingdom), Albion may be set free.

P. 30, l. 41.—So Los, lamenting, followed Albion. Albion covered his Western Heaven—instinctive life—with clouds of death and despair. In the account in Vala, it is Urizen who falls—(another portion of the same idea)—as the effect of his casting down of Ahania; and Tharmas, of the West, utters the cries of fury and becomes the "cold wave of despair" (Night III., 181).

The identity of the story is shown in the incident ("Vala," III., 104) of Albion closing his Western Gate,—equivalent to the Western Heaven of this page.

P. 31, ll. 2 to 39.—Then Los, as the spirit of prophecy, began to explore the interior of Man's nature as it was under the churches (compare p. 71, l. 9). He found to what his loves and graces had become, his minute particulars, hardened to make pyramids, of Heber and Terah (see previous chapter on the Twenty-seven Heavens). He walks towards the Parent Power,—London, from the North—(Highgate, &c.)—or outer regions. He found that the jewels of Albion, his precious and tender imaginations—("the countless gold of a merry heart; the rubies and pearls of a glancing eye," as elsewhere described)—were called vile and suppressed by stern Moral Virtues. He finds the Tower of London,—place of punishment and death and war, made by the Satanic Luvah for himself in the Eastern Gate of Jerusalem, the heart of love,—now given over to ideas of Vengeance. (According to the law of the Selfish, Head—Heart—Loins, that become Envy—Revenge—Cruelty.) Los debates how to change the heart from the state of Revenge without taking vengeance on those who had brought it to that state.

By his prophetic power he saw Jerusalem on the closed Western Gate, closed by the ruins of the Temple (Fallen Man), ruined by the narrowed senses, morality and reason,—faithless. And he saw Vala,—the shadow of faith, whose veil is Law itself,—the law that springs from generation only.

He heard Jerusalem tell Albion that she could not be his
wife.   He had entered another atmosphere, not hers, but
Vala's whose veil (it is of iron) had for its three parts, Love,
Jealousy, Despair,—the Western form of Envy, Revenge,
Cruelty. (Compare MS. Book, last quotation. Note on Tree
of Life and Tree of Knowledge.)

Vala replies, claiming Albion and telling of the Eastern
wars (opposite to the " Wars of Eden").

P. 31, l. 55.—It is the strife of Albion and Luvah in the
mingling, as afterwards appears, of their spectres,— (the
Punisher, as Luvah is become, now mingling with his victim's
spectre,—p. 41, l. 15).   These are wars of the East because
the fallen Luvah has become the selfish affection that, seeking
her dominion, has got into the region of the Laws, Moralities,
Demonstrations.   Thus Luvah will be slain (p. 57) by the cold
Urizen aiding the darkened Albion.   Vala calls Jerusalem a
Daughter of Despair, forgetting that she is, as the spiritual
female, Hope, opposite of Despair,—and rails at her for being
the cause of all these shakings on Euphrates (sexual passions
on red river of blood).   And so she is a sinner and a harlot to
be cast out, that man may be purified by the death of Imagination,—Jerusalem's " delusions."

P. 31, ll. 66 to 70.—After her speech Albion, pale at heart,—
Eastern Gate,—stood while her iron threads of mortal love
were cast over his southern counties,—region of Vision.

P. 32, l. 1.—Through this he became ready to fall into Non-
Entity, or outer Nature.

P. 32, l. 5.—The interiors of Albion presented only petrified
surfaces,—he had nothing in his mind but what the sight of
exteriors had placed there.   His four points—senses—were
reversed inwards upon the false centre composed of the
imported impressions of outer things.

P. 32, l. 9.—So Los, shouting for aid, aroused the fires of
his heart.

P. 32, l. 10.—At this Albion's sons,—the warriors of his fallen
mind,—his reasonings and arguments came forth and on a couch

of gold—(this couch is dogma, on which the mind sleeps that has ceased to be prophetic)—they laid him and built ecclesiastic systems, Druid temples, round his limbs, his ideas.

P. 32, l. 15.—Though Albion's—Man's—intellect be now a rocky (reasoned) shore (limit), yet it is the place where all things begin and end.

P. 33, l. 1.—So, turning his back to the True Inward that is expansion, the surrounding Divine Vision, as a result of the reversal to the false inward of his points, his mind divided under experience between the formed and unformed memory; the unformed, equally spectrous, appeared before his face. (He was in the state of Urizen, tracing the wonders of Futurity "in horrible fear of the Future." Compare "Vala," Night VII., l. 26, or Night III., l. 11.)

The Unformed Memory calls itself the reasoning power and utters the word of scepticism, telling Albion that he is mortal and that nothing of his affections (cities) will remain. The South and East (Battersea and Chelsea), Eyes and Heart, mourn, and London and Canterbury (the larger form, the Zoas), tremble. London is Urizen and Luvah; Canterbury, Luvah and Urizen. See chapter on English names of Zoas.

The Unformed Memory is the Devouring Power, (contrasted with the Prolific in the Marriage of Heaven and Hell). He is the Spectral Tharmas through whom Christ was slain— (compare preface to " Milton ")—and is bodily instinct, enemy of Imagination and also the Personal God, or Satan worshipped under the Divine Name, as well as the destroying Reason worshipped as Intellect.

P. 33, l. 28.—He appears to Albion by the power of Jerusalem (hidden on the Thames and Medway), for only Imaginative Love can make bodily love visible, even to fallen Man,—or Albion.

P. 33, l. 36.—In his female appearance he reveals himself as Vala. (Compare Ololon's visibility in female form in "Milton," p. 36, l. 16.) She describes herself and her unity with Jerusalem in the state of Innocence.

Albion, replying, protests with her on being an outward
feeling and vitality that has entered his inward region, not
knowing that her visibility is a portion of Jerusalem's "ruins."
(See above, p. 29, l. 81.)

Then Los shows that in separating the feminine,—the outer
chambers, the dark region of instinct,—Albion has created a
female will, instinct with his jealousy. He complains that if
we go that way we must seek truth in symbol, imagination
in experience, the Unity of God in the child born of uniting
of sexes. He sees there the birth also of the most unimaginative or disunionized thing of all, the false centre, the
Self-hood. Hand is born when Reuben is rooted in the heart
—(see chapter on the Story of Reuben). Then Los divides
Reuben—(the vegetative heart)—cutting his fibres and sending
him forcibly to the West. Reuben is seen to be a detail of the
great story of Redemption. His cutting and passage over are
like "Milton's" descent into his shadow, or Christ's putting
on of Luvah's robes of blood.

P. 34, l. 57.—Sixty years is mentioned as the age of the
Human Worm, as later (p. 36, l. 3) the period during which
Los raged in the division of Reuben. This is not only the
6 × 10, or completeness and multiplicity multiplied by the
creative period, but presumably about Blake's age at the time
of printing, since the first page is dated 1804, and in 1803 he
was still "about to print" the whole book, while 1757 is the
date of his birth.

P. 35.—The voice of prophecy in Blake,—speaking from
the furnaces, the region of the heart,—utters his central
doctrine and paradox,—that lest the punisher should commit
the unpardonable sin of revenge, the state of Law shall be
made permanent, and all mind pass through it and arise free
from it. The female portion of this state is the "Law,"
Christ's "Mother" (compare conversations with Crabb
Robinson in the Memoir), and the passing through is once
more incarnation which is redemption, being crucifixion in
right of the fact that it is a nailing of mind to the divided
passions of sex,—the cross.

P. 36.—The story of Reuben and the Tribes is then told in its chief incident. Reuben, the imaginative force which makes vegetative instinct generate, goes in the horrible slumber of the mind whose dreams are daily experience, to the region of the West,—Prolific of body, Devouring of Mind,—the valley of Hinnom, of Destruction, of Giants, of Vision,—to bring its four biblical names together.

All the sons of Albion in horror of Reuben fled, but eventually by Los's power they all became Canaanites. (See below.)

Meanwhile Man became enslaved to experience and law—the female and vegetative—and hardly dared to imagine anything, for this is fructifying (it is embracing his own wife).

P. 37.—The whole of page 36 is an interpolation. It is an elaboration of what is now briefly told in p. 37, namely, that Albion (to mass Reuben, his brethren, and Hand and his brethren in one word) fled, covering his face, when Los spoke from the furnaces on the madness of isolation in mind, and threatened him with a punishment of absolute entombment in rocky demonstrative barrenness if he insisted on the reign of Moral Laws in the regions of Eternity.

P. 38, ll. 1 to 7.—As a consequence of his state, he feels more by personality, less by sympathy, and lives more in experience, less in imagination, and his personal ideas propagate. (His emanation trembles within, closed with iron, but his limbs shudder on mountains.)

P. 38, ll. 8 to 14.—A paradox is given. Cold rages with fever (in Albion), warring against warmth (of Eden) with fires of smoke. Jealousy and egotistic love, origin of the moral law, and the darkness of vegetative nature, contained all the intemperate temperatures. By contrast, the Divine Vision is displayed in the only form in which it can reach those given over to experience,—in loves and tears of affectionate families.

P. 38, ll. 15 to 29.—The tears, and the affections in guise of the Divine Vision, speaking, protest with Albion against Revenge, and in favour of Forgiveness.

P. 38, ll. 30 to 40.—London, the name of the chief, the guardian,—who is geographically the South of the East, and here is as the Eyes of the Heart,—as the Urizen (in Eternity's position) of Luvah, speaks. As Luvah he is in robes of blood. As Urizen (in South) he is the Parent of Ideas. He is the body of the Redeemer, with the Redeemer inside it. He is thus every individual who uses his imagination to widen the brotherly sympathy of his emotions for non-selfish purposes, for this is the thing symbolized by all the stories and symbols of the Redemption which consists in Incarnation, of which the cross is merely the sexual condition.

Blake, as a portion of this same London, tells that his visions in whatever place, Felpham, Lambeth, South Molton Street, are to be understood as in Regions of Humanity corresponding to those places, he believing that he was sent to the places for the sake of the correspondences attaching to them.

Cities are Men, so are rivers and mountains. Their place is not in true existence outside, but inside the human bosom.

In the same sense is to be understood the gate unseen by mortals, vegetations ; unfound by Satan's watch-fiends,—the reasoning and spectrous men.

The gate, passing from Oxford Street, over Hyde Park, to Tyburn, the place of this gate is symbolic. Comparing the ideas of West, Tharmas, tongue, throat, devouring, and the crucifixion mentioned in Milton as work of Tharmas, a symbol is found by suggestion that Hyde Park is a mouth, Oxford Street a throat, Tyburn the place, in Blake's time, of execution, or death of victims, and food the symbol of destruction of life to support life,—the whole of the suggestions, though a team of symbols so diverse as to be difficult to drive, reveal themselves when all sent together down the one mental road now traversed, as a complicated correspondence for Redemption. "Every kindness to another is a little death in the Divine Image" (p. 96, l. 26). "Life lives on death" ("Urizen," VIII., stanza 5). The life of Humanity lives on the countless surrenders of, so to speak, atoms of imagination to sympathetic purpose, as a man lives on food, whose spirits (for if food were not full of spirits it could not support life) yield to the inexorable law, the great gallows (Tyburn), and die that he may live.

P. 39, ll. 1 to 11.—It is the Gate of Los,—place of division by mental as well as bodily digestion, where vital food is absorbed and unvital rejected, where the heart takes up blood and the bowels cast forth what cannot be so taken up, as Prophecy (Los) gathers from experience for Life what mere Reason or Analysis (Satan) presently casts out for death, while in the moral correspondence the same contrasted parts are played by Brotherhood and Egotism, which in the moral world within also digest the food of experience. And Forgiveness is life-absorbed material, while Moral Virtue (or Revenge, so masked) is the life-ejected material,—the former being Jesus, in scriptural terms, the latter Rahab. Thus true religion has a correspondence or counterpart in digestion.

P. 39, ll. 12 to 27.—Los now, as Brotherhood, is the type of life. He combines the four Cities which are the Zoas in English equivalent, who, with the twenty-four cities, symbols of the affections that correspond to the Sons and Daughters of Albion, form the twenty-eight here spoken of, in the aggregate as the Divine Family. Los bears Albion going, unwillingly, to the eternal death of mental and moral isolation. He cries out that Atonement is not Mercy, but Moral Severity, and in doing so is speaking as pure prophecy, not infected with error. The Victim of Atonement is Mercy, offering itself. The Acceptor of Atonement in destroying the Victim, by the atoning death, is a destroyer of Mercy. Thus, ultimately, God the atoner is Mercy, and Satan, the Acceptor of Atonement, is mistakenly called God, whereas he is the Accuser.

P. 40, ll. 1 to 10.—The twenty-four hours of the day are resumed in Time from whom comes the Motion without which the Four Points and Four Seasons are nonentity, having no relation to one another. This is merely a symbolic correspondence. Now Albion's friends, the twenty-eight, are all resumed finally in Los, in whom Albion sees the likeness and similitude of Christ (p. 96, l. 22). They swear the "Oath of God." This oath is used as meaning the promise to die, and it is equally employed as the promise to forgive. The first implies incarnation : the entrance of the mind into the senses, dying out of imagination into feeling that it may return to imagination with fresh powers, having incidentally redeemed feeling from its isolated egotism, and made it an instrument of brotherhood, without which Man *is not*. The second implies the death of justice and law and righteousness in favour of pity, mercy, love, who cannot live unless it dies for their sake. The oath is also referred to in " Milton," p. 12, l. 13.

P. 40, ll. 11 to 24.—Albion in disease of doubt (of imagination) and despair (of comprehending truth without vision) sat dying, into materialistic thought, while the four senses, with darkened flames, saw him in the Porch of Sixteen Pillars,—the Scriptures, as appears later, and they swore the Oath of God (that one must die for another through all eternity).

Every valley calls on every city,—every spontaneous on every considered affection, to save Albion.

P. 40, ll. 25 to 44.—The twenty-four, the considered affections, came to sacrifice themselves, borne by the four Zoas of Tharmas (for each Zoa is fourfold)—or the Living Creatures of the third, or Western Region or Procession.

For but that sympathy helped imagination not to die, visionary life might never have been ours, but Man might have become as that " fiend hid in a cloud "—a new-born baby.

Had the Body of Albion,—the Organized Idea of Man,—fallen down, lost all coherence of Vision or Sympathy, nothing but the Spectre could have sprung from its ruins, as it is said that only Individualism can proceed from Rationalism.

P. 40, ll. 45 to 61.—The Twenty-four are named—

Selsey	Lincoln	Chester		
Winchester	Durham	Worcester		
Gloucester	Carlisle	Lichfield	Verulam	
Exeter	Ely	St. David's	London	
Salisbury	Oxford	Llandaff	York	Bath
Bristol	Norwich	Asaph	Edinburgh	Canterbury
Bath	Peterborough	Bangor		
Hereford	Rochester	Sodor		

P. 45, ll. 1 to 14.—The object of the "Triple octave taken to Reduce Jerusalem to Twelve," is equivalent to reducing the Bible to the Old Testament, or Book of the Tribes, without living by the New Testament, or Book of the Evangelists. The Tribes standing for Mosaic Law, the Evangelists for Forgiveness. Bath is both East and West, Canterbury both North and South. See chapter on English names for Zoas. Jerusalem cast out to Malden and Bow is the emanative emotion put to the Druid uses of the East (false centre), while in an evil aspect, the West, Bath, puts on the darkness of Tyburn's river that flowed past the gallows. The daughters of Beulah hid Jerusalem in Lambeth—the West of the South, —place symbolic of Vision, the gate outwards to Eden.

In the many lost books of Blake it is probable that the visions here called by the names of cities were made the personages of some more complete and self-explained myth.

Here only a passing hint about Bath explains its name being used as both the East and West of the South. The normal position would be West, as is suitable to a place of healing springs, but the mingling of its spectre with that of Luvah has an Eastern allusion.

In its character of seventh—spiritually manifest personality in emotion, as Schofield, as the Mandrake—Bath causes Kox, Kotope, and Bowen to appear in line, and they are Eastern names in the division of Reuben. The symbol is obvious, and accounts for the question addressed to Schofield when (above, p. 17, line 61) he was asked whether he was Bath or Canterbury—the female poisonous yet healing spring, or the male venerable parent of men that yet taught a religion of Atonement, not of forgiveness. Canterbury is used as an equivalent for London in its religious, not affectionate aspect. So that the list of the four cities that stand for the Zoas reads in several ways. The Wheel of Religion goes from Canterbury to Bath; that of Creation from Bath to Canterbury (p. 77).

| Bath | Canterbury | } York | Edinburgh |
| Verulam | London | | |

These are two ways of the same thing.

As a result of Albion in his darkened state resting on the couch of sixteen pillows, or personality feeding its hopes on a literal non-mystic reading of the Scriptures—the twenty-eight trembled in caves of death, the affections in mortality, while the four Zoas themselves, grown elemental, fought with each other, and tried in turn to obtain the worship of man.

The last line of this page was originally intended to precede the first of page 43. But page 42 was inserted, as the subject of page 40 was not exhausted and more needed to be said to elaborate it.

Page 40 began with Albion's disease. Page 42 goes on with details of the disease.

P. 42, ll. 1 to 9.—Albion brooded on evil, and saw that what he looked on as accursed were his sons and daughters—his own affections. He was in the state of Urizen in North, and of Tiriel. The curse he laid on them was Law. The Divine Vision appeared with tears of pity among them.

P. 42, ll. 11 to 19.—In his dismal dreams (daily life, experience), Albion accused Los of deceit, as matter-of-fact always accuses prophecy, and darkness rolled round his South, where his eyes ought to have been, but where his skirts were, from Dover to Cornwall—for he was head-downwards, or Northwards.

Prophecy in answer showed how Albion had destroyed his three Zoas, turning Head, Heart, and instinctive Loins to destruction, and the fourth, yet though the most earthly, had the Divine element in it—(" God is even in the depths of hell ")—for Urthona had Los for his vehicular form. He showed Albion the philosophy of personality and of matter, under the figures Adam and Satan, and of Redemption under the pity and forgiveness and innocence that are revealed through what infancy teaches, though this also is the means of evil. The infant is not only Schofield, the ninth, but Reuben, the first, and Bath (healer and destroyer), the seventh, in its various aspects. Los invited Albion to look on him as an enemy, for Albion's self-hood was for ever accursed, but wept for him after speaking.

P. 42, ll. 55 to 81.—The spectres of the dead are furious against the spectres of the living. The systems of reason fought systems of mysticism. The personality of law fought that of rebellion (p. 17, l. 15). The one spectre is certain to arouse the other to fury (p. 37, l. 4). (Los is called the Spectre of the Living in "Vala," Night VII., l. 306.) The one effort of the "dead" is to construct a religion of law and punishment, instead of sympathy and forgiveness. Thus the affections, the twenty-four, suffer, and Rahab and Babylon are constructed instead of Jerusalem. Such is the net and veil of "Vala," the religion and covering of the loins, among the souls or passions of the dead, or unforgiving and unprophetic.

P. 43, l. 1.—So the Twenty-eight (who are only spoken of as "They," without explanation, if page 43 be not, as it certainly was, the sequel of page 41), saw their wheels—their Zoas—in antagonism against Albion, endeavouring to keep him only in connection with their spectrous tendencies, the cold of Urizen, the indolence of Tharmas, the despair of Urthona, the dominating pity of Luvah, acting each as a separate quality, not as portions of a united humanity; so that Albion, yielding to the idea that each mood was an ultimate, might be prevented walking about among them in the four complexions.

P. 43, ll. 7 to 11.—They saw America, the Western or instinctively productive region, closed out from the soul by the physical organs that should admit it. (Compare "Vala," Night III., l. 104, where the allusion to the Western Gate follows the part of the story given in "Jerusalem," p. 27.) They saw Tharmas, the Zoa, destroyed in fragments, each of which was a rocky or physical portion of an organ of the central West (a victim of Mexico), and they revolted from entering into their spectres—their isolated vitalities—and called on the god of Albion to deliver joy from the body, Jerusalem from the oak.

P. 43, ll. 12 to 80.—Los replies that they must help themselves by the aid of God in their own bosoms. Were they not four?—for the twenty-eight's last four included all. Then under various names the struggle is told of the mental forces which made the body a solidity, that man might be separate from man. Out of this grew moralities and demonstrations, the infection of sin and repentance, for the body is Luvah's sepulchre, and the tomb of all that mingles with his spectre.

P. 43, ll. 80 to 82.—When Los had spoken the affectionate twenty-four, as resumed in the four, stand a moment, pale, before Albion's House of Death—the bodily form.

P. 44, ll. 1 to 17.—With one accord the Divine family—the four quarters of Imagination disguised as Albion's twenty-four friends—attempted by force to induce Albion to go out to Eden,—the circumference, the universal expansion, back through the gate of Los, which Albion had passed, going Eastward (p. 39, l. 11), toward the Satanic void, in which Urizen had built his world, going, that is to say, into rationalism. But Albion was given up to the literal interpretation of Scripture and acceptance of experience. (He saw with, not through the eye, and refused to come.) The Atlantic waters, the male physical powers that should be but a thin stream between man and the Atlantic mountains, became an impassable gulf. Man,—Albion,—could not pass generation or see regeneration beyond it. Poetry in vain spread its wings. Albion's sons were literal ideas and in the world of phenomena, Satan's world, the void, they passed up and down.

P. 44, ll. 18 to 21.—But Will—even evil will—is sacred except from inspiration. Education,—the " friendly force " brought to bear on Albion—must not compel it. The Divine family of poetic idea simply hovered over Albion waiting.

P. 44, ll. 22 to 36.—By the nature of Ulro, the Eastern or Central Error, every idea entering becomes matter of argument, contest and trouble; that is to say, is sexual,—the sexes being symbol for the divided and the contesting portions of disunited truth. Meantime the mingling of love and jealousy brought to birth as offspring an idea miscalled religion,—a mere restraint, a law, not an inspiration or an energy. So Los's prophecy in poetry was set to watch, and called Elijah.

P. 44, l. 37.—The twenty-four fell under the influence of Religion (they are cathedral towns), and among the oaks of Albion or Druid, vegetable errors fell away into nonentity from the truth of inspired vision, impersonal love or Jerusalem, the universal joining Emanation.

P. 44, ll. 43, 44.—And they wept, being mild—not wicked, being feminine—and presently Bath spoke.

P. 45, ll. 1 to 9.—Bath, her healing water flowing, spoke through the gate of instinctive emotion, the West, and said that this gate was closed in Albion and he could no longer pass through it to eternity. Self-hood and passion, together, however noble the one, however mild the other, cannot attain to the immortal states of mind but by aid of Jesus, the inspiring faculty, or Imagination.

P. 45, l. 20.—When Africa, the merely emotional self-hood, fell into sleep, belief in matter, and bound-down sun, male desire or wish to propagate ideas, and moon, female desire, or wish to propagate emotions, requiring these things to be chained to experience, his friends broke his chains. His own tendencies delivered him from mental delusion, and his sympathies, untrammelled by dogma, broke loose into brotherhood again. But Albion is Humanity that has been in this state and has fallen into sexual delusion from a height,—he is headdown. He is religion once mystic, now literalized, so his machines of argument are woven with his life.

P. 46, ll. 1 to 15.—Many of the friends join their voices. They bid Albion repose, since he cannot awake,—that is they urge man fallen into the night of uninspired mind to cease manufacturing erroneous ideas from literal error, to cease argument, to rest in instinct,—till the night is passed. The

plough and harrow will go over. The Northern constellations
—the experience-mind-moods—will not rule for ever.

P. 46, l. 16.—But Albion refused peace as he had refused
Imagination, and remained conscientious, wretched, moral,
mistaken.

P. 46, ll. 16 to 22.—The females,—cities,—grew weak, the
instincts and mild passions trembled and fainted. The male
potencies, furnaces raged.

P. 46, l. 23.—The four Zoas—called now by their female
names, Verulam, London, York, Edinburgh—mourned to each
other and foresaw that a man's ideas in the conscientious
muddle wrought by non-mystic religion would become his
enemies, though, like his own house and family, they should
have been his friends, and ·mutual love in the world would be
checked by a religion which, designed only to regulate generation, would simply kill Imagination,—as though revenge
(which is morality unmasked) were the true character of God,
the Father of Imagination. (Compare poem " To the Jews,"
on p. 27, stanza 21.)

P. 47, ll. 1 to 9.—But from the regions of experience in man
(Northern quarters of London), where the passions are propagative (Thames shudders) where friendship and love are alike
forms of fleshy desire (Jerusalem and Vala howl), Luvah came
forth from Albion's loins.

The sun rose on a world that saw it only *with* the eye. It
was therefore Satan, the Greek Apollo, and was Luvah entered
into the state called Satan. This is the contrary mood or
story from the mild watery Luvah rising as a shadow from
man's weaned intellect. It now tears from his loins. Religion
has led on to war. The hidden harlot is surrounded by the
dragon red. Mild religious error is going to be persecution.
It will offer up children in the wicker man of Scandinavia,—
that is to say, innocences will be burned in a cage of vegetation, in a network of physical organs. Compare p. 27,
stanza 10, the Druids are always those defined in the essay on
the Vision of the last Judgment ("Gilchrist," Vol. II.), namely

the literal readers of symbolic words who thus mistake their meaning.

Luvah rising into the clouded heavens of Albion, shows the emanative Love growing physical by mingling with the blood (p. 31, l. 3).

P. 47, ll. 9 to 17.—The souls of the dead, the passions of the unimaginative break forth from Beulah's hills,—dream-land,—into sexual contests,—scythed chariots. The veil of Vala is composed of their law-making personalities, for she is natural love and her veil is restriction or moral law.

So with cries Luvah, once female heart, mingles with intellectual energies. Luvah is become punisher, as Satan, and mingles with his victim's spectre. The last living part even of passive or female mind,—Hope, the female,—is banished from Albion, while the other female,—Nature, or rationalism—takes her place and will presently cause the mingling of Luvah's and Albion's spectres to be Hermaphroditic or self-contradicting (p. 58, l. 20.—Compare "Vala," Night VIII., l. 109 and 245). When the Hermaphrodite is of feminine sorrow, and masculine thought, it is as in "Vala," Night VII., l. 155.

P. 48, ll. 1 to 11.—Albion having uttered his last words, the pale limbs, or ideas, of his eternal individuality, or imagination, are reposed on the Rock of Ages, Scripture carried into a couch of sixteen pillars,—books. (They correspond to the sons of Jerusalem also.)

P. 48, l. 12.—Imagination groaned and was troubled at the literal acceptation of these mystical writings—an image, not of life, but of eternal death.

P. 48, ll. 13 to 20.—Beneath the bottoms of the graves,—elsewhere called places of human seed,—("Vala," Night VII, l. 610),—we escape sexual life with its divisions, and there its contraries, not revealed as enemies, not slaves to the elements, are equally true, and feminine emotion and masculine imagination stand on the same basis, both being "true."

Here is the ultimate protection from the warlike sports of

intellect, and here images defined, dogmatized, or adapted to period,—killed in fact, revive, putting on their original form, adapted for imaginative or mystic communion.

P. 48, ll. 21 to 52.—From here, as a result of Albion's dying on the Rock, Jerusalem separated and went out of his human heart, whose gates closed with a solemn sound; in a word, as Albion himself said, " Hope is banished."

P. 48, l. 53.—From here onwards, just as the above elaborates the banishment of Albion's hope, this narrative elaborates the story of Albion's fall into the Ulro of imputing sin and righteousness, as already sketched in the speech of Bath. Erin, who includes all the cities, is now the speaker. She tells how, in the darkening of Albion and his narrowing perceptions, the vision of Eternity, the symbolic cities, plants, animals, herbs, are become visions of Time and Space, and fixed into furrows of death. That is to say, the fall of Humanity from imagination itself created what we call the material world; which is merely a narrowed vision and has no existence but as a result of this disease of the soul. (P. 49, l. 24.) Among such diseases morality is one, for it is a tranference to the soul of the intellect's error, while pity and forgiveness at least leave the soul unclouded and not turned into that "limit of opaqueness," the "one great Satan," which all things *may* become. ("Milton," p. 40, l. 1.)

P. 49, ll. 25 to 45.—The four Zoas are now only mortal senses —Ear, Eye, Nostrils, Tongue—rooted in Egypt and kindred places of mortal perception in the Erythrean, or Red Sea,— or Luvah's robe of blood, their uncircumcision, their want of cutting round or outline, or imaginative definition, shall be lost by self-annihilation, for the story is always the same. It is Redemption, the Saviour,—eternal imagination becoming as we are, blood, that we may be as he is, eternally delivered from blood.

P. 49, l. 46.—The laws of cruelty may be bent to peace by the discovery of Divine Analogy as the meaning of the body of Moses, Law (into which Los, poetry, led Vala, natural passion). But Law was the Mother of Christ, after the

flesh,—that is to say, Divine Analogy brought forth Divine
Imagination. (For Vala, in a sense, is Mary, so far as Mary
was only the origin of the temporary part of the Gospel's
meaning, not that which transcends time and outspeeds the
need of sermons.)

The terrible apparent surfaces, or meanings, of prophecy as
of the natural perceptions that close Jerusalem (the regenerate
Vala) away from Albion are got rid of when sin and righteousness are attributed to states, not individuals. Christ enters
the state of Satan in order to have them attributed to him, so
that in dying he may put them off, and that is the meaning of
the birth of us all and our deaths.

It is also the meaning of every lapse from Imagination (the
Lord who was not there when our brother died) into intellect,
sense, morality. But if Jerusalem remain undelivered,—if
she be only a personal emotion, not a mystic perception as
well,—she will change from friendship to self-righteousness
and become mother of war,—falling, in her turn, to be Babylon
as Albion fell to be Satan.

P. 50, ll. 25 to 30.—So Erin spoke. Then in a rainbow, sign
of Hope, symbol of Beulah, possessor of the Three Colours,
the daughters replied that to sin,—that is to believe in and
feel through the body as though it were not a symbol, and to
hide that sin in matter,—in the organs,—which are "sweet
deceit"—leaving themselves only an apparent fleshly existence is lovely, but it is evil to let the Sun, inspiration, go
down and the mind brood darkly on the blood's business.
Imagination must come and release the mind from remembrance (the spectre) of personal or sensual states.

PREFACE TO CHAPTER III.

The third chapter of "Jerusalem" has, for preface, a little
prose essay, or manifesto, whose argument is to the effect that
natural morality and religion, and a belief in the natural good-
ness of man, are all evil states of mind, belonging to the symbols

Rahab and Satan, and their detailed symbols, Voltaire, Rousseau, Gibbon, Hume, &c., while experiment and reason are the mental equivalents. Christianity on the contrary being truth, its morality, forgiveness, its conviction, a disbelief in nature, and its mental equivalent Imagination, called Jesus, as its contrary is Satan.

In the poem of the "Monk of Charlemagne" War and Fortune are attributed to the Satanic convictions,—that is to say to Natural Reason, Morality, and Religion. It has seven verses. The number suggests that it is a complete account of a spiritual manifestation. The seven were selected, probably for this purpose, from the MS. book. The poem from which they are taken includes that published under the title of the "Grey Monk" in the Aldine edition. Blake seems to have intended at first to use fourteen stanzas, but the double seven seemed, perhaps, unnecessary, and their matter too explanatory. At present the page "To the Deists" is as nearly pure explanation in its prose as Blake knew how to make a page, while the verse is frankly symbolic.

A comparison of the various readings of the verses finally chosen by Blake is of itself an explanation of them. The personages are seen to be names of States—one repentant, and on his way to be imaginative, others proud, reasoning, and, as the eighteenth century believed, philosophic. The monk, like the figure of War, is a visionary creature, as is seen by comparison of the first and third verses.

As printed by Blake.	Readings rejected by Blake.
I saw a monk of Charlemagne	——— of Constantine.
Arise before my sight,	
I talked with the grey monk as he stood	
In the beams of infernal light.	
Gibbon arose with a lash of steel,	Gibbon armed with a lash of steel,
And Voltaire with a wracking wheel.	And Voltaire with a racking wheel;
The schools in clouds and learning rolled,	Charlemagne and his warriors bold
Arose with war in iron and gold.	Arose with war in iron and gold.

Gibbon plied his lash of steel,
And Voltaire turned his racking
   wheel;
Charlemagne and his warriors bold
Stood by and mocked in iron and
   gold.

The wheel of Voltaire whirled on
   high;
Gibbon aloud his lash does ply;
Charlemagne and his clouds of war
Must now arouse the polar bear.

A Grecian scoff is a racking wheel;
The Roman pride is a sword of steel;
Glory and victory platted whips.

Thou lazy monk they sound afar,
In vain condemning glorious war;
And in your cell you shall ever dwell.
Rise, War, and bind him in his cell.

"Seditious monk," said Charlemagne,
"The glory of war thou cursedst in
   vain."

The blood red ran from the grey
   monk's side;
His hands and feet were wounded
   wide;
His body bent, his arms and knees
Like to the roots of ancient trees.

When Satan first the black bow bent
And moral law from the gospel rent,
He forged the law into a sword,
And spilled the blood of mercy's Lord.

Titus, Constantine, Charlemagne,
O Voltaire, Rousseau, Gibbon; vain
Your Grecian mocks and Roman
   sword
Against the image of his Lord.

O Charlemagne! O Charlemagne!
O Voltaire, Rousseau, Gibbon; vain
Your mocks and scorn and Roman
   sword
Against the image of his Lord.

For a tear is an intellectual thing,
And a sigh is the sword of an Angel
   King;
And the bitter groan of a martyr's
   woe
Is an arrow from the Almighty's bow.

The connection of ideas between the symbols, Reason, Morality, Covering Cherub, Rahab, Satan, the churches, righteousness and war, and the hermaphroditic dragon and harlot, with the rationalism of the day and its advocates, will be evident on comparing these verses with any other passages where the symbols are found.

The following set of verses which Blake seems to have decided not to use at all, continuing as they do the story of the monk, are apparently the narrative of a vision. They do not contain corrections and re-writings as the above lines do, for here the labour of forming a system (of symbols), not from vision but from intellectual philosophizing on vision, lest the mind should be "enslaved" by the system of another man, is apparent on the surface.

The arrangement of verses in the Aldine edition is specious, but has no countenance in anything to be found on the page from which they are taken. Two are omitted altogether for no apparent reason except the difficulty of placing them, yet they are important, connecting, as they do, the monk and the tyrant with the symbols Milton and Satan, in "Milton," p. 39.

As originally sketched by Blake, the entire poem of fourteen stanzas began with the words "I saw a Monk of Constantine." Its first four stanzas were the first four of the seven he printed in "Jerusalem." But instead of the last three, were the following ten :—

5.

"I see, I see," the mother said,
" My children shall die for lack of bread ;
What more has the merciless tyrant said ? "
The monk sat him down on her stony bed ;

6.

His eye was dry, no tear would flow,
A hollow groan bespoke his woe ;
. . . . *(line illegible)*
He trembled and shuddered upon the bed.

7.

When God commanded this hand to write
In the shadowy hours of deep midnight,
He told me that all I wrote should prove
The bane of all that on earth I love.

8.

My brother starved between two walls ;
Thy children's cry my soul appals.
I mock at the rack and the grinding pain ;
My bent body mocks at their torturing pain.

9.

Thy father drew his sword in the North,
With his thousands strong he is marched forth.
Thy brother has armed himself in steel,
To avenge the wrongs thy children feel.

10.

But vain the sword and vain the bow,
They never can work war's overthrow.
The hermit's prayer and the widow's tear
Alone can free the world from fear.

11.

The hand of vengeance found the bed
To which the purple tyrant fled ;
The iron hand crushed the tyrant's head,
And became a tyrant in his stead.

12.

Until the tyrant himself relent,
The tyrant who first the black bow bent,
Slaughter shall heap the bloody plain ;
Resistance and war is the tyrant's gain.

13.

But the tear of love and forgiveness sweet,
And submission to death beneath his feet ;
The tear shall melt the sword of steel,
And every wound it has made shall heal.

14.

For the tear is an intellectual thing,
And a sigh is the sword of an Angel King ;
And the bitter groan of a martyr's woe
Is an arrow from the Almighty's bow.

Such were the fourteen stanzas of the poem. Constantine
and Charlemagne are simply the Eastern and Western regions
of the churches, when Paul and Luther stand for the Southern
and Northern. Hence the correction. The Monk was rightly
of Charlemagne, of the West, the sorrowful region. (Compare
"Milton," p. 23, l. 32.) The verses called "Morning," beginning, "To find the western path," were put down next, and
then, later, the alterations and various forms and final cutting
down to seven stanzas, of the previous poems arranged
wherever space was left on the paper. It is easy to see that
in the "Monk," as in "Milton," Blake had his own career
in mind. "He told me that all I wrote should prove the
bane of all that on earth I love," recalls some lines written
at Felpham about the same time and sent in a letter to
Mr. Butts—

> " Must my wife live in my sister's bane
> And my sister survive on my love's pain? "

The word "bane" is so rare in Blake, that though the use of
it is not the same here, both belong to the threat of evil
accompanied by command to work that Los, in one, God in
the other, gives, though in the case of Los the threat only is
in the verses, which relate an incident afterwards turned into
an "ornament" in "Milton," p. 16, where Los opposes
Milton, the command to write being indicated in the same
book, p. 36, line 21, &c. Voltaire and Rousseau and the
mocking of confessors, &c., is referred to also in "Milton,"
p. 20, line 36, &c.

As the verses go on, the father and brother in the north are
recognizable by their sword and steel as states of whom
Gibbon and Voltaire are divisions. They are part of Urizen's
war, of the jealousy of Theotormon and the deceitful side of
Milton's religion ("Milton," p. 20); while ver. 11 contains
the symbol of Milton, p. 39, line 29. It was a quick second
thought, the first correction of the original improvisa-
tion. The stanza as written having ended " And assumed

the tyrant's crown and fled," the correction was made at once and the poem went on.

At the bottom of the page occurs the first form (with its corrections made on the lines themselves) of the quatrain about the spectre which occurs in " Jerusalem," page 41, written in reverse on the scroll held by a bending figure representing Albion.   Here are the two forms :—

CORRECTED.	FIRST DRAUGHT.
" Each man in his spectre's power	" This world is in the spectre's power
Until the arrival of that hour	Until the arrival of that hour,
When his humanity awake	Until the Humanity awake
And cast his own spectre into the lake."	And cast the spectre into the lake."

The spectre is Satan, bender of the black bow, and the quatrain finally unites all that is essential in the teaching of the Monk, for Humanity is the tear of Forgiveness.   It also unites the whole with " Milton " through the lines 10 to 13, p. 40 :—

> " Awake! Albion, awake! reclaim thy Reasoning Spectre.   Subdue
> Him to the Divine Mercy.   Cast him down into the lake
> Of Los that ever burneth with fury, ever and ever.   Amen."

And with Jerusalem by the picture, p. 95, of Albion as a youth arising while garments that develop into the face of an old man slide from his limbs towards a place on whose brink he kneels, which is seen by the flames that spring from it to be the Lake of Los.

CHAPTER III.

In so far as these loosely cohering chapters have separate and particulars of subjects at all, that of the third is Judgment, as that of the first was Creation, and of the second, Redemption.

P. 53, l. 1.—In the beginning we hear of Los weeping over

Albion as he howled over Urizen, and the roots of Albion's tree entered his soul. It is the tree of Moral Virtue and Natural Growth,—these roots he afterwards thrust out to oppose Milton. Man, the furnace of Beryl, and woman, the emerald, are described in their sevenfold attributes as seen by the visionary and the Hammer and Bellows of the furnace as having for physical symbol the Heart and Lungs. South to North,—Head to Loins, the furnaces are ranged. But Man, Albion, is now head-downwards.

P. 53, ll. 15 to 29.—Therefore beneath Beulah, outside or beneath the heart, where contraries are equally true, Los built Golgonooza,—or the spiritual fourfold London, the friendly cities helping. Golgonooza is a space, or created feminine quality continued for the male potency to inhabit. It means the propagative power of the mind and of the love of man even when fallen into the clutches of daily unimaginative experience. It has the symbol of Parentage in the Thames, and by it man sees the typical quality of experience and is saved from passive acceptance of its details in unimaginative memory. From this, imagination may have birth as generation from its symbolic organs. From Surrey to Italy and Greece to the Valley of Hinnom signifies from sight by thought and beauty to love,—from eyes by heart and organs to passion.

P. 54, ll. 1 to 14.—And then we are told of the enwrapping light round all things that is Jerusalem and Liberty,—of Albion's fallen position, for instead of his spectre being thrown by him into the lake of fire it has thrown him on the rocks,—demonstration.

P. 54, ll. 14, 25.—And as memory it mildews his imagination and frosts his inspiration, and claims to be his mental god. And it hardens into experience round Canaan, place of seed, of promise, and Egypt, of earthly limitations.

P. 54, l. 27.—Albion drew England into his bosom, and in her drew in Jerusalem and Vala. She is seen like a serpent of space, the shape of Nature itself, they like sad figures in the expanses that dragon wings, personal thoughts, made in his emotional regions.

P. 55.—Then we learn of the multitude of the spiritual forces, how they descend into life, sitting even in the furrow of generation. How the seven, called the seven eyes of God, keep visionary life in darkness of the blood and of the creeds ; how an eighth (Milton, Los, Blake, Elias) is named (but we are not told by what name here), and though he kept his majesty he came not. How all resumed their stations by right of the knowledge that they were one family, were all of the Imagination, of the body of the Divine One. Their conscience bids them labour well at art with the plough of the graver, that those who are unimaginative may not be so long, and all may be eventually released from delusions of matter by the influence of symbol. And as each mood works each shall be judged. (The loins, the furrow, is the "place of the last Judgment.")

P. 55, ll. 1 to 43.—The fifty-fifth page is an interpolation of a later date. It tells of voices at the plough, of spiritual forces in physical passion. The scythed chariot, the moon on the British ocean, are obvious symbols. The babe, the clod weeping (like the "dog," another name for natural desire used elsewhere), at the wintry door, or gate of maternity, reveals the rest. At the end Los suddenly addresses Paul, the symbol of the early church, and showing him the feminine in all the three regions—as three women round the cross—cries out to reproach Albion, or the downward mind of man, for creating a "female," or personal, natural, non-mental Will.

P. 57, ll. 1 to 18.—The voices at the ploughing are again heard—Bath, Canterbury. The spring of physical healing, the centre of ecclesiastical healing—feminine ; and the great voice of the Atlantic, the sea of male potency (when the male is seen as himself a female, a breeder of seed) is heard (p. 64, l. 12). Then it is seen how Albion, so entirely was he head-downwards, fled beneath the plough, and getting indeed to

the centre (the "selfish centre," which is outside) found
that the Divine Vision rolled it into an expanse and placed the
Rock of Ages there, the primæval experience, selfish in each,
common to all, sought for self, and found it led to brotherhood, on which he sat. For inspiration, the highest, widest
thing is found in the symbol of the narrowest and lowest.
("God is within and without, He is even in the depths of
hell.")

P. 58, ll. 1 to 12.—For the daughters of Albion, his natural
emotions, mix and change, divide and unite. Now as he
grows to one condition he is cut off by them and sent to
another, and so kept always free from final bondage.

P. 58, ll. 12 to 30.—Philosophy and Demonstration, mixed
together, are Luvah's and Albion's Spectre. Hermaphroditic
when mingled, sexual when divided, they create the world of
Generation, which shall be put off in the end.

P. 58, ll. 31 to 51.—Urizen, the human mathematic or logical
mind, gets form and order out of the confusion of experience.
Through his influences the countries, spaces, or organs,
become possessions of a being, generated man. They are his
halls, steps, pillars, fountains, and so forth. The countries
named are all symbols for organs or regions. (As in the
verses from Felpham where "every nation felt affliction,"—
that is every organ, or region of the body.)

And the body is indeed a world, the world of the unimaginative mind,—of Urizen when in the North. It is a world
of rocky destiny, and is "continually created" by being
continually perceived; for creation (of the impressions called
in aggregate the body) is an act of mind.

P. 39.—The Veil of Vala,—at once the flesh, and its morality
and sorrow, religion, which Albion cast into the Atlantic deep,
began to vegetate and became in its turn the other aspect of
nature, known as Los's or Urizen's mundane shell,—the
cavernous reflection of things that seem to surround man.
But in truth it is the mysterious place of redemption, the
centre, that seems an expanse.

P. 59, ll. 10 to 21.—But Albion is not yet awake, and the Zoas are not for him four living creatures, but chaotic universes still, by their regions or their names, they are only warring elements.

P. 59, ll. 22 to 55.—In the Northern region, the deep world of generation, female powers spin the integuments—the threads of emotion which the Spectres, the centres of personality, are to put on. Sorrowfully they weave the mortal instrument of sorrow. It is, in truth, the Veil of the Temple.

P. 60, ll. 1 to 9.—At the same time in the world of the deserted Heart, now the Satanic Void, the cloud and the fire, —corporeal and spiritual energy—fill the tormented blood. Yet from the fire, or lust, the Divine Vision, or Imagination, is seen, coming and caring for innocent higher emotions,—Jerusalem's children—as a shepherd for his sheep.

P. 60, ll. 10 to 38.—Jerusalem and Vala are inseparable. Vala sometimes rises into Jerusalem, and Jerusalem wanders into Vala. This latter is her error. She is here called a shadow, while Vala is properly her shadow (p. 44, l. 40). But Albion's sleep has darkened her into Vala-like qualities. Here (l. 29, 30) it is the moralities of Vala that Jerusalem mistakenly imitates, and thus defaces her beauty and requires to be led through the wilderness, by the Lamb, by Forgiveness. (Compare the everlasting Gospel—

" My sin thou hast forgiven me ;
Canst thou forgive my blasphemy ? ")

P. 60, ll. 39 to 65.—Jerusalem, closed in the dungeons of Moral Law, faintly saw the Spirit of Forgiveness. She spoke and asked if he indeed suffered, or if he was, as they told her, a delusion. She says the turning mills of argument have deluded her.

P. 60, ll. 66 to 69.—He tells her she does well to pity the visions he shows her, and that he is able to raise Albion, as Lazarus, from the dead.

P. 61, ll. 1 to 52.—The sixty-first page, which follows, is an interpolation, of later date than the rest. It enlarges the idea, and shows the vision that will raise Albion. It is the sight of forgiveness, of Joseph receiving Mary to wife after her Divine fructification, and of the Resurrection when identity is not changed by sin.

P. 62, ll. 1 to 17.—In page 62 the conversation goes on between the Lamb and Jerusalem. She is to repose on him. Divine emotion is to rest on Divine inspiration. That is to say, love whose origin is the conscious union of all for Imagination's sake, is to rest on the source of all Imagination as natural emotion on her. (Mary leaning against Jerusalem, p. 61, l. 47.) She speaks, asks if the chaste shall be ashamed,— if Vala shall bring forth love? She says she herself is called a harlot and sold in the streets. Yet she knows that Albion will yet arise, and that in her flesh—he is her flesh as well as she his light—she shall see God; sin, forgiveness, love, being the steps that lead to the sight.

P. 62, ll. 18 to 29.—Imagination answers that it will yet create, or give mental existence to Vala, the body-mother, and Luvah, the love-father, for it cannot leave them altogether corporeal, quite in the gnawing grave. Meantime Jerusalem, the universal love and soul-mother, must walk through mortal things, and the cloud (blood) and the rock—personality—shall give her food and drink, though they are not of her nature, if she have faith.

P. 62, ll. 30 to 42.—So spoke the Lamb, while blood and reason fought, yet their battles only ended in more and more of the error called materialism, and the sin called punishment. And Los even in the furnaces then saw the Divine Vision walking among the mortal passions, and so went to his labours strengthened, though himself suffering, as prophecy suffers in time of sorrow and restriction.

P. 63, ll. 1 to 25.—The story of Reuben,—that is, of birth redeeming sex, of innocence rising from passion, of the great law that contrary calls up contrary,—is told again in this segment. Jehovah, among the Druids, introduces the paradox.

Cheviot, place of sword-forging, is the place where this is seen. It is the symbol of male reason, with its desire for destruction of imagination whether by training or by indulgence.

The Zoas trembling before the Spectre when they have fallen toward the centre is regeneration trembling before generation,—the Universal before the Momentary. Luvah slays Tharmas,—East dominates West,—Heart, passion. But it is selfish heart dominating universal instinct. Vengeance follows violence, however holy. Vala—natural emotion that does not know itself to be passion (for Vala is more related to Tharmas than she thinks)—takes vengeance. Religions of slaughter— the slaughter that slays the pitying heart in man—triumph.

P. 63, ll. 26 to 36.—Los, in his prophetic spirit, says that the female—that is to say, the natural or material man—cannot be chaste. (The reason is elsewhere given that the body is woven over the mind, and a chaste body cannot be woven over an unchaste mind.) Thus, forgiveness is the lesson taught by the presence of sin. The victims are to be of flocks and herds. That is, those appetites which do not help, however indirectly, to join man to his fellow man, may go,—but not those, even if sinful, which serve this great purpose.

London and Canterbury—(here standing for heart and eyes, Luvah and Urizen)—groan in fear. While the lions and tigers rage against imagination of Gwendolen (who is both Rahab and Tirzah, as we know, the typical mother of mortal blood) sport before her on the Thames and Medway,—nerves of feminine natural instinct.

P. 63, ll. 37 to 39.—Los, prophet though he was, did not see at first the meaning. He thought all this a " vision of the atmospheres "—a symbol in the region of Luvah. But Canaan —the natural, the seed-producing Canaan—rolled apart from Albion (as a result of Luvah slaying Tharmas), and this murder was put apart in Enitharmon's looking-glass.

This is not, therefore, finally formed into a portion of the main myth, but as in other places the symbolic statement of a

piece of Blake's experience out of which he is endeavouring to
extract eternal truth. It has had the aquafortis of prophetic
fury poured on it to melt away apparent surfaces and make it
an "ornament." But it must stand apart. No prophet can
digest *all* his experience into growing vital mind. But what
Los saw clearly was that Revenge is always the knife, and
always associated with the shrinkage of the "numerous
senses" into the "five" of the mortal worm, the life of
blindness, sleep, reason (p. 94, l. 22). This knife is the
contrary of the balm of Forgiveness. So in this subtle interchange of functions Vala is seen doing the work of Satan,—
Luvah's emanation that of his spectre. The symbolism is less
intricate than it seems at first, however, though to finally
paraphrase every part of it would be long, Blake's *names* being
condensed paragraphs in themselves.

In a general way this page refers to the eternal struggle
between what moralists call the higher and lower parts of
mind, and contains a partial justification for their classification
from the opposite point of view of the mystic.

P. 63, l. 54.—Reuben went head-downwards taxing the
nations. Reuben being in a sense birth, head-downwards
being mind in experience, this line is the Blakean acknowledgment of an analogy between political economy and symbolism.

P. 64.—But since body is woven over mind, covering over
cherubim, the mundane shell over the living world (the impressions of man over impression-receiving man), in a word, all
the affairs of ages and generations reach from good to evil in
their infinite extent from the outside spread without to the
outside spread within.

Vala, with the united voice of natural instinct and productivity, speaking as all the daughters of Albion shows
individual men, whether of papal or lesser dignity, to be, on
this side, female—that is organic, vegetable. Scorn and Pride
being essentially mortal, the vegetable or mortal despises and
scorns itself in the spectrous.

Los explains love and the sexual in the mental symbol of

sex,—and ends by the only solution, Forgiveness. Then his personality, his Spectre, draws Vala into his bosom: The dragon red and hidden harlot becoming thus constituted, the dark Hermaphrodite appears. The plough (lost sight of since seen in its good aspect on p. 55, c. 67), is seen to be in the Spectre's hand, and the distaff in the Emanation's. The sexual act, whether of passion or of mind, is thus always a double death. Reuben alike is the result. In all the above there is a constant interchange between good and evil aspects. Los, Albion, Canterbury and Luvah are good aspects in a bad temporary condition,—that of reason or revenge. Tharmas, the Spectre, Cheviot, Derby Peak, &c., are varieties of the male,—himself a female, and thus, in view of the ultimate aim of life, evil. For female stands finally for division, and male for unity. Male is essentially unity even in destruction. Female essentially division even in construction. Her part is to construct the body, type of individualism, or division into separated persons who have not the capacity of joining into a Divine Family, though ultimately to be joined by Christ or inspiration breaking through the circle of destiny or Reason.

P. 65.—But besides all the lesser contraries, there are the two great ones of Humanity—wrath and pity. Now a huge effort is made by the daughters of Albion to cast Albion into the Pity,—to make manhood a prey to its feminine softness that they may have dominion,—and Luvah, naturally the feminine heart himself, into the wrath. This is a symbol for the Coming Again in which Christ, who assumed Luvah's robes of blood at the Incarnation, puts on the wrath of Satan or Urizen as Judge, as thus as accuser or condemner,—as anything opposite to pitier and forgiver. For while pity "Divides the soul and man unmans" yet it "joins what wrath divides,"—the divisions of wrath being unproductive even of such produce as Reuben. It only propagates by the law that "we become what we behold."

These leading ideas cover the whole of this page, and join it to the essay on "Last Judgment" in its spiritual mani-

festation, and thus with Night VII. as predecessor of Night IX.
in the "Book of Vala."

All the symbolism here is a sexual myth:—the plough
has become the spear; Vala trembles; Luvah is slain;
incarnation is seen to be the prelude to judgment; it is a
death into cruel roots, and the tree is Albion's tree of moral
virtue. It is the gallows sign of judgment; the battle round
Vala is that of passion; the Spectre is identified with the
priest, who is a symbol of male intention as upright serpent,—
and is the completion of the many symbols,—plough,
spear, serpent Prophet, warrior, priest. All is seen as a
vision of the atmospheres now, for it is "In the depths of
Albion's bosom, the Eastern Heavens." The analogy between
reason and the feminine is never lost sight of. Lines 5, 11,
show passion and love the slaves of materialism. 12 to 28,
reason taking advantage and usurping mind. 29 to 55
passion usurping love. Then 56 to 62 show how reason, or
moral law (always the same thing in two aspects) in deceiving
a victim takes possession of his sympathetic feeling until, in
the power of Liberty,—or Jerusalem, the victim rending his
bonds, casts off the veil of law and of delusion and enters
into the Universal Mental Humanity. In lines 64 to 79 the
reaction comes. Reason perceives that Mortal passion and
moral law,—(double yet one female, Vala) is its own mother.
It becomes what it beholds.

P. 66.—This page tells of the "female will" which is not
"in eternity," that is to say, the will of the reason that is not
in imagination. It, in the persons of the daughters of
Albion, cuts off inspiration, wounds as well as covers, enters
the heart of man, makes the sun Vision,—or the South, drunk
with doubt, sends the stars—lesser mental illuminations—far
off, covers the soul with mental disease and acts in perpetual
Druid sacrifices of those who mistake Imaginative significance
for corporeal command—an error never easier to commit than
when we are reading Blake's own prophecies. In lines 1 to 15,
the relation of the feminine to Natural Morality and Rational

religion, and of these to the Personal Spectre, is given by making Luvah the victim of Albion's Spectre,—Reason and War,—and making him France,—who was such a victim in the beginning of the nineteenth century. This is attributed to Voltaire and Rousseau, who between them are Vala's covering cherubim,—the two curtains of the feminine ark, Rationalism—taking the place of Rahab and Tirzah, who divide Guendolen and all the daughters between them. The rest of the page is rather itself the key to others than need of explanation.

P. 67.—Continuing, the subject enforces again and again the idea that all evils,—nature being the essence of evil,—flow from the Reasoning part of mind, deluding the sensations into being mistaken for imaginative fact and so enabling them to enter into humanity when they should stay outside, thus giving them existence, thus, as we say, creating the world, requiring its redemption and leading to its judgment. Thus is formed the Polypus or Generation whose head—here said to be in Verulam, elsewhere, or Salisbury plain—is equally in the West and the North, the place of instinct, and of experience and its result,—cold Law where Rocks are called Fathers of men and Druids slay in their great stone circle.

In the last lines daughters of Zelophad,—blood-weaving forces, portions and sisters of Tirzah,—speak lovingly to the human being whom they enslave, whose freedom would be their death.

P. 68.—For, as in the next page,—when Chemosh, Bacchus, and Venus triumph, man is a victim, the State yields to the Space. The Emanation plays the Spectre's part, and is ravenning. Lines 62 to 70 give the key. The female passions eat up the male energies. Desire usurps the " time " of imagination. (Compare p. 77, first line of prose.)

P. 69.—Then the males begin their united destruction. Jealousy, that female form of personality and reason, has entered the male. It becomes at variance within itself. The dragon red and hidden harlot reappears with a new re-creation

of itself from new origin. The male refuses liberty to the
male, for the female within him makes him do so, for it is a low
female jealous of Liberty who is Jerusalem, the highest female.
The reason is that we are still struggling head downwards, to
solve the problem of life otherwise than by forgiveness. In
Beulah, which is not such a feminine place as Verulam or
Salisbury Plain, because it is of Vision (South), there were
sexes but no unhappiness (lines 15 to 25) till the Spectres entered
Beulah (line 32), because jealousy had entered through the law
that female bliss was allied to Generation and vegetation (31),
and these to the Tree of Mystery and Morality which causes
the sexes of Beulah, since they had sweetly stolen delight from
imagination (no crime), to "receive punishment to make them
commit crimes" (27), and so they became murderers (36) (or
Druids "demanding in the name of Chastity the slaughter of
the sweet Infant Joys"). We learn in the last lines that this
is all part of the result of Reuben's wandering.

Jerusalem yearns over him, for liberty yearns over the errors
that make the rocks of experience, and Reuben, when wandering and head down, is Hand, for he is all the sons of Albion
whom Hand absorbed, for they are the Male in Limit, just as
Vala is the Female in Limit.

P. 70.—Therefore, in the seventieth page follows a description of Hand, who is the whole world of Male Reason and
personal claims and envy, plotting to devour Albion's
Body of Humanity (or Imagination which is Brotherhood)
and love.

Hand, the twelvefold, dividing threefold into the three
dark creations of Bacon, Newton, and Locke, through vegetation (the oak groves) is related to Rahab, whose object, whether
with morality or reason is always the same (19), to destroy
Imagination, the Divine Humanity. In imagination (*or* eternity)
she is seen to be Vala,—the beauty and love of Nature, but in
fact, and Time, she is seen to be Rahab, its disgrace.

Thus the subject of the poem has come round, as it were,
from near the end to the beginning—compare lines 17, 20,

with page 5, line 57, page 6, lines 14, 15, page 8, line 44, and page 9, lines 1, 2, page 18, lines 36 and 39.

It will be noted that page 70 does not continue exactly the style or matter of page 69. There is some reason to suppose that it was meant at first for an earlier portion of the book. The three terrible heads, mentioned in line 5, are symbolic of the same truths as the three wheels, page 18, line 6. The whole action related in page 70 is that of page 18, differently told. The last word in it,—His, indicated by its place as being the first of the following page, is not the word that commences page 71, while it does commence page 19, and the whole of page 19 perfectly continues, in style, matter, and handwriting, the whole of page 70. Page 20 does not continue page 19, but continues page 18.

However, taking the pages as they come, an intention is found even in their disarrangement, or rather in their re-arrangement, though it is to be regretted that the matter of the great poem was not better kept in hand from the first. Had the work been more deliberately intellectual and less an ill-assorted note-book reporting intermittent visions, it would have been more verbally continuous though less mystically coherent.

Page 71 continues the account of places associated with various States and Places which is found on p. 16. Perhaps its number was 17 and was miscopied 71 by Blake when writing in reverse on his copper plates. There has evidently been more error and change of mind in the arrangement of the pages than conjecture can satisfactorily set right now, for p. 72, and not 71, is both by style of handwriting and matter the follower of p. 16. Pages 73 and 74 follow 72, but the page that should have followed that numbered 70 began with the word *His* as indicated. Page 19 will do. It is clearly out of place where it stands. That its first line should have come from "Vala," Night IX., l. 99, is of itself a hint that it is placed too early in the present work. But what should have followed it? We must be content that we know now what Blake meant by what he wrote and give up in despair, as he himself did, the final arrangement of his ponderous but sublime scrap-book. (Compare above " About Jerusalem.")

P. 71, ll. 56 to 62, return to the story, but find no continuation in those that follow them, that is to say,

P. 73, ll. 1 to 22, attempts to touch on the great list of the condensations of the furnaces,—the Creation, in fact, and gives up the task; but the nature of the subject strongly points to its place being in Chapter I., not Chapter III.

P. 73, ll. 22 to 30.—In a general way they are " limits." The limits that the Divine Hand found and called Satan and Adam (see p. 35) were not God's work. He found and removed them by the aid of Los's Hammer. Voltaire insinuates that they are the work of God,—yes; of the God of this world, not of God as an ultimate. Compare note in MS. book; section " Literary Period."

P. 73, ll. 31 to 40.—The spirit of Reason creates kings, that of prophecy successive churches or patriarchs and prophets; the one to enslave more and more, the other to release.

P. 73, ll. 40 to 52, explain some symbolic terms, and the end of the page suggests that the next following should have been that numbered 16 at present.

P. 73, ll. 42, 43.—These two lines are the key to Blake's belief in the possibility of imputing sin and righteousness to states and not to individuals, and so attaining the power of forgiving sins.

P. 74, at any rate, does not even pretend to follow 73. Its true place in the book is difficult to fix. It should have been probably among the very first few. It shows (ll. 1 to 9) how a spectre is produced by separation, and (ll. 10 to 13) explains the destructive character of the separated spectre.

P. 74, ll. 15 to 39, is an invocation, clearly for the beginning of the poem. It bears the stamp of early printing, but is not the earliest of all. It probably represents a method for introducing the story of Reuben, printed from scraps of MS. whose intended order had been forgotten.

P. 74, ll. 40 to 51, in presenting Reuben and the lost tribes, this page shows even these as they are when made spectral by separation, and tells parenthetically of the sight of a visionary form of Jerusalem in a minor aspect, as Dinah, the youthful form of Erin, and places the experience in South Molton Street, —not Felpham. It is therefore an early London page of the poem, about 1804.

P. 75, ll. 1 to 27.—This little page of twenty-seven lines about the twenty-seven heavens is explained in the chapter devoted to this subject. Their purpose, and the purpose of all creeds, to release the prisoners of reason, and bring man into the eternal life of the Imagination, is here given. ·

PREFACE TO CHAPTER IV.

P. 77.—The first verse is the motto of the whole book, placed at the head of this fourth chapter, whose title should be Regeneration, the only fourth phase of growth when Creation, Redemption, and Judgment have been passed. It is a manifesto to the Christians, that is to those united in the brotherhood of Imagination, and dwelling in consciously mental regions by choice and by liberty.

The prose essay explains itself. It is an argument needing no support, if it be true that Imagination is the world of eternity, that its moral side is forgiveness, and its feminine emanation love. In this world clearly the entrance is by mental act, and the virtues come of themselves; for where all brotherhood is spontaneous, any punishment is inadmissible, and all reward or sense of merit and virtue is absurd.

The blank verse passage was probably the foundation of the whole work, and belongs to the time indicated in the preface to the first chapter, when Blake intended to write the entire poem, in what he does himself the injustice to call "a monotonous cadence."

It is curiously complete as a manifesto. Its claim is emphatic. It describes the new direction of illumination and life as from West to East,—once the direction of darkness and devouring fire. Such is Regeneration, and such the creed it was Blake's mission to announce. When this was the direction of the "wheel of religion" it was symbolized by the passage of the sun during the night;—by Urizen not in the south but the north, where the tree of morality grew over his head, on which the dark storms of ice fell while he read his terrible books. Caiphas, who said that it was expedient that one should die, was its preacher. Brotherhood and Imagination personified were the One who so died. The beginning of "Milton" tells that Christ became the victim of Tharmas: East of West, Heart of Loins, Regeneration of Generation.

But the night is over. The passage under the earth of the sun, the days of Christ in the tomb, of Albion head downwards in his cliff, of the mind of man in the religious delusions of the twenty-seven heavens, and the moral errors of self-righteousness, and the mental mistake of thinking the Reasoning Memory and its produce to be Mind instead of Eternal Vision, have gone by. It is time to awake. The Prophet calls to the Man. Adam returns to Paradise. The Angel of Obedience leaves the Tree life. Such, whether in the words here used or in those of the preface to the "Marriage of Heaven and Hell," is always Blake's one great Message. This alone can break the Circle of Destiny that Tharmas, even with holy hand, cannot but turn round for ever, from Adam to Luther, with sighs and bitter tears. The circle of creation is justified as the image of the circle of Regeneration. The Satanic creation, called that of God, is cruelty in itself, and only so far Mercy that it enables error to be put off. The Nature Created by Christ is that which treats the fiery law of vegetation (growth being ceaseless burning, though disguised in a green tree) as a chaos, whence to achieve the new heavens and new earth, where the peace of sinners is respected and the magic of happiness cures the disease of experience.

This, in words all found in Blake in one place or another, is the paraphrase of this piece of verse, which, even had it stood alone, would have indicated what Blake's other writings

have so abundantly proved, that his claim to be a prophet
was as well founded as that of any Eastern in Biblical times,
while its general comprehension would be no less of an epoch
in the world's history than the era of any public acceptance of
the inspiration of any period.   It is new only in its symbolism
and in its bold unmasking of that symbolism.   It is new as
consciousness is always new; old as life is always old.

Chapter IV.

The chapter begins with a description of darkness and
sorrow, prelude to light.

P. 78, ll. 1 to 9.—In the first lines the formula of the great
contest is repeated.   The Spirit of Prophecy in the form of
Time arrays both the inner expansiveness of mind and the
outer mutability of sense against the self-righteous Reasoning
Power.

P. 78, ll. 10 to 20.—The separated mental states attempt to
make themselves human, and to have connection with imagination by means of Vala, called Rahab, and exalted : that is
to say, natural love lifted into chastity, and made the subject
of contemplation.   (This would be well if well done, but is
ill when it pretends that the truth of matter and untruth of
imagination are demonstrated by the purifying effects of
outward morality demanded by reason.   Life depends on
imagination and the great importance given to conduct for
virtue's sake,—contrary of the importance of forgiveness for
love's and unity's sake—leads straight to exaltation of the
mortal, his possessions, his tyrannies, his wars, his generalised
law, till death alone unites man with man,—death or any
other similarity that is not sympathy.)

Why has Erin forty-two gates ?   This is obscure.   Blake
does not clear the point.   It may be a clerical error, thirty-two
being intended.

P. 78, ll. 21, 22.—Mount Zion, the ancient promontory, or

holy place, where dwelt the giant Mental Energies that formed this world, was the place of Jerusalem, the mother of giants. But as the giants destroyed feminine affection they destroyed her, pleading that she, being of the same nature, was so far an outcast from the divine presence of Imagination. So Vala is the aspect of her that triumphs, by corporeal morality, contrary of her physical nature, a pretence. Jerusalem is the morality of universal liberty, as conceived by the Christian ideal. But in practise she, as all, need forgiveness, for the sin of loving the lower mind, called matter.

P. 79.—But in the next page,—Jerusalem suffers; all the symbolism of Nations and Cities and the tribes being wrought together. She describes her grief. The sexual delusion is that part of mental life, is complete in itself, with a right to exist at the expense of another part.

This is an appropriation of "universal characteristics" (p. 90, l. 30), whereas the sexual division is merely an occasion for re-uniting, and thus a chariot for the Divine Power (p. 98, l. 11). The whole book of "Jerusalem" (see the first lines) is about Ulro,—the place where whatever enters becomes sexual and vegetated and born. In the resurrection, at the end of this chapter, we shall hear of the end of the sexes, and shall be free of Ulro (p. 61, l. 51; 64, ll. 20 to 25).

P. 80, ll. 1 to 5, end the story of Jerusalem's loss. She is lost by entering into natural life, to realise herself there. This is "harlotry," the sin of mixed convictions and mixed mental states.

P. 80, ll. 6 to 15.—So important to salvation is a distinct repudiation of the delusion called Nature, that if this cannot be attained on account of the attractiveness of natural pleasures, it were better that these, and all that belongs to mortal blood,—the feminine,—should cease and be no more.

P. 80, ll. 16 to 31.—Luvah, the now fallen and separated love, having gone to outer spheres, to the false centre, has given

Vala in her character of the weaver of the moral veil, the knife to slay Albion, and bring him under the subjection of unforgiving Law.

To be a punisher and judge *is* to be dead: dead to the life of brotherhood.   She embalms his body in soft odours of jealous stupefaction, and so keeps his system of thought fixed. She dares to beg the Lamb not to raise him from the dead.

P. 80, ll. 32 to 36.—Then Vala disguised Jerusalem like herself (compare "Vala," Night II., l. 37), and female influence over the whole earth made its great effort against the Lamb of God.   The device was that Forgiveness should be got rid of by becoming unnecessary, Moral Virtue (opposed to the Lamb) taking its place.   The sin of this lies in the fact that Forgiveness is also a dweller in the Human breast, as well as sin, and that to cast out Forgiveness, even if righteousness be formally substituted, is necessarily the reverse of real righteousness, and is the great crucifying sin.

First Vala, then those divisions of her called daughters of Albion, enslave Luvah, then those divisions of his and Albion's Spectre (Satan), called Sons of Albion, or mental materialistic convictions, are enslaved by the daughters of Albion.   They are feminine now in the sense of being affiliated to the dark religion of prohibition, not the bright religion of Forgiveness.   Sinai, not Zion, is the mountain whose divisions are called the Peak of Derbyshire, Skiddaw, Welsh hills, &c.   Such is the act of female will, and the raving and the desire of the male mind is its result.

P. 81.—This leads to the destruction of Reuben, who was wandering,—the natural infant of male innocent love that put itself under material conditions, and being "named" Jehovah, —who was seen among the Druid temples in the Reuben vision (page 63, line 1) was obliged to incarnate as an infant that Forgiveness might also have a body.   It will be noticed that this is in reference to one of the supposed origins of the Biblical name Reuben, namely *ráû béonyi,* "Jehovah hath seen

my affliction," or " Roubel," explained by Josephus as the
" Pity of God." Page 81 also contains a few of Blake's
dicta about the sexes, and about " Heaven," and " Earth," in
which one pair is used as symbol for the characteristics of the
contrary displayed by the other.

P. 82, ll. 1 to 9, explains the reason why nature (or the
feminine side of man's mind) acts on mind. It seeks
command lest it should be discovered to be a delusion, and so
its power vanish.

P. 82, ll. 10 to 21.—Guendolen, in Rahab's cloud, takes a
falsehood in her left hand behind her loins. She thus speaks
from the very essence of the material world of delusion. She
tells about eternal divisions of the universal energy,
" forgetting that falsehood is prophetic,"—forgetting that
symbols may be used with intent to deceive, but that they
have in themselves a truth-generating power that appeals to
vision, and so enters the light of imagination in which the
ultimate of all is found.

P. 82, ll. 21 to 45.—She claims Enitharmon as having will
like hers (true, when Enitharmon's will is " separate "), and tells
that Jerusalem is thus to be changed from imaginative into
mortal love.

P. 82, ll. 47 to 77.—As a result the feminine powers grow
jealous of each other, and Hyle, the son of Albion, most
characteristic of Luvah, is woven into a worm and an infant,
and another form is seen of the same visionary symbol told of
at length in the " Book of Urizen " as the birth of Orc. To this
work the feminine will that desires to enslave the strong,
yields, giving itself away to the weak.

P. 82.—Los sees, and his mind—as that of Urthona, keeper
of the gates that are of heaven in their result, but northern
or material in place, and that are indeed, at once the gates of
Reuben and of Jerusalem—is comforted, but yet he is bound
to pangs of maternal feeling on which he has looked.

P. 83, ll. 1 to 5.—For this is part of the story of Los entering
by paternity into Orc, and by sympathy becoming closed in

Albion's cliffs. The power that thus binds him is the chain that also bound Orc, in the older vision.

P. 83, ll. 5 to 65.—Yet he is still the watchman, though Amalek, Canaan, and Moab (the outer, the Eastern, and as such the egotistic or false-central head, heart, loins) triumph over the cities of Albion that are daughters of Jerusalem and change their functions. This Canaan is not the " Heavenly Canaan " that is " over Albion's Land," and is " Divine Analogy." Los will prepare a place on Euphrates, river of life in blood. In Cathedron's dome,—the body,—the feminine powers weave for the ultimate use of Jerusalem the web of maternal life which goes glistening with soft affections to the place where reason makes all mind into darkness, —Entuthon's Vale.

P. 83, ll. 65 to 84.—So Los, having told the daughters of Albion, goes forth in golden sandals (protecting even the lower parts of imagination with the shield of visionary material) and walks from mountain to mountain, from one to another of the places of loveless convictions, whether of unreality or of reason, while the dogs (natural desires) of Leutha (child of natural beauty) lap the trembling Thames (river of parental generation).

P. 83, ll. 85 to 87.—And Los calls to Albion to awake,— calls to man to perceive prophetically, not materialistically.

P. 84, ll. 1 to 16.—Page 84 is an afterthought,—an elaboration of the scheme. The portions of London, especially the North, West and East,—all suffer, and London grows old, as do the mortal portions of man, whether of the loves that are brought to him by experience (north) or generated from him by loins or heart (west or east). An infant leads the old, as it commands the female, through whom age comes to man as well as infancy. This still means always the history of the portions of mind, so named.

P. 84, ll. 17 to 25.—The night falls thick. Hand is seen as Molech and Chemosh, the gods that destroy infancy by the fire of tyrannous vegetative painful passion (Molech) or

pleasurable passion (Chemosh) with their contraries, or
moral laws, equally destructive to innocence. The feminine
calls to the prophetic at last for the sound of his voice.

P. 84, ll. 26 to 29.—Gwendolen's falsehood, an infant also, a
body fit for Hyle, or Reuben, grows.

P. 85, ll. 1 to 7.—It becomes revealed as divine by analogy.
But its date is restricted. It is only for six thousand years.
It is symbol trying to live for its own sake, compelled to live
for truth's sake. Prophecy leads wandering ignorance and
innocence into it. (If prophecy had not done so the incarnation would not have meaning for each of us, nor we ourselves
be members through it of Christ's body, according to the
early Christian doctrine.)

P. 85, ll. 8 to 9.—Spectre and emanation, male and female,
times and spaces again are explained.

P. 85, ll. 10 to 21.—And Los' position towards the east (the
same as the once wicked wheel of religion) repeated. Los
replies and sings.

P. 85, ll. 22 to 32.—His voice calls Jerusalem forth from her
hiding place in Babylon on Euphrates, where she was hidden
when (in equivalent symbol) Albion, the sleeping man, in his
jealousy,—for sleep is sexual, and the sexual is jealous,—hid
her, on the Thames and Medway,—the parental nervous
system that is the counterpart of the Euphrates, the sanguine
parental system.

P. 86, ll. 1 to 14.—The visionary symbolic form of Jerusalem,
as shown in the title-page of the book, is described. It is the
general form of true daughters of Beulah, but in her case has
a more extended symbolism, as being the form of one of those
in whom multitudes are united. It will be noticed that the
cities and valleys of Albion are mental spaces in the head of
Jerusalem. In no other sense has the geographical nomen-
clature used here any meaning. The interpretation must be
content to deal in aggregates, and drive the symbols before
it like flocks,—it cannot carry them each separately in its
hands. Space is lacking, and the clue is sometimes not

made clear by Blake himself. The points of the compass
generally will be found to indicate the "region" and thus
the symbolic meaning of the different towns, lands, seas and
streams.

P. 86, l. 15.—Here is the clue to the mixture of Holy Land
and English names in the text. The tribes of Israel in the
heart are equivalent moods or states to the places of England
in the head. Jerusalem is now within Albion. What is in
her heart is above (or within, see page 71, lines 1 to 10) what
is in her head. Her bosom is "the cloud of the sun's tabernacle,"—the rainbow. It is thus also a universal in itself, and
has within it the sun, true head, and the light cloud, true loins.
In fact, the rainbow is symbol of that true "circumference
which is within," when the "selfish centre is outside." Its
three colours are on the wings of Beulah,—(compare title-
page of "Jerusalem," and "Vala," Night VIII., ll. 6 to 15).

P. 86, ll. 22 to 32.—Her third region, here called reins,—also
shows a universal. It has its four points. Its northern
Libanon, southern Egypt, eastern Assyria, western Islands
and Coast Towns. Egypt is the North of the South. It is
science. It is the ear of the loins. It is experience in the
world of imagination. It is the name of that from which the
salt ocean rolled englobed. ("Book of Urizen," last line.)
It is the knees and feet, the lower parts of imagination.
These loins show Israel in her tents. We see the meaning
by comparing the end of the sixth chapter of the "Book of
Urizen,"—when a tent was made for Los, the symbol of the
female organs,—ark and curtains,—and the lid of the eye, the
eye being the Feminine South, Beulah, vision,—the emanative
function of mind. The fluency of the stream of symbolism
is evident, and the current is obvious, bearing as it does
a whole fleet of images all in one mental direction.

P. 86, l. 32, 50.—The great fact is that while we are in
(the state of mind, or mood, called) this world, the Spirit of
Prophecy and Eternity is in the form of Time the Labourer,
and the Spirit of Home and Unity, is in the form of Jerusalem,

who, because she includes Vala, is a Wanderer. Each contains and is its own opposite. A Wanderer is a mood going from impression to impression and not firmly placed in good mystic permanence. (Compare "Milton," p. 14, l. 16.)

P. 86, ll. 50 to 61.—And the Labourer only able to see as much of the Wanderer as belongs to him, sees her as Enitharmon, the Rainbow that came from the Water-region, his Loins. He is in the fire-region by personality, but she drags him out of himself by sympathy. In the world of temporary division, fire and water have two intellects and two wills, not one, as in eternity.

P. 86, ll. 62 to 64.—This division enables them to desire one another, as well as to oppose (such is the origin of Orc, their child,—who is Desire). But before his birth they are like two infants of the ancient mother Enion,—a phase of Eno. (See "Stories of the Zoas.")

P. 87, ll. 1 to 11.—Enion is silently maternal,—the speech of love repels her. Los speaks. He tells Enitharmon that soon their action on one another will drag them from the inner to the outer world,—from heart to loins (for such is Growth, the inevitable action of Time on Space in the World of Generation), and he bids her make the heart eternal in the loins,— love in sensation before he is obscured from her mental sight by the roof (the tent, the body, the senses, the flood, the blood) growing over him. Love in the heart (East) will thus be an element of eternal sunrise, even should blood roof it over (as with a covering cherub).

P. 86, ll. 12 to 24.—But this is not to be done in a moment, the beast of the flesh,—of the feminine nature in man,—contains pride and jealousy. The lower love is proud of not being the higher and jealous that the higher is nearer than itself to that element of mind that was its origin. Los is origin of Enitharmon ; as infants they are twins, but in the mature sense, Space is from Time, and Love from Imagination. Jerusalem is higher than her own rainbow,—and in this the three colours are more than the one,—the red. The lower

falsely accuses the higher. Albion's daughter is said to be set
in Los' path. The lower is always the Satan,—or Accuser,
of the higher.

P. 88, ll. 1 to 36.—Only at the thirty-sixth line of this page
is the key given to the eternal (or ornamental) meaning of the
contest between the male and female. It is the struggle
between the non-creative emotions through which companionship of complete personalities must be begun, and the
creatively mental attributes with its own Emotion of Existence,—to coin a description which Blake does not use, but
includes in the word "real Human" Humanity. The Man in
Man fights the God in Man, for the merely man is woman, and
has no will in Eternity, though in Time it can fight the
Eternal Will.

As the outer is the symbol of the inner, conjugal life is the
book in which this may be read.

The reference to the Spectre probably coincides, both in
idea and in date, with that in the Truchsessan letter, printed in
the Memoir here, and belonging to 1804, the date of the title-
page of "Jerusalem," containing the pictorial form of the vision
described just before.

P. 88, ll. 36 to 50.—The concluding lines complete the account
of the symbol of the strange paradox, continually recurring in
Blake, that sexual love springs from spiritual hate (p. 54, l. 2).
The three regions of Los are now Justice, Mercy, Wrath.
Those of Enitharmon are Jealousy, Scorn, Love.

From the point of view of narrative, all the intervening
portion of the poem might be wiped out, and the opening
scene between Los and his Spectre, made the prelude of this
scene.

P. 89, ll. 1 to 8.—Under six names Pharasaion, Grammateis,
Presbiterion, Anhiereus, Jereus, Saddusaion, the twelve
divisions,—each name being double, or hermaphroditic,—are
symbolized of Satan,—of the body, of the Jealousy (sometimes called God, by mortals), the scorn (also called righteousness), the love (also called sin), now to be further described as

the Covering Cherub. This is also a companion symbol to
the Serpent of the "Everlasting Gospel," and some of the
words of that poem recur here. He is here called "dragon,"
but is equivalent to serpent,—in whose guise elsewhere appears
not only the "self-hood" but its outer symbol, the "Vast form
of Nature."

P. 89, ll. 9 to 23.—The Covering Cherub being all that he
should not be, has his loins in his head,—a reflexion of Eden,
and other loin-symbols, Egypt,—the Gihon (a river of Paradise, used by Jeremiah ii. 18, as an equivalent for Sichor, or
Sihor, the Nile), "many tongued," Tongue: Tharmas.
He is outwoven from the loin-streams, Thames, Tweed, Severn,
—and having for twelve-fold palace the twelve stones, not those
that "give light in the opaque" ("Europe") but the Druidical
circles. And the forests of melancholy cover the Earth (north,
loins) from pole to pole.

P. 89, l. 24.—His heart, too, is full of loins and of stone.
Moab, the desert is in it, more Druid buildings. The River
Pison (called Amon in "Milton" and Storge: it is the stream
of generative and parental affection), and Hiddekel, whose
Biblical interpretation is a "sharp cry,"—River of Child-birth,
—for the heart of nature also emanates its kind,—and here,
too, are Islands of Greece, beauty in unbelief,—heathen,
perverted visionary art, merely mortal love.

The last verse of "Cupid" given in the chapter on the MS.
book was written not long after this chapter. The "Grecian
mock" of the Monk of Charlemagne in the rejected stanzas
will be remembered also. Wings,—the great space-makers,
are here of iron and brass and full of eyes; they are of
experience and passion, and these elements surround their
marriage powers (eyes).

P. 89, ll. 38 to 42.—The loins are given eye-less wings.
Impotent eternally is the exterior productivity of the temporary Covering—the dragon-Cherub. Yet Babylon is within,—
morality and immorality,—that strange mixture which pretends
to be, and is not, innocence. Yet they also have their own

beauty: for the genitals are always producers of beauty. Compare the sixty-second Proverb in the "Marriage of Heaven and Hell." The remainder of the story of this symbol and its relation with others is to be found in the "Book of Milton," and in the chapter here on the Twenty-seven Heavens.

P. 89.—But Jerusalem is hidden on the inward rivers, in the midst of the devouring Stomach (Tharmas), her natural opposite, sheathed and surrounded by the Covering Cherub, as a hundred miss-statements surround one truth, and all the churches surround one ideal Love. As for all the errors of Love, whether of Rahab and Tirzah or the Kings of Canaan and Baalim of Philistea which correspond to them (in right of their numbers seven and five), all these at the entrance to the world of generation were overwhelmed by the sea of the blood, bodily instincts,—that came up the vale of Rephaem (East to West: heart to loins), and it overwhelmed all the separate tyrants of the world and arguments of naturalism.

P. 89, ll. 52 to 62.—We cannot help seeing that a vision is implied of the Satanic double quality, the tears and the destructiveness which corresponds to the Hermaphroditic wine-press of love and wrath, the wine-press of Los in the aspect of Luvah, when he yields to female love, and of Luvah in the state called Satan, when he mingled with Albion's Spectre who was also that of Los. In fact, mortal love conceals itself in mortal egotism. This is the dragon red and hidden harlot,—double female, yet also female within male,—for the temporary in the male is female. In the chapter on the Twenty-seven Heavens, the especial aspect of the Cherub belonging to this symbol is analyzed.

The last lines of the page are somewhat broken and difficult to read. They are as follows:—

> "For multitudes of those who sleep in Alla descended,
> Lured by his warlike symphonies of tabret, pipe, and harp,
> Burst the bottoms of the graves and funeral urns of Beulah
> Wandering in that unknown night beyond the silent grave,
> They become one with Antichrist, and are absorbed in him."

The description recurs with a difference in " Vala." It has more than one meaning. As a symbol it contains a mystic visionary perception of the spiritual forces that pass from the region of digestion and blood to that of pro-creation and blood, and so pass out from the place where nature is still a part of man, beyond the region of himself by its grave's broken boundary,—the rent limits of fleshly individuality. And it is also philosophic,—the sexual being the Destroying and the Imagining, the Reasoning and the Desiring,—and so forth. The same class of " Spirits" permeate the breaking of both boundaries.

P. 90, ll. 1 to 16.—The " Everlasting Gospel " describes the crucifying of Christ's pride, his Satan, when he humbled God in himself,—the subtle paradox can be retraced here. There is another Redemption performed by Satan when we behold his double Male-female nature, and in doing so are redeemed from our own separateness into sexes, and so taken down from the cross, the tree of mystery, of morality, the gallows on which we were hung. He imitates the Divine. He has his union of sexes in the form of Hermaphroditic doubt,—the war of reason and the harlot of mixed moral and immoral emotion. Nothing can be so far from the Divine as the Hermaphrodite, its opposite. The one is Certainty : the other is Self-Contradiction. But we learn from this the evil of the separation of the masculine from the feminine and both from Man, who then no longer is that "Man" of whom the " Everlasting Gospel " says—

" Thou art a Man, God is no more."

Even the masculine of Eternity is covering to a feminine within, who exudes and covers him, as the torch contains the heat which comes out as a flame and wraps the torch. But when the torch and flame are separate this is the Evil. For Masculine and Feminine are not only Sublime and Pathos, Wrath and Pity, but they reverse their functions when separated. Each tries to devour the " body " of man,—

Reason and Imagination, separated do so also, and strive to become the Two insanities, Delusions, Self-hoods,—the belief in unimaginative reason, unreasonable imagination till a " Delusion is found, woman perishes, and the heaven of heavens shall be no more."—P. 80, l. 14; compare also p. 67, l. 14.

P. 90, ll. 15 to 38.—And then Bowen and Conwenna, the most divided forms of Reason and Feeling cut the weakest prophetic impulse, the youngest son of Jerusalem from the instinctive Western River of Chester,—place of a camp once, —and Innocence of Birth (Reuben) was taken from the South (Eyes), and all went to separated states of Evil, and there grew the great danger that generation should swallow up regeneration,—and the blasphemous self-hoods swallow ultimate unity. So Christ,—the Ultimate Imagination is prayed to take on himself the divisions of Reason, so that he may put them all off. (Compare " Everlasting Gospel.")

P. 90, ll. 39 to 57.—So Los cried. Then the Reasoning that seeks for dominion commingled with the Pity that seeks for Dominion, and became one great Satan. The marrying loves, the daughters of Beulah ran along the rivers of parentage in cruelties of moral law. But Los forced them into mortal bodies, to give them something temporary to be moral with, that the error might die with the vegetated body's death. Hand and Hyle helping the daughters made stones of their shrunken victims, their curbed appetites, and built a temple of reasoning therewith, even to the stars. Then Los showed that they were worshipping the Dragon-Harlot Cruelty-Law, a Hermaphroditic God. Such were the Demonstrations of Prophecy.

P. 90, l. 58.—So Los spoke, but the reason of man rested its ideas in a circle (of prejudice), and mocking God and eternal life in private, in public called themselves religious and worshipped Satan (Nature), which is the Maternal Humanity, or Female God.

P. 91, ll. 1 to 30.—This whole page seems to have been an interpolation, an after-thought. It cannot be assigned to any other place in the book, but its last line was evidently not intended to precede the first line of the next page, and its first paragraph, though made part of what Los cried at his anvil,—Los was doing so on page 90,—is in another and more explanatory, less mythic style. The reference here is evidently to the incident of the *Examiner*, and all the troubles with Hayley and Flaxman. The artistic symbol of "general form" and "particular" is chiefly to be understood in connection with Blake's notes on the third Discourse of Sir Joshua Reynolds. The Book is in the British Museum, and most of the notes are still legible.

P. 91, ll. 31 to 46.—Here is a suggestion that Blake had now reached the time of his life when he knew Varley, the astrologer. If so, this would make the present page a very late one. Gilchrist dates the notes on Reynolds, "from internal evidence," about 1820. This is probably too late. Gilchrist assumes that "Jerusalem" was published entire on the date of its title-page, 1804, but this was evidently not the case. The first dated evidence, so far given, of a complete number being in existence is in the allusion to the book by Wainwright, in the *London Magazine*, September, 1820.—("Gilchrist," Vol. I., page 324.)

The idea that the Spectre read the voids while Los read the stars, and that it used the smaragdine table of Hermes to draw Los down, must be considered as most probably an "ornamental" version of Blake's conversations with Varley,—while the subduing of the eye and ear of the Spectre may well refer to more than the taming of his egotism to the needs of actual and visionary marriage (or act), but may have to do with his complaisance in drawing "visionary heads" at this time.

P. 91, ll. 46 to 52.—Certainly Blake was trying hard now to do what he called in conversation with Mr. Crabb Robinson "thinking rightly,"—and this is strongly shown by the phrase "dividing the Spectre into a separate space." The word *space* implying feminine, while Spectre is usually masculine.

But by tears, by yielding to the Delusive Goddess Nature, it grows feminine, and in this form only can be divided. Then naturalism is cast out, as a mental tendency, from that part of the mind's activity rightly devoted to visionary effort. Blake's acquaintance believed that the process was the reverse, and that the visionary faculty had begun to usurp in Blake the mental position and mood that should belong to the naturalistic; in other words, Crabb Robinson and the *Examiner* were in the right about him. His intimate record of this poem, not intended for any argumentative purpose, shows how different was the fact.

P. 91, ll. 53 to 58.—The page ends with the injunction to the Spectre,—the reason,—to put off holiness,—in the sense of passivity,—and egotism and restriction, and put on intellect,—in the sense of emanative sympathy with all minds. Compare the last lines in the prose passage on p. 77.

P. 92, ll. 1 to 7.—The reason why Albion is taken as symbolic name for Man : he is a four-fold,—a nation the result of unity, and so typical of the great unity in the realms of imagination which shall make the whole human family One Man. He is thus inheritor of Abraham, the individual in whose loins was the seed of the promise before it was divided into tribes. "Abraham fled from Chaldea," and Reuben took refuge in his loins, *but first* (showing that these events are to be taken in symbolic order, derived from but not following historic order) Albion must sleep. (See above, "Jerusalem," page 15.)

P. 92, ll. 8 to 12.—Enitharmon foresees that if Man indeed be about to rise in Albion, prophecy is to merge in fulfilment, and she, as a separate Will, shall be no more. In another sense Enitharmon as a mythic impersonation belonging to the poem ends with the poem.

P. 92, ll. 13 to 27.—It is of the nature of sexes that they attribute sin and righteousness to individuals and not to states, and this is part of the sleep of Ulro, and will end when Albion awakes. Ulro is this world in which you shall not find where to live if you forgive. P. 81, reversed inscription on the cloud. Awakening is passing out of it, first by philosophic change of mind,—only fit preparation to passing out of it by getting rid of that unphilosophic portion of mind called body.

P. 93, ll. 1 to 27.—This whole page is the last word of the sexes before they are no more. On Mam-Tor the conversation is held. It is a mountain of female beauty and virtue,— of Nature's holiness in fact. Compare page 82, line 45. The graves that thunder under their feet are the graves in whose caverns are the places of human seed,—the ultimate of the body. Enitharmon begins,—"Oh! Ruler of Day, and of Night (Rintrah and Palamabron), Plowman of Art, Harrowman of Poetry, do you mean to flee away entering the fleshly passion, losing the sympathetic? Do you mean to plough as when Satan drives the team—or when pride (woman's delight) meets pride, as sexual emotion meets itself? How can love follow its impulses,—little ones,—when they flee along the valley,—the furrough,—the place of seed-sowing, weeping,—as Urizen wept when he would 'form man to his image,' and how can I see tents,—the fleshly places where they are hidden?"

With this,—and more to the same effect,—sympathetic love laments, and as it ceases, enthusiasm replies:—

"The vitality of generation is the promise of the vitality of regeneration. The darkest hour of passion precedes the dawn of imagination. The "waking death," the aroused flesh, becomes one (through the Everlasting Incarnation) with the spirit of prophecy. Let us see in the region of materiality not the Baconian philosophy, but, on the contrary, a symbol and a promise,—even though in this region the male appears as Satan, and the female as Babylon,—the Accuser, and the Moralist—two opposites of the Sympathetic and Unity, Imagination and the Forgiveness, as the passions that give them birth by reaction, and make of them coverings are opposites of inspiration."

P. 94, ll. 1 to 27.—Albion, cold, lies on his rock, and storms

# # #

beat on him. That is, Man, unimaginative, rests his mind on the hard apparent surfaces of things in this world of appearances; he gives his belief to common sense, and time and space beat on him as a tempest. The weeds of death,—the growths of experience, wrap round his mind. The feminine, or material nature, seeking good by regulation of evil,—instead of by absorbing the mind in beauty,—lay beside him and his body, his organised mind, was closed from all nations,—outer truths. Over them, Genius, like a famished eagle, flaps its wings (compare "Marriage of Heaven and Hell," page 9, proverb 55), and the feminine nature coming to self-consciousness after seven faintings, perceived it had killed the masculine as restriction kills exuberance, and as the Satanic combat of Good and Evil,—or tree of knowledge, kills the Christian contest of truth and error,—or tree of life. (This explanation of the "killing by moral law," is from the erased passage given at the end of the chapter on the MS. Book.)

P. 95, ll. 1 to 24.—Albion awoke. His words took Human forms. The feminine entered his bosom. (Eve returned to Adam's side, and Adam returned to the Creator. The rib threw off the semblance of woman. The man threw off the dust of the image. The Human remained.)

P. 96, ll. 1 to 15.—Imagination as the Saviour, stands by Albion, now the awakened man, and explains his own use as the producer of Brotherhood without which Man is not.

P. 96, ll. 16 to 40.—Albion, notwithstanding that the Covering Cherub still tried to darken them (the eternal circle of the faiths), perceived this, and saw it through the prophetic element in Los, whose similitude became that mental instrument, a figure, whereby he saw Christ. Thus he also saw the meaning of the paradox that he who would lose his life should save it, for just as morality being negative is death, so sacrifice being positive, and of the very essence of love, is life, nor is their life, because there is no unity, without it. He saw that he had slept (in materialism and morality) while his imagination, his spiritual friend, was in danger. For Los had become Time

when roofed in Albion's cliffs, dying thus for him for kindness. He roused up all his affections (his cities) and his sons
and daughters became as pleasant clouds, for the flesh, when
mind is free from the mistaken belief in its opacity, is a
pleasant cloud, and so are all its reasonings (sons) and its
loves (daughters).

P. 96, l. 41.—Then Man became alive in all his fourfold
regions, and so walked in their unity in the vision of God, not
in the mere delusive light of Time and Space.

P. 97, ll. 1 to 17.—Awake Jerusalem! (was this page intended
to follow page 83 ? The intermediate ones cannot be spared,)
with this cry the last and final vision is described in symbols
that explain themselves as a picture of truth, such as only by
vision can we know for certain.

P. 98, ll. 1 to 56.—It covers the next page.

P. 99, ll. 1 to 5.—Finally the released Jerusalem is seen as
the love that when made alive by mind, unites its living
members into one body, for such is the act of love when
aroused by sympathy, which is Imagination, or Christ.

Of the "Milton" we only know that it was planned as a work in twelve "books," and finished in two. We surmise that this was due to the events of the years succeeding Blake's Felpham period. We know that such books as "Milton" and "Jerusalem" were not written all at once, or engraved all at once. Whichever of these two was actually the great poem suggested by the acts of the enemies of Blake's "spiritual" life alluded to in his letters from Felpham, dated April 25th and July 6th, 1803, what he says about the printing being "progressive" was true of both works, and the date on the title-page does not apply to every page of the one any more than of the other.

Both should belong to 1804, were this the case, but he alludes obscurely to one of them in the passage from the Public address which refers to the *Examiner* attacks that did not begin till August, 1808. Even then the poem is said to be one which he "would soon publish."

It may possibly be that the poem referred to in the letters was "Milton," and that intended to be understood in the sentence from the "Public Address" was "Jerusalem." It is almost certain that a great deal of matter intended for Milton was never used in that work, and some of it may have gone to "Jerusalem." "None can know," Blake wrote to Butts, "the spiritual acts of my three years' slumber on the banks of the ocean unless he has seen them in the spirit or unless he should read my long poem." The most interesting part of the allusion in the letter is the phrase—"Unless he has seen them in the spirit." This matter-of-course reference to what is still a rare faculty, sometimes called Thought-reading, says more for the peculiarly *clairvoyant* quality of Blake's mental organism than many allegories. In alluding to the mortals who represented the States of Spiritual Enmity with which he struggled, he would often write regardless of their date. Thus, in 1803, he made a poem about these enemies. They included Titian, Rubens, and Hayley, as well as Sir Joshua Reynolds, all viewed as *states* and all included in "the state called Satan." Then in 1808 he added Leigh Hunt to them, and referred to the poem written in 1803 as being (*by anticipation*, though he does not think it necessary to explain this) an extirpation of the nest of villains of whom Leigh Hunt was one.

The exact point in the poem at which the idea of twelve books was abandoned must be left to conjecture, until more biographical material comes to light. The letter printed here after the postscript to the "Memoir" is of some help in the matter.

At the end of the facsimile some extra pages will be found which are reproduced from tracings of a copy in America in the Lennox Library. These were made some years ago for Mr. Muir, the able and enthusiastic facsimilist, some of whose reproductions in colour of Blake's works, already becoming scarce, are still in the hands of the publishers of the present work. We are indebted to Mr. Muir's courtesy for their appearance here. They are of great help for the explanations they contain of some of the symbols,—notably the harrow of Palamabron (on p. 3), called the Harrow of Shaddai (or the "Almighty "), and its linking together with the Plough of Rintrah on the first line of that page. For here may be found the hint of a companion incident or vision, nowhere related in full, and only alluded to in " Jerusalem," p. 93, l. 10.

The plough is one of the scarce symbols most difficult to trace in its fourfold meaning, as a comparison of other places where it is introduced will show. For example, Satan (reason) drives the team in Jerusalem," p. 33, l. 9. A physical symbol is suggested in " Jerusalem," p. 34, ll. 12, 13, and the same occurs in " Vala " I., 124. The plough is distinguished from the harrow in " Jerusalem," p. 46, l. 14; in p. 55, l. 39 (line 38 is mis-numbered 33), and ll. 54, 67 on the same page. On p. 57, ll. 2, 13, 14, 15 the symbol recurs, and in p. 63, l. 3, and p. 64, l. 30. These references are elsewhere referred to, but are collected here as important to " Milton," and the connection between Rintrah as the Reprobate in whom Orc lived again, the Satanic Luvah, the Naturalistic Satan, the fire of vegetative generation and decay, and so forth.

To a certain degree the character of the mild "Satan" in "Milton," who seemed a brother while he was "murdering the just," was partly suggested by Hayley with his depressing action on Blake's art, afterwards forgotten and forgiven in view of his assistance at the trial for treason. But the furious Satan is Blake's own "Spectre," always States are "combinations of individuals," and another constituent of the complex Satan will be found in Blake's notes to Sir Joshua Reynolds's Discourses. The suggestion is explained in the chapter on Blake's critical opinions where the notes are printed entire. Without them the full meaning of the myth of Satan and Palamabron in the early pages of "Milton" cannot be understood.

In "Milton" it is easy to see that page 4 is an interpolation of late date, and that from p. 25 to the end of Book I. all was engraved after the matter up to the end of p. 24 had been done and laid aside. Much of Book II. is earlier than these pages. The very long page 35 seems to be of their period, and to indicate a desire to force in more matter than in a twelve-book poem would be required on a page, though the subject of it recalls Felpham days, and it was probably written at Felpham before the engraving of the work began. The same may be said of pp. 37, 39 and 40, while the hasty and poor illustration on p. 41 seems also a late engraving. In fact, all the remainder of the poem after 35, except 36, and the illustration on 38, is evidently printed after the change of plan.

In "Milton" Canaan, 1st and 2nd, *appear* to be used with the same significance as Cainan 1st and 2nd. But it would be unfair to Blake to take this for granted, as in the Bible Canaan, always the fourth son of Ham, or his land, is used in two senses, a broader and a narrower, and cannot be taken as equivalent to Cainan I., son of Enos, and Cainan II., son of Arphaxad, any more than the term Canaanite applied to Simon Zelotes in Matth. vi. 4, and Mark vii. 26, means that he was an Old Testament character.

THE Preface to Milton springs from Blake's central idea, namely, that Imagination is common to all, is the future basis of brotherhood, is inspiration, heaven, and Christianity. But there is true and false imagination, and much that pretends to be of the true, notably classic art and myth, has only been stolen from it, and perverts what was once visionary creation of states of mind into allegoric reference to the changes of matter. Matter, or the lower mind of the five senses, should be used as symbol for the higher mind, and not *vice versâ.*

In "ancient time" visionary freedom and the conduct of life were one. Christ, the Imagination, stood with Albion, the ancient Man. He shall return again aided by the Bow, sexual symbolism, the arrow, desire, the spear, male potency, the chariot, joy. The mental weapons shall build Jerusalem in England, that is to say, shall give mental freedom to man, once more.

Book I.

P. 1, ll. 1 to 5. Blake bids the daughters of Beulah, the beautiful forms of mental life, to descend through his right arm, and so on to the paper before him, that is to say through the executive portion of his mind, so into manifestation as poetic utterances.

The labouring inspired man, as Los, faces towards the east; his right arm is therefore southern and mental.

They are to tell the history of Milton's journey through the realms of thought and dream, and also of that sensuous world below or outside the realms of Beulah which makes Jesus, that is the Imagination, its prey, for it is the sense of touch which gives the delusive power to Nature and nails Imagination on the stems of vegetation, and makes it an atonement for the sins of matter. The higher portion of mind is sacrificed to the lower, but in the end triumphs by spiritualizing it.

P. 3, ll. 16 to 24. He bids them tell what caused the spirit of religious poetry—symbolized by Milton—to leave its world of silent inner mood and come forth as manifest utterance. They answer it was the song of a bard or the creative imagination still dwelling in the natural man which persuaded Milton's poetry of supernatural mind to descend. (A Druid is the reasoning—a bard the creative side of Nature's life, before the various coverings or churches have developed.)

P. 3, l. 25, to p. 4, l. 7. The daughters of Beulah, now speaking through Blake, bid the reader note well these things, for they tell of his salvation from the body, or the non-mystic and temporary doctrines of art and poetry.

Before they relate the descent of Milton they describe the world into which he had to descend. Los and Enitharmon—time and space—make these classes of men. Space weaves them out of the mental unity of man, symbolized by London, various suburbs being mentioned to represent its zons and "London Stone" expresses its most "natural" portion because of the association of London stones with Druidism. The corporeal portion of mental space—"the weights of the loom"—play alluring music to overpower the souls.

P. 4, ll. 18 to 23. Time—the eternal present—"eternal mind," labour making, not only the three classes but "schemes of conduct," of art and literature, which are mental conduct, "the plough" to prepare the way for the souls' journey and "the harrow," to wrap it round as in a close furrow. His four sons, or forms of action corresponding to the intellectual, emotional, instinctive and energetic powers, work with him, and their labours go on in all parts of mind symbolized by districts of London and of the world, when Babel—or war of man upon man, thought upon thought—has taken the place of imaginative unity, Jerusalem, southward, the least corporeal portion of mind, " Lambeth," glows with aspiration, though it has been so long given over to demonstration and the sacrifice of mind to body ("oak groves" and "druid temples"). All things, he says, are contained within man, "Albion," although he be now given over to demonstration (become "rocky").

P. 4, l. 27, to p. 5, l. 14. When the spectral forms of life have been burnt in the mental furnace the emotional side of the eternal mind weaves them into affections and soft moods. The masculine side makes out of materialistic faculties which are too individual to become ashes, the force of the mind, " the sinews of life." The result of this double labour is to make the three classes, the elect, those who are wholly given over to reason and its god—" the redeemed," those in whom imagination struggles with reason, " the reprobates," those who sin against law whether for selfish or for high motives, while mental space weaves their affections together. Corporeal space, " Targum," drags their emotion into purely physical life or into mere length and breadth, and separates them one from another, that they may be destructive of each other's existence. The regions of the mind where these three classes dwell, are symbolized by Western and Eastern portions of London to show that they are all three confined, the first willingly, the last unwillingly in " length and breadth." Blake bids the reader consider his scheme of expression or "follow his plough."

P. 5, ll. 5 to 17. After this warning Blake begins the true action of the poem by describing Satan—the opaque non-imaginative, who belongs to the first class. He pities imaginative emotion, Palamabron, and wishes to give it rest by taking its place, that is to say rule and method; and the generalizing, analytical and formal allegories of classic models or nature, each to do the work of imaginative impulse, as Hayley tried to help Blake, regulating both his art and his life for him. The creative mind permits him to do so, wearied out by his repeated offers.

P. 5, ll. 18 to 31. After again warning the reader to attend to his words—for they deal with the salvation of his soul from opaque reasons—Blake tells how the secondary or elementary powers through which the arts, whether of life or literature, work, rebel against this rule of the generalizing reason of the opaque and become egotisms ("madder") and strive for their own life against the power of Satan. The imaginative impulse, hearing their complaints, grows angry. He calls on the eternal mind to judge what has occurred.

P. 5, ll. 32 to 41. Impulse calls mind into action by its destructive vehemence, but the opaque rules and laws make it appear as if imaginative impulse was itself the means of breaking them, and mind is made believe that imaginative impulse is their enemy.

P. 5, ll. 42 to 47. Mind bids Impulse work at the Arts free from the rules of the opaque, or bids the powers of the opaque do their own work by themselves. Again Blake bids the reader mark his words.

P. 6, ll. 1 to 10. Satan excuses himself with inner speech for rules, and corporeal reasonings are always mild or without that chafing of the spirit with limitation which is wrath. Here is this insidious quality. When he returns to his mills, that is when he, leaving the work of impulse, returns to his own work of mechanical drudgery and mechanical arguments, he finds all in disorder. He had persuaded Palamabron to do his work as the easier task, as Hayley had set Blake to the drudgery of miniature paintings, and the like, and impulses had set all in confusion. Two days—of a thousand years a-piece—equivalent to the first two days of creation, and corresponding to the eyes of God, Lucifer, and Moloch, have now been described. Impulse has sought the "mills" as light fell in the beginning, and on the second, corresponding to Moloch, the flame-filled idol, the power of "mills" and "harrow," are alike enraged. The next three days, needed to carry us to birth, are passed over without special mention, and we are about to reach a sixth

day when water will cover the earth, and "the rains of
Jehovah "—the sixth eye—contend with the fires of Moloch.
Another correspondence associates the present story with the
Churches. "The rains of Jehovah " close the history of the
first church with the flood of time and space.

P. 6, ll. 11 to 15. The mind, Los, has to choose from labour
of imagination, and covers itself with the external world
symbolized by Los placing his left shoe above his head. The
feet are the lower and most outward part of the mind, and
the left foot means that part of the mind nearest to the
Northern darkness, for Los has his face to the East. The
lower mind is placed above the higher. This is not done
because Los has become enamoured of matter, but as a
" solemn mourning," or period of repentance spent in mere
outward life, that the confused mental powers may return to
themselves. The powers of the mill of reason rest, also the
Imaginative well—Reuben—and ideal's space.

P. 6, ll. 16 to 26. Mind speaks of the power of rule, and
tells them that it is itself to blame, for it should have known
that the rest offered to the spirit by mechanical assistance—
"pity"—"divides the soul" into two contending parts, one
of imagination, one of reason, and " man unmans," that is,
contracts him down from the universal, and imaginative, to
the limitations of his life of the moment. He bids them
therefore rest for this day from their labours, following the
track of his thought—his " plough "—passively, for this
day will be " a blank in Nature," that is a period without
creative effort. They follow mind and its will accordingly,
and the Elect, who belong to rule, and the Redeemed, who
belong to imaginative impulse, tormented by mechanical
reason, mourn, that is, remain inactive. (It is as though an
artist having tried to do the creative part of his work by
mere reason and patience, and to do the mechanical part with
the impulsive side of his mind, got all into such confusion
that he had to cease from his work and merely observe.)

P. 6, ll. 27 to 33. We now find this blank in nature

identified with the flood. The tears become "Jehovah
rain," and its object is revealed by its contending with "the
fires of Moloch." (Tears are formative in the corporeal
sense, and they are now shed in order that corporeal order
may be substituted for mental disorder—physical vitality
and sensuous life are to save man from dead reason—the
persuasions of Satan. It is the same story as that told in
America when the Atlantic mountains—purely imaginative
life—are submerged in the contest of reason with passion, &c.
It is also the flood which sweeps away the first churches, and
prepares the way for the substitutes of the second Canaan,
the physical world for the first Canaan, this mental world.)
Blake's vision now changes, and he sees the story in the form
of a contest of the imagination and the opaque. The side of
mind most allied to instinct, Theotormon, and that most allied
to pleasant energy, Bromion, are persuaded by the fascination of the opaque "Satan" to take his side. Michael, of
whom we hear nowhere else in Blake, and who is evidently
spiritual fire, contends against "Satan," and Thulloh, also
mentioned nowhere else, but almost as certainly, procreative instinct, reproves his friend "Satan." (The
word Thullius, the female Leviathan, in the Kabala closely
resembles Thulloh, and like him is "first slain" or first
enclosed in corporeal function. The female Leviathan is
the procreative side of opaque existence in the Kabalá, and
is "slain," lest it should overrun spiritual life with its
offspring. Imagination is alone permitted to create mental
forms. Reason can but copy them from the external.
Thullius is wife to Satan, the male Leviathan is the Zohas,
but Thullah is here merely his "friend," friendship being a
symbol for mental life that does not deal with the sexual
thing—argument, or contradiction. Even Satan has such a
state, and therefore a "friend." He is made masculine
because the male is the creation in Blake's philosophy, and
this involves the dropping of the feminine "in" at the end of
this word. (See chapter on the names.) He reproves Satan

because he, too, objects to the rule of reason. Both Michael and Thulloh reprove the faculty for the "tears" of outer natures have weakened their impulse.

P. 6, ll. 34 to 44. The Imaginative Will, "Rintrah," however, is full of anger against the opaque, and it flames above the tracks of thought, "the ploughed furrows," and slays Thullah, watery or instinctive naturalistic conception, with its own fiery creative power, "its spear," thereby confining procreative instinct to physical function by driving it out with the energy of the mind. He compels Michael, who had grown weary, to begin again his contest with Satan. He then weeps, becoming himself infected with corporeal life by the law that makes us "become what we behold." Mind—"Los"—hides new corporeal procreative instinct from the sight of the purely mental emotions and affections, "Enitharmon," lest they beholding it might "die of grief," that is, become opaque also. The mental emotions and affections weave a world for rest and peace about the contending states, and shut man out from war and contest by Love, "a tender moon." Amid this world, woven by the affections, buries Thullah.

P. 6, l. 46, to p. 7, l. 6. All the corporeal side of the mind is now becoming unvital, non-mental, and in order to make it live again, imaginative impulse calls the mental faculties to descend into the corporeal, that it may become vital once more, even though that vitality be only "to defend a lie." The corporeal functions may thus be "grown" and "caught" and "taken" by mental life. The powers of vision, "All Eden," descend into the dwelling Imaginative Impulse has made for itself, among the forces of unimaginative life. Imaginative Impulse prays that God may protect it from the powers that pretend to be its friends, like generalizing reason and mechanical labour. It can protect itself against its avowed negations. (The descent of "All Eden" reminds us that we are now in the Second Church, the church of redemption, and invites comparison with the descent of "the Divine

Family," of Los, and the Divine Vision in the second book of
"Jerusalem," and of the formation of Urizen into personality
in the fourth book of " Urizen and Vala.")

P. 7, ll. 8 to 12. Imaginative Will—Rintrah—in order
that the enemies of Imaginative Impulse may be open and
not pretended friends, and in order that those who will not
defend truth may defend a lie—namely, assert the existence
of corporeal life separated from mind, descends into Satan,
or the opaque, so that he appears to be among the reprobate,
instead of more passive and lifeless matter, as he really is.
(Now is seen the meaning of the Reprobate. They are those
who sin imaginatively or enthusiastically, either by indulgence
or by fierce strictness. Among these Blake would perhaps
have put his "brother John, the evil one," reserving for James
a place in the "elect," who surrender themselves to the opaque
without enthusiasm. It was in contrast to this latter class
that he spoke to Mr. Crabb Robinson of " the vices " as
" highest sublimities.")

P. 7, ll. 13 to 19. Mind rises against the opaque, and in
its struggles collections of mental "states," or nations, and
collections of mental "spaces," or continents, are moved aside
from their old positions, and the vegetative sensations,
"oceans," are compelled to give way before him, and the
Zoas revolve. But he keeps mental space separate from all
other things which happen in corporeal and reasoning spaces.

P. 7, ll. 19 to 29. The reason of his rage is that Imaginative Will, which has now entered into Satan, accuses Imaginative Impulse of making disorder, and invents a punitive
law of the mind and a bodily law of restriction, and the war
of bodily forces and the diseases of mind and body, and by
their means perverts the divine voice, which is its own
enthusiasm, and cries that it rends away the divine families
of loves and emotions, and will belong wholly to the covering
cherub or nature.

P. 7, ll. 30 to 35. By thus making a law against imaginative freedom, Satan is shut off wholly from imagination, and

becomes utterly dark. The fires of Rintrah are within him, but the stones or reasons of which he is built up darken wholly. A deeper Ulro—Or Ulro that is—is now formed. (The Third Church has now developed—the Church in which the soul no longer remembers even that natural laws and objects are but symbols.)

P. 7, ll. 36 to 48. For a time sadness and silence—uncreative life—fills the mind, and Satan accuses the creative power for shutting imaginative impulse in the mind. Rintrah creates entrenchments of philosophy and law about Satan; but Satan, being essentially uncreative and without enthusiasm, at last tears them asunder, and sinks down absolute death and negation, for he now no longer lives with the borrowed life of Rintrah. He is now merely mechanical force—whether of the mind or the body—and not the enthusiastic denial of the earlier stage. (The opaque Reason sooner or later destroys the impulse that gives it the power to think at all, as Tiriel, growing old and feeble, curses his own sons and daughters. Impulse is always of the imagination.)

P. 7, ll. 49 to 52. He sinks down to the "spaces" especially associated with the cherub—to Rome, Babylon, and Tyre, the Loins, Heart, Head. (The Third Church is now complete, and the world is ready for redemption.) For Rome, compare Song of Liberty after "Marriage of Heaven and Hell." Here the "extra page," numbered 8, is fortunately rejected by Blake. It helps the interpretation if read in this place, but not the continuity of the myth, as it does not read on into the beginning of p. 9. It connects Analogy with the moving space.

P. 9, ll. 1 to 15. Satan will destroy the spiritual identity—the core—of humanity, unless help comes. The spiritual emotion, Enitharmon, is hid from all these things by the imaginative mind in a pleasant region of mental space.

P. 9, ll. 6 to 14. A special region of material or maternal—"moony"—space receives the logical and mechanical part of the mind, and thus the emotions—human victims—

are sacrificed, and Satan is proclaimed God within these boundaries.

P. 9, ll. 15, 16. It is asked by the assembled thoughts of the higher mind, why the innocent emotions are sacrificed thus as an offering for the Satanic faculties? (Why the spiritual nature is compelled to be intermixed with and imprisoned by the lower?)

P. 9, ll. 17 to 26. The answer is that if the imaginative and innocent life did not descend into, "die for," the guilty life, then the condemnation would fall upon the guilty un-imaginativeness itself, and it would be cut off wholly from the imaginative, and become "an Eternal Death." The Satanic life has to be constantly "recreated," or reorganized by this descending life, or it would cease to be life. The class of living things that belong to it are called "the elect," those of wrathful Rintrah—the imaginative energy entangled in physical things—the Reprobate, and those of Palamabron the Redeemed, because he is outside of Satan's law—material restraint—being of the obedient mental life alone. Palama-bron, fearing that the condemnation might have fallen on him for being other than assertive, convinced imagination, does not dare to assemble the thoughts together to consider the state of man until Satan had put on the anger and assertive-ness of Rintrah, and so drawn off the condemnation. As against pure imagination Palamabron is material, as against pure matter asserting its separate life in spectral "pride" he is imaginative. The spiritual state, who tells this, confirms it by "an oath," or by the assertion of his own unity with God or pure imagination.

P. 9, ll. 28 to 31. When the sexual formation—Leutha—sees Satan condemned, she, who is essentially imaginative, descends into corporeal life, takes on her the sin of Satan; for sexual love is the last outpour, as it were, of imagination in the bodily life. Again the reader is bid to mark that the story is the story of his salvation.

P. 9, ll. 32 to 38. Leutha tells how she loved Imaginative

Mind—Palamabron—but was repelled by his purely mental emanation, the formation of the internal emotions, as Leutha herself is of the external sensations.

P. 10, ll. 1 to 15. She asks why it is that the spectral life issues from her to seize the children of the mind. To prevent this, sexual love enters into the brain of pleasant life or into the lower mind and fills it with that apparent love for the higher mind which made it attempt the work of the imagination and so cause the confusion already described. Instead of imagination, hater of corporeal mind and sexual love,—she makes them have a feminine or passive love for this love. Thus Hayley was fascinated by the mind of Blake, through the least corporeal part of his own mind—its desire for sensations. Leutha having thus entered the imaginative world, through Satan driving the horses of Palamabron. Leutha, now the emanation of Satan, tries to do the work of Elynitria, the emanation of Palamabron, that is to say, to give rest (in emotional life) to the horses, or unfeeling thoughts. They are, however, maddened by the corporeal fascination, bodily beauty, ll. 16 to 30. Satan filled with a power, reflected from the internal life, controlled the harrow and tried to stay its maddened course by the observations of generalized reasons—banks of sand—and all the classifications of external things. "Chaos and Ancient Night," the life of mere memory, came from under the harrow, and the lower mind filled with egotistic pride drives the harrow of personal emotion among "the stars of Jehovah," the once creative centre of the intellect. It was then that Leutha made the serpent of corporeal life—the deceiving bodily activity that crawls upon its belly, and through length and breadth, not from Nadir to Zenith, or Zenith to Nadir, ll. 31 to 40. The gnomes, the forces of the energetic life of thought, answered the creation of the deceitful serpent by an egotism of the imagination which attacks the corporeal. They refused to labour more in the harrow now that Satan drives it, and to fascinate them into obedience, Leutha says that she revealed herself before them, coming out of the mind of Satan. She is now corporeal emotion separated from corporeal reason, and her name is Sin. Leutha, Rahab, Vala, are the Female counterparts of the Head, Heart, and Loins of Satan. (Ll. 40 to 50.) Now that Leutha has separated from Satan, Elynitria, the emotional mental nature, enters into Satan, and fills him with a perverted prophetic power under the influence of which he assumes holiness, and drives Leutha from him. (As soon as corporeal emotion separates from corporeal reason they become contending powers, and instead of uniting to draw down the imaginative mind, they war with each other.)

P. 11, ll. 1 to 11. But separated emotion acknowledges the source of all things in God, whereas the low-born reason believes only in itself. Emotion asks how Reason is to be saved, and then becomes silent for a moment, only to cry out the next instant that she is the spectral side of Luvah—love. She began in the eternal life of the mind, and cannot end until "two eternities"—the spectral and emanative—meet in one.

P. 11, ll. 12 to 29. In order that Satan may be saved from eternal death or enters separation from spirit, he is formed into a symbolic body corresponding to the internal spiritual body, the imagination or the lamb, every one of the six stages of creation passes over him, and is under an especial mental state (see "Work of Urizen," also the chapters on the Cherub). Leutha "hides," or clothes herself with organized form—the fascination of corporeal life finds a dwelling-place in corporeal beauty. The Imagination is now "punished" to save Satan, by its taking on his sin. (The incarnation into the midst of the Third Church has taken place.)

P. 11, ll. 30 to 35. The self-righteous see that they only live from God, and lament in, or grow "creative" in bodily sensations, in the region of vegetative fruitfulness. The bodily life is changed into a symbol of the bodiless, and so brings the fallen mind back to the universal perceptions.

P. 11, ll. 36 to 44. The purely mental emotions now no longer war on the bodily, but lead the bodily emotions into the presence of the creative energy of the mind, and from the bodily attraction and the inventive energy are born the organization of the corporeal mental condition. Death, the recurring period of unimaginativeness, is made, that death may be separate, a part to be learned and refused, and the bodily restriction is given a place apart and called Rahab, that she may be known as other than Jerusalem, and so cast out when the time comes. Oothoon, spiritual beauty, is made the guard of heathen corporeal beauty to protect it from the destroyer, force of reason. (Palamabron, though he is the inventive mental personality in general, is, in a special sense, the writer in Blake himself, his harrow being the pen. Oothoon is the spiritual beauty whereby Blake seeks to win the corporeal beauty and fascination of merely natural things.)

P. 11, l. 45 to 50. Having been told the stages whereby the personal Blake was made, and the personal method of his philosophy invented, the history of thought and life carried on from the creation to modern times, the poet in Albion ceases to speak for a moment, or from being creative becomes possible. Some say that Pity—corporeal creation—Love, or Leutha, are too high to be charged with this guilt of unimaginativeness. Others say his words are true, and ask where he had his song.

P. 12, ll. 12 to 19. He replies that he knows it is truth because he speaks from the poetic genius which is good. The bard takes refuge in Milton—Religious poetry—from the confusion of many speculations caused by his revelation.

This "refuge" in Milton's bosom is a symbol occurring elsewhere. Later on, we find it revealed as "repentance," p. 19, l. 50, and the symbol of nature's and analogy's period, six thousand years, enables us to trace it once more in "Vala," Night VII., l. 395, where it appears as "self-denial and bitter contrition," and Los is found as larger than the symbol Milton, for only a portion of him goes to eternal death.

Going to the extra page, numbered 3, intended to be placed
where the later and interpolated p. 3 stands before it was
written, and after Blake had concluded not to fill that space
otherwise (presumably with a full-page illustration), allowing
the book to read on so that l. 1 of p. 5 followed the last line
of p. 3 as now numbered, (p. 3 was p. 2, p. 5 was p. 4, and
the extra page 3 was designed as the first of two after-
thoughts to come between them,) we find a hint of the
biographical correspondence or personal meaning below the
myth almost as plainly as in the scene between Los and
Enitharmon in " Vala," Night VII.

Compare all this with the letters, and especially verses,
written to Butts from Felpham, quoted in the explanation of
the ballad " William Bond" and with that of " Mary," not
forgetting that Enitharmon stands for the lovable side
of Naturalism in life and art, just as Satan is its dangerous
side, and the story of Blake's personal and emotional
experiences at Felpham stands before us, from the time
when he was " very much degraded " by Hayley, who
even sought to act on his art by arraying the needs and the
opinions of his wife against him, to the reconciliation before
the *Examiner* period, and a fourfold vision indeed is given to
the reader of " Milton."

It will then be easily understood that although the above
explains to a certain degree the coherence of the symbolism, the mystic framework of the " Bard's prophetic song,"
it does not exhaust the relations between this and other
portions of Blake's books and life. It hardly touches the
artistic symbolism, a counterpart which may be considered in
relation to each part separately, and it only indicates faintly
the biographical suggestions.

It is impossible to work out in full extent each of these forms
of comment. None of the books can in anything short of a
whole bookshelf full of commentary be paraphrased three
or four times over. In treating all it has been necessary to
select some stream of interpretation and follow it from source

to sea, only glancing here and there at the other roads that lead the same way, and carry freights of meaning by other means of transport.

The book of "Milton," however, demands more than any to be read in several meanings at once. The comment may, therefore, go backwards for a moment and very slightly trace the companion methods.

In "Vala," Night VIII., l. 345, Los, in the same words as are found in "Milton," p. 20, l. 15, speaks to the delusive female forms who are Rahab, and identifies himself with the Bard, and Blake, and by a single quality. The Bard taking refuge in the bosom of Milton, and Milton in the foot of Blake, are seen all to signify phases of the one great Spirit, whose sacrificial side is perfect in Christ, and whose prophetic voice was called Elijah before it was named Los.

Los conversing with Rahab is, in her, conversing with Milton's wives and daughters through the first of them. ("Milton," p. 16, l. 11.) Thus he is, in a degree, Milton telling the myth of Satan and Palamabron to the triple form or division of the twenty-seven heavens when he relates it to Rahab.

The account in "Vala" slightly differs from that in "Milton," but is essentially the same. (Night VIII., l. 362, &c.) We are able to follow the artistic thread, and to a certain extent the biographical thread, by remembering that Hayley was occupying Blake with painting a head of Homer in his library at the time, as well as with the attempt to persuade him to study the classics, and by enforcing on him the duty of following any and every branch of art except symbolic design.

Satan—or the Greek Apollo (see conversations with Crabb Robinson), or classicality, as explained in the Preface to "Milton," and naturalism in art—accused Palamabron before his brethren. These were sons of Los belonging to the group whom Los refused to coerce, though their liberty caused him to go in fear of his own life. ("Vala," Night VII., l. 476.)

To realize who Rintrah and Palamabron are, we must look a few lines higher up for their origin (ll. 451, 458 and 470).

Rintrah and Palamabron, both "flames" or inspirations, cut Satan or naturalism off from Art, or Golgonooza. Satan in tears is equivalent to the soft side of Tharmas, whose spectre was eternal death.

Enitharmon (who has a right to tears, being Pity, and female) made him a moony space as he rolled down beneath those "fires of Orc" (Night VIII., l. 366), who were Rintrah and Palamabron, to whom Orc was a father as well as brother (Night VII., ll. 474, 475), just as Schofield was, in his turn, in "Jerusalem," p. 7, l. 43. Schofield is a Felpham name, and here stands for Adam (also a gardener).

Orc, it will be noticed, had been the means, in his serpent-form, of Luvah's entry into the state called Satan (Night VIII., l. 377), who is, in a sense, his irredeemable human remains. Thus a clue is found in the following table:—

Spirit of Opacity   ...   ... · Limit of contraction.
Satan ...   . Adam.
Orc (father of his brethren)... Schofield (father of his
                                            brethren).

The Satan of Milton has lost the fire of Orc through the great Separation or Division alluded to in "Jerusalem," p. 65, ll. 1 to 5, where it is connected with Albion whose Eon was to have been destroyed by Satan, "Milton," p. 9, l. 1, as the spectrous Luvah, *ibid.* p. 11, l. 8, and in "Milton, p. 7, l. 46 to 48, where we have the "sinking down" of Satan that brings the story to the incident of the "rolling down" of Vala, VIII., 366.

Then Orc as the father of his brethren who wanted to chain them to the rock, "Vala," Night VII., l. 475, becomes identified with Satan, who tempted them to flee away. The flight, which is out of the prophetic into the vegetative region, is only the action of the chain disguised in suavity. It is

Vala's veil, the net, and so forth ("Milton," p. 22, l. 61). Los only just contrived that four sons of his, (and Jerusalem's) sixteen, should not "flee,"—namely, the four "unvegetated," Rintrah, Palamabron, Theotormon and Bromion.

Enitharmon breathed Satan into Golgonooza (VIII., 377), though Rintrah and Palamabron had cut him off. It was her "moony space," and when he rolled down he rolled down in it (l. 388).

Jerusalem there who was created in Golgonooza from the very spectres who were Satan in the aggregate (Night VIII., l. 136, and elsewhere), wove them mantles of life and death (VIII., 391), being herself a building of Human Souls,— "Milton," p. 4, l. 19, actuated by Pity.

Thus Jerusalem and Enitharmon grow one, and have the good aspect of Pity, which joins what wrath has rent asunder, while its bad aspect being the "false pity," ("Milton," p. 5, ll. 27 and 43, p. 6, l. 19,) "divides the soul and man un-mans."

"Driving the harrow in Pity's paths" ("Milton," p. 10, l. 28,) has an artistic reference also. Driving inspiration in realism's paths is one of the equivalents.

"Divine Pity" supports Leutha, ("Milton, p. 11, l. 7,) the feminine self-sacrifice, or Christ. She is a daughter of Los and Beulah (Vala, VIII., 357, and "Milton," p. 9, l. 28). Here, examples may cease. The usual truth that everything has two aspects, according as it is used to serve God,—the true imagination, or mammon, the matter-believing intellect of the five senses, must needs apply to pity as to other things.

It has been noticed that Orc and Schofield were on a level by being father of their brethren. It will be remembered how Reuben "enrooted" and Hand "absorbed" their brethren. This gives them all a quality in which they resemble one another in a degree that suggests that missing fragments of the story of any one of the four may be restored by consulting the story of another and using it appropriately.

This leads to an understanding of the contradiction that Satan

(Orc's human remains) was cut clear off from Golgonooza, for both accusation of sin and mere naturalism are cut from symbolic art, yet he rolled down in it with his companions.

Golgonooza is not only delineative art but interpretative art in its milder, passive, or feminine aspect. It is the moony space of Enitharmon, and it is where Los's furnaces stand, but it is also Divine analogy, into which wandering Reuben was led at last (" Jerusalem," p. 85, l. 1, &c.).

Reuben's symbolic equivalence to Satan is through Hand and Albion, not through Orc and Los, though every spectre when alone and "ravening" is Satanic and of the Eating Cancer, or evil aspect of the Polypus.

One aspect of Divine analogy is the "body" or system of Moses (" Jerusalem," p. 49, l. 58). In the passage where this is told several other suggestions containing the explanation are to be found.

Beth Peor, the mountain whose counterpart is the valley where this body is built, is in the loins of Los, place of war. Compare " Vala," Night I., l. 442, and " Jerusalem," p. 67, l. 29.

War reaches the valley also,—having its own male and female aspect, as told in "Jerusalem," p. 43, l. 7. A little way above in the same page, l. 31, a line will be recognized as also belonging to "Milton," p. 35, l. 2. The whole page 67 of " Jerusalem " is closely woven into the subject of " Milton," the struggle of classic with symbolic art.

P. 12, ll. 10 to 14. Milton takes off the robe of promise and ungirds himself of the oath of God. This is presumably the " oath of the covenant "—the covenant being that referred to in " Jerusalem," p. 61 (a very late page written during the time when "Milton" was being printed), l. 25,—" If you forgive another so shall Jehovah forgive you." When he goes to self-annihilation he ceases to seek forgiveness, or anything else ; on the contrary, he fulfils the covenant, and thus is no more bound by it, for self-annihilation and the forgiveness of sins are the same thing (" Jerusalem," p. 98), l. 23. He passes out of pure or passive spiritual existence into spiritual labours, in order to lift corporeal into spiritual life. The last thing he takes off when he does this is the covenant of truth. He puts on the twenty-seven heavens instead,—all of them belonging to Rahab, being, as they were poisonous modifications of truth, mixed with realism and moralism (compare "Jerusalem," pp. 1 to 22). That is to say, when the religious impulse of poetry assumed the form of Milton's works it put on sin, as Christ put on death in the Virgin's womb.— It also, as will presently be seen, put on repentance.

The act may be, and has been, considered as also a passing of the power here called "Milton" from the narrower spiritual life that condemns the bodily life, and entering into that larger form of the same that accepts all. In this secondary sense the girdle and the robe are the "covering" (see chapter on "Christ") of the life and that which holds it together. The covering is the man of tradition, dogma, custom, &c., which any idea or emotion gathers round it in the course of time. It is held together by the resolve of men to serve that idea, hence Milton, God himself in one aspect, has to ungird himself of his oath to himself or to his self-hood, before he can get rid of the mass of religious traditions which make it impossible for him to expand beyond himself." (Now begins again in another aspect that story of the churches which Blake is for ever dwelling upon. Milton, religious impulse, descends and will in time become again tradition and rule.)

P. 12, l. 14 to 32. The states and moods of man are still given to the worship of natural fact and of mere brute force. He will enter into this evil world lest he becomes a self-hood by being separated from his emanative portion. He has constructed but a narrow tradition, and so becomes wholly masculine and repulsive, and must now redeem the feminine and attractive portion. He must leave memory and enter inspiration, which is born of the union of memory (the spectre) and hope (the emanation).

P. 12, ll. 33 to 35. He takes the corporeal journey (the outside course) among the unimaginative (the dew), and the eternal wave of imagination within him shadowed at the opaque world he was entering.

P. 12, ll. 36 to 42.   He enters into the body (the covering cherub) and the seven angels of the Presence, or the seven-fold light of the mind, wept over this body.

P. 14, ll. 1 to 7.   The seven angels go with him and give him perception of the bodily life (the last five are the five senses—the first two are thought and feeling—the brain and the blood). He walks with them in Eden, in the beginning of vegetative life.

P. 14, ll. 8 to 16.   The body grows, as it were, into the earth (like a polypus). To those in the spiritual world he seems asleep, but to himself he seems lost in night.   The emanations of the spiritual moods feed him with beautiful emotions.

P. 14, ll. 17 to 20.   His body journeys through the satanic world, the spirit thoughts see the poet like a warning light —a comet.

P. 14, ll. 21 to 35.   All we have yet to pass sucks us into it as into a vortex, while that we have left takes definite shape in the memory or in the perception which repeat experience and was moulded upon experience.   (There can be no form without thought and no thought without experience.) The earth is not yet a form, because we have not yet made it intellectual and imaginative with our experience.   It is a great plain (Blake alludes to the lower limit of man when he uses this term earth).   The heaven we have already passed through (by heaven he means here the mentor's world), and it is accordingly full of images of beauty and truth.

P. 14, ll. 36 to 46.   Milton sees sleeping Humanity asleep in matter, but sustained by the power of God—the "rock of ages" —from sinking wholly into that matter, "the sea of time and space."   Milton, in descending into this humanity, goes head-foremost, so that what is below "soon seem above," the lower vegetative life seemed to enclose him above as well as below, as the sensuous wave encloses us all.   His body falls like a globe—a self-hood.

P. 14. ll. 47 to 50. Blake changes the plain of the symbolism, and sees Milton descend unto himself—thus identified with humanity—as a falling star, or descending inspiration which enters the lower part of his mind, that portion which is towards the northern darkness, and which is symbolized by the left foot.

P. 14, l. 50. Milton's arising and going forth is seen to be his entrance into Blake's mythic system. From then, the part of that system called "Milton" understood itself and the meaning of the story of its personage when he was a vegetated mortal, not yet perceived as a state. In this meaning is included a set of minor significances for his wives and daughters. For these, in their symbolic sense, as Rahab, i.e. the symbolic power, this form of religious poetry gives itself.

P. 16, ll. 1 to 20. The word Human must be noted as meaning "belonging to the imagination,"—in this page. Milton as a thought perceives backwards himself as a man, and knows himself a symbol. He sees his wives and daughters symbols also, though, as such, they are not merely six, but numberless. His body (for now the fleshly idea of body definitely vanishes,) is the rock that Urizen shot at Fuzon,—his system is the law. (He would justify the ways of the God who was Satan misnamed,—the God of darkness, jealousy, and vindictive law, to men). His female symbols being named twice over, once for his system or shadow, and once for the symbolic or human element in his life.

P. 16, ll. 21 to 30. The mundane shell is described, and it is shown how Milton, as an influence, travels from erroneous morality towards eternal art, going to Golgonooza, that is, from the graves, or flesh, outside, by way of Midian, the desert, among the moral rocks of Horeb.

P. 16, ll. 31 to 36. It seems to the feminine portion of Los that he will surely let loose Satan from bondage in Analogy, and cause him to dominate mankind, Albion. So the masculine portion opposes him.

P. 17, l. 5. And Los frowned, but it was not his true self but the personal spectre in him, the Satan, the accuser, the Urizen, the taskmaster who really opposed Milton.

P. 17, ll. 6 to 14. This Urizen who opposed Milton was the very same whom Milton had praised under the name of Jehovah—thus giving life to his opposer. The red clay of the Adamic man in Milton fills out the image,—for without it Urizen could assume only the appearance of age, not the beauty of even the most false and unforgiving ideal of God-head.

P. 17, ll. 15 to 26. The position of Golgonooza in the four-fold Humanity is explained, and the opposition of Urizen. Afterwards, at p. 32, is a diagram showing how Milton reached Golgonooza between the worlds of Urizen and Luvah and passed to Adam, the elementary Humanity, his best goal and highest ideal, having no power to terminate his mental journey otherwise.

P. 17, ll. 27 to 60. Rahab seeing this endeavours to divert him into entering her world of unideal life, not having Adam, but Satan for the goal of his journey, thus never escaping the rocks of Horeb but taking them with him. Then, indeed, Satan would have been unloosed on Albion. The beauty of Morality, Love, and Flesh in strange juncture allure him. She forms them all.

P. 18, ll. 1 to 6. These lines belong to the above account of Rahab.

P. 18, ll. 7 to 24. But Milton worked on as before. The poetry of his words idealised the dark God of Sinai. The words of his poetry were frozen into the rock itself of the law, the real Human, the symbolic influence inhabited the symbolic region where Blake by prophetic power has perception of him, as though he saw himself through the seven eyes of God.

P. 18, ll. 7 to 25. A fourth Milton,—the "elect" portion already satanic in idea, but continually saved through election and made a redeemer,—by inspiration that astonished and mistook itself—(Milton wrote of the Messiah under the idea that he was writing of Satan,—compare " Marriage of Heaven and Hell," p. 5)—came down to earth to Blake, who feels unable rightly to tell so strange and fourfold a story in mortal language.

P. 18, ll. 25 to 50. And Albion in Blake was aroused by his descent, which is re-described, and the gates referred to and partly explained. But many of the spiritual powers rushed into the arena of mortal effort and passed to Ulro.

P. 18, ll. 50 to 62. This grieved the prophetic spirit of poetry. But he, fixing his perceptions on the symbolic influence of Milton, saw, as by memory, that he had always known that it should do what Enitharmon feared, only in a different sense, not letting loose Orc's Human remains in a Satanic sense, but in the sense of enthusiasm freed from restrictions of rule, especially in art and poetry, rule of dogmatism and realism, and classicalism,—the triple Tongue, all false ; the triple chain, all jealousy.

P. 19, ll. 1 to 3. So Los went down after Milton, passing the seat of Satan, who slept in Udan Adan,—the lake into which, as Blake's or Los's Spectre, he was cast.

P. 19, ll. 4 to 14. And Blake, by Los's power, being Los, and going down with him, saw the vast extent of the Human proportion of his mind, and where Milton's influence reached in his imagination, and where the influence of the world had power,—both in the nether regions of the imagination. Fearless of being controlled by either, he bound on experience as a sandal with which to walk through imagination.

P. 19, ll. 15 to 36. At this point a new poem practically commences. As at the entrance of Leutha, who claimed Satan's blame, a fresh view of the first myth was made perceptible, so now Ololon, the sorrowful feminine power, comes forth, and joins the story of Milton's journey.

It appears at first as of both sexes, lamenting with its female tears that its male fires had driven Milton (the State called Milton) into Ulro,—the moral error that attributes sin and righteousness to individuals.

P. 19, ll. 37 to 44. The multitudes that make up the State called Ololon called the Divine Family which appeared as four suns, then joined in one, and wept, as Christ over Lazarus. They grieved at Milton's going to this error, which is death, being opposite of the " only means to Forgiveness " (" Jerusalem," p. 49, l. 75), which is life, and is the force of the hammer of Los himself. (*Ibid.*, p. 88, l. 50.) In fact they grieved for the sacrifice of Christ (the portion of him in the State called Milton) to Tharmas, the false tongue seen on its moral, not sensuous or artistic, side.

P. 19, ll. 45 to 50. Then Ololon took refuge in Milton's bosom of sacrifice from the efforts of poetic creation,—the wars of eternity, even as the Bard did from outer wrangling.

P. 19, ll. 51 to 57. The Divine family made watchmen of the people of Ololon for the lower world's sake. Such is the best that imagination can make of contrition. It cannot restore poetry gone to error, even though it went there in one only of its fourfold phases as a sacrifice.

P. 19, l. 58. And the self-sacrifice of Ololon identified it with Christ also, though it be but a cloud, an outward thing of the life of instinct and blood.

P. 20, ll. 1 to 25. Blake tells what he felt in Lambeth when he saw with what and with whom his symbolic perceptions had identified him. (Here the tale touches " Vala," as above noted, Night VIII., l. 345, and dates that portion of the poem, incidentally, as after 1803.) He tells us the temporary things of nature become permanent in the mind, the world being bound on as a sandal.

From here, l. 26, to the end of p. 23, the forces of imagination and contrition, of the sacrifice that turns itself into mental labour, and that which gives its ease away to suffer for what it deems to be moral truth,—a miracle in human nature,—and the attractions of all contraries and their dangers are sketched in reference to all the myths and mingled with the names of historic personages who illustrate. At the end, the classified symbols Bowlaboola and Allamanda,

Los and Enitharmon, give imaginative purpose to blood and nerves, to Time and Space.

Then (pp. 24, 25 and 26) Los is allowed in the myth to assume his full stature of gigantic proportions; war is his wine-press and printing press, and the whole mental world is the place of his vintage and harvest. He calls all the forces that live, to be one with him, delighting in prophecy and despising all other pleasure. They are discontented. Then his sons are seen as stars above the sea, and as little flies dancing in the field. Then some towns of England are used to hint the regions, south or north, and show how the instincts of man become ideas as souls put on body. And the inner expansiveness of the symbolic body is asserted, and the great central truth declared that Nature has no cause or causes in her (unless in the word Nature we include the idea Spirit,—an over-straining perhaps), but that Spiritual force alone has. This awakes and will re-awake ideas when Memory itself has gone to destruction with the brain in which it dwells, both being perishing and vegetable.

P. 27. And Los has other sons than those that wear the look of stars, flies, or flowers.—These are the spiritual forces themselves. They form the corporeal, and they divide Time into its divisions and unite it again like a healed wound till six thousand years are seen to be less than a moment, notwithstanding the tent of its minutes, the golden entrance to its hours, the adamantine gates of each of its days and nights, the pure terrace of the months, the high towers of the years, the deep moats around the ages, the all other work of Fairy hands, that do the bidding of the Spirit of Prophesy.

P. 28. And the unity of art with the source of time, and of nerves with their meanings and of all with one another in the great polypus is told,—in brief, Nature is sketched in a few architectural strokes as a mental fact,—the Science of the Elohim."

Book II.

P. 30, ll. 1 to 20. In the second book it appears that Ololon, intending to enter into the pangs of repentance in Milton's bosom (see above, p. 19, l. 50) thinking such to be the refuge from the intellectual wars of eternity, found that she had entered Beulah, which, rightly viewed, is not repentance but innocence. It is sexual and is the "three-fold," but is not a place of war, but the exterior of Eden, the veil, so to speak, of the joys that belong to the wars of eternity,—a sort of Mundane Shell, not made of rocks and tears, but sweet emotions. It is created by the wars, as contraries create one another.

P. 30, l. 32 to p. 31, l. 7. It is, like all the temporal world, of which it is a portion, a creation of mercy, and is the Mercy Seat itself. Therefore its symbol is the emotion of marriage, given to enable the weaker form of love to endure itself, and not be blinded by the light of the stronger form. It is the innocent Vala before she became Rahab.

P. 31, ll. 7 to 11. It is an emotion that ends in realism,— terminates in Rocky Albion.

P. 31, ll. 11 to 17. And as Beulah weeps with the sorrow of Ololon, all nations, all ideas feel with her, and the Zoas, the Los's halls, generation and regeneration, stand visible in all their relations and their contrasts. ("A tear is an intellectual thing.")

Once more at this point we see the story of the poet through the veil of his writings, we see the contrition of Los, and his reconciliation with Enitharmon in "Vala," and we read the "Truchsessan letter" over Blake's shoulder.

P. 31, ll. 17 to 63. We see also Blake's art reconciled to make some use of Nature, not hating nor fearing, for this is the wider meaning of the reconciliation of Los and Enitharmon. He finds wonderful things in the sandal which he has bound on his foot to walk forward through Eternity,—he hears the birds and sees the flowers, and they form part of the

harmless pleasures of the eye—(of sight, which is the
"happy" realization of marriage—or Beulah (compare Visions
of the Daughters of Albion)—and the lamentation of innocence
over self-sacrifice turns to beauty. Here "extra page" 32
was to have come in. It is invaluable as explanation, but
needs no comment. Extra page 17 can well be read here as a
counterpart.

P. 32, l. 24. And the Divine Voice was heard in all the
songs of Beulah, saying, "When I first saw nature and married
it, and in it married you, and I gave it, and you, my whole
heart. But nature did not joy in the pleasures of the spirit,
but was jealous of them and sought her own sower. It refused
to allow corporeal life to be lived on the principle of spiritual
life. Then it was Rahab, binding the red cord in the window,
—crossing vision with the streak of blood. Therefore I, said
the Divine Voice, show you my jealousy. It is seen as the
death of Milton, who annihilated himself, which now means
that he ceases to love nature, or to feel or claim self-righteousness, and so ceases all personal life. He labours, by this
withdrawal from "female loves" or love of self-righteous
holiness, to be able to enter into the moral and religious life of
the exterior, and so redeem his own contrary, the twenty-seven
heavens of Rahab. He praises the jealous and dark god, and
gives life to Urizen. At this in fear, nature, who gives to those
who ask nothing, places herself at the service of the new
religious poet and both are happy. So sang the Divine
Voice when Ololon repented for Rahab, and took on her fault,
and so the voice of Imagination instructed Blake to sing, not
as Milton.

P. 34, l. 7. Thus Beulah sounded "comfortable notes,"
terror being changed to pity. The reason is given where the
first line of this page occurs in "Vala," Night VII., l. 781.
It is because the Divine Voice no longer suffered doubts to
rise up from the Shadowy Female, who is the real driver-down
of Milton into the Ulro.

P. 34, ll. 8 to 49. The divisions of Ulro and Beulah are ex-

plained. All are evil and satanic except when in repose. They are
essentially female. Their "will" has no place in Imagination.
They belong to Bowlahoola. Law, itself, is innocent in Repose.
They are the "maternal humanity," taken together. They
unite spirit and body, and lower spirit, and are the bridge
between mind and "matter," or lower mind, and digestion
and gestation are their physical symbols, and law and morality
their invention.

Blake's mythic system being explained, we are able to look
down into matter with Ololon.

P. 34, ll. 50 to 55. We see that while the wars of eternity
give life, those of time and space give death, even if we include
marriage among the wars, for mortal birth gives death.

P. 35, ll. 1 to 25. And female forms weave the woof of
death, which is that of unforgiveness in the moral world, as in
the physical, in all the quarters of humanity symbolised under
portions of London, or of the world. But there is a spiritual
life that cannot be had except by putting on the mortal and
allowing it to destroy you. This is Golgonooza. Christ only
can be both mortal and spiritual, alive and dead at once.

P. 35, ll. 26 to 30. Ololon's multitudes expressed their
contrition to the starry eight—Milton and the seven eyes.

P. 35, ll. 30 to 35. They rejoiced, for they saw that the
contrition of Ololon had opened a road to eternity, just as
morality of Rahab closes the road.

P. 35, ll. 42 to 47. There is a moment in every period
of time which cannot be found by the powers of external
nature, and in this moment the Divine influx descends into
man to make beautiful the other moments also. It is in the
symbolic morning, just at the time when the sun reaches the
point midway between Zenith and Nadir (see chapter on the
Zodiacal symbolism of the Cherub) at the point of the commingling influences of reason (Urizen) and love (Luvah) where
masculine influx had already descended (see diagram on page
32 of present poem), and makes the beauty (the wild thyme)
of the earth send up its aspirations towards the Zenith.

P. 35, ll. 48 to 53.   In this moment a fountain of influence flows from the mind of man outward into the external physical, and inward into the external mental, worlds, into the world of sensation and the world of custom and dogma, awakened by the inspired moment this purifying stream from the mind, and in this final union is in art (Golgonooza), the union of symbol and thought.

P. 35, ll. 54 to 61.   The Wild Thyme is the messenger o the formative mind to length and breadth.   He is not greater because he would overpower the world with his merely earthward tendency if he were.   This Thyme covers the rock or individualized tendency, which is over the abode of the Divine aspirations (the lark), and beside the source of the two streams of influence already described.

P. 35, ll. 61 to 67.   The aspirations—the lark—mount upward to the place in the symbolic Heavens which is called Leutha (see chart of symbolic Heavens in chapter on the Zodiacal symbolism of the Cherub). (This Heaven named last, when the Heavens are enumerated, is now named first, for it is considered in its capacity as a gate where influx can enter, rather than as the place for the removal of accumulated abstractions of dogma and symbol).   Adam is now the second, and so on. The aspiration—the lark—is the messenger that keeps the eyes of God—the Divine senses descended into formalism and dogmatism and materialism—from forgetting their office.   It rises from the side of imaginative life or Art, which faces to the East or towards Love.

P. 36, ll. 1 to 12.   When the lark reaches the gate of Leutha he meets another lark, that is to say he meets and becomes one for a moment with his own symbol or external expression. They both then descend to their different abodes—the first lark to his home in imagination pure and simple, the second lark to his place in symbol and dogma.   Each Heaven is not only a sub-division of the day that is made up of all the Heavens, but contains within itself the twenty seven-fold Heavens on a smaller scale, and is a complete day in itself, and in every one of these smaller days, at the moment when the sun reaches Leutha, the lark ascends, and so the message is carried from Heaven to Heaven one after another, until the twenty-eighth lark, that is to say the lark that rose when Luther had come round again, met the Divine feminine influence, Ololon, descending. (Milton—the Divine man—descended in the first moment, and when the circle is completed again, Ololon—the Divine woman—follows him.)

P. 36, ll. 13 to 32. Here direct autobiography mingles with the poem. The contrition of Ololon was an experience of Blake's. When it came to put on a natural or feminine form he sent it into his cottage to comfort his wife, who was sick with fatigue,—presumably much worried both by rheumatism and by Blake's "absences in Eden," which she said once were the only faults for which she ever had to blame him, all other reports and gossip notwithstanding.

P. 37 presents a new appearance. It was not done directly after page 36. What we have lost between them is unknown.

Lines 1 to 3 gives an answer of Ololon. She has come to seek Milton.

Lines 3 to 60. She finds him, he has entered into the accuser of sins and destroyer of joys. The whole symbolic connection between the Churches, Spectres, Cherub, and Mundane Shell is then declared. Read with the other parts of the myth and commentative chapters, it explains itself.

P. 39, l. 8. The number of the starry regions explains why Los first opposed Milton with forty-eight fibres. Milton appears in visionary form as historically known.

P. 39, ll. 9 to 27. Satan is seen both within and without, and further explained.

P. 39, ll. 27 to 49. Milton in Eastern porch,—place where the lark mounts,—speaks as a State and identifies Satan, as Los does in Jerusalem, as his spectre, his self-hood, self-righteousness, and utters Blake's own manifesto upon the purposes of his poetry.

P. 39, ll. 50 to 57. Satan claims to be the Messiah,—as in Milton's poems.

P. 40, l. 1. Milton is seen on Blake's path with the starry seven whose words are forms.

P. 40, ll. 10 to 52. The appeal to Albion to awake. This seems to have been written for a page of "Jerusalem," perhaps to follow l. 83.

P. 40, ll. 53 to 61. Urizen's struggles with Milton continue, notwithstanding the presence of the visionary Milton on Blake's pathway.

P. 42, l. 3. Milton and Ololon perceive each other, but Blake only imperfectly perceives what they do. The *naïveté* of this and the manifest honesty of the vision as narrative, are here so evident as to form the best of excuses for the fragmentary nature of this and all Blake's later poems viewed as literature.

P. 42, ll. 3 and 4. Ololon tells Milton all she sees of him and admits herself to be "Natural Religion," an absurdity. She weeps lest the little ones of Jerusalem should be lost, because the Satanic Milton who was annihilated, is the moral personage, the "wicker man of Scandinavia," to and in whom they are sacrificed.

At her words Rahab is revealed within Satan, whose regions are a mingling of city and desert—Babylon and Midian.

Milton tells Ololon the secret of annihilation, which is the putting off of the "false body" or incrustation.

P. 43, l. 28. It is in fact the not-human. With all his faults Milton at least tended against the classic and in favour of the symbolic, and as such is allowed to be a State,—that of self-annihilation,—and now he comes to awake Blake and retire or vanish while a more purely mystical Christianity than his own is put forward. The result is to be the swallowing up of generation in regeneration, of the symbol in the symbolized.

P. 43, ll. 29 to 38. Then Ololon declares herself as the contrary of Milton, who is masculine Hope. She is feminine Despair. (She is like Theotormon, he like Oothoon.)

She enters into the void outside existence and finds it to be Milton's shadow. She enters as a dove, thus counterparting the Annunciation as Satan counterparted the coming again.

The covering cherub is revealed as Luvah's robe of blood. The starry seven become one man, and the clouds of Ololon, which were the heavens, are put on by him and the clouds are seen as the literal expression of Scripture,—the word of the Word.

Then the vision of the four Zoas, who included the twenty-four cities, is seen as they arose into Albion's bosom,—as in the last pages of "Jerusalem," Blake falls on the path, his soul returning to his body, and sees Mrs. Blake beside him trembling. Then Time and Space arise over them, and all their physical powers (animals) are made ready to go forth to gather into poetry the truths that they have learned, the great vintage and harvest of the nations.

Such are the last words of the last prophetic book that Blake eft to us. Merely to measure his power is a task. Who will emulate it now ?

A FEW of the seventy pages of the MS. of "Vala" are reproduced here in facsimile, by the courteous permission of the Linnell brothers. They are enough to give some conception of the appearance of the MS., with its close and rapid writing, and hasty, slight, but poetic, sketches, designed for future illustrations.

It will be noticed that pages 1, 2 and 3 contain many erasures; that 4 and 5 are neatly written, evidently a fair copy, while later on we have what is clearly a first draft of the poem.

The title page, portions of which are almost too faint for reproduction, showed several changes of an important character. The work seems at first to have been intended to bear the name of

THE DEATH AND

JUDGMENT

OF THE

ANCIENT MAN.

A DREAM

OF NINE NIGHTS.

BY WILLIAM BLAKE.

1797.

In the first lines, however, it is Los, and not the Man, who is made the hero of the tale. This was a much later idea. It seems to have arisen from the perception that the Spirit of

Prophecy is the portion of man essentially capable of falling without completely losing its characteristic quality. It is the " Shadowy Prophet who six thousand years ago fell from his station," who "now returns," and through whose voice Blake himself claims to speak, whether under his own name or under that of Los, Elijah or Milton.

The statement that Los was the Friend of Albion, in whom Albion should eventually see the lineaments of the Eternal Friend, from whom he had separated ("Jerusalem," p. 46, l. 22) was the result of long contemplation, and had not been considered by Blake at the outset.

"Albion," as a name for the Ancient Man, or, as he is sometimes called, the " Fallen Man," was also an after-thought. It first appears as a correction in pencil on the title-page, and an imperfect attempt to carry the new name through the MS. was made probably during the Felpham period, when Blake may have picked up patriotic ideas with regard to the symbolic usefulness of ancient English names, and those of English towns from books in Hayley's library. In Night II. of " Vala," l. 3, *Man* is altered to *Albion*, and the name is substituted in the same way in Night III., ll. 68, 69, 71, 79, 81, 83, &c. Where these passages occur in "Jerusalem," whose printing was not begun till 1804, the name "Albion" is definitely adopted, p. 29. It is, however, still alternated here and there with the more general term, which we have retained in the text of " Vala."

Another title was considered as better suited to the poem and was written higher up on the page. It was to have been called

THE FOUR ZOAS
OR
THE TORMENTS OF LOVE AND JEALOUSY.

This idea was afterwards absorbed in the explanation that Los falls into division and arises into unity; he is fourfold. The title was only faintly pencilled. An almost invisible design on the page represents figures with fiends in a

chaldron at the bottom of the page, and along the margin
a trumpet-bearer is descending, to call to the Last Judgment.

Finally the name

VALA

was boldly penned as the true title, and repeated as the
heading of the poem's first page.

The value of these changes in assisting the interpretation
of the poem itself is evident. They almost explain it without
further key.

The motto of the work may be called that of Blake's
artistic life. It is taken from the Epistle to the Ephesians,—
"For we wrestle not against flesh and blood, but against
principalities, against powers, against the rulers of the darkness of this world, against spiritual wickedness in high places."
He has printed it very carefully and legibly in Greek, though
the faintness of the letters causes the words to have a broken
appearance as they stand at the head of the first page in our
facsimile. The reference, Ephesians 5, comes out more distinctly.
It is one of Blake's few mistakes, as we cannot readily believe
that he possessed a Greek testament in which the sixth
chapter of the Epistle was numbered as the fifth. The reason
for his use of the Greek is probably that he felt it to be more
evident in its meaning than the English, especially in the last
words, where our "high places" does not indicate mental
height, or the height of heaven with any particular distinctness,
but rather seems to carry on the social suggestion of exaltation
which the non-mystic and perhaps courtly translator derived
from the words he has rendered as "principalities and powers."
These also Blake would have us remember are not intended
to be understood as of the kind made of flesh and blood.
"Mental" warfare was his constant occupation. Nor had he
any doubt as to the kind of peace which he trusted it would
acquire. Against the sixth line of the poem is a reference
to the Gospel of St. John, Chap. xvii.-20, 21, 22, 23. "Neither
pray I for these alone, but for them also who shall believe on

me through their word, that they may be one in us, that
the world may believe that thou hast sent me. And the glory
which thou gavest me I have given them, that they may be
one, even as we are one, I in them, and thou in me, that they
may be made perfect in one, and that the world may know
that thou hast sent me, and hast loved them as thou hast
loved me."

This "glory" is what Blake meant by the "emanation," in
particular " Jerusalem," as in the poem of that name, p. 54,
l. 5. Here is the ultimate object of his art expressed. Side
by side with this, Milton's high and cold desire to "justify the
ways of God to Man," strikes with a tomb-like chill.

On the margin of the first page can also be detected a
reference to the verse about the Word being made flesh and
dwelling among us (John i.-14), with the central term of the
phrase in Greek added. This practically dates Blake's Greek
studies as between 1797 and 1804, probably more near the
latter than the former date, as the quotations do not belong to
the first draught, but to the corrections which were added
along with the later pages of " Vala." The language was
fresh to him then, and its novelty gave its words the emphasis
belonging to terms of endearment. As late as the date of
Night IX., years after the beginning of the poem, he quotes
Ephesians xiv.-10 against line 634 and following lines, which
tends to show that he was much occupied with the Epistle at
this time, though by what slip of the pen he gave it fourteen
chapters is incomprehensible. There is hardly a word in the
whole of its few pages that is not evidently a source of
inspiration to much that is to be read in " Vala,"—even
its metaphors and figures of speech being adopted with sympathetic enthusiasm.

In the text of " Vala " here printed an attempt has been
made to offer the early portions as nearly as possible in the
form in which Blake sketched them, even restoring many
paragraphs which he afterwards erased, blotted, or crossed
out in large blocks. Nevertheless his later insertions are

included, and the whole put in as nearly consecutive order as
possible. Of course the text thus produced is a sort of hybrid.
It contains matter belonging to two different poetic periods
and two different manners. But the poem could not be printed
twice over, and therefore is presented to the reader not exactly
as it was left by Blake's furiously rapid pen, nor is it re-
written according to the fancy of the editors, but an attempt
has been made to print it as nearly as may be in the form in
which Blake seems to think he had written it. His ear appears
to have been so filled with the cadence of the passages he was
writing, that he continually left unaltered the most evident
clippings or overgrowth of syllables, without seeming to have
been aware of what he had really done. It is the old story
of the " Poetical Sketches." Blake could improvise when in
the state which he called "the heat of the spirit"; but the
only idea of finish in any act which had been held up to him
was that of a tame and silly polish into a dead level, and re-
belling against this, he neglected too often the true finish
which consists in re-considering a work with the object of so
treating its errors, that its beauties may have free play to
follow their own organic tendencies, and move in the freedom
of their own natural freshness and beauty. It is quite probable that, if Blake's attention had been called to the
corrections made in this text, he would have been furious.
But the editors venture to think that if the revised form now
printed had been read aloud to him without any hint of
editorial treatment, he would have not been conscious that his
sketch had received a single re-touch, but would have claimed
all the work. His own corrections are always changes of
symbol or insertion of fresh figure,—never are they the much-
needed literary emendations of his evident slips.

It must suffice for the moment to indicate in a table apart
the earlier and later lines and other changes.

In a general way the more simple part of the story is
earlier, and the scraps of explanation and allusions to the

tribes of Israel and English or Welsh names are later, as
where Reuben is suddenly intruded at l. 47, Night II., or
Snowdon, or in Night IX., l. 626, " Science " for "Nature,"
or the insertion of the words "of Orc" into l. 634 of
Night VII., to the utter destruction of the music.

The MS. was never properly looked over by the author, or
even finally sorted into chapters or "Nights." Some nights
have more than one beginning and more than one ending
indicated. It is only possible to conjecture the sequence.
The numbering of the lines which occurs here and there on
the manuscript pages is so continually thrown wrong by insertions and erasures as to offer but little guide. When the
present editors received the MS. from the brothers Linnell it
was un-paged and unsorted. An attempt had been made to
put it in order, but without success. The arrangement of the
loose sheets occupied us during several long days.

There remained a more delicate task. Blake had not,
though he says in the first lines that he had done so,
marshalled the long-resounding, long-heroic verse, in order of
intellectual battle. He had, however, left many passages
of perfect sound and emphasis. The restoration of the halting
or stumbling lines to a condition in which they could equal the
musical quality and cadence of their neighbours was an
exceedingly irksome task, but not, in most cases, particularly
difficult. One system has been pursued. Wherever a correction was obvious and was almost forced upon the mind by the
evident metrical intention, it has been made. But all the lines
that did not practically correct themselves have been left
untouched however much their irregularity seemed to cry
aloud for revision. But that the reader may take nothing
through the editors without an opportunity to judge for
himself, the corrections are all indicated in the notes, and any
one who pleases may restore from them every slip and blot
that the manuscript contained without fear of suppression or
falsification. Any one who does so will see that at least we

are free of the blame of attempting to insert any fresh poetical matter that our author did not supply in order to beautify his work. "Beautify," since the days of Shakespeare's Polonius has most justifiably been considered "a vile phrase."

For the paraphrase-commentary of "Vala," see Stories of the Zoas where it is given as the story of Urthona.

BLAKE THE ARTIST.

I.

BLAKE'S artistic misfortune was that he did not live where he could habitually study good and varied specimens of human form. He made the most of his own and his wife's, as every drawing shows. The elegant sketch of Mrs. Blake dressing shows where he got the type of his strong and lithe female figures. The portrait of himself as Los in "Jerusalem," p. 6, shows where he got his males.

But unhappily he had so powerful an imagination that he vitalized in his own mind every work of art that he saw, and contemplated each through the glass of this vitalization unti all that he loved in art seemed perfect to him. That which he hated, he refrained from so contemplating, because it required him to yield himself body and soul to the influence of the work to be studied. Therefore, in what he hated he found no good quality. Yet he knew himself to be in danger of finding no evil even in this also. He says of his pet aversion—Rubens —in his Descriptive Catalogue: "Rubens is a most outrageous demon, and by infusing the remembrances of his pictures and style of execution hinders all power of individual thought, so that the man who is possessed of this demon loses all admiration of any artist but Rubens, and those who were his imitators and journeymen." (Note to picture No. IX.)

It is not everyone who is capable of carrying in his mind really "infused remembrances" of works of art. But children dream at night that the pictures they have seen by day step out of their frames and walk about. Fairy-tales habitually employ this incident. The Roman Church tells it again and again as a miraculous favour accorded to this or the other saint. Christ has come off a wooden cross to embrace a praying devotee. The Virgin of the panel weeps. In a contrary sense, tradition tells of a priest who believed that he lived on immoral terms with a statue of Venus, which became alive every night for his soul's destruction ; and the classic tale of Pygmalion attests the usual experience in a more pleasing form.

This power which works of art possess of exciting the imagination till the moveless figures on the walls produce visions of figures that move, is what enables the student of a given master to learn from his works to produce attitudes in original drawings, other than those to be found in the compositions of the master himself. Were it not so, the lessons to be learned from the great monuments of art would be sterile, and have no result beyond teaching the student to repeat the same figures in the same positions.

It is precisely the most imaginative student who, when deprived of sufficient natural stimulus, is most in danger of repeating, even in his most individual and original work, the qualities of " infused remembrances " and of getting to think them his own. Thus Blake at one time gives us vitalized gothic, at another vitalized antique, at another vitalized Fuseli, and believes that he is presenting a perfect view of an original vision. But at moments he knew (as he says in the essay on the Last Judgment) that his vision was " infected."

He believed that he had only to learn the "language of art" from his masters, and that he could use it to tell the story of his spiritual experiences. But for the native power of his constitution, and the sight of his own vigorous frame and his wife's well-contoured form, he would never have escaped from the accidents of his artistic surroundings at all.

For it must also be remembered that exactly in proportion as an artist's imagination is vivid is the probability great that he will never know when a given drawing of his own is right and when it is wrong. He sees, not the drawing, but the vision which came along with it, and which is called up by it, just as an author when reading over his book as it first comes from the press often leaves the most absurd misprints uncorrected because his eye beholds, not the erroneously composed words or phrases, or the misplaced letters, but the ideal page that he intended should be put in type, and whose presence is too clearly before his mind's eye for his body's eye to know at what it is looking.

Were it not for the fact that by mere muscular balance and nerve-sympathy, a vivid vision tends to draw itself vigorously in proportion as it is vivid, the possession of this faculty of pictorial conception would be so great a danger to an artist that *all* works of art would be likely to be as tame as those of what Blake called the "idiot high-finishers," for every man would need to review and alter in cold blood, an indefinite number of his own first designs. But unless he could preserve when cool the exact remembrance of the inspiration given in the heat of the spirit, and unless this remembrance had an equal power to stimulate his hand into giving the quality of touch and the stamp of form needed, he would produce nothing finished except poor plagiarized polished imitations of his own inventions. This, as we see too often, is commonly the case at the present day when the age demands neatness, and the designer's nerves are weakened by industry, till his knowledge becomes the enemy of his originality, and one promising young genius after another is educated down into flat helplessness. Against this tendency the "Pre-Raphaelite Brothers" fought by allowing error and finish to go hand in hand and to be equally excused if poetic intention could be found in them. Against this tendency the talented rebels of the "Impressionist" camp are now at war. Against this tendency the clever illustration and magazine drawers have successfully combated because they have ceased to strive to put more poetry into their work than the daily charm of the beautiful in ordinary drawing-room or country life will renew in their minds from external impressions as fast as the employment of it for artistic arrangement wears off the edge of its freshness.

It is only to be wondered at that Blake's art was not more unequal than we find it to be. It is not in the least surprising that he constantly joined the well-drawn parts of strangely posed figures by morsels of form that are like nothing ever seen *or imagined*, though this was hidden from him. There is wonderfully little in his work that bears the horrible and nauseating quality of later eighteenth century idealism, and among those who realize the conditions of Blake's life most clearly and feel his slips, errors, and mannerisms with most pain, will be found the admirers that feel certain with the strongest assurance that his name belongs to the first rank of genius, and has no lower place on the scroll which the artists of the world have signed.

II.—His Critical Opinions.

THAT Blake was, before all things, what men agree to call a "Genius," is so universally admitted that the glamour of the word has hitherto been sufficient to excuse both students and connoisseurs from the task of looking for any secondary merits in his art. In fact, there is a generally received opinion that, apart from its "genius," his art is either actually bad, or good in an erratic way, which it would ill become our modesty to attempt to follow. As for Blake's artistic *opinions*, these are supposed to be mere nonsense, the result of ignorance and irritability.

Those of us who are not, in our own turn, quite free from the disadvantages attaching to imperfect knowledge and hasty indignation, have long ago turned with angry despair from the critical writings of a man who called Rubens an outrageous devil, Correggio an effeminate demon, and the Venetian masters, in general, journeymen and knaves.

It seems the merest wrong-headedness and partisanship to take up the cudgels in defence of such an irreclaimable savage. But there is something else to be done with Blake's views besides arguing about them. There is the duty of ascertaining what they meant, and whether they were important.

To find meaning in them it is only necessary to remember that Blake's ambition was not merely to record his visions, but to do so in a manner that should contain the great and only preservative of artistic productions—namely, *style*. One of the greatest of French critics has gone so far as to lay down that nothing, in art, was immortal *except* style. Blake, from his youth, attached the highest importance to it.

The illustrations to the Book of America are enough, of themselves, to give to the artist who produced them the right to speak about style with the voice of a master. Their manner of employing that most useful, yet most dangerous method, the *thick line*, together with the feeling and intention, the self-control and the mingled impulsiveness and judiciousness in every stroke, show a mind made up beforehand, and a will not dulled by this foresight,—qualities in which may be found the true secret of style. Of the Job series these qualities appear again with the same masterly daring, giving vitality and originality to a more finished, if not a more difficult kind of execution.

Blake's views on the subject were not of cast iron. They were slightly modified as his knowledge grew, and under different artistic conditions would probably have undergone still greater change. But what unites all he has recorded on the subject, so that it becomes a single utterance, is the motive with which all was spoken.

Style was good, to Blake, if it lead to an improvement of the capacity of art to preserve and to express imaginative conceptions of the kind which take the Human Form for the one Word whose varieties of expression contain the entire language. One test of success was to be found in the effect that art had in stimulating the higher faculties of the artist who used it, and of the spectator who looked at what it

brought before him. Another criterion was to be looked for
in the accuracy, simplicity and beauty of the result produced
—the means, or technical devices employed, being judged
according to their tendency to help these qualities to present
themselves without hindrance and without disguise.

Blake found that the typical in art had a higher effect on
his mind than the individual. He sees the typical not only in
Chaucer, as we learn from his criticism on the Characters in
the "Canterbury Pilgrims," but in Raphael and Michel
Angelo, and the individual (in the form of the "model" who
"sat" for the figures painted), in Titian, Rembrandt, and
Rubens, in whom he also finds "generalization," or a substitute
of effects of colouring, texture and shadow so grouped as to
make a picture something else than a clear presentation of
each of its own individual parts, limbs, or features.

He did not consider that a picture might be, itself, a unit,
and that its individuality might be imaginatively complete and
permanent though mist, or glow, or gloom wrapped up every
head, hand, arm, and leg. His idea of execution is the
"making out of parts" and the nobly conceived and typical
individuality of those parts. He needs no further induce-
ment to commence a warfare of aggrandizement for the
artistic kingdom of his favourites, and of exterminating
hatred against his hinderers and oppressors. Titian used to
assail his mind with doubts when he was trying to draw from his
own visions. The "doubts" suggested to him that he ought
to have a "model." He could not take a model without
partly obliterating the imaginative impression, and substi-
tuting a memory of some individual peculiarities of anatomy
or physiognomy that were inimical to his originating artistic
impulse. At the same time a secret conscience within him told
him that his drawing was not what it should be. Titian's work,
put beside it, by superior strength, notwithstanding that this
strength was partly weakness—namely, the weakness that had
not sufficed to keep the accidental individualisms of his model
out of the typical expression of his subject—could still so

batter the pale form of Blake's wearied imagination that the Vision would be " snatched away."

The remedy was to anathematise "doubt" and to abuse Titian.

It is easy for us now to see that this is a bit of O'Neil faction-fighting, rather than a dictum of sublime wisdom. It is not difficult to remember that Raphael and Michel Angelo studied from life assiduously, and then, when a typical or allegoric figure was to be produced,—turned out of the studio the individual whose muscles and bones had served for the study of the work produced. But it was not easy in Blake's own time for people to realize that the imposing and really noble work of Titian, Rubens, Rembrandt, &c. (all "Venetians" by equality of solid worldliness in style) were not the mental companions whose influence exalts or purifies the art of a visionary,— admittedly the highest of all arts, could it only be successful as the lower art can be. Their massively moulded, heavily decorated, and solidly illuminated pictures required genius indeed in the producers, as one glance at the insipidity that results when imitators would handle their dignified, though mundane splendour, is enough to prove. But after all, they were, though followers of " Christ " in their degree, far more like the rich youth, who turned away sadly when offered the kingdom of heaven, than the fishermen who knew not where to go if they were once to leave Him who could speak the " words of eternal life."

Half a century and more has gone by since Blake rebelled against the Venetian supremacy. A generation has seen his rebellion succeed in other hands. We praise Titian now without dispraising Raphael. We do not base all our criticism on the text, " He that is not with me is against me," as Blake avowedly based his. On the contrary, we are almost in danger of being over-obedient to the other Divine command, that bids us " render unto Cæsar that which is Cæsar's."

But it is sometimes well to turn back and read at first hand a protest from a pioneer. Blake's " Notes on Reynolds," which are printed here in full enable us to trace the story of what may be called the great crisis of Blake's life. It has been referred to already in the Memoir, but may with advantage be re-told here, more narrowly confined to its purely artistic aspect.

When Blake was at Felpham he went through a period of mental anxiety which almost deprived him of his artistic self-confidence, without whose support his talents would not have been of any practical use to him. For a while he drew and painted badly. Almost everything that he touched went through a phase of failure. All the commissions he received required a much longer time and much harder labour in the execution than he had expected before hand. He was obliged continually to write to Mr. Butt's requesting his forbearance, because drawings that were ordered had not been produced. He attempted to paint in a style unsuited to his genius. "Experiment pictures" to which he was urged by the temptations of "blotting and blurring demons," were undertaken in the doubtfulness and perplexity of his mind. They gave no satisfaction either to himself or to any one else. He fell into changeable moods, alternating violent self-assertion with pitiable fits of the lowest spirits and the most abject melancholy. At times he feared that he might be obliged to give up imaginative art altogether and take to realism.

The fact of the matter,—the artistic fact,—was this. He was overstraining his imagination by attempting to make it do the work of a model while working in a style that wearied it, instead of in a style that refreshed it. So long as he used a sweeping line and a luminous tint, not only did his imagination produce his drawing, but the drawing itself excited the imagination to greater vividness, and the artistic impulse to greater fullness of power. Such an action of expression on idea is familiar enough in a different sphere when we see people who imagine that they have a wrong to complain of, and who "work themselves into a rage," as the phrase goes, in the very act of complaining, until the bitterness of their own outcry affects themselves to astonishment and enthusiasm as they exaggerate their trouble in the telling. But these same people are sometimes induced by an adroit questioner to so speak of their troubles that the effect of utterance shall be the direct opposite. They are reduced to hunting about for something to cry over, and finally are more miserable at their failure to present a satisfactorily tragic appearance than at all the original cause of their woe and grief.

Such was the effect on Blake of attempting to put a prosaic picturesqueness and a Venetian solidity into his own pure scheme of tint, until his tortured mind, driven into a corner by pride and a mis-applied transcendentalism that forbad the right and simple remedy of alternating imagination with passive study of fresh material, was goaded like a bull in a bull-fight till it became blinded, sick, faint, furious and helpless.

The sufferings that are undergone by men who have to work hard when hungry are known, and those of us who do not know them claim that we can imagine them. Such pains, we feel sure, must be dreadful. We do not dream of making light of them.

It is different with the mental torture of an over-taxed imagination, working without proper artistic nourishments and always ready to respond by fresh efforts to the admiring, but perfectly uncomprehending and unsympathetic demands of those who sit near and say,—" He is a genius—let him go on and do something wonderful. Why should he not?" So long as the artist can conceal his weakness from himself and go on in the strength of his belief in his own powers, it is matter of amazement to see how far a talent may be over-taxed and underfed,—used as though it were nature as well as art, and not supplied with food of new impressions of form and colour. But at last mannerism and errors become almost the whole of the achievement, and one day a comparison of his own with another talent, not of greater natural strength perhaps, but of more adroit avoidance of great difficulties, and of more patient reception of natural aids, comes suddenly to the poor idealist. In a moment of disgust with himself,—not necessarily in admiration of his happier brother,—he falls trembling. His will is like a rudder whose cords are broken. He can no longer use it to steer. It bangs against the side of his swaying ship, and adds to the dangers of the rocks and waves.

Such was the position of Blake at Felpham, and so great was his innocence in artistic self-analysis that notwithstanding his genius he could not think what was the matter with him. He found out that he could not paint a portrait of Mrs. Butts when she was not sitting for it, and he discovered that he soon obliterated his own ideas when he tried to "go on" with a picture made from the mental image, as though it were being done from something corporeal. But he does not seem to have discovered that he need never have worried and overworked himself until he grew so nervous that the reading of Reynolds's Discourses or a quiet conversation with Hayley was almost enough to drive him to frenzy. He struggled through his mental errors into final daylight, as he ended by adopting a style of art suited to his own genius, and to the wasteful folly with which he weakened and overstrained it.

One sign, which will be noticed in all the notes to the discourses is sufficient of itself to show the concentrated anger and rebellion of mind in which they were written. The name of Raphael is continually recurring. Sir Joshua always printed it *Raffaelle*. Blake invariably changed it to *Rafael*.

This is a portion of the "indignation and resentment" which he says at the beginning the reader "must expect." In the same paragraph the artists and critics of his day are generally alluded to as the "gang of cunning hired knaves," belonging to Sir Joshua, under whose oppression Blake has spent his youth and manhood.

These notes were written at three different times. At first the majority were made in pencil. Then they were read over. In doing so Blake "found" with satisfaction that his opinions had not changed since early youth (see note on flyleaf to Discourse VIII.). Then he inked almost all the pencillings, and added a few sentences and epigrams with the pen. He did not remove the pencil marks, which are still to be seen under the ink. This was done at Felpham in the year 1803. Out of a mistaken desire not to contradict our predecessors more than we could help, we have vaguely placed the notes as not later than 1808, but this is stretching compliance too far. There can be no doubt that at the time Blake was writing extracts from the Discourses to Butts, and reconsidering, as he says, all his thoughts on art, he was looking over his pencilled notes and adding to them.

At first he penned epigrams in verse here and there on the margins, but the restricted space being inconvenient for the purpose, the epigrams gradually flowed over into the MS. book. All those on Sir Joshua belong to this period, as do the first lines of the "hired villain" epigram. So also do the opening pages of "Milton," where the "hired gang" of Sir Joshua, afterwards made responsible by Blake for the *Examiner* attacks, and called a "nest of villains," were "rooted out," that is to say, summarized and "ornamented" under the title of "Satan."

This, as noted already, in reference to the book of "Milton," reconciles the puzzle arising from the fact that the *Examiner* articles were written several years after the poem in which the "nest of villains" was "rooted out." Blake afterwards merely referred to the *Examiner* as an example of their style. The great villainy was the oppression they had exercised on his genius during all his youth and manhood,—"these thirty years."

Many phrases and catchwords from the epigrams and the "Public address" may be recognized in these notes, especially in those to Discourses VII. and VIII. The exclamation "Mocks," relate them to the "Monk of Charlemagne."

But there were three periods to the notes. Only one of them belongs to the third. Much later than the rest, the epigram was added in a markedly different handwriting, which begins,—

> " When nations grow old, &c.,
> The arts grow cold, &c."

Because this occurs at the beginning,— a convenient space of blank paper having remained there, and because the verse ends with the words "aged sixty-three," and because Blake was born in 1757, Gilchrist has dated the whole of the notes to Reynolds 1820,—with the remark that he does so "from internal evidence." He thus deprived himself and his readers of a valuable means to the comprehension, not only of Blake's general mode of thought and of the story of his Felpham days, but of the "Book of Milton" itself. Mr. Swinburne recoils from the attempt to understand the myth of Pala-mabron and Satan, as he does from the Zoas, but he at least recognizes its existence, calls it "beautiful" and "intricate," and then with praiseworthy caution says that he "will not enter into it."

Gainsborough and Reynolds, as the note on the flyleaf to the first volume shows, are the "blotting and blurring demons" referred to in the Descriptive Catalogue.

They were "demons" because enemies of the imaginative and pure style believed by Blake to be inspired, and to lead to eternal life.

The same idea underlies the connection of Sir Joshua with Satan, and Satan with the Greek Apollo, and with the stealing and perversion by the Greeks of Biblical allegory. It explains the artistic side of the Bard's song in "Milton." The early note immediately following the quotation from Voltaire gives the clue to all this. It was written at Felpham.

The gang of hired knaves, who are the "Satans" of another note, are also the "oppressors" of Blake's genius, the "multitudes of tyrants" of "Vala," Night VIII., line 250, and the "Satans" of Night VII., last line. All the part in Night VIII. about Rahab and Satan, and the summary in it of the Bard's song from "Milton" is late in date, and belongs to the Felpham period.

It is probably not without intention that Blake began to put into the seventh and eighth Nights of "Vala," references to the ideas aroused in him by re-reading his notes to the

seventh and eighth Discourses of Reynolds. He appears to
have abandoned the idea of making them run quite together,
and to have re-arranged Night VII. several times, always
adding. The pages about Rahab and Satan in Night VIII.,
are also very recent, and were probably inserted into the
original myth during these Felpham meditations. When we
read of the Lamb of God standing before Satan Opposite, we
know that, on the artistic side of the fourfold idea involved
in the myth, Imagination is the Lamb, and Florentine,
Roman, Blakean art, while Satan is Dutch, Venetian, Sir
Joshuan art. So, also, when Los and Rahab are opposed (in
Night VIII.), we find Blake and Reynolds again behind
these masks. We even find that in later years Blake added
Jehovah and Wordsworth, or landscape-poetry to the list of
opposites under the same myth, as the incident of the
dropping of Los's tear as he followed Rahab (Night VIII.,
line 405,) shows by comparison with the note on Wordsworth,
given by Gilchrist, Wordsworth " passed Jehovah unalarmed,"
while Jehovah " dropped a tear and followed him into the
Newtonian void," for Jehovah is here " The Poetic Genius "
of the " Marriage of Heaven and Hell."

Rahab we have long been accustomed to associate with
Locke, and the reference to Locke in the notes to Discourse VII., just after the note in which Blake claims to be
the Contrary of Sir Joshua, shows at once how the train of
thought which was started in Blake's mind led to the passages
about Los, Rahab, and Satan in the Felpham parts of
" Jerusalem," " Milton," and " Vala."

At the end of Discourse VI. we find in the quotation about
oppression making " the wise man mad," the source of the
madness of the horses of Palamabron's harrow when Satan
had been driving the team.

Gradually, as the whole connection of ideas unrolls before
us, we see how natural and inevitable was Blake's belief
in the eternity of Imagination, and the Atheism of ideas
or arts that worked against it (compare note to Discourse

VII.), and the consequently logical connection of imaginative art with salvation, as announced in the recurrent line of the Bard's song in "Milton." We understand how terrible to him was the solitary struggle which his mind went through with all that was, in his day, accounted most authoritative and irrefutable in the canons of art and poetry. Then the words about his spiritual warfare from the letter to Hayley published here after the Postscript to the Memoir; can be understood as in no way exaggerated or high-flowing. Then we admit his phrase in another letter to Butts, where he says that he had gone through his troubles "not unlike a champion," and we feel grateful to the visionary beings who " praised Los for having kept the Divine Vision in time of trouble," and vainly regret that we live too late to add our voice to theirs in time to be heard by the unassisted wrestler who fought with his opponents as " Spirit of the Awakener, with the Spirit of the Oppressor," in "Milton," "the one giving life, the other giving death."

<hr />

MARGINAL NOTES

TO

THE DISCOURSES OF SIR JOSHUA REYNOLDS.

<hr />

WORKS OF REYNOLDS, 1798.

(*On title-page.*) " This Man was Hired to Depress Art."   This is the opinion of Will. Blake.   My proofs of this opinion are given in the following notes.

(*At foot of page.*) Advice to the popes who succeeded to the age of Rafail (*sic*)—

> Degrade first the Arts, if you'd Mankind Degrade.
> Hire Idiots to Paint with cold light and not shade.
> Give high Price for the worst, leave the best in disgrace,
> And with Labours of Ignorance fill every place.

(*On fly-leaf.*) Having spent the vigour of my youth and genius under the oppression of Sir Joshua and his gang of cunning hired knaves, without employment, and, as much as could possibly be, without bread, the reader must expect to read in all my remarks on these books nothing but indignation and resentment.   While Sir Joshua was rolling in riches, Barry was poor and unemployed except by his own energy.   Mortimer was called a madman, and only portrait painting applauded and rewarded by the rich and great. Reynolds and Gainsborough blotted and blurr'd one against the other and divided all the English world between them. Fuseli, indignant, almost hid himself. I am hid.

(On table of contents.) The arts and sciences are the destruction of tyrannies or bad government. Why should a good government endeavour to depress what is its chief and only support.

To: " Much copying discountenanced."

Blake: To learn the language of art, copy for ever is my rule.

(At foot of first page of table of contents.)

Blake: The foundation of empire is art and science. Remove them, or degrade them, and the empire is no more. Empire follows art, not *vice versâ* as Englishmen suppose.

(At foot of table.)

On peut dire que le Pape Lion Xme en encourageant les Etudes donna les armes contre lui même. J'ai oui dire à un Seigneur Anglais qu'il avait vu une lettre du Seigneur Polus, ou de la Pole, depuis Cardinal, à ce Pape : dans laquelle on le fólicitant sur ce qu'il etendait le progrès de Science en Europe, il l'avertissait *qu'il était dangereux de rendre les hommes trop savants.*

> Voltaire, Mœur de Nattes (?) *(illegible.)*
> (?) Tom. 4.

O Englishmen, why are you still of this foolish Cardinal's opinion ?

(On fly-leaf—opposite Dedication to the King, and over it.) Who will Dare to Say that Polite Art is Encouraged or Either Wished, or Tolerated in a Nation where the Society for the Encouragement of Art Suffered Barry to give them his Labour for Nothing. A Society Composed of the Flower of the English Nobility and Gentry —— Suffering an Artist to starve while he Supported Really what They under Pretence of Encouraging were Endeavouring to Depress.— Barry told me that while he did that Work he Lived on Bread and Apples. O Society for the Encouragement of Art, O King and Nobility of England, Where have you hid Fuseli's Milton ? Is Satan troubled at his exposure ?

The Bible says that Cultivated Life existed First. Uncultivated Life came afterwards from Satan's Hirelings. Necessaries, Accommodation and Ornaments are the whole of Life. Satan took away Ornament first, Next he took away Accomodations, and then he became Lord and Master of Necessaries.

NOTES TO MEMOIR OF REYNOLDS.

(This is written as note to the statement in the dedication that " the regular progress of cultivated life is from necessaries to accommodations, from accommodations to ornaments.")

" To give advice to those who are contending for Royal liberality has been for some years the duty of my station in the Academy "—says Reynolds.

To this, Blake: Liberality ! We want no liberality. We want a Fair Price and proportionate value, and a General Demand for Art.

(At foot of page.) Let not the Nation where Less than Nobility is the Reward Pretend that Art is encouraged by that Nation. Art is First in Intellectuality, and ought to be First in Nations.

(At head of account of Reynolds' life.) Invention depends altogether upon Execution or Organisation, as that is right or wrong, so is the Invention perfect

or imperfect. Whoever is set to undermine the Execution of Art is set to destroy Art. Michael-Angelo's Art depends on Michael-Angelo's Execution Altogether.

To: "Raffaelle appeared to him superior to the most illustrious names."

Blake: Why, then, did he not follow Rafael's Track?

To: "The better taste of Reynolds put an end to Hudson's reign."

Blake: Hudson drew correctly.

To a long account of how first impressions of Raffaello at the Vatican disappointed Reynolds and other students and visitors.

Blake: Men who have been Educated with the Works of Venetian Artists under their Eyes cannot see Rafael, unless they are born with Determinate Organs.

I am happy that I cannot say that Rafael Ever was from my Earliest Childhood hidden from Me. I saw, and I knew immediately the difference between Rafael and Rubens.

> Some look to see the sweet Outlines,
> And beauteous Forms that Love does wear :
> Some look to find out Patches, Paint,
> Bracelets and Stays and Powdered Hair.

To: "I found that those persons only, who, from natural imbecility, appeared to be incapable of ever relishing those divine performances made pretensions to instantaneous raptures on first beholding them."

Blake: Here are Mocks on those who saw Rafael.

To: "Not relishing them" (the works of Raffaelle) "as I was conscious I ought to have done . . . . . . I felt my ignorance and stood abashed."

Blake: A liar. He never was Abashed in his Life, and never felt his Ignorance.

To: "I viewed them again and again. I even affected to feel their merit and admire them more than I really did. In a short time a new taste and new conceptions began to dawn upon me, and I was convinced that I had originally formed a false opinion of the perfection of art, and that this great painter was entitled to the high rank which he holds in the estimation of the world."

Blake: All this concession is to prove that Genius is Acquired as follows on the next page.

(*On next page.*) "I am now clearly of opinion that a relish for the higher excellencies of art is an acquired taste. . . . . We are often ashamed of our apparent dullness; as if it were to be expected that our minds, like tinder, should instantly catch fire from the divine spark of Raffaelle's Genius."

Blake: A Mock.

To: "The excellence of his style is not on the surface, but lies deep, and at the first view is seen but mistily."

Blake: A mock.

To: "It is the florid style which strikes at once, and captivates the eye for a time."

Blake: A lie.

The Florid Style such as the Venetian or Flemish Never struck Me at Once nor At All. The style that Strikes the Eye is the True Style, But a Fool's Eye Not to be a Criterion.

To : " I consider *general copying* as a *delusive style of industry*."

Blake (after underlining the words) : Here he Condemns Generalizing, which he almost always Approves and Recommends.

To : " How incapable of producing anything of their own those ar who have spent most of their time in making finished copies. . . . ."

Blake : Finished. What does he Mean ? Niggling Without th Correct and Definite Outline. If he means that Copying Correctly is a hindrance, he is a Liar, for that is the only School to the Language of Art.

To : " It is the thoughts expressed in the works of Michael Angelo, Correggio, Raffaelle, Parmegiano, and perhaps some of the old Gothick masters, and not the invention of Pietro di Cortona, Carlo Maratti, Luca Giordano, and others whom I might mention, that we seek after with avidity."

Blake : Here is an Acknowledgment of all that I could wish. But if it is True—Why are we to be told that Masters who could Think had not the Judgment to Perform the Inferior parts of Art, as Reynolds artfully calls them. But that we are to learn to Think from Great Masters, and to Learn to Perform from Underlings? Learn to Design from Rafael, and to Execute from Rubens?

(*More is added, but cut off by the binder.*)

To a description of " Mr. Mudge, the clergyman," often seen at Sir Joshua's house, as a " learned and venerable old man," very conversant in the Platonick Philosophy, and very fond of that method of Philosophising.

Blake : Hang villainy.

To an account of two different reports, one saying that Dr. Johnson and the other that Burke had written Reynolds's Discourses.

Blake : The Contradictions in Reynolds's Discourses are Strong Presumption that they are the work of several Hands. But this is no Proof that Reynolds did not write them. The Man, either Painter or Philosopher, who Learns or Acquires all he knows from Others, Must be full of Contradictions.

To a note on Mr. Moser, Keeper of the Royal Academy, of whom it is said that he " might in every sense be called the Father of the present race of Artists."

Blake : I was once looking over the Prints from Rafael and Michn Angelo in the Library of the Royal Academy, Moser came to me and said, " You should not study these old Hard, Stiff, and Dry Unfinished Works of Art. Stay a little, and I will show you what you should Study." He then went and took down Le Brun's and Rubens' Galleries How did I secretly rage. I also spoke my mind.

(*A line follows, cut off by the binder, so as to be illegible.*)

I said to Moser, These things that you call Finished are not even Begun, how can they then be Finished? The Man who does not know the Beginning never can know the End of Art.

To the statement of Sir Joshua that he " consoled himself by remarking that these ready inventors are extremely apt to acquiesce *in imperfection*."

Blake (after underlining " imperfection") : Villainy—a Lie.

To : " How difficult it is for the artist who possesses this faculty (invention) to guard against carelessness and common-place invention is well-known, and in a kindred art Metastasio is an eminent instance, who always complained of the great difficulty he found in attaining correctness in consequence of having been in his youth an *Improvisatore*."

Blake : I do not believe this anecdote.

To : " There is nothing in our art which enforces such continued exertion and circumspection as attention to the general effect of the whole. It requires much study and much practise ; it requires the painter's entire mind : whereas the *parts* may be finishing by nice touches, while his mind is engaged on other matters : he may even hear a play or a novel read without much disturbance."

Blake : A Lie. Working up of Effect is more an operation of Indolence than the Making out of the Parts as far as Greatest is more than Least. I speak here of Rembrandt's and Rubens's and Reynolds's Effect. Real effect is Making out of Parts, and it is Nothing Else but That.

To an editor's note on the lost secrets of colour-mixing known to the old Masters.

Blake : Oil colours will not do. Why are we told that Reynolds was a great colourist and yet inferior to the Venetians ?

To an editor's note on a list of prices obtained by Reynolds, stating that being " without a rival, he continues to add thousands to thousands."

Blake : How much did Barry get ?

To : " Many of the pictures of Rubens being sold in 1783, in consequence of certain religious houses being suppressed by the Emperor, he (Reynolds) again in that year visited Antwerp and Brussels, and devoted several days to contemplating the productions of that great painter."

Blake : If Reynolds had really admired Mich. Angelo he never would have followed Rubens.

To : " His (Reynolds's) deafness was originally occasioned by a cold he caught in the Vatican, by painting for a long time near a stove, by which the damp vapours of that edifice were attracted, and affected his head. When in company with only one person he heard very well without the aid of a trumpet."

Blake : A Sly Dog. So can everybody ; but bring Two People, and the Hearing is Stopped.

To a note from " Retaliation," a poem by Dr. Goldsmith, in which he has drawn the characters of several of his friends in the form of epitaphs to be placed on their tombs — with the quotation—

> " Here Reynolds is laid, and to tell you my mind,
> He has not left a wiser or better behind.
> His pencil was striking, resistless, and grand ;
> His manners were gentle, complying, and bland ;
> Still born to improve us in every part,
> His pencil our faces, his manners our heart.
> To coxcombs averse, yet most civilly steering,
> When they judged without skill he was still hard of hearing ;
> When they talked of their Raffaelle's, Correggio's, and stuff,
> He shifted his trumpet, and only took snuff. "

Blake : Such Men as Goldsmith ought not to have been Acquainted with such Men as Reynolds.

To an editor's note saying of Reynolds : " It is clear from his manners and his writings that in the character of his eloquence he would have resembled the perspicuous and elegant Lælius, rather than the severe and vehement Galba."

Blake: He certainly would have been more like a fool than a wise man.

To: "He was a great generalizer . . . . generalizing and classification is the great glory of the human mind."

Blake: To generalize is to be an Idiot. To Particularize is the Alone Distinction of Merit.—General Knowledges are those Knowledges that Idiots possess.

To: "Such was his love of his art and such his ardour to excel that he often declared he had, during the greater part of his life, laboured as hard with his pencil as any mechanick working at his trade for bread."

Blake: The Man who does not Labour more than the Hireling must be a poor Devil.

To a quotation from Pope, appropriate to "the ferocious and enslaved Republick of France," ending in these words:—

> "They led their wild desires to woods and caves
> And thought that all but savages were slaves."

Blake: When France got Free, Europe, 'twixt fools and knaves,
    Were savage first to France, and after—slaves.

To a note on the prosperity of England, stating that the national trade having doubled between 1784 and 1796, amounted then to THIRTY MILLIONS, and that the price of land, war notwithstanding, was nearly as high as in times of profound peace, and that these FACTS ought to be sounded from one end of England to the other, and furnish a complete answer to all the SEDITIOUS DECLAMATIONS that have been or shall be made on this subject.

Blake: This whole Book was written to some Political Purposes.

To the account of Reynolds' death in 1792.

Blake: When Sir Joshua Reynolds died
    All Nature was degraded;
    The King dropped a Tear into the Queen's Ear;
    And all his Pictures Faded.

To the account of his funeral, where the pall was borne up by three Dukes, two Marquises, and five other noblemen.

Blake: A Mock.

To: "Sir Joshua Reynolds was, on very many accounts, one of the most memorable men of his time."

Blake: Is not this a Manifest Lie.

To: "In taste, in grace, in facely, in happy invention, in the richness and harmony of colouring, he was equal to the great masters of the renowned ages."

Blake: Barry Painted a Picture for Burke, equal to Rafael or Mich. Ang. or any of the Italians. Burke used to shew this Picture to his Friends and say, "I gave Twenty Guineas for the horrible Daub, and if any man would give . . . . . ."

(*The rest cut off by the binder.*)

Such was Burke's patronage of Art and Science.

(*So ends the notes to Reynolds's Memoir. Then on the fly-leaf of the dedication of the Discourses to the Members of the Royal Academy, and on the blank spaces of that dedication.*)

Blake: I consider Reynolds's Discourses to the Royal Academy as the Simulations of the Hypocrite who smiles particularly when he means to Betray. His Praise of Rafael is like the Hysteric Smile of Revenge. His Softness and Candour the hidden trap, and the poisoned feast. He praises Michel Angelo for qualities which Michel Angelo abhorred: and He blames Rafael for the only qualities which Rafael Valued. Whether Reynolds knew what he was doing is nothing to me: the Mischief is the same whether a man does it Ignorantly or Knowingly. I always considered true Art and true Artists to be particularly Insulted and Degraded by the Reputation of these Discourses. As much as they were Degraded by the Reputation of Reynolds's Paintings, and that such Artists as Reynolds are at all times hired by the Satans for the Depression of Art. A Pretence of Art: To destroy Art.

The Neglect of such as Milton in a Country pretending to the Encouragement of Art is Sufficient Apology for my Vigorous Indignation, if indeed the Neglect of My own Powers had not been. Ought not the Employers of Fools to be Execrated in future Ages. They Will and Shall. Foolish Men, your own real Greatness depends on your Encouragement of the Arts, and your Fall will depend on their Neglect and Depression. What you Fear is your true Interest. Leo X. was advised not to encourage the Arts. He was too wise to take this Advice.

DISCOURSE I.

The Rich Men of England form themselves into a Society to Sell and Not to Buy Pictures. The Artist who does not throw his Contempt on such Trading Exhibitions, does not know either his own Interest or his Duty.

> When Nations grow Old the Arts grow Cold,
> And Commerce settles on every Tree;
> And the Poor and the Old can live upon Gold,
> For all are Born Poor, Aged Sixty-Three.

To the commencement of the first Discourse.

Blake: Reynolds's opinion was that Genius May be Taught, and that all Pretence to Inspiration is a Lie and a Deceit, to say the least of it. For if it is a Deceit the whole Bible is Madness. This opinion originates in the Greeks calling the Muses Daughters of Memory.

The Enquiry in England is not whether a Man has Talents and Genius! But whether he is Passive and Poetic and a Virtuous Ass, and obedient to Noblemen's Opinions in Art and Science. If he is, he is a Good Man: if Not, he must be Starved.

To: " After so much has been done by His Majesty, &c."

Blake: 3 Farthings.

To: " Raffaele, it is true, had not the advantage of studying in an Academy, but all Rome, and the works of Michael Angelo in particular, were to him an Academy. On the sight of the Capella Sistina, he immediately from a dry Gothick, and even insipid manner, which attends to the minute accidental discriminations of particular and individual objects, assumed that grand style of painting which improves partial representation by the general and invariable ideas of nature."

Blake: Minute Discrimination is not Accidental. All Sublimity is founded on Minute Discrimination.

I do not believe that Rafael taught Mich. Angelo, or that Mich. Ang. taught Rafael, any more than I believe that the Rose teaches the Lily how to grow, or the Apple tree teaches the Pear tree how to bear Fruit. I do not believe the tales of Anecdote when they militate against Individual Character.

To: " I would chiefly recommend that an implicit obedience to the *Rules of Art*, as established by the practice of the GREAT MASTERS, should be exacted from the *young* Students. That those Models, which have passed through the approbation of ages, should be considered by them as perfect and infallible guides ; as subjects for their imitation, not their criticism."

Blake: Imitation is criticism.

(On a page on the importance of directing the studies of youth at first to what is substantially necessary for their artistic knowledge, lest they should pick up brilliant and superficial tricks early on, and not have the courage to go back afterwards, and learn essentials.)

To: " A facility in composing . . . a masterly handling . . . . are captivating qualities to young minds."

Blake: I consider the following sentence is Supremely Insolent, for the following Reasons :—Why this Sentence should begin by the words, A Facility in composing, I cannot tell, unless it was to cast a stigma upon Real Facility in composition by assimilating it with a Pretence to and Imitation of Facility in Execution. Or are we to understand him to mean that Facility in composing is a Frivolous pursuit. A Facility in composing is the Greatest Power of Art, and Belongs to None but the Greatest Artists, the Most Minutely Discriminating and Determinate.

(To the next pages which are about the "useless industry" that makes execu- tants of mere boys with mechanical facility, about its danger as a source of corruption and error as shewn in Foreign Academies, about frivolousness of the ambition of a student who wants to show dashing effect, not to attain exactness — and about a warning against the impetuosity of youth seeking short paths to excellence, and needing to be told that labour is the price of fame, and that how- ever great their genius, there is no easy method for them to become painters.)

Blake: Mechanical Excellence is the only Vehicle of Genius.

This is all False and Self-Contradictory.

Execution is the Chariot of Genius.

This is all Self-Contradictory ; Truth and Falsehood Jumbled Together.

To: " When we read the lives of the most eminent Painters, every page informs us that no part of their time was spent in dissipation. . . . . . They pursued their studies . . . ."

Blake: The Lives of Painters say that Rafael Died of Dissipation. Idleness is one Thing and Dissipation is Another. He who has Nothing to Dissipate Cannot Dissipate. The Weak Man may be Virtuous Enough, but will Never be an Artist.

Painters are noted for being Dissipated and Wild.

To : " When they (the old masters) conceived a subject, they first made a variety of sketches, then a finished drawing of the whole ; after that a more correct drawing of every separate part,—head, hands, feet, and pieces of drapery ; they then painted the picture, and *after all re-touched it from the life.*"

Blake (after underlining) : This is False.

To : " A Student is not always advancing because he is employed ; he must apply his strength to that part of the art where the real difficulties lie.   .   .   .   . The Students, instead of vying with each other which shall have the readiest hand, should be taught to contend who shall have the purest and most correct outline."

Blake : Excellent.

To : " I must beg to submit . . . . . to Visitors . . . . . a matter of very great consequence. . . . . .   The students never draw exactly from the living models which they have before them . . . . . drawing rather what a figure ought to be than what it appears. . . . . This obstacle has stopped the progress of many young men . . . . I very much doubt whether a habit of drawing correctly what we see will not give a proportionable power of drawing correctly what we imagine."

Blake : This is Admirably Said.   Why does he not always allow as much.

To : " He who endeavours to copy nicely the figure before him not only acquires a habit of exactness and precision, but is continually advancing in his knowledge of the human figure."

Blake : Excellent.

(*At the close of Discourse I.*)

Blake : The Laboured Works of Journeymen employed by Correggio, Titian, Veronese, and all the Venetians, ought not to be shown to the young Artist as the Works of original conception, any more than the Engravings of Strange, Bartolozzi, or Woollett.   They are Works of Manual Labour.

DISCOURSE II.

(*At the head of Discourse II.*)

Blake : What is laying up materials but copying.

To : " When the Artist is once enabled to express himself . . . . he must collect subjects for expression . . . . . amass a stock of ideas . . . . learn all that has been known and done before . . . . perfections which lie scattered amongst various masters . . . . . united in one general idea . . . . to enlarge his imagination."

Blake : After having been a Fool, a Student is to amass a Stock of Ideas, and, knowing himself to be a Fool, he is to assume the Right to put other Men's Ideas into his Foolery.

To : " Though the Student will not resign himself blindly to any single authority when he may have the advantage of consulting many, he must still be afraid of trusting to his own judgment, and of deviating into any track where he cannot find the footsteps of some former master."

Blake : Instead of Following One Great Master, he is to follow a Great Many Fools.

To : " A Student unacquainted with the attempts of former adventurers is always apt to over-rate his own abilities ; to mistake the most trifling excursions for discoveries of moment, and every coast new to him for a new found country."

Blake : Contemptible mocks.

To : " The productions of such (*i.e.* uneducated) minds are seldom distinguished by an air of originality ; they are anticipated in their happiest efforts ; and if they are found to differ in anything from their predecessors, it is only in irregular sallies and trifling conceits."

Blake : Thus Reynolds Depreciates the Efforts of Inventive Genius. Trifling Conceits are better than Colouring without any meaning at all.

To : " How incapable those are of producing anything of their own, who have spent much of their time in making finished copies, is known to all who are conversant with our art."

Blake : This is most false, for no one can ever design till he has learned the language of art by making many finished copies both of Nature and art, and of whatever comes in his way from earliest childhood. The difference between a bad artist and a good one is : the bad artist seems to copy a great deal ; the good one really does copy a great deal.

To : "The great use of copying, if it be at all useful, seems to be in learning to colour ; yet even colouring will never be obtained by servilely copying the model before you."

Blake : Contemptible. Servile copying is the great merit of copying.

To : " Following these rules, and using these precautions, when you have clearly and distinctly learned in what good colouring consists, you cannot do better than have recourse to nature herself, who is always at hand, and in comparison of whose true splendour the best coloured pictures are but faint and feeble."

Blake : Nonsense. Every eye sees differently. As the eye, such the object.

To : " Instead of copying the touches of those great masters, copy only their conceptions. . . . Labour to invent on their general principles."

Blake : General Principles again ! Unless you consult particulars you cannot even know or see Michael Angelo or Raphael or anything else.

To : " But as mere enthusiasm will carry you but a little way . . . ."

Blake : Mere enthusiasm is the All in All ! Bacon's philosophy has ruined England. Bacon is only Epicurus over again.

To : " Few have been taught to any purpose who have not been their own teachers."

Blake : True.

To : " A facility of drawing, like that of playing upon a musical instrument, cannot be acquired but by an infinite number of acts."

Blake : True.

To : " I would particularly recommend that after your return from the Academy . . . . you would endeavour to draw the figure from memory."

Blake : Good advice.

To : " But while I mention the port crayon as the student's constant companion, he must still remember that the pencil is the instrument by which he must hope to obtain eminence."

Blake : Nonsense.

To : " The Venetian and Flemish schools, which owe much of their fame to colouring, have enriched the cabinets of the collectors of drawings with very few examples."

Blake : Because they could not draw.

To : " Correggio and Baroccio have left few, if any, drawings behind them. And in the Flemish school, Rubens and Vandyck made their drawings for the most part in colour or chiaroscuro. . . . . Not but that many finished drawings are made under the names of those artists. More, however, are undoubtedly the work either of engravers or their scholars, who copied their works."

Blake : All the paintings said to be by these men are the laboured productions of journey-work. They could not draw.

To : ". . . he who would have you believe that he is waiting for the inspirations of Genius is in reality at a loss how to begin, and is at last delivered of monsters with difficulty and pain."

Blake : A stroke at Mortimer.

To : The well-grounded painter . . . . is contented that all shall be as great as himself, who have undergone the same fatigue . . ."

Blake : The man who asserts that there is no such thing as softness in art, and that everything in art is definite and determinate, has not been told this by practice, but by Inspiration and Vision, because Vision is determinate and perfect, and he copies that without fatigue. Everything being definite and determinate, softness is produced alone by comparative strength and weakness in the making out of forms. I say these things could never be found out from nature without con—— or innate science.

DISCOURSE III.

At the head of Discourse III.) *Blake* : A work of genius is a work " not to be obtained by the invocation of memory, and her syren daughters, but by devout prayer to that Eternal Spirit who can enrich with all utterance and knowledge, and sends out His Seraphim with the hallowed fire of his altar to touch and purify the lips of whom he pleases."—*Milton.*

The following discourse is particularly interesting to blockheads, as it endeavours to prove that there is no such thing as inspiration, and that any man of a plain understanding can, by thieving from others, become a Michael Angelo.

To : " The genuine painter . . . instead of endeavouring to amuse mankind with the minute neatness of his imitations, must endeavour to improve them by the grandeur of his ideas."

Blake : Without minute neatness of execution the sublime cannot exist. Grandeur of ideas is founded on precision of ideas.

To : " The moderns are not less convinced than the ancients of this superior power existing in their art (the power of a fixed idea of perfect beauty)."

Blake : I wish that this was true.

To : " Such is the warmth with which both the ancients and moderns speak of this divine principle of the art : but, as I have before observed, enthusiastic admiration seldom promotes knowledge. Though a student by such praise may have his attention roused, and a desire excited of running in this great career, yet it is possible that what has been said to excite may only serve to deter him. He examines his own mind and perceives there nothing of that divine inspiration with which, he is told, so many others have been favoured. He never travelled to heaven to gather new ideas, and he finds himself possessed of no other qualifications than what mere common observation and a plain understanding can confer. Thus he becomes gloomy amidst the splendour of figurative declamation, and thinks it hopeless to pursue an object which he supposes to be out of the reach of human industry."

Blake: And such is the coldness with which Reynolds' speaks ! And such is his enmity. Now he begins to degrade, to deny, and to mock. Enthusiastic admiration is the first principle of knowledge and its last. The man who on examining his own mind finds nothing of inspiration ought not to dare to be an artist. He is a fool, and a cunning knave, suited to the purposes of evil demons. The man who never in his mind and thoughts travelled to heaven is no artist. It is evident that Reynolds wished none but fools to be in the arts and in order to this, he calls all others vague enthusiasts and madmen. What has reasoning to do with the art of painting ? Artists who are above a plain understanding are mocked and destroyed by this President of Fools.

To : " Most people err not so much from want of capacity to find their object, as from not knowing what object to pursue."

Blake : The man who does not know what object to pursue is an idiot.

To : " This great ideal of perfection and beauty are (*sic*) not to be sought in the heavens but on the earth . . . . upon every side of us . . . . only to be acquired by experience."

Blake : A lie. A lie. A lie.

To : " . . . . and the whole beauty and grandeur of the art consists, in my opinion, in being able to get above all . . . . details of every kind."

Blake : A folly; singular and particular detail is the foundation of the sublime."

To : The most beautiful forms have something about them like weakness— minuteness, or imperfection."

Blake : Minuteness is their whole beauty.

To : " But not every eye can perceive these blemishes. It must be an eye long used to the contemplation and comparison of these forms."

Blake : Knowledge of ideal beauty is not to be acquired. It is born with us. Innate ideas are in every man, born with him; they are truly Himself. The man who says that we have no innate ideas must be a fool and a knave, having no conscience, or innate science.

To : " . . . . from reiterated experience an artist becomes possessed of the idea of a central form."

Blake : One central form composed of all other forms being granted, it does not, therefore, follow that all other forms are deformity. All forms are perfect in the poet's mind, but they are not abstracted or compounded from nature, but are from imagination.

To : " The great Bacon treats with ridicule the idea of confining proportion to rules . . . . Says he : ' . . . . The painter must do it by a kind of felicity and not by rule.' "

Blake : The great Bacon he is called—I call him the little Bacon—says that everything must be done by experiment. His first principle is unbelief, and yet he says that art must be produced without such method. This is like Mr. Locke, full of self-contradiction and knavery.

What is general nature ? Is there such a thing ? What is general knowledge?   Is there such a thing?   Strictly speaking, all knowledge is particular.

To: " . . . . it may be objected, there are various central forms . . . Hercules . . . . Gladiator . . . . Apollo."

Blake: Here he loses sight of a central form, and gets to many central forms.

To: "There is one central form belonging to the human kind at large . . in each class there is one . . . . central form . . . . common form in childhood . . . common form in age."

Blake: Every class is individual.   There is no end to the follies of this man. Childhood and age are equally belonging to every class.

To: " . . . . highest perfection not in Hercules . . . . Gladiator . . . . Apollo . . . . taken from all . . . . activity of Gladiator . . . . delicacy of Apollo . . . . strength of Hercules."

Blake: Here he comes again to his central form!

To: " There is likewise a kind of symmetry or proportion which may be said to belong to deformity."

Blake: The symmetry of deformity!   Here is a pretty foolery.   Can any man who thinks talk so?

To: "A figure lean, or corpulent, tall or short, though deviating from beauty, may still have a certain union of the various parts which may contribute to make them, on the whole, not unpleasing."

Blake: Leanness and fatness is not deformity.   But Reynolds thought character itself extravagance and deformity.   Age and youth are not classes but properties of each class.   So are leanness and fatness.

To: " . . . . when he has reduced the variety of nature to an abstract idea . . . ."

Blake: What folly!

To: " The painter must divest himself of . . . . age . . . . country . . . local and temporary ornaments . . . . he addresses his work to people of every country and every age . . . . and says with Zeuxis *in æternitatem pingo.*"

Blake: Generalizing in everything the Man would soon be a Fool, but a Cunning Fool.

To: " Albert Dürer—as Vasari has justly remarked—would have been one of the first painters of his age . . . . had he been initiated into those great principles . . . . practised by his contemporaries in Italy."

Blake: What does this mean?   " *Would have been one of the first painters of his age!* "   Albert Dürer Is!   *Not would have been.*   Besides, let them look at Gothic Figures, and Gothic Buildings, and not talk of Dark Ages, or of any Age. Ages are all equal, but Genius is always above The Age.

To: "Though the painter is to overlook the accidental discriminations of nature, he is to exhibit distinctly, and with precision, the general forms of things."

Blake: Here he is for Determinate, and yet for Indeterminate.   Distinct General Form Cannot Exist.   Distinctness is Particular, Not General.

To: " A firm and determined outline is one of the characteristics of the great style in painting, and, let me add, that he who possesses the knowledge of the exact form which every part of nature ought to have, will be fond of expressing that knowledge with correctness and precision in all his works."

Blake: A Noble Sentence! Here is a Sentence which overthrows all his Book.

To: " I have endeavoured to reduce the idea of beauty to general principles . . . . . the only means to . . . . . give rest and satisfaction to an inquisitive mind."

Blake: Bacon's Philosophy makes both Statesmen and Artists Fools and Knaves.

DISCOURSE IV.

(At the head of Discourse IV.)

The Two Following Discourses are Particularly Calculated for the Setting Ignorant and Vulgar Artists as Models of Execution in Art. Let him who will follow such advice; I will not. I know that The Man's Execution is as his Conception and not better.

To: " Gentlemen, the value and rank of every art is in proportion to the mental labour employed in it, or the mental pleasure produced by it. As this principle is observed or neglected, our profession becomes either a liberal art or a mechanical trade."

Blake: Why does he not always allow This?

To: " I have formerly observed that perfect form is produced by leaving out particularities, and retaining only general ideas."

Blake: General Ideas again!

To: " Invention in painting does not imply invention of subject, for that is commonly supplied by the poet or historian."

Blake: All but Names of Persons and Places is Invention, both in Poetry and Painting.

To: " The usual and most dangerous error is on the side of minuteness."

Blake: Here is Nonsense!

To: " All smaller things, however perfect in their way, are to be sacrificed without mercy to the greater."

Blake: Sacrifice the Parts; what becomes of the Whole?

To: " Even in portraits the grace, and we may add the likeness, consists more in taking the general air than in observing the exact similitude of every feature."

Blake: How Ignorant! (*Unknown commentator*—" No; 'tis true!")

To: " A painter of portraits shows the individual likeness. A painter of history shows the man by showing his actions."

Blake: If he does not Show the Man as well as the Action, he is a poor Artist.

To: " He cannot make his hero talk like a great man. He must make him look like one. For which reason he ought to be well studied in those circumstances which 'constitute dignity of appearance in real life."

Blake: Here he allows Analysis of Circumstance.

To: " Certainly nothing can be more simple than monotony, and the distinct blue, red, and yellow colours which are seen in the draperies of the Roman and Florentine schools, though they have not that harmony which is produced by a variety of broken and transparent colours, have the effect of grandeur which was intended. Perhaps these distinct colours strike the mind the more forcibly from there not being any great union between them, as martial music which is intended to arouse the nobler passions has its effect from the sudden and strongly marked transitions from one note to another, which that style of music requires. Whilst in that which is intended to move the softer passions the notes imperceptibly melt into one another."

Blake : These are Fine and Just Notions. Why does he not always allow as much ?

To : " In the same manner as the historical painter never enters into the detail of colours, so neither does he debase his conceptions with minute attention to the discriminations of drapery."

Blake : Excellent Remarks.

To : " Carlo Muratti was of opinion that the disposition of drapery was a more difficult art than that of drawing the human figure."

Blake : I do not believe that Carlo Muratti thought so, or that anybody can think so. The Drapery is formed alone by the Shape of the Naked

To : " Some will censure me for placing Venetians in this inferior class . . . . Though I can by no means allow them to hold any rank with the nobler schools of painting, they accomplished perfectly the thing they intended . . . . elegance."

Blake : They accomplished Nothing. As to Elegance, they have not a Spark.

To : " Paul Veronese, although a painter of great consideration, had—contrary to the strict rules of art, in his picture of Perseus and Andromeda represented the principal figure in the shade . . . . His intention . . . . effect of light and shadow . . . . everything sacrificed to that . . . . capricious composition suited . . . . style."

Blake : This is not a Satisfactory Answer. To produce an effect of True Light and Shadow is Necessary to the Ornamental Style, which altogether depends on Distinctness of Form. The Venetian ought not to be called the Ornamental Style.

To : " The powers exerted in the mechanical parts of the art have been called *the language of painters* . . . . The language of painting must be indeed allowed these masters (the Venetians)."

Blake : The language of Painters cannot be allowed them. If Reynolds says right at p. 97. He there says that the Venetian Will Not Correspond with the great style. The Greek Gems are in the Same Style as the Greek Statues.

To : " Such as suppose that the great style may be happily blended with the ornamental,—that the simple, grave, and majestic dignity of Raffaelle could unite with the glow and bustle of a Paolo or Tintoret, are totally mistaken. The principles by which each is attained are so contrary to each other that they seem in my opinion impossible to exist together, as that in the same mind the most sublime ideas and the lowest sensuality should be at the same time united."

Blake : What can be better said on this Subject ? but Reynolds contradicts what he says continually. He makes little Concessions that he may take Great Advantages.

To : " . . . . the Venetians show extraordinary skill . . . . their colouring . . . . I venture to say . . . . too harmonious to produce that solidity, steadiness, and simplicity of effects which heroic subjects require, and which simple or grave colours only can give to a work."

Blake: Somebody else wrote this for Reynolds. I think Barry or Fuseli wrote it—or dictated it.

To: " . . . . the principal attention of Venetians, in the opinion of Michael Angelo . . . . study of colour . . . . neglect of ideal beauty of form . . . . general censure from the sight of a picture of Titian's."

Blake: Venetian attention is to a Contempt and Neglect of Form Itself, and to the Destruction of all Form or Outline, Purposely, and Intentionally.

As if Mich. Ang. had seen but One Picture of Titian! Mich. Ang. knew and despised all that Titian could do.

On the Venetian Painter.

He makes the Lame to walk we all agree,
But then he Strives to blind all who can see.

If the Venetian Outline was right, his Shadows would destroy it and deform its appearance.

A pair of stays to mend the shape
Of Crooked, Humpy Woman ;
Put on, O Venus ! Now thou art
Quite a Venetian Roman.

To: "When I speak of Venetian painters . . . . . I mean . . . . to the exclusion of Titian. . . . . . There is a sort of senatorial dignity about him."

Blake: Titian, as well as other Venetians, or far from Senatorial Dignity appear to me to give always the Characters of Vulgar Stupidity. Why should Titian and the Venetians be Named in a Discourse on Art? Such Idiots are not Artists.

Venetian ! All thy Colouring is no more
Than Boulstered Plasters on a Crooked Whore.

To: " The Venetian is indeed the most splendid of the schools of elegance."

Blake: Vulgarity and not Elegance. The Word *Elegance* ought to be applied to Forms—not Colours.

To: " . . . . . elaborate harmony of colouring . . . . brilliancy of tints . . . . . . soft transition . . . . . merely a gratification of sight. Properly cultivated where nothing higher than elegance is intended . . . . . unworthy . . . . . when work aspires to grandeur and sublimity."

Blake: Broken Colours, --Broken Lines,—and Broken Shapes are equally Subversive of the Sublime.—Well Said Enough.

To: " Rubens,—formed on Venetians . . . . . took figures from people before him . . . . . more gross than they (the Venetians) . . . . . all err from the same cause. Paolo introduced gentlemen, Bassano, boors of district of Bassano . . . . . called them patriarchs and prophets."

Blake: How can that be called the Ornamental Style of which Gross Vulgarity forms the Principal Excellence.

To: " Some inferior dexterity,—some extraordinary mechanical power is apparently that from which they seek distinction."

Blake: The words Mechanical Power should not thus be Prostituted.

To: " An History-Painter Paints man in general : a portrait painter a particular man,"

Blake : A History-Painter Paints the Hero, and not Man in general, but most minutely in Particular.

To : "Thus, if a portrait painter desires to raise and improve his subject . . . . he leaves out all the minute breaks and peculiarities . . . and changes the dress from a temporary fashion to one more permanent which has annexed to it no ideas of meanness from being familiar to us—&c."

Blake : Folly ! Of what consequence is it to the Arts what a Portrait Painter does.

To : "Of those who have practised the composite style,—the foremost is Correggio."

Blake : There is no such thing as a composite style.

To : ". . . . The errors of genius."

Blake : Genius has no Error. It is Ignorance that is Error.

To : "On the whole it seems to me that there is but one presiding principle which regulates and gives stability to every act. The works which are built on general nature live for ever."

Blake : All Equivocation is Self-Contradiction.

DISCOURSE V.

(*On fly-leaf.*) *Blake* : Gainsborough told a Gentleman of Rank and Fortune that the Worst Painters always chose the Grandest Subjects. I desired the Gentleman to Set Gainsborough about one of Rafael's Grandest Subjects, Namely, Christ delivering the Keys to St. Peter, and he would find that in Gainsborough's hands it would be a Vulgar Subject of Poor Fishermen and a Journeyman Carpenter.

The following Discourse is written with the Same End in View that Gainsborough had in making the Above assertion, Namely To Represent Vulgar Artists as Models of Executive Merit.

To : "Nothing has its proper lustre but in its proper place. That which is most worthy of esteem in its proper sphere becomes an object, not of respect, but of derision, when it is forced into a higher, to which it is not suited."

Blake : Concession to Truth for the sake of Oversetting Truth.

To : "If you mean to preserve the most perfect beauty *in its most perfect state* you cannot express the passions."

Blake : What Nonsense ! Passion and Expression is Beauty Itself. The Face that is Incapable of Passion and Expression is deformity Itself. Let it be Painted and Patched and Praised and Advertised for Ever, it will only be admired by Fools.

To : . . . . . . "Cartoon and other pictures of Raffaelle where the excellent master himself may have attempted the expression of passions above the powers of art . . . . . ."

Blake : If Reynolds could not see varieties of Character in Rafael Others Can.

To : "The ancients . . . . when they employed their art to represent Jupiter confined his character to majesty alone."

Blake : False ! The Ancients were chiefly attentive to Complicated and Minute Discrimination of Character. It is the Whole of Art. Reynolds cannot bear Expression.

To : "A stature in which you endeavour to unite stately dignity, youthful elegance and stern valour, must surely possess none of these to any eminent degree."

Blake: Why not? O Poverty!

To: "The summit of excellence seems to be an assemblage of contrary qualities, but mixed in such proportions that no one part is found to counteract the other."

Blake: A Fine Jumble!

To: " . . . . transcendent, commanding, and ductile genius . . . . is fitter to give example than to receive instruction."

Blake: Mocks!

To: "The principal works of modern art are in *Fresco*, a mode of painting which precludes attention to minute elegancies."

Blake: This is False. Fresco Painting is the Most Minute. Fresco painting is like Miniature Painting. A Wall is a Large Ivory.

To: "Raffaelle . . . . owes his reputation to fresco . . . . His easel works stand on a lower degree of estimation . . . . he never aimed at such perfection as to make him an object of irritation."

Blake: Folly and Falsehood. The Man who can say that Rafael knew not the smaller beauties of the Art ought to be Condemned, and I accordingly hold Reynolds in contempt, and his critical Pretences in particular.

To: "When he painted in oil his hand seemed so cramped and confined that he lost, &c."

Blake: Rafael did as he Pleased. He who does not Admire Raffaelle's Execution does not Ever See Raphael.

To: "I have no desire to degrade Raffaelle from the high rank which, &c."

Blake: A lie!

To: "Michael Angelo considered art as consisting of little more than sculpture . . . . He never attempted those lesser elegancies or graces in art."

Blake: According to Reynolds Michael Angelo was worse Still, and Knew Nothing at all about Art as an Object of Imitation. Can any Man be such a fool as to believe that Rafael and Michael Angelo were incapable of the mere Language of Art, and that Such Idiots as Rubens, Correggio, and Titian knew how to Execute what they could not Think or Invent.

To: Along with these he rejected all the false, though specious, ornaments which disgrace the works of even the most esteemed artists."

Blake: Here is another Contradiction. If Mich. Ang. Neglected anything that Titian or Veronese did, he Rejected it for Good Reasons. Sir Joshua in other places owns that the Venetian cannot Mix with the Roman and Florentine. What does he Mean when he says that Mich. Ang. and Rafael even are not worthy of Imitation in the Lower parts of Art?

To: "Raffaelle had more taste and fancy, Michael Angelo wise genius and imagination."

Blake: What Nonsense!

To: "Michael Angelo's works have a strong, peculiar, and marked character. Raffaelle's materials were chiefly borrowed. . . The . . . structure is his own . . . . the propriety, beauty, and majesty of his characters, the judicious contrivance of his composition, the correctness of drawing . . . . &c."

Blake: If all this is true, why does not Reynolds recommend The Study of Raphael, and Mich. Angelo's Execution? At page 17 he allows that the Venetian Style will Ill correspond with the great Style.

To : . . . "Such is the great style, in this search after novelty has no place . . ."

Blake : The great style is always Novel or New in all its Operations.

To : " But there is another style, the characteristic . . . . Salvator Rosa, . . . has that sort of dignity which belongs to savage nature . . . ."

Blake : Original and Characteristic are the Two Grand Merits of the Great Style. Why should the words be applied to such a Wretch as Salvator Rosa ? Salvator Rosa is precisely what he Pretended to be. His Pictures are high laboured Pretensions to Expeditious Workmanship. He was the Quack Doctor of Painting. His Roughnesses and Smoothnesses are the Production of Labour and Trick. As to Imagination, he was totally without Any. Savages are Tops and Fribbles more than any other Men.

To : " Everything is of a piece, even to his (Salvator Rosa's) handling."

Blake : Handling is all that he has, and we all know that Handling is Labour and Trick. Salvator Rosa employed Journeymen.

To : "Rubens . . . . a remarkable instance of the same mind in all the various parts of art. The whole is . . . of a piece . . ."

Blake : All Rubens' Pictures are Painted by Journeymen, and so far from being all of a Piece, are the most wretched Bungles.

To : "His colouring, in which he most excelled . . ."

Blake : To my eye Rubens's colouring is most Contemptible. The shadows are of a Filthy Brown, somewhat of the Colour of Excrement. These are filled with tints of yellow and red. His lights are all the colours of the Rainbow laid on Indiscriminately, and broken into one another. Altogether his Colouring is Contrary to the Colouring of Real Art and Science.

To : " Opposed to this, . . . Poussin . . . . &c."

Blake : Opposed to Rubens's Colouring, Sir Joshua has placed Poussin. But he ought to put all men of genius who ever painted. Rubens and the Venetians are Opposite in everything to Fine Art, and they Meant to be so. They were hired for this Purpose.

To : "Poussin in the latter part of his life changed from his dry manner to one richer . . . . not at all comparable to his dry manner. . . ."

Blake : True.

To : "The favourite subjects of Poussin were ancient fables, and no painter was ever better qualified to paint such subjects."

Blake : True.

To : " Poussin seems to think that the style and language in which such stories are told is (*sic*) not the worse for preserving some relish of the old way of painting. . . ."

Blake : True.

To : " If the figures which people his pictures had a modern air or countenance, ... if the landscape had the appearance of a modern view, how ridiculous would Apollo appear instead of sin, an old man, or nymph, with an urn to represent a river or a lake ? "

Blake : These remarks on Poussin are Excellent.

To: " It is certain that the lowest style will be the most popular, as it falls within the compass of ignorance itself, and the vulgar will always be pleased with what is natural in the confined and misunderstood sense of the word."

Blake : Well said.

To: "I mention this because our Exhibitions, while they produce such admirable effects by nourishing emulation, and calling out genius, have also a mischievous tendency by seducing the painter to an ambition of pleasing indiscriminately the mixed multitude who resort to them."

Blake: Why, then, does he talk in other places of pleasing Everybody?

DISCOURSE VI.

(*On fly-leaf.*) *Blake*: When a Man talks of Acquiring invention, or of learning how to produce Original Conception, he must expect to be called a Fool by Men of Understanding. But such a Hired Knave cares not for the Few. His eye is on the Many—or, rather, on the Money.

To: "Those who have represented art as a kind of *inspiration*, a gift . . . . more captivating than he who attempts to examine whether . . . . art may be acquired."

Blake: Bacon's philosophy has Destroy'd true Art and Science. The Man who says that Genius is not Born but Taught, is a Knave.

> O, Reader, behold the Philosopher's grave!
> He was born quite a Fool, but he died quite a Knave.

To: "To derive . . . . nothing from another . . . . is the praise which men bestow . . . . naturally lightened by a supercilious censure of the low, the barren, the grovelling, the servile imitator."

Blake: How ridiculous it would be to see the Sheep Endeavour to walk like the Dog, or the Ox striving to trot like the Horse—just as Ridiculous it is to see one Man Striving to Imitate Another. Man varies from Man more than Animal from Animal of Different Species.

To: "The truth is that the *degree* of excellence which proclaims genius is different in different times and different places."

Blake: Never! Never!

To: "We are very sure that the beauty of form, the expression of the passions, the art of composition, even the power of giving a general air of grandeur to a work, is at present very much under the dominion of rules. These excellencies were heretofore considered merely as the effects of genius, and justly, if genius is not taken for inspiration, but as the effect of close observation and experience."

Blake: Damned fool.

To: "He who first made these observations . . . . had that merit . . . . as art shall advance its powers will be still more and more fixed by rules."

Blake: If art was Progressive, we should have had Mich. Angelos and Rafaels to Succeed and to Improve upon each other. But it is not so. Genius with its Possessor, and comes not again till Another is born with It.

To: "Even works of genius, like every other effect must have their cause."

Blake: Identities, or things, are Neither Cause nor Effect. They are Eternal.

To: "Our minds should be habituated to the contemplation of excellence . . . . the substance which supplies the fullest maturity of our vigour."

Blake: Reynolds thinks that Man Learns all that he knows. I say on the Contrary, that Man Brings All that he has or Can have Into the World with him.

To : " The mind is but a barren soil . . . ."

Blake : Man is Born Like a Garden ready Planted and Sown. This World is too poor to produce one Seed. The Mind that could have produced this sentence must have been a Pitiful, a Pitiable Imbecility. I always thought that the Human Mind was the most Prolific of All Things, and Inexhaustible. I certainly thank God I am not like Reynolds.

To : " (The mind) will produce no crop or only one, unless continually fertilized with foreign matter."

Blake : Nonsense.

To : " Nothing can come of nothing."

Blake : Is the Mind Nothing ?

To : " We are certain that Michel Angelo and Raphael were equally possessed of all the knowledge in art which had been discovered in the works of their predecessors."

Blake : If so, they knew all that Titian and Correggio knew. Correggio was two years older than Michel Angelo. Correggio, born 1472 ; Michel Angelo, born 1474.

To : " It is not that I advise any endeavour to copy the exact peculiar colour and complexion of another man's mind . . . . . The copy will be ridiculous."

Blake : Why then Imitate at all ?

To : " Art in its perfection is not ostentatious. It lies hid, and works its effect itself unseen. It is the proper study and labour of an artist to uncover, and find out the latest cause of conspicuous beauty, and from them form principles of his own conduct. Such an examination is a continual exertion of the mind ; as great, perhaps, as that of the artist whose works he is studying."

Blake : This is a Very Clever Sentence. Who wrote it God knows.

To : " Peculiar marks I hold to be generally, if not always, defects."

Blake : Peculiar marks are the Only Merit.

To : " They are always so many blemishes, both in real life and in painting."

Blake : Infernal Falsehood.

To : " The great name of Michel Angelo may be used to keep in countenance a deficiency, or rather a neglect, of colouring. . . . In short, there is no defect that may not be excused, if it is a sufficient excuse that it can be imputed to considerable artists."

Blake : No Man who can see Michel Angelo can say that he wants either Colouring or Ornamental parts of Art in the highest degree, for he has everything of Both. He who Admired Rafael, must admire Rafael's Execution. He who does not admire Raphael's execution, Cannot Admire Raphael.

To : " In this (strength of parts) certainly men are not equal, and a man can bring home wares only in proportion to the capital with which he goes to market."

Blake : A confession.

To : " In order to encourage you to imitation . . . a skilful painter . . . in no danger of being infected . . . under the rudeness of Gothic essays, will find original, rational, and even sublime inventions."

Blake : This sentence is to Introduce another in Condemnation and Contempt of Albt. Durer.

To : " The works of Albert Durer . . . afford a rich mass of genuine materials, which, wrought up and polished to elegance, will add copiousness to what perhaps, without such aid, could only have aspired to justness and propriety."

Blake: A polished Villain, who Robs and Murders!

To: "The greatest style . . . would receive an additional grace by the elegance and precision of pencil."

Blake: What does Precision of Pencil mean? If it does not mean Outline it means Nothing.

To: "I can easily imagine that if he (Jan Stein) had lived in Rome, and been blessed with Michael Angelo and Raphael for his masters . . . he now would have ranged with the great pillars and supporters of our art."

Blake: Jan Stein was a Boor, and neither Rafael nor Mich. Ang. could have made him any better.

To: "Men, who thus bound down by the almost invincible powers of early habit . . ."

Blake: He who can be bound down is no Genius. Genius cannot be Bound. It may be Rendered Indignant or Outrageous. "Oppression makes the wise man mad."—*Solomon.*

DISCOURSE VII.

(*On fly-leaf.*) *Blake*: The purpose of the following discourse is to Prove that Taste and Genius are not of Heavenly Origin, and that all who have supposed that they Are so, Are to be considered as Weak-headed Fanatics. The obligations which Reynolds has laid on bad Artists of all classes will at all times make them his Admirers, but most especially for this discourse, in which it is proved that the stupid are born with Faculties Equal to other Men, Only they have not Cultivated them, because they have not thought it worth the trouble.

To: "We allow a poet to express his meaning, when his meaning is not well known to himself, with a certain degree of obscurity, as it is one source of the sublime."

Blake: Obscurity is Neither the Source of the Sublime nor of anything Else.

To: "But when in plain prose we talk of courting the muse in shady bowers, waiting the call and inspiration of genius, ... we generally rest contented with mere words, or at best entertain notions not only groundless but pernicious."

Blake: The Ancients, and the wisest of the Moderns, are of the opinion that Reynolds condemns and laughs at.

To: "I am persuaded that scarce a poet is to be found who preserved a sound mind in a sound body . . . . whose latter works are not all replete with the face of imagination as those which he produced in his more youthful days."

Blake: As Replete, but not More Replete.

To: "To understand literally these metaphors or ideas expressed in poetical language seems as absurd as to conclude that because painters sometimes represent poets writing from the dictates of a little winged boy or genius, that this same genius did really inform him in a whisper what he was to write. . . . ."

Blake: The Ancients did not mean to Impose when they affirmed their belief in Vision and Revelation. Plato was in earnest. Milton was in earnest. They believed that God did visit Man really and Truly, and not as Reynolds pretends,

How very Anxious Reynolds is to Disprove and Contemn Spiritual Perceptions!

To: "Genius and taste . . . . pretend . . . . that great works are produced . . . . and an exact judgment is given, without our knowing why . . . . one can scarcely state these opinions without exposing their absurdity. . . . ."

Blake: Who ever said this? He states Absurdities in Company with Truths, and Calls both Absurd.

To: "The prevalent opinion . . . . considers the principles of taste as . . . less solid . . . . than really . . . ."

Blake: The Artifice of the Epicurean Philosopher is to Call all other Opinions Unsolid and Unsubstantial than those which are derived from Earth.

To: "We often appear to differ in sentiment from each other from inaccuracy of terms."

Blake: It is not in Terms that Reynolds and I disagree. Two Contrary Opinions can never by any Language be made alike. I say Taste and Genius are Not Teachable nor Acquirable, but are both born with us. Reynolds says the Contrary.

To: "We apply the term *taste* to . . . . like or dislike . . . . we give the same name to our judgment on a fancy . . . . and on unalterable principles. However inconvenient this may be, we are obliged to take words as we find them."

Blake: This is False. The Fault is not in Words but in Things. Lock's Opinions on words and their Fallaciousness are hurtful opinions and Fallacious also.

To: "The same taste relishes demonstration . . . . resemblance of a picture . . . . and harmony."

Blake: Demonstration, Similitude and Harmony are Objects of Reasoning Invention. Identity and Melody are Objects of Intuition.

To: ". . . . as true as mathematical demonstration. . . . ."

Blake: God forbid that Truth should be Confined to Mathematical Demonstration. He who does not know Truth at sight is unworthy of Her Notice.

To: "In proportion as prejudices are . . . . long received, ... taste . . . . approaches certainty . . . ."

Blake: Here is a great deal to do to Prove that All truth is prejudice, for all that is Valuable in Knowledge is Superior to Demonstrative Science, such as is Weighed and Measured.

To: "As these prejudices become more narrow, this secondary taste becomes more fantastical . . . ."

Blake: And so he thinks he has proved that Genius and Inspiration are All a Hum.

To: "Having laid down these propositions I shall proceed with less method."

Blake: He calls the Above, proceeding with Method.

To: "We will take it for granted that reason is something invariable."

Blake: Reason—or a ratio of all we have known—is not the same it shall be when we know More. He therefore takes a Falsehood for granted to set out with.

To: "We will conclude that whatever goes under the name of taste which we can fairly bring under the dominion of reason must be considered as equally exempt from change."

Blake: Now this is supreme Fooling.

To : " The arts would lie open for ever to caprice and casualty if those who are to judge of their excellencies had no settled principles . . . ."

Blake : He may as well say that if man does not lay down settled Principles the Sun will not rise in a Morning.

To : " My notion of nature comprehends . . . . the internal fabric . . . . of the human mind and imagination."

Blake : Here is a plain Confession that he Thinks Mind and Imagination not to be above the Mortal and Perishing Nature. Such is the End of Epicurean or Newtonian Philosophy. It is Atheism.

To : " This (Poussin's Perseus with Medusa's head) is undoubtedly a subject of great bustle and tumult . . . . the eye finds no repose anywhere . . . . I remember turning from it in disgust . . . ."

Blake : Reynolds's Eye cannot bear Characteristic Colouring or Light and Shade.

To : " This . . . . I hold to be improper to imitate. A picture should please at first sight."

Blake : Please whom ? Some Men Cannot see a Picture except in a Dark Corner.

To : " No one can deny that violent passions will naturally emit harsh and disagreeable tones."

Blake : Violent Passions emit the Real Good and Perfect Tones.

To : " If it be objected that Rubens judged ill . . . . to make his work so very ornamental . . . ."

Blake : Here it is Called Ornamental that the Roman and Bolognian Schools may be Insinuated not to be Ornamental.

To : " No one will dispute that the Roman or Bolognian Schools would have produced a more learned and more noble work."

Blake : Learned and Noble is Ornamental.

To : " This leads us to weighing . . . . the different classes of art . . . ."

Blake : A fool's Balance is no criterion, because though it goes down on the heaviest side, we ought to look what he puts into it.

To : " If a European who has cut off his beard, put false hair on his head, or tied up his own, and . . . . with the help of the fat of hogs covered the whole with flour . . . . issues forth and meets a Cherokee Indian, who has bestowed as much time on his toilet . . . laid on his ochre . . . . whichever of these two despises the other for this attention to the fashion of his country . . . . is the barbarian."

Blake : Excellent.

To : " In the midst of the highest flights of the fancy or imagination, reason ought to preside . . . ."

Blake : If this is True it is a devilish Foolish Thing to be an Artist.

DISCOURSE VIII.

(*On fly-leaf.*) *Blake* : Burke's treatise on the Sublime and Beautiful is founded on the Opinions of Newton and Locke. On this Treatise Reynolds has grounded many of his assertions in all his Discourses. I read Burke's Treatise when very young. At the same time I read Locke on the Human Understanding, and Bacon's Advancement of Learning. On every one of these Books I wrote my opinion, and, on looking them over, find that my Notes on Reynolds in this book are exactly similar. I felt the same Contempt and Abhorrence then that I do now. They mock Inspiration and Vision. Inspiration and Vision was then, and now is, and I hope will always remain, my Element, my Eternal Dwelling-place. How can I then hear it condemned without returning Scorn for Scorn ?

To : "Principles of art . . . in their excess become defects."

Blake : Principles according to Sir Joshua become Defects.

To : "Artists should learn their profession from endeavouring to form an idea of proportion from the different excellencies which lie dispersed in the various schools of painting."

Blake : In another discourse he says that we cannot mix the Florentine and Venetian.

To : An instance occurs to me of two painters—Rembrandt and Poussin . . . . . Rembrandt's manner was absolute unity. . . . . Poussin has no principal light at all."

Blake : Rembrandt was a Generalizer ; Poussin a Particularizer.

To : "The works of Poussin are as much distinguished for simplicity as those of Rembrandt for combination."

Blake : Poussin knew better than to make all his pictures have the same light and shade. Any fool may concentrate a light in the Middle.

To : "We may compare . . . . the portraits of Titian, where dignity, seeming to be natural and inherent, ... has the appearance of an inalienable adjunct. . . . ."

Blake : Dignity an Adjunct.

To : "When a young artist . . . . is told . . . certain animating words of Spirit, Dignity, Energy, Grace, greatness of Style and brilliancy of Tints . . . he becomes suddenly vain of his newly acquired knowledge."

Blake : Mocks.

To : "Art in its infancy, like the first work of a student, was dry, hard, and simple. But this kind of barbarous simplicity would be better named Penury, as it proceeds from mere want ; from want of knowledge, want of resources, want of abilities to be otherwise. Their simplicity was the offspring, not of choice, but of necessity."

Blake : Mocks. A lie.

To : "In the second stage they are sensible of this poverty . . . . ran into a contrary extreme. But . . . . . we cannot recommend them to return to that simplicity . . . . but to deal out their abundance with a more sparing hand . . ."

Blake : Abundance of Stupidity.

To : " . . . . it is not enough that a work be learned ; it must be pleasing."

Blake : If you Endeavour to Please the Worst, you will never Please the Best. To Please all is Impossible.

To : "Again, in the artificial management of figures, it is directed that they shall contrast each other according to the rules generally given. . . . . But when students are more advanced, they will find that the greatest beauties of character and expression are produced without contrast. St. Paul preaching at Athens, far from any affected academical contrasts of limbs stands equally on both legs, and both hands are in the same attitude ; add contrast, and the whole energy and unaffected grace of the figure is destroyed. Elymas the Sorcerer stretches both hands forward in the same direction, which gives perfectly the expression intended."

Blake: Well said.

To : " It may not be improper to give instances where the rule itself, though generally received, is false. . . . It is given as a rule by Fresnoy : That *the principle figure of a subject must appear in the midst of a picture, under the principal light, to distinguish it from the rest.*"

Blake: What a Devil of a Rule.

To : " . . . . what those proportions are cannot be so well learned by precept as by observation on pictures, and in this knowledge bad pictures will serve as well as good."

Blake: Bad pictures are always Sir Joshua's friends.

To : " It ought, in my opinion, to be indispensably observed that the masses of light in a picture be always of a warm mellow colour—yellow, red, or yellowish white; and that the blue, the grey, or the green colours be kept almost entirely out of these masses, and used only to support and set off these warm colours, and for this purpose a small proportion of cold colours will be sufficient."

Blake : Colouring formed on these Principles is destructive of All Art, because it takes away the possibility of Variety, and only promotes Harmony, or Blending of Colours one with another.

To : " The conduct of Titian in the picture of Bacchus and Ariadne has been much celebrated, and justly, for the harmony of colouring."

Blake: Such Harmony of Colouring is Destructive of Art. One Species of General Hue over all is the Cursed Thing called Harmony. It is like the Smile of a Fool.

To : " The illuminated parts of objects are in nature of a warmer tint than those that are in the shade."

Blake: Shade is always cold, and never, as in Rubens and the colourists, hot, and Yellowy Brown.

To : " . . . fulness of manner found in perfection in the best works of Correggio and, we may add, of Rembrandt. This effect is produced by melting and losing shadows in a ground still darker than those shadows. . . ."

Blake : All this is destructive of Art.

To : " A picture I have of Rubens ; it is a representation of moonlight. . . . The Moon in this picture does not preserve so great a superiority in regard to the object which it illumines as it does in nature. This is likewise an intended deviation, and for the same reason. If Rubens had preserved the same scale of gradation of light between the moon and the objects which is found in nature, the picture must have consisted of one small spot of light only, and at a little distance from the picture nothing but this spot would have been seen."

Blake : These are Excellent remarks on Proportionate Colour.

To : " Before and above all things it is necessary that the work should be seen, not only without difficulty, but with pleasure and satisfaction."

Blake: If the Picture ought to be Seen with Ease, surely the Nobler parts of the Picture, such as the Heads, ought to be Principal. But this is never the case except in the Roman and Florentine Schools, not, I (?) trust the German in the Florentine school.

To: " . . . . Sketches give the pleasure of imagination . . . . the imagination supplies more than the painter probably could produce."

Blake: What Falsehood!

To: " . . . . Everything shall be carefully and distinctly expressed as if the painter knew with correctness and precision the exact form and character of whatever is introduced into the picture. This is what, with us, is called Science and Learning, which must not be sacrificed and given up for an uncertain and doubtful beauty which, not naturally belonging to our art, will probably be sought for without success."

Blake: Excellent, and contrary to his usual opinion.

To: "Mr. Falconet has observed in a note . . . . that the circumstance of covering the face of Agamemnon was probably not in consequence of fine imagination of the painter . . . . he thinks meanly of this trick of concealing . . . ."

Blake: I am of Falconet's opinion.

In all this we see the temperament of a partisan, the limited knowledge of a man who has not travelled, and the pleading of an advocate who held a brief for impulse against the accusations of authority. We see Blake's "spectre," his "pride and self-righteousness" coming forward over and over again, "with all the fury of a spiritual existence." We see general condemnations passed for particular deficiencies, and things declared to be true of other men because they were true of the author. In fact, we feel continually the horrible "oppression" of "one law for the lion and the ox." We find particularity praised, and portrait painters despised, while masters are accused of hiring sometimes and of being hired on the strength, as we more than suspect, of pictures which were indeed produced for hire, but as much in accordance with the convictions of the artists as with those of the patrons. We find the eloquence and the unfairness of an enthusiast, but we also find the penetration into essentials which no one without the personal experience belonging to the possessor of genius could have attained. There is no variety of critical merchandise in Blake's market, but as we stumble through the empty bazaar a strange light from among the overturned tables reveals to us that the goods were not battered in vain, and that here at last is the Great Pearl in their place.

IV.—Our Illustrations.

The books by which Blake won his fame are almost as full of pictures as of written lines. The subjects of the designs will be spoken of later. But the manner of their production and reproduction must be noted first.

The method of printing from raised lines on copper, which the spirit of Robert dictated in a dream to his brother, supplied, as a rule, little more than the foundation on which the works were built. The rough and thick strokes, which indicate the figures with such determination and yet such sensitiveness, in "America" and in the colourless editions of "Jerusalem," were entirely hidden in "Ahania," "Urizen," and "Los,"—the colours here having been first laid on solid— it is said by pressing on the face of the drawing a piece of paper or cardboard on which the design had already been painted in oils. This leaves a mottled and crummy surface. A picture can be finished up over it in water-colours by the mixing of a little glue and oxgall, and the effect is very solid and mysterious. Blake used plaster in his glue, on paper, to make a preparation like that which the Italians called *gesso.* He used to call water-colours painted on this *fresco.* The books worked up in this way are, in the present series, only three. An attempt has been made to represent in lithographic chalk the effects so produced. The reproductions of these books are the same size as the originals.

"Jerusalem" has been differently treated. The book was sometimes printed in brown, as in Lord Houghton's copy mentioned by Gilchrist, sometimes in dark slate-coloured ink, as in the British Museum copy. A facsimile, the exact size of the original, has been published of the uncoloured form of the work.

In the copy possessed when the present reproductions were made by Mr. Quaritch, probably the copy alluded to as the last treated in colour by Blake himself, the outlines and black spaces were printed in pale yellow-brown, and then elaborate finish in water-colour was added over this, and fresh outline, often much thinner, added. The result was that the contrasts of light and shade were wholly altered. For example, the distinguishing quality of the woman-swan on page 12 is a massive but soft whiteness. In the uncoloured copies it is black, and the outline is indicated by thin white strokes as though it were drawn on a school-slate.

In the figure of Albion lying on the ground, at the foot of page 19, the uncoloured copies are so roughly lined that it is practically impossible to distinguish the smaller figures, one of which is lying on him while he lies on two others.

In some, such as the crucifixion on page 76, and the cock-headed watcher awaiting the sunrise on page 78, the coloured examples lack the simplicity, strength, and statuesque grandeur of the simple lines, as anyone may see by comparing the shaded drawings in the example here given with the facsimile of the uncoloured plates in Gilchrist's life. Somewhat the same may be said, but in a less degree, of the most beautiful design of all, that on page 32 of "Jerusalem." This also may be compared with facsimiles given elsewhere of the untouched plate, while some of the pictures, such as those on pages 46 and 75, gain very much by being less archaic, and lose none of their supernatural fascination, their visionary weight and emphasis by being made more intelligible. Others, such as that on page 74, are at least capable of being comprehended in the present edition, whereas in the facsimile of the untouched plate they are masses of confusing bars of black.

This edition was prepared in the following manner. The exact facsimile of the uncoloured plates, as reproduced on stone by photography, was laid beside the highly finished copy coloured by Blake's hand. Wherever Blake had sacrificed any of his heavy black in painting over, the black in the facsimile was hidden under a coat of solid white laid on with a brush. When this was dry the drawings were shaded with a few strokes,—not more than would indicate the effect of the painting. These were added with pen and ink. The pages so treated were then photographed on to stone once more (reduced from quarto size), and are printed here. Wherever the reader sees a line of heavy black, or a solid piece of black shading, he is looking on the touch of Blake, unaltered except by mechanical reduction in the camera. Where he sees the sketchy shading of a pen, laid on and handled in the style of an ordinary pen-and-ink draughtsman of to-day, he sees the editor's work indicating the effect of shading given by Blake in his elaborate and unphotographable painting. No alterations have been made. The outlines of every figure, the expressions of face, &c., are Blake himself. No attempt has been made to forge his style of shading in the pen-and-ink part—on the contrary. The object was to indicate truly the painted effect in a style of work quite manifestly belonging to a technique that was never Blake's so that on every page the eye can analyze at a glance the entire effect, separating the indication added from the foundation of the picture. No reader need worry himself by wondering how far what he sees is Blake. In *effect* all is Blake. In *touch* the masses and the forms are from Blake's own hand,—while the shading, which is not black mass, is carefully copied, and that is all. The reason why this method was adopted was that while it made the rougher parts of the foundation-drawings capable of being understood as Blake intended them to be,—a thing impossible in their first state,—it enabled most of what was there to be preserved, and the modern treatment, to be easily distinguishable. But for the fact that the outlines in the uncoloured plates were so wildly daubed as sometimes to be incomprehensible,—and for the loss that would occur were no record of the changes Blake made in them while painting, put before the public at once, the editor would very gladly have let the plates alone. He touched them most unwillingly, and in some, such as that on p. 41, could not see any necessity for

adding anything at all. This is exactly the uncoloured block
as left by Blake. That on p. 14 is hardly changed at all. The
sea from below and the kneeling angels are cleared a little as
in the coloured copy. The roughnesses, the extravagances,
and mannerisms,—the bits of white on black that stick out
from behind figures, as on pp. 47 and 100, are Blake himself.
Pure Blake also is the massive dignity of even the most con-
torted and fragmentary figure, and the clear-eyed and living
directness of the expression in every face.

Leaving the subjects of the designs for another chapter,
something more should be told of the reproductions, as the
system described above has been followed in no other case.

In the " Book of Milton " it was found that though tints had
been laid over the outlines, these showed through with enough
clearness to be photographed at once on stone. Then in a few
places where a yellow tone had made blackness where light
was intended, the stone was scraped with a knife, as in the
rays between the upper figures on page 15.

On other pages, the effect of the black-and-white drawings
here presented is not always exactly that of the page as
tinted, but at least it was intelligible and was Blake himself.
Therefore no additional lines of black by way of shading or
for any other purpose have been added. Here are Blake's
plates as he had them before tints were added, and anyone
with a water-colour brush and a little patience may make
them into facsimiles of those in the Print room of the British
Museum. Page 1 and page 41 are interesting, as examples
of Blake's work when almost at its best and its worst. When
page 1 was drawn and engraved, the poem, as the white
lettering on the clouds tells us, was to have been in twelve
Books. Blake was in high spirits about it. There is a loving
luxuriance of innocent satisfaction in the very handwriting
of the signature. Note the style of the words " Author and
printer, W. Blake," with the date, 1804. Page 41 must have
been done during the struggles and angers of the years
succeeding, when the poem was compressed into two Books,

and hurriedly abandoned to its fate. The wild scratches on the last page show the hand of a man whose whole artistic power is wrecked by the unnerving effect of anger, apprehension, agitation, and disturbance of mind. Poetry can flourish in this atmosphere, but wo have Michel Angelo's own word for it that art cannot.

In other books, such as "Europe," where a black outline and shading mingled with very slight tinting which in no way disguised it,—the line has been reproduced as line, and the tinting as shadow added with chalk, and given hastily where the touch of the brush was hasty, and with careful completeness where the original displayed a more elaborate treatment. Excepting the Pope's face on page 9 of "Europe," and the diabolic King's face on page 5 of the same book, in both of which the editor failed to catch the true quality of the original, wherever queer faces and spoiled limbs or impossible draperies are found, the reader may be sure he is looking at an accurate representation of Blake, even where the editor was suffering the extremest torture of temptation to touch him up just the least bit in the world. There is nothing truer and stranger about Blake's art than this,—that while his merits are so vital and so vitalizing to others that to know his work is to be exalted into a new being and taught as no student can be taught who goes to any other of all the thousands of Masters, great and small, who each deserves his meed of praise and wonder, and scholarly following, yet so childish are Blake's errors that, far from being difficult to correct, the most stern self-control is needed by any copyist who desires to refrain from correcting them. In this his art is exactly like his verse. In the verse we have here and there edited and offered a text, giving the original for comparison, to show that only the "ifs and ans" had been manipulated. But in drawings to improve is often to replace. Sometimes it is only to continue. But the public cannot be expected to know the difference. We all read and write, but only a small group draw,—even in this day of art schools,

—and of those few how many do so really and truly " out of
their own heads," as Blake did ? In no other experience can
the knowledge be acquired that should analyze him. Therefore the illustrations have been reproduced, or copied, but
never edited.

" America " is an untouched repetition from the colourless
copy of the British Museum. This, like " Jerusalem " and
" Europe," is somewhat reduced to accommodate it to our
pages, while all the rest are the same size as the originals.
The few specimen pages of " Vala " were also reduced, the
originals being the size of an ordinary page of music for the
piano. They were photographed to the size of our pages, and
then it was found that the drawings were too faint in their
pencilling and the paper about them too much toned by age
to enable a direct transfer to stone for printing to be made
from the photograph. The few lines were carefully traced
with lithographic chalk, and so transferred without alteration.
In some of them, as in the arms of the central figure of the
frontispiece, the vague strokes may still be seen doubling the
outline where Blake's hand h..d outrun his mind, and he had
not yet quite decided where the limb should come, although
he had already begun to put it on paper.

V.—Subjects of Blake's Designs.

The greater number of Blake's designs have been left
hitherto without any explanation. Those which illustrate
his Prophetic books are seldom placed near the part of the
text to which they refer. No sub-title or foot-note, no
separate list is to be found to make up for the difficulty in
deciding the subject which is caused by this. Here and there
a word on the background gives a clue. Usually there is not
even this amount of indication. The result is that for nearly a
century critics have been looking at his designs, and no one
has had a word to say about what they were intended to
represent.

The following descriptions of the subject of a large number of unnamed drawings in illustration of the various books is not given on Blake's own authority, as are our explanations of the myths themselves. They must be considered as suggestions on the part of the editors, offered to the reader, and left for future study to supplement or to correct.

TO MARRIAGE OF HEAVEN AND HELL.

1. (Title-page.) Desire and Blood meeting and kissing. (Flame and cloud.) Enthusiasm and instinct are equally to be understood, and all that is grouped symbolically under the points of the compass, East and West. Imagination and instinct are also appropriate names for the figures which are placed below the earth, and the roots of the trees, in that place " beneath the bottoms of the graves where contraries are equally true." (" Jerusalem," p. 48, l. 14.)

2. On the margin beside the Argument. Orc feeding Vala (in her scarlet veil worn as a skirt) with the fruit of the tree of Mystery.

The smaller figures may be merely the human forms of vegetations.

3. The upper figure repeats the subject of the title-page, only the flame is not personified, and the cloud, as the Female, is. The picture may be called Orc embracing Enitharmon. Los here has the form of Orc. The " Eternal Hell," in the act of " reviving " seems also to be intended as the subject.

The lower figures illustrate lines from the Mental Traveller :—

> They cry,—" The babe—the babe is born ! "
> And flee away on every side.

4. Los is seen bearing a child across the sea of Time and Space to deliver him up to Orc, for none can behold Los's world till he has passed the Polypus, and the Polypus in its passionate aspect is Orc, and Orc is fire.

5. The fall of Urizen and of one of the horses of light.

7. (on page 10.) The Devil's proverbs being written down in—and by—the brass and iron books of Urizen.

8. (on page 11.) Thel and the Lily of the Valley, from the " Book of Thel." The golden cloud in the background. (There is a separate copy of this in the book of designs without letters in the British Museum.)

9. (on page 14.) The soul hovering over the body : a variation of the design to Blair's grave. Here the soul is feminine, and is " the indulgent self of weariness." It hovers in flames. It is vague passion and appetite without mind, —counterpart of the " Spectre " that lies dead beneath.

10. (on page 15.) Luvah and Tharmas as the Eagle and the Serpent, or air and water, fighting. It is the expansive power bearing away the mundane shell or Christ removing the Veil of Druid Law.

11. (on page 16.) The four Zoas and Albion as five senses in darkness,—the Giants who formed this world into its sensual existence. They are locked up in black marble of Egypt,—chains of the mind. Albion is in the middle. Urizen and Luvah exterior to his right and left—(the left and right of the

picture)—Tharmas and Urthona nestled against him. When not in darkness
Urizen and Luvah would be within, and Tharmas and Urthona exterior.

12. (on page 20.) The War-by-Sea or Leviathan.

13. (on page 21.) The spiritual form on the mortal (whose skull is just
perceived beneath his knee). This also is the design in Blair's Grave, otherwise
treated, and done years before it was used for that work.

14. (on page 24.) Urizen attempting to live as Urthona,—under type of
Nebuchadnezzar. He is exploring the dens, but the globe of light is not in his
hand, but shines through him as red blood.

TO BOOK OF LOS.

(Frontispiece.) The hoar-frost's wife the aged snow. (Compare: "Vala" Night
IX., l. 810.)

1. Los roofed in Albion's cliffs.

2. Urizen's nets involving the sexes.

3. Los as Urizen casting the globe of light, and heat into the depths.

TO BOOK OF URIZEN.

1. Urizen writing his books, under the tree of Mystery. ("Vala," Night VI., l. 85.)

2. Urizen in infant weakness with Vala. ("Vala," Night VI., l. 153.) He is
the son of Vala—first-born of generation. (Night VII., l. 242.)

3. Orc.

4. "Urizen answered, Read my books, explore my constellations. ("Vala,"
Night VII., l. 90.)

5. This differs only in the presence of the serpents or "worms" from the
sixteenth design to the Book of Job, where Satan falls with sin and death. It
includes some further ideas, and symbolizes the crucifixion of the serpent,—Man
is the cross on which Satan is slain. It shows a "worm going to eternal
torment" ("Jerusalem," p. 80, l. 4), and it also suggests the "furnaces of
affliction," in which the sisters of Guendolen "began to give their souls away,"
in order to give the worm a "form of love." The subject, without furnaces, is
differently treated in the margin of "Jerusalem," p. 80.

6. Orc, or Los in torments of Orc.

7. The bones of Horeb.

8. Urizen's journey in the dens.

9. Beginning of Urizen's journey.

10. Los binding the changes of Urizen.

11. Urizen passing the world of Tharmas.

12. Ahania.

13. Man head-downwards, or Urizen going north.

14a. The fall of Los from the Book of Los.

14b. The four Zoas. Tharmas turning round the circle of destiny. ("Vala,"
Night I., l. 106.)

15. The Female.

16. Los.

17. Los and Enitharmon.

18. The bulk of Orc.

19. Los, Enitharmon, and Orc.

20. Enslaved Humanity,—Forgetfulness, Dumbness, Necessity.

21. Urizen with the globe of light to explore the dens.

22. The sons of Urizen,—Fuzon, Tiriel, Utha, Grodna.

23. Harlotry: the *Virgo-scorpio*, also the "Shadowy Female," and the worm, Orc. Compare "Vala," VIII., ll. 60, 82 and 109.

24. Virginity : the " dog at the wintry door."

25. Urizen followed, as he journeyed, by a white web.

26. Urizen in his own net.

TO AHANIA.

(Frontispiece.) To Chap. I. stanza 7, Urizen groaning and calling his parted soul " Sin."

(On title-page.) To Chap. V. Ahania on the margin of nonentity.

(At the end.) To "Urizen," Chap. V. stanza 3, ruinous fragments of life.

TO TIRIEL.

One design to Tiriel only has been seen by the present editors. Tiriel in straight skirts, with mild face, stands in a sparse forest of thin trees outside the gates of Har and Heva. It is not reproduced. It marks Tiriel as a very early book, now printed not in chronological position, but so as to bring the three eyes—Hela, Thel, Oothoon—together.

TO THEL.

The designs to the book of Thel explain themselves by help of the Text, all but the last, Innocence ruling Nature, which is repeated in America, p. 11.

TO VISIONS OF THE DAUGHTERS OF ALBION.

1. (Title-page.) The spectrous figure with the clasped arms which appears with wings in the " Europe," and in the MS. book in several forms, seems to have been considered a fire-spirit by Blake. The page here is full of elementals, and the motto implies that the artist was not always certain of the meaning or mission of every form that presented itself to him in vision.

2. The second drawing shows Oothoon plucking the flower of Leutha, and illustrates the lines above.

3. The design at the foot of the first page shows Bromion and Oothoon resting.

4. The figure on page 2 is Theotormon, dressed in his own sadness and gloom.

5. On page 5 is the design which should have been on page 4. The Eagle rends Oothoon's breast.

6. Oothoon chained with the chain of jealousy. She pleads to Theotormon from the " watery Flame," the symbol of Tharmas.

7. Oothoon in-despair.

8. Theotormon scourging Oothoon with accusation of sin. (See chapter on minor symbols, the Serpent and the Whip.)

9. Fourfold sorrow of Theotormon, in " Daughters of Albion."

10. Oothoon telling her story. She is symbolized as fire in cloud.

11. Bromion and Oothoon in the cave, and Theotormon at the threshold.

TO AFRICA.

In this book the one design represents the male saving the female from the watery region—her own. This contrasts with the last design to Europe. The work is of a very rugged and unchiselled character, and is accurately represented by the lithograph.

Between Africa and Asia—Oberon and Titania. The painting is much obliterated, and the lithograph shows fairly well what is left of it.

TO ASIA.

The male is seen in a cave rescuing the female from Earth. This makes the third of the series. The fourth seems to have been lost. Man, as Urizen, weeping, or Los, and the same person falling, is also found on the margin.

TO AMERICA.

(Frontispiece.) Urizen as Albion's Angel chained to the wall that became the Mundane Shell, or the " finite wall of flesh." Enion sits outside with Los and Enitharmon as children.

(Title-page.) Upper figures.—A male and female figure reading in books (evidently of law) back to back. Lower figures.—Law as a female repentant of jealousy striving to revive dead men in a storm with kisses.

(Preludium.) Los, Orc, and Enitharmon. Below, the winding worm.

(After Preludium.) Orc about to burst from earth, on the left the winding vine of humanity.

(Beginning of the poem—on page 3.) Corn and the vine are indicated on the letters. A released figure floats up with bonds dropping off him. Below, a released family look behind at every step, and see that nature is but a dream. Between the two an angel blows fire from the trumpet of the last judgment.

(On page 4.) War chasing religion. The fall of Vala. Men below call on the rocks to cover them.

(On page 5.) Man, as Ijim, bearing Tiriel on his shoulders between the east and west, between the angel with the flaming sword (who is Tharmas, angel of the tongue), leaving his guard at the Tree of Life, (see " Marriage of Heaven and Hell,") and the eastern angel, Luvah, who " rent the scales from the faint heart of man." (" Vala," Night II., l. 139.)

The balance is natural morality, and the angel who has torn it from the human heart, indicates to man that he should cast his spectre, his moral pride, into the lake of fire. The angel with the flaming sword leaves his guard at the Tree of Life, that all things may appear holy. Then the western gate, that was closed in moral pride, is unclosed.

Below are seen two falling spectres or human errors. " To be an error, and to be cast out, is part of God's plan." The man holding his head as he falls is a Greek philosopher. His thoughts bring only pain now. The other is a different variety of the strong, wicked man, and of all who, head-downwards, reason from the loins as Albion when fallen. The serpent surrounds him, and its tail takes the form of the downward spiral that leads to death, as the senses of Reuben appeared when bent outwards.

(On page 6.) Regeneration. Awakening of Albion. Below are the thistle, newt, and fly, types of mortality.

(On page 7.) Vala, while yet the sinless soul, asleep among the Flocks of Tharmas. ("Vala," Night IX., l. 450.)

(On page 8.) Above, the Spirit of God, as Angel of the Divine presence. Below, the dark waters on which the Spirit brooded, as in Genesis.

(On page 9.) Jehovah, as Humanity, became a weeping infant. ("Jerusalem," p. 81, l. 14.) Around it the void, as a womb, "heaves in enormous circles."

(On page 10.) Orc.

(On page 11.) What is innocence on earth is freedom in the air. The power of Childhood over the Serpent, is that of Manhood over the Bird. The Swan is used in design only here, in "Jerusalem," p. 11, and in its black and diabolic form on p. 71. It is mentioned as a symbol of purity and happiness in "Vala," Night V., p. 194.

(On page 12.) Urizen in the North,—or Old Age. Companion picture to that on p. 6, and other half of the design as given in Blair's grave.

(On page 13.) Oothoon rent by the eagles above. Below, Theotormon devoured by his own jealousy and drowned in his own melancholy.

(On page 14.) Natural Religion. The woman is Rahab. The serpent is Nature. The tree is Mystery. The youth adoring her and listening to her teaching, rests his elbow on a closed Bible.

(On page 15.) The fires of vegetation,—the wine-bearing flames.

(On page 16.) Natural Religion again,—Earth worshipping the void, and the people on her doing the same. This is an old Vala, with her locks spread on the pavement. Below, the inhabitants find themselves among the branches of a snake-bearing thorn tree, whose flowers are lilies.

TO EUROPE.

1. (Frontispiece.) Los as Urizen dividing the space of love with brazen compasses. ("Jerusalem," p. 88, l. 47.) He has here the attributes of Urizen the Architect. He is in the Sun, as Angel of the Divine presence. The symbol is that of the male powers dividing the female, wherever found, whether as the Spirit of God in Genesis on the Dark Waters, or in any minor vision.

The idea is as follows. God, when including all things, was motionless, because motion implies division of the universe into a whence and a whither. He could not desire to move, but he could desire to divide. He divided into Time and Space. As Time, Angel of the Sun, he then desired to generate, and divided Space, who was seen to be female, and whose unity was virginity while her division, so accomplished, was fructification. Thus the sexes are not the image of original Godhead, but of God and the external, or divided Godhead. Thus they are not eternal, and will vanish and cease when the original unity is restored.

2. (title-page.) The Serpent.

3. (page 1.) The idiot questioner who sits so sly, like a thief in a cave. ("Milton," p. 43, ll. 12 to 20.)

Below, a spectre from Vision, first sketched in the MS. book, and a man dragged head-down, or out into the world of experience by the iron weight of love.

4. (page 2.) Elemental spirits of the air.

5. (on page 3.) On the top two groups contrast bodily and mental ideas of

love. In the first Jerusalem (naked) is dragging Vala (clothed) heavenwards. In the second, two winged figures kiss freely. Below an angel flies weeping. Type of inspiration in a corporeal region. At foot of page Urizen released from chains glowing like a meteor in the distant north.

6. (on page 4.) It is difficult to be certain here that the figure lying on its face with flames issuing from its hair is female. On the presumption that it is so, conjecture would explain the design as a repetition of the little group on the title-page,—a contrast between mortality and imagination, morality and liberty, body and spirit veiled, and unveiled,—Vala and Jerusalem.

7. (page 5.) The spectre as Og. Angels of pity and compassion behind him. This seems to have been the figure seen by Blake on the top of his staircase and mistaken by him for a ghost, so that he was frightened and ran away. ("Memoir," p. 47.) The lithograph of this design does not do it justice.

8. (on page 6.) This seems to represent Ona returning to her father from the "Song of Experience," A Little Girl Lost. There was only a tree, and no figure on the plate, on which this song is engraved in the original edition.

9. (on page 7.) Usually called Mildews blighting ears of corn. The figures belong to Urizen's "armies of disease."

10. (on page 8.) The very serpent into which thought changed the infinite.

11. (on page 9.) The only allusion to papal dignity in Blake's writings is to be found in "Jerusalem," p. 64, l. 15.

12. (on page 10.) Creatures from the Wine-press of Luvah.

13. (on page 11.) The human fly on page 10, re-drawn as a captive in a dungeon.

14. (on page 12.) Insects again, caterpillar and butterfly, no symbolism seems suggested beyond what usually associates itself with them.

15. (on page 13.) A first form of the group in the centre of the third of the "Job" series. The masculine, or intellect, saving the feminine, or body, and the infantile or innocent from the fire of corporeal destruction. In the copy of "Europe" in the British Museum are some extra designs not belonging to the poem, and some MS. notes from various poets given as the subjects of the illustrations.

TO JERUSALEM.

1. (on page 1.) "Los took his globe of fire to search the interior of Albion's bosom" (p. 31, l. 2).

2. (Title-page.) Jerusalem in various positions as "all Beulah." The figures are described when watching over Albion in "Vala," Night VIII., ll. 7 to 15.

3. (on page 4.) Law, as the veiled figure of Vala or Rahab clutching at man. Liberty, as the naked figure of Jerusalem (without wings) setting him free.

4. (on page 6.) Portrait of Blake as a young man, in the character of Los, disputing with his own Pride and Self-Righteousness as his Spectre.

5. (on page 8.) Feminine desire entering the loins in the form of a Fairy dragging the moon along the valley of Cherubim (p. 63, l. 14).

6. (on page 9.) The five senses as the five daughters of Zelophahad—Tirzah and her sisters —" sighing to melt Albion's giant beauty on the moony river."

6. (on page 11.) This has been called Schofield as the man-drake on the Lake of Udan Adan. This has been suggested as the subject, but it has rather

the appearance of an involuntary vision of the Feminine viewed as a combination of Air and Water, East and West, which do not meet as in the title-page of "Heaven and Hell," but mingle as a Leda-Swan.

7. (on page 11.) Vala, or America, as Oothoon, taking " her impetuous course o'er Theotormon's reign."

8. (on page 14.) Masculine and Feminine as the Sleeper, with a daughter of Beulah watching him within the rainbow, whose three colours are those of the three Zoas, Urizen, Luvah, Tharmas (yellow, red, and blue), while his sleep takes the colour of the fourth, who was not slain—Urthona, black.

9. (on page 5.) Abraham fleeing in fires from Chaldea, and Reuben enrooting himself in his loins—the narrow Canaanite valley.

(This is another form of what is also seen as Los opposing with fibres the path of Milton. Abraham had the seed of Christ the Awakener in him. Reuben, the slumberer, tried to take its place.)

10. (on page 18.) Purity and Love, as the Lily and Rose, sending forth their spiritual human forms to meet and mingle.

11. (on page 19.) Albion's children, exiled from his breast, pass to and fro before him. (First line of same page.)

12. (on page 20.) Energy dragging thoughts at the command of instinct.

13. (on page 21.) Accusation, as Hand, driving natural instinct, as daughters of Albion, with repentance, as scourges, through moral law, as the streets of Babylon. (Line 30 of the same page.)

14. (on page 22.) The female sendeth forth love as an angel from her body.

15. (on page 22.) Punishment and Forgiveness weaving rival veils. (Last lines of the same page.)

16. (on page 23.) A weary feminine spirit resting from the task of supplying animal forces to man, by managing his digestion.

17. (on page 23.) Urizen in the form of multitudes of prisoners in Urthona's dens,—or Los roofed (by the affections read from the understanding) in Albion's cliffs.

18. (on page 24.) The moon, a ship in the British ocean (p. 56, l. 18).

19. (on page 25.) The daughters of Albion weeping and weaving his body of vegetation.

20. (on page 26.) Jerusalem perceiving with astonishment that Hand himself, the great accuser and destructive reasoner, is clothed with the flames of desire.

21. (on page 28.) Jerusalem and Vala made one through love and innocence in the Lily of Havilah.

22. (on page 30.) Urthona and Enitharmon about to enter the bosom of Los (Line 16 of the same page.)

23. (on page 32.) Jerusalem asking Vala, with tears, what is sin (p. 20, l. 21).

24. Reason, as Urizen in old age, laboriously ploughing the earth.

24. (on page 35.) Creation of Eve.

25. (on page 37.) The Divine Saviour receiving the pale limbs of man's eternal individuality in His arms, and reposing them on the Rock of Ages (p. 48, ll. 1 to 3; also "Vala," I., 393). Between the oak of weeping and the palm of suffering is seen in the background a portion of that mighty wall the Veil of Moral Law, or of Vala, which in process of time became the beautiful Mundane Shell (p. 59, ll. 2 to 9).

26. (on page 37.) The Spectre howling over the body, and in particular the spectre of Los prevented from devouring Enitharmon (p. 18, l. 17).

27. (on page 39.) Death and despair, as an archer of three bows and a sunset.

28. (on page 41.) Death and despair again expressed in the attitude of a man in his Spectre's power.

29. (on page 42.) The human vine.

30. (on page 44.) Angels pointing out the holiness of the organs of generation, seen as a winged ark. Below, the serpent revealing himself as animated vegetation, the head, devouring the body, passing from flames to leaves.

31. (on page 45.) The net and veil of Vala among the souls of the dead (p. 42, l. 81), seen as veins, twigs and cords, which grow out of a humanized earth, as the result of rain poured on it by a cloud, whose human, or female, form floats away after doing its work. In general it is the male, when fallen, and become captive of the female, who from childhood spreads nets in every path. The female, as elsewhere, is the blood of man,—the male, his mind. Below, fishes devour one another. In woman's world life lives on death.

32. (on page 46.) The regenerate man served by nature as a serpent-wheeled chariot, drawn by human-headed horses—intellectual powers—goaded by gnomes with pens, and guided by hands which grow from their heads. These are the "living creatures of the plough."

33. (on page 47.) The sufferings of the flesh in restraint, as Albion turning from Jerusalem and casting down Vala. He is seated on the rock of despair, by which man is separate from man (p. 28, ll. 10 to 12), and treading on a cloud—his own blood ("Vala," Night IX., l. 276). The Male figure stands also for each Zoa casting out or down his counterpart.

34. (on page 50.) Hand on Albion's cliffs and his brethren.

35. (on page 51.) Vala, Hyle, and Schofield.

36. (on page 53.) The mixture of love and jealousy called by the female Religion, as Vala, the triple-crowned, being also Rahab, and Babylon, or Mystery, enthroned on the sunflower, type of mental desire in physical organs.

37. (on page 54.) Albion as a rock hurled from eternity.

38. (on page 54.) The giants who formed this world into its sensuous existence, and now live here in chains (as in "Marriage of Heaven and Hell").

39. (on page 57.) Female forms of cities,—York, London, and Jerusalem.

40. (on page 58.) A spectre.

41. (on page 58.) The mortal consumed.

42. (on page 59.) The females spinning,—or sensuous experience, weaving rational ideas, called the body, in sorrow.

43. (on page 62.) Spectre of Tharmas in torment; image of eternal death humanized.

44. (on page 63.) Mortality triumphant over experience without mind,—or the winding worm and the female, Hyle and Guendolen.

45. (on page 64.) Daughter of Beulah taking care that the sleeper does not fall into the abyss.

45. (on page 64.) The sleeper pretending to be awake, and in the abyss in spite of them, reading the scriptures in a literal sense.

46. (on page 65.) The chain of jealousy.

47. (on page 66.) A daughter of Albion and her victim.

48. (on page 67.) A victim as Orc chained to the rock.

49. (on page 69.) A victim sacrificed on Druid rocks,—his brain cut round with flint, and his senses shrunk from imagination by the cruelties of the female, experience.

50. (on page 70.) Bacon, Newton, and Locke as the triple female going under a Druid arch. The dark moon in the sky.

51. (on page 71.) Spectre and Emanation divided, and both faint and miserable.

52. (on page 72.) The world of Los.

53. (on page 73.) Los at the forge.

54. (on page 74.) Reuben taking root.

55. (on page 75.) War, the Hermaphrodite, as Rahab, the Dragon, and Harlot.

56. (on page 76.) Christ as the Humanity of Luvah bound down on the stems of generation to die a death of six thousand years. The spirit of prophecy worshipping.

57. (on page 78.) A watcher, as Albion on his rock in the first winter. His head, the crested cock, one of the forms of life offered to the Spectre who takes refuge in the human form, finally.

58. (on page 80.) Giving the worm a form of love (p. 82, l. 14).

59. (on page 81.) Guendolen hiding a falsehood behind her loins, and speaking to her sisters (page 86, ll. 82 and following).

60. (on page 82.) Hyle.

60. (on page 83.) Reuben wandering.

61. (on page 84.) London, blind and age bent, "begging through the streets of Babylon" (led by a child), or humanity under morality asking a little food of love, and guided by innocence to where this may be obtained (line 11 of the same page).

62. (on page 85.) The female as the emanation weaving the vine by which man is adjoined to his fellow man.

63. (on page 87.) Enion, blind and age bent, seeking Los and Enitharmon in vain. Tharmas old, lamenting her absence. ("Vala," Night I., l. 181.)

64. (on page 91.) Man between passion and instinct,—the blood-dropping sun, and the cornfield englobing.

65. (on page 92.) Jerusalem in Babylon, weeping.

66. (on page 93.) The three-fold female as three males or Satan accusing the just, and the fiery male as one female in the grave consumed.

67. (on page 94.) The three-fold female as the Satanic Hand, or Bacon, Newton, and Locke, cast down.

68. (on page 94.) England awaking on Albion's bosom (line 20, same page).

69. (on page 95.) Albion arising (line 5, same page), also Urizen arising,—("Vala," Night IX., l. 189, &c.) Also Blake casting off the rotten rags of memory by inspiration,—("Milton," p. 43, l. 4). Also the renewal of the soul as in Blair's grave.

70. (on page 96.) Wisdom and love united, as God and Jerusalem.

71. (on page 97.) The regenerate man.

72. (on page 98.) Outcast forms of lower nature.

73. (on page 99.) Love rescued from nature, or salvation of Vala, who was not "left in the gnawing grave," but, like "Babylon, come up to Jerusalem," was "elevated inwards."

74. (on page 100.) Sun, Time, and Moon. Behind, the Druid Serpent Temple.

TO MILTON.

1. (on page 1.) Milton entering his shadow.

2. (on page 3.) Milton as a star. Below, the corn and vine of the human harvest.

3. (on page 4.) A traveller passing through the state called Satan, or Eternal Death,—the Druid Law.

4. (on page 8.) Los, Enitharmon, and Orc. Time, Space, and Man.

5. (on page 13.) Milton ungirding himself of the oath of God.

6. (on page 15.) Milton struggling with Urizen.

7. (on page 16.) Milton's three wives and three daughters.

8. (on page 16.) Los opposing with fibres the path of Milton.

9. (on page 21.) Los in the Sun behind Blake.

10. (on page 24.) Creatures from the Wine-press of Luvah.

11. (on page 26.) Albion's rocks.

12. (on page 29.) Milton entering Blake by the foot (or lower portion of the imagination).

13. (on page 32.) The Four Zoas, or Universes, or regions of Humanity, and the egg of Los. A diagram.

14. (on page 33.) Milton entering Robert Blake.

15. (on page 36.) Ololon entering Blake's cottage at Felpham.

16. (on page 38.) Man in mortality, on the rock, the finite wall of flesh, in the sea of time and space.—A more complete vision of this is described in "Vala," Night VIII., ll. 505 to 515.

17. (on page 41.) "But I, thy Magdalen, behold thy spiritual risen body." ("Jerusalem," p. 62, l. 14.) "Oh, Melancholy Magdalen, behold the morning over Malden break." ("Jerusalem," p. 65, l. 38.)

18. (on page 43.) Milton performing the journey of Urizen through the dens of Urthona. ("Vala," Night VI., l. 252.)

19. (on page 42.) The waters of life,—joy.

20. (on page 44.) The waters of death,—sorrow.

21. (on page 45.) The Human harvest.

TO VALA.

The productions here given are chosen from the most interesting and least scribbled of about sixty. The greater number are so slight as to represent little to any eye but that of the artist.

Man bearing the sun on his head, surrounded by the four Zoas, as four states of himself, seems to have been intended as the subject. The crouched figures are hardly intelligible. The floating form on the right will be recognised as belonging to the Book of Urizen.

1. Vala.

2. Desire.

3. Obedience or restraint.

4. Vala growing up, and becoming a dragon. (Night II., l. 78.)

5. Albion seeing his softer passions outside of himself in odorous stupefaction.

6. Urizen as a dragon. (Night VIII., l. 419.)

8. When the sons of Urizen have wielded the scythe (of the south), the corn lies on the ground.

9. On the rock. (Pencil shading in the background of an early date, but seemingly not by Blake's hand, obliterates the proof that in the design as first drawn this figure was masculine.)

10. Vala exalting her power even to the stars.

11. The Prester Serpent.

12. Enitharmon and Los.

13. The spectre as the cock.—The crest omitted. Compare " Milton," p. 27, l. 24.

14. Chaste youth.

15. The female turning the circle of the eyes of God. She is the labourer at the Nine Months with which the Seven Eyes, when Elohim is triple, are counted.

FROM THE MS. BOOK.

1. " As Daphne was root-bound." This sketch has been chosen as the most elegant and least formless of the little pencil sketches made in the MS. book while it was still a sketch book.

2. " —— reared his mighty stature." This was the first design for the " Fire," afterwards engraved in the Gates of Paradise, of which there is a copy in the Print-Room of the British Museum.

3. Mrs. Blake dressing. This is sketched on the title-page designed for the " Ideas of Good and Evil." Those words may be faintly traced above it. These little artistic fragments are gathered from three separate pages of the MS. book. See Vol. I., p. 208.

4. The flying figure with the human being in its mouth is thus repeated by Blake, on several pages, growing larger with each repetition. The vision seems to have actually appeared to approach the artist as he contemplated it,— " coming on with all the fury of a spiritual existence." The subject seems taken from the " Screw-much " lines printed in the Memoir, p. 78.

5. A doubled-up figure sketched five times. Was evidently drawn also from a vision that developed itself as contemplated. One form is given wings, and produced on page 1 of " Europe." The most developed shape suggests the " enormity " called " Luvah-and-Vala."

6. Below is seen, apparently, Urizen flying away with a debilitated Vala, Reason capturing Beauty and Art, or Cromek, as he imagined himself, with the soul of Stothard as Blake perceived it.

7. The full-page illustration representing a monster with protruded tongue, carrying a helmet in one hand and a sting in the other, is copied, and only slightly reduced from the full-length painting, now very dark, of the " Ghost of a Flea," also called " A Vampire," and really signifying the military spirit, or the ideal form of bloodthirstiness. That even this is a " fallen son of Eden " is indicated by the falling star in the background.

The engravings from Blair's Grave are described in the Memoir, p. 110.

The Laocoon engraving is referred to in the Memoir, p. 120.

A DESCRIPTIVE CATALOGUE

OF

PICTURES

Poetical and Historical Inventions

PAINTED BY

WILLIAM BLAKE

IN

WATER COLOURS

BEING THE ANCIENT METHOD OF

FRESCO PAINTING RESTORED

AND DRAWINGS FOR

PUBLIC INSPECTION

AND

𝔉𝔬𝔯 𝔖𝔞𝔩𝔢 𝔟𝔶 𝔓𝔯𝔦𝔟𝔞𝔱𝔢 ℭ𝔬𝔫𝔱𝔯𝔞𝔠𝔱

London : Printed by D. N. Shury, 7 Berwick Street, Golden Square. 1809.

CONDITIONS OF SALE.

I. *One third of the Price to be paid at the time of Purchase and the remainder on Delivery.*

II. *The Pictures and drawings to remain in the Exhibition till its close, which will be on the 29th September, 1809. And the Picture of the Canterbury Pilgrims, which is to be engraved, will be sold only on condition of its remaining in the artist's hands twelve months, when it will be delivered to the Buyer.*

PREFACE.

THE eye that can prefer the Colouring of Titian and Rubens to that of Michael Angelo and Rafael ought to be modest and to doubt its own powers. Connoisseurs talk as if Rafael and Michael Angelo had never seen the colouring of Titian or Correggio. They ought to know that Correggio was born two years before Michael Angelo, and Titian but four years after. Both Rafael and Michael Angelo knew the Venetians and contemned and rejected all he did with the utmost disdain, as that which is fabricated with the purpose to destroy art.

Mr. B. appeals to the Public from the judgments of those narrow blinking eyes that have too long governed art in a dark corner. The eyes of stupid cunning never will be pleased with the work, any more than with the look, of self-devoting genius. The quarrel of the Florentine with the Venetian is not because he does not understand Drawing, but because he does not understand Colouring. How should he who does not know how to draw a hand or a foot know how to colour it.

Colouring does not depend on where the colours are put, but on where the lights and darks are put, and all depends on Form or Outline,—on where that is put. Where that is wrong, colouring can never be right, and it is always wrong in Titian and Correggio, Rubens and Rembrandt. Till we get rid of Titian and Correggio, Rubens and Rembrandt we shall never equal Rafael, and Albert Durer, Michael Angelo, and Julio Romano.

No. I.

The spiritual form of Nelson guiding Leviathan in whose wreathings are enfolded the nations of the Earth.

Clearness and precision have been the chief objects in painting these pictures. Clear colours, unmudded by oil, and firm, determinate lineaments, unbroken by shadows, which ought to display and not to hide form, as is the practice of the latter schools of Italy and Flanders.

No. II.—*Its Companion.*

The spiritual form of Pitt guiding Behemoth. He is that Angel who, pleased to perform the Almighty's orders, rides on the whirlwind, directing the storms of war. He is ordering the reaper to reap the vine of the Earth, and the Ploughman to plough up the Cities and Towers.

This picture is also a proof of the power of colours unsullied with oil or with any cloggy vehicle. Oil has falsely been supposed to give strength to colours. But a little consideration must show the falsity of this opinion. Oil will not drink or absorb colour enough to stand the test of very little time and of the air. It deadens every colour it is mixed with at its first mixture, and in a little time becomes a yellow mask over all that it touches. Let the works of modern artists since Ruben's time witness the villany of some one of that time who first brought oil painting into general opinion and practice; since which we have never had a picture painted which could show itself by the side of an earlier production. Whether Rubens or Vandyke, or both were guilty of this villany is to be inquired in another work on painting, and who first forged the silly story and known falsehood about John of Bruges inventing oil colours; in the meantime let it be observed that before Vandyke's time and in his time, all the genuine pictures are on plaster or whiting grounds, and none since.

The two pictures of Nelson and Pitt are compositions of a mythological cast, similar to those Apotheoses of Persian, Hindoo, and Egyptian Antiquity which are still preserved on rude monuments, being copies from some stupendous

originals now lost, or perhaps buried till some happier age.   The artist having
been taken in vision into the ancient republics, monarchies, and patriarchates of
Asia has seen those wonderful originals, called in the sacred scriptures the
Cherubim, which were sculptured and painted on walls of Temples, Towers,
Cities, Palaces, and erected in the highly cultivated states of Egypt, Moab, Edom,
Aram, among the Rivers of Paradise—being the originals from which the Greeks
and Hetruvians copied Hercules Farnese, Venus of Medicis, Apollo Belvedere,
and all the grand works of ancient art.   They were executed in a very superior
style to those justly admired copies, being, with their accompaniments, terrific
and grand in the highest degree.   The artist has endeavoured to emulate the
grandeur of those seen in his vision, and to apply it to modern Heroes on a
smaller scale.

No man can believe that either Homer's Mythology or Ovid's was the production of Greece or Latium; neither will any one believe that the Greek
statues, as they are called, were the invention of Greek Artists: perhaps the
Torso is the only original work remaining; all the rest being evidently copies,
though fine ones, from the greater works of the Asiatic Patriarchs.   The Greek
Muses are daughters of Mnemosyne or Memory, and not of Inspiration or
Imagination, therefore not authors of such sublime conceptions.   Those wonderful originals seen in my visions, were, some of them, one hundred feet in
height: some were painted as pictures, and some carved as basso-relievos and
some as groups of statues, all containing mythological and recondite meaning,
when more is meant than meets the eye.   The Artist wishes it was now the
fashion to make such monuments, and then he should not doubt of having a
national commission to execute these two Pictures, on a scale that is suitable to
the grandeur of the nation who is the parent of his heroes, in high finished
fresco, where the colours would be as pure and as permanent as precious stones,
though the figures were one hundred feet in height.

All Frescoes are as high-finished as miniatures or enamels, and they are
known to be unchangeable; but oil, being a body itself, will drink, or absorb
very little colour, and changing yellow, and at length brown, destroys every
colour it is mixed with, especially every delicate colour.   It turns every
permanent white to a yellow and brown putty, and has compelled the use of
that destroyer of colour, white lead, which when its protecting oil is evaporated,
will become lead again.   This is an awful thing to say to Oil Painters: they
may call it madness, but it is true.   All genuine old Little Pictures, called
Cabinet Pictures, are in fresco and not in oil.   Oil was not used except by
blundering ignorance, till after Vandyke's time: but the art of Fresco painting
being lost, oil became a fetter to genius and a dungeon to art.   But one convincing proof among many others that these assertions are true is that real gold
and silver cannot be used with oil as they are in all the old pictures and in
Mr. B's frescoes.

No. III.

*Sir Jeffrey Chaucer and the nine and twenty pilgrims on their journey to
Canterbury.*

The time chosen is early morning, before sunrise, when the jolly company are
leaving the Tabarde Inn.   The Knight and Squire with the Squire's Yeoman

lead the Procession ; next follow the youthful Abbess, her nun, and three priests ;
—her greyhounds attend her,—

> " Of small hounds had she, that she feed
> With roast flesh, milk, and wastel bread."

Next follow the Friar and Monk, and then the Tapiser, the Pardoner, and the
Sompnour and Manciple. After this " Our Host," who occupies the centre of
the cavalcade, and directs them to the Knight, as the person who would be
likely to commence their task of each telling a tale in their order. After the
Host follows the Shipman, the Haberdasher. the Dyer, the Franklin, the
Physician, the Ploughman, the Lawyer, the Poor Parson, the Merchant, the
Wife of Bath, the Miller, the Cook, the Oxford Scholar, Chaucer himself; and
the Reeve comes as Chaucer has described : —

> " And ever he rode hindermost of the rout."

These last are issuing from the gateway of the Inn; the Cook and the wife
of Bath are both taking their morning's draught of comfort. Spectators stand
at the gateway of the Inn, and are composed of an old Man, a Woman, and a
Child.

The Landscape is an eastward view of the country from the Tabarde Inn,
in Southwark, as it may be supposed to have appeared in Chaucer's time ;
interspersed with cottages and villages. The first beams of the sun are seen
above the horizon ; some buildings and spires indicate the position of the Great
City. The Inn is a Gothic building which Thynne in his glossary says was the
lodging of the Abbot of Hyde by Winchester. On the Inn is inscribed its title,
and a proper advantage is taken of this circumstance to describe the subject of
the Picture. The words written over the gateway of the Inn are as follows :—
" The Tabarde Inn, by Henry Baillie, the lodgynge house for Pilgrims who
journey to St. Thomas' Shrine at Canterbury."

The characters of Chaucer's Pilgrims are the characters which compose all ages
and nations. As one age falls another rises different to mortal sight, but to
immortals only the same ; for we see the same characters repeated again and
again, in animals, vegetables, minerals, and in men. Nothing new occurs in
identical existence ; accident ever varies. Substance can never suffer change
or decay.

Of Chaucer's characters as described in his Canterbury Tales some of the
names or titles are altered by time, but the characters themselves ever remain
unaltered ; and consequently they are the physiognomies, or lineaments of
universal human life beyond which Nature never steps. Names alter ; things
never alter. I have known multitudes of those who would have been monks in
the age of monkery, and who in this deistical age are deists. As Newton
numbered the stars and as Linneus has numbered the plants, so Chaucer
numbered the classes of men.

The Painter has consequently varied the heads and forms of his personages
into all Nature's varieties. The horses he has also varied to accord to their
Riders ; the costume is correct according to authentic monuments.

The Knight and the Squire and the Squire's Yeoman lead the procession as
Chaucer has also placed them first in his prologue. The Knight is a true Hero,
a good, great, and wise man ; his whole length portrait on horseback as written

by Chaucer cannot be surpassed.   He has spent his life in the field, has ever been a conqueror, and is that species of character which in every age stands as the guardian of man against the oppressor.   His son is like him with the germ of perhaps greater perfection still as he blends literature and the arts with his warlike studies.   Their dress and their horses are of the first rate, without ostentation, and with all the true grandeur that unaffected simplicity when in high rank always displays.   The Squire's Yeoman is also a great character, a man perfectly knowing in his profession :

> "And in his hand he bore a mighty bow."

Chaucer describes here a mighty man ; one who, in war, is the worthy attendant on noble heroes.

The Prioress follows these with her female chaplain.

> "Another Nonne also with her had she,
> That was her Chapelaine, and Priestes three."

This Lady is described also as of the first rank, rich and honoured.   She has certain peculiarities and little delicate affectations, not unbecoming in her, being accompanied with what is truly grand and really polite : her person and face Chaucer has described with minuteness ; it is very elegant and was the beauty of our ancestors until after Elizabeth's time, when voluptuousness and folly began to be accounted beautiful.

Her companion and her three priests were no doubt all perfectly delineated in those parts of Chaucer's work which are now lost ; we ought to suppose them suitable attendants on rank and fashion.

The Monk follows these with the Friar.   The Painter has also grouped with these the Pardoner and the Sompnour, and the Manciple, and has here also introduced one of the rich citizens of London ; characters likely to ride in company, all being above the common rank of life, or attendants on those who were so.

For the Monk is described by Chaucer as a man of the first rank in society, noble, rich, and expensively attended ; he is a leader of the age, with certain humourous accompaniments in his character that do not degrade but render him an object of dignified mirth,—but also with other accompaniments not so respectable.

The Friar is a character of a mixed kind :

> "A Friar there was, a wanton and a merry ; "

but in his office he is said to be a 'full solemn man ;' eloquent, amorous, witty, and satirical ; young, handsome, and rich ; he is a complete rogue, with constitutional gaiety enough to make him a master of all the pleasures in the world.

> " His neck was white as the flour de lis,
> Thereto was he strong as a champioun."

It is necessary here to speak of Chaucer's own character that I may set certain mistaken critics right in their conception of the humour and fun that occur on the journey.   Chaucer himself is the great poetic observer of men who in every age is born to record and eternize its acts. This he does as a master, as a father, and superior, who looks down on their little follies, from the Emperor to the Miller, sometimes with severity, oftener with joke and sport.

Accordingly Chaucer has made his monk a great tragedian, one who studied poetical art. So much so that the generous Knight is, in the compassionate dictates of his soul compelled to cry out:—

> " Ho," quoth the Knyght,—" good sir, no more of this;
> That ye have said is right ynough I wis,
> And mokell more; for little heaviness
> Is right enough for much folk, as I guesse.
> I say, for me, it is a great disease.
> Whereas men have been in wealth and case
> To heare of their sudden fall,—alas!
> And the contrary is joy, and solas."

The Monk's definition of tragedy in the proem to his tale is worth repeating:—

> " Tragedie is to tell a certain story,
> As old books us maken memory,
> Of hem that stood in great prosperity,
> And (who) be fallen out of high degree
> To miserie, and ended wretchedly."

Though a man of luxury pride and pleasure he is a master of art and learning though affecting to despise it. Those who think that the proud Huntsman and Noble Housekeeper Chaucer's Monk is intended for a buffoon or a burlesque character, know little of Chaucer.

For the Host who follows this group, and holds the centre of the cavalcade, is a first-rate character, and his jokes are no trifles; they are always,—though uttered with audacity, equally free with the Lord and the Peasant,—they are always substantially and weightily expressive of knowledge and experience; Henry Baillie, the keeper of the greatest Inn of the greatest City, for such was the Tabarde Inn in Southwark, near London,—our Host was also a leader of the age.

By way of illustration I instance Shakespeare's Witches in Macbeth. Those who dress them for the stage consider them as wretched old women, and not, as Shakespeare intended, the Goddesses of Destiny. This shows how Chaucer has been misunderstood in his sublime work. Shakespeare's Fairies, also, are the rulers of the vegetable world, and so are Chaucer's. Let them be so understood and then the poet will be understood, and not else.

But I have omitted to speak of a very prominent character, the Pardoner, the Age's Knave, who always commands and domineers over the high and low vulgar. This man is sent in every age for a rod and scourge, and for a blight, for a trial of men, to divide the classes of men. He is in the most holy sanctuary, and he is suffered by Providence, for wise ends, and has also his great use and his grand leading destiny.

His companion, the Sompnour, is also a Devil of the first magnitude, grand, terrific, rich; and honoured in the rank of which he holds the destiny. The uses to Society are perhaps equal of the Devil and the Angel. Their sublimity, who can dispute.

> " In danger had he at his own gise,
> The yonng girls of his diocese,
> And he knew well their counsel,"—&c.

The principal figure in the next group is the Good Parson; an Apostle, a real Messenger of Heaven, sent in every age for its light and its warmth. The man is beloved and venerated by all and neglected by all. He serves all and is served by none. He is according to Christ's definition the greatest of his age, yet he is a Poor Parson of a town. Read Chaucer's description of the Good Parson and bow the head and knee to Him, Who in every age sends us such a burning and a shining light. Search O ye rich and powerful for these men and obey their counsel; then shall the golden age return. But alas! you will not easily distinguish him from the Friar, or the Pardoner. They, also, are "full solemn men," and *their* counsel you will continue to follow.

I have placed by his side the Sergeant at Lawe who appears delighted to ride in his company, and between him and his brother the Ploughman, as I wish men of law would always ride with them, and take their counsel, especially in all difficult points. Chaucer's Lawyer is a character of great venerableness, a Judge, a real master of the jurisprudence of his age.

The Doctor of Physic is in this group, and the Franklin the voluptuous country gentleman, contrasted with the Physician, and on his other hand, with two Citizens of London. Chaucer's characters live age after age. Every age is a Canterbury Pilgrimage. We all pass on, each sustaining one or other of these characters, nor can a child be born who is not one or other of these characters of Chaucer. The Doctor of Physic is described as the first of his profession; perfect, learned, completely Master and Doctor in his art. Thus the reader will observe that Chaucer makes every one of his characters perfect in his kind. Every one is an Antique Statue, the image of a class, not of an imperfect individual.

This group also would furnish substantial matter on which volumes might be written. The Franklin is one who keeps open table, who is the genius of eating and drinking, like Bacchus. As the Doctor of Physic is the Æsculapius, the Host is the Silenus, the Squire is the Apollo, the Miller is the Hercules, &c. Chaucer's characters are a description of the eternal Principles that exist in all ages. The Franklin is voluptuousness itself, most nobly portrayed.—

> " It snewed in his house of meat and drink."

The Ploughman is simplicity itself with wisdom and strength for its stamina. Chaucer has divided the ancient character of Hercules between his Miller and his Ploughman. Benevolence is the Ploughman's great characteristic. He is thin with excessive labour, and not with old age, as some have supposed:

> " He would threash, and thereto dike and delve,
> For Christe's sake, for every poure wight,
> Withouten hire, if it lay in his might."

Visions of these eternal principles or characters of human life appear to poets in all ages. The Grecian gods were the ancient Cherubim of Phœnicia, but the Greeks, and since them, the Moderns, have neglected to subdue the gods of Priam. These gods are visions of the eternal attributes or divine names, which, when erected into gods become destructive to humanity. They ought to be the servants and not the masters of man or of society. They ought to be made to sacrifice to Man and not man compelled to sacrifice to them; for

when separated from man. or humanity, who is Jesus, the Saviour, the vine of
eternity? They are thieves and rebels; they are destroyers.

The Ploughman of Chaucer is Hercules in his supreme eternal state, divided
from his spectrous shadow, which is the Miller, a terrible fellow, such as exists in
at all times and pes for the trial of men, to astonish every neighbourhood
with brutal strength and courage, to get rich and powerful, and to curb the
pride of Man.

The Reeve and the Manciple are two characters of consummate worldly
wisdom. The Shipman, or Sailor, is a similar genius of Ulyssean art, but with
the highest courage superadded.

The Citizens and their cook are each leaders of a class. Chaucer has been
somehow made to number four citizens, which would make his whole company,
himself included, thirty one. But he says there were but nine and twenty in his
company,—

"Full nine-and-twenty in a company"

The Webbe, or Weaver, and the Tapiser, or Tapestry Weaver, appear to me
to be the same person, but this is only an opinion, for 'full nine-and-twenty'
may signify one more or less. But I daresay that Chaucer wrote, "A webbe
dyer" that is, a Cloth dyer:—

"A Webbe Dyer, and a Tapiser."

The Merchant cannot be one of the Three Citizens, as his dress is different
and his character is more marked, whereas Chaucer says of his rich citizen

"All were y-clothed in o liveric."

The characters of Women, Chaucer has divided into two classes, the Lady
Prioress, and the Wife of Bath. Are not these leaders of the ages of men?
The Lady Prioress in some ages predominates, and in some the Wife of Bath, in
whose character Chaucer has been equally minute and exact, because she is also
a scourge and a blight. I shall say no more of her, nor expose what Chaucer
has left hidden. Let the young reader study what he has said of her. It is
useful as a scare-crow. There are such characters born,—too many for the
peace of the world.

I come at length to the Clerk of Oxenford. This character varies from that
of Chaucer as the contemplative philosopher varies from the poetical genius.
There are always these two classes of learned sages, the poetical and the philo-
sophical. The painter has put them side by side as if the youthful clerk had
put himself under the tuition of the mature poet. Let the Philosopher always
be the servant and scholar of inspiration and all will be happy.

Such are the characters that compose this picture which was painted in self-
defence against the insolent and envious imputation of unfitness for finished
and scientific art,—and this imputation most artfully and industriously
endeavoured to be propagated among the public by ignorant hirelings. The
painter courts comparison with his competitors, who, having received fourteen
hundred guineas and more, from the profits of *his* designs in that well-known
work Designs for Blair's Grave, have left him to shift for himself, while others,
more obedient to an employer's opinions and directions, are employed at great
expense to produce works in succession to his, by which they acquired public

patronage. This has hitherto been his lot, to get patronage for others and then to be left and neglected, and his work, which gained that patronage, cried down as eccentricity and madness,—as unfinished and neglected by the artist's violent temper. He is sure the works now exhibited will give the lie to such aspersions.

Those who say that men are lead by interest are knaves. A knavish character will often say,—" Of what interest is it to me to do——so and so ? " I answer, " Of none at all, but the contrary, as you well know. It is of malice and envy that you have done this, therefore I am aware of you, because I know that you act, not from interest, but from malice, even to your own destruction." It is therefore become a duty which Mr. B. owes to the Public, who have always recognised him, and patronised him, however hidden by artifices, that he should not suffer such things to be done, or be hindered from the public exhibition of his finished production by any calumnies in future.

The character and expression in this picture could never have been produced with Rubens' light and shadow or with Rembrandt's or anything Venetian or Flemish. The Venetian and Flemish practise is broken lines, broken masses, and broken colours : Mr. B.'s practise is unbroken lines, unbroken masses, and unbroken colours. Their art is to lose form. His art is to find form and keep it. His arts are opposite to theirs in all things.

As there is a class of men whose sole delight is the destruction of, so there is a class of artist whose sole art and science is fabricated for the purpose of destroying Art. Who these are is well known. " By their works ye shall know them." All who endeavour to raise up a style against Raphael, Michel Angelo, and the Antique, those who separate Painting from Drawing, who look if a picture is well drawn, and, if it is, immediately cry out that it cannot be well coloured,—those are the men.

But to show the stupidity of this class of men nothing need be done but to examine my rival's prospectus.

The five first characters in Chaucer, the Knight and the Squire he has put among his rabble, and indeed his prospectus calls the Squire the " fop of Chaucer's age." Now hear Chaucer,—

> ' Of his stature he was of even length,
> And wonderly deliver, and of great strength
> And he had been some time in chivauelry,
> In Flanders, in Artois, and in Piccardy,
> And borne him well, as of so litele space,'

Was this a fop ?

> ' Well could he sit a horse, and faire ride,
> He could songs make, eke well indite
> Joust, and eke dance, portray, and well write,'

Was this a fop ?

> ' Curteis he was, and meek and servicable,
> And kerft before his fader at the table.'

Was this a fop ?

It is the same with all his characters. He had done all by chance, or perhaps his fortune,—money, money! According to his prospectus he has three monks. These he cannot find in Chaucer who has only One Monk, and that, no vulgar character, as he has deavoured to make him. When men cannot read they

should not pretend to paint. To be sure Chaucer is a little difficult to him who
has only blundered over novels, and catch-penny trifles of booksellers, yet a
little pains ought to be taken even by the ignorant and weak. He has put the
Reeve, a vulgar fellow, between his Knight and Squire, as if he was resolved to
go contrary to everything in Chaucer who says of the Reeve,

> ' And ever he rode hindermost of the rout.'

In this manner he has jumbled his dumb dollies together and is praised by
his equals for it, for both himself and his friend are equally masters of Chaucer's
language. They both think that the wife of Bath is a young, beautiful, bloom-
ing damsel, and H—— says, that she is the ' Fair Wife of Bath,' and that ' the
Spring appears in her cheeks." Now hear what Chaucer has made her say of
herself,—who is no modest one.

> But Lord (Christ) when (that) it remembreth me
> Upon my youth and on my jolcity
> It tickleth me about the hearte-root,
> Unto this day it doth my hearte boot
> That I have had my world as in my time,
> But age, alas, that all will envenime
> Hath me breft my beauty and my pith,
> Let go! Farewell! The Devil go therewith,
> The flour is gone; there is no more to tell
> The bran, as best I can, I now mote sell.
> And yet to be right merry I will fond,—
> Now forth, to tell about my fourth husband."

She has had four husbands; a fit subject for this painter. Yet the painter
ought to be very much offended with his friend H——, who has called his, ' a
common scene,' and ' very ordinary forms,' which is the truest part of all, for
it is so, and very wretchedly so indeed. What merit can there be in a picture
of which such words are spoken with truth ?

But the prospectus says that the painter has represented Chaucer himself
as a knave who thrusts himself among honest people to make game of and
laugh at them; though I must do justice to the painter and say that he has
made him look more like a fool than a knave. But it appears in all the writings
of Chaucer, and particularly in his Canterbury Tales that he was very devout,
and paid respect to true enthusiastic superstition. He has laughed at his knaves
and fools, as I do now, but he has respected his True Pilgrims, who are a
majority of his company, and are not thrown together in the random manner
that Mr. S—— has done. Chaucer has nowhere called the ploughman old, worn
out with ' age and labour' as the prospectus has represented him, and says that
the picture has done so too. He is worn down with labour but not with age.
How spots of brown and yellow, smeared about at random can be either young
or old I cannot see. It may be an old man; it may be a young man ; it may be
anything that a prospectus pleases. But I know that where there are no lineaments there can be no character. And what connoisseurs call touch, I know by
experience must be the destruction of all character and expression and of every
lineament.

The scene of Mr. S——'s picture is by Dulwich Hills, which was not the way to Canterbury, but perhaps the painter thought he would give them a ride round about because they were a burlesque set of scarecrows not worth any man's respect or care.

But the painter's thoughts being always upon gold, he has introduced a character that Chaucer has not, namely, a Goldsmith, for so the prospectus tells us. Why he introduced a Goldsmith and what is the wit, the prospectus does not explain. But it takes care to mention the reserve and modesty of the painter. This makes a good epigram enough—

> Tho fox, the mole, the beetle, and the bat
> By sweet reserve and modesty grow fat.

But the prospectus tells us that the painter has introduced a 'Sea-Captain.' Chaucer has a ship-man, a sailor, a trading Master of a vessel, called by courtesy Captain, as every master of a boat is; but this does not make him a Sea Captain, Chaucer has purposely omitted such a personage, as it only exists in certain periods: it is the soldier by sea. He who would be a soldier in inland nations is a sea-captain in commercial nations.

All is misconceived, and its mis-execution is equal to its misconception. I have no objection to Rubens and Rembrandt being employed, or even to their living in a palace. But it shall not be at the expense of Raphael and Michael Angelo living in a cottage, and in contempt and derision. I have been scorned long enough by these fellows who owe me all that they have. It shall be so no longer;

> I found them blind: I taught them how to see;
> And now they know neither themselves nor me.

No. IV.

The Bard, from Gray.

> On a rock whose haughty brow
> Frown'd o'er old Conway's foaming flood
> Robed in sable garb of woe
> With haggard eyes the Poet stood:
> Loose his beard, and hoary hair,
> Streamed like a meteor to the troubled air,
>
> Weave the warp and weave the woof
> The winding sheet of Edward's race.

Weaving the winding sheet of Edward's race by means of sounds of spiritual music, and its accompanying expressions of spiritual speech, is a bold, and daring, and most masterly conception that the public have embraced and approved with avidity. Poetry consists in these conceptions, and shall painting be confined to the sordid drudgery of fac-simile representations of merely mortal and perishing substances and not be as painting and music are, elevated to its own proper sphere of invention and visionary conception? No: it shall not be so! Painting, as well as poetry and music exists and exults in immortal thoughts. If Mr. B's Canterbury Pilgrims had been done by any other power than that of the poetic visionary it would have been just as dull as his adversary's.

> The Spirits of the murdered bards assist in weaving the deadly woof:
> With me in dreadful harmony they join
> And weave with bloody hands the tissue of thy line.

The connoisseurs and artists who have made objections to Mr. B's mode of representing spirits with real bodies would do well to consider that the Venus, the Minerva, the Jupiter, the Apollo, which they admire in Greek statues are all of them representations of spiritual existences,—of Gods immortal,—to the ordinary perishing organ of sight; and yet they are embodied and organised in solid marble. Mr. B. requires the same latitude, and all is well. The Prophets describe what they saw in Vision as real and existing men, whom they saw with their imaginative and immortal organs; the Apostles the same; the clearer the organ, the more distinct the object. A Spirit and a Vision are not, as the modern philosophy supposes a cloudy vapour, or a nothing. They are organised and minutely articulated beyond all that the mortal and perishing nature can produce. He who does not imagine in stronger and better lineaments and in stronger and better light than his perishing and mortal eye can see, does not imagine at all. The painter of this work asserts that all his imaginations appear to him infinitely more perfect, and more minutely organised than anything seen by his mortal eye. Spirits are organised men. Moderns wish to draw figures without lines and with great and heavy shadows. Are not shadows more unmeaning than lines and more heavy? O who can doubt this?

King Edward and his Queen Eleanor are prostrated, with their horses at the foot of a rock on which the Bard stands; prostrated by the terrors of his harp, on the margin of the river Conway, whose waves bear up a corpse of a slaughtered bard at the foot of the rock. The armies of Edward are seen winding among the mountains.

> ' He wound with toilsome march his long array.'

Mortimer and Gloucester lie spell-bound behind their king.

The execution of this picture is also in water colours, or fresco.

No. V.

The Ancient Britons.

In the last Battle of King Arthur, only Three Britons escaped; these were the Strongest Man, the Beautifullest Man and the Ugliest Man. These three marched through the field, unsubdued, as Gods, and the sun of Britain set, but shall rise again with tenfold splendour when Arthur shall awake from sleep and resume his dominion over earth and ocean.

The three general classes of men who are represented by the most Beautiful, the most Strong, and the most Ugly, could not be represented by any historical facts but those of our own country,—the Ancient Britons,—without violating costume. The Britons (say historians) were naked civilized men, learned, studious, abstruse in thought and contemplation; naked, simple, plain in their acts and manners; wiser than after ages. They were overwhelmed by brutal arms, all but a small remnant. Strength, Beauty, and Ugliness escaped the wreck, and remain for ever unsubdued, age after age.

The British Antiquities are now in the Artist's hands,—all his visionary contemplations relating to his own country and its ancient glory, when it was, as it shall be again the source of learning and inspiration. Arthur was a name for the constellation Arcturus, or Boötes the keeper of the North Pole; and all the fables of Arthur and his Round Table, of the warlike naked Britons, of Merlin, of Arthur's conquest of the whole world, of his death, or sleep, and promise to return again, of the Druid monuments or Temples, of the pavement of Watling Street, of London stone, of the caverns of Cornwall, Wales, Derbyshire and Scotland, of the Giants of Ireland and Britain, of the elemental beings called by us by the general name of Fairies, and of these those who escaped, namely Beauty, Strength, and Ugliness, Mr. B. has in his hands poems of the highest antiquity. Adam was a Druid, and Noah; also Abraham was called to succeed the Druidical age, which began to turn allegoric and mental signification into corporeal command, whereby human sacrifice would have depopulated the earth. All these things are written in Eden. The Artist is an inhabitant of that happy country, and if everything goes on as it has begun, the world of vegetation and generation may expect to be opened again to Heaven, through Eden, as it was in the beginning.

The Strong Man represents the human sublime, the Beautiful Man represents the human pathetic, the Ugly Man represents the human reason. They were originally one man who was fourfold. He was self-divided and his real humanity slain on the stems of generation, and the form of the fourth was like the Son of God. How he became divided is a subject of great sublimity and pathos. The Artist has written it under inspiration, and will, if God please, publish it. It is voluminous and contains the ancient history of Britain, and the world of Satan and Adam.

In the meantime he has painted this Picture, which supposes that in the reign of that British Prince who lived in the fifth century there were remains of those naked Heroes in the Welch Mountains. They are there now. Gray saw them in the person of his Bard on Snowdon. There they dwell in naked simplicity. Happy is he who can see and converse with them above the shadows of generation and death. The Giant Albion was Patriarch of the Atlantic. He is the Atlas of the Greeks: one of those the Greeks called Titans. The stories of Arthur are the acts of Albion, applied to a Prince of the fifth century who conquered Europe, and held the Empire of the world (in the dark age) which the Romans never again recovered. In this picture, believing with Milton the ancient British History, Mr. B. has done as all the ancients did, and all the moderns who are worthy of fame,—given the historical fact in its poetic vigour, so as it always happens, and not in that dull way that some Historians pretend, who, being weakly organised themselves, cannot see either miracle or prodigy. All is, to them, a dull round of probabilities, and possibilities. But the history of all times and places is nothing else but improbabilities, and impossibilities,— what we should say was impossible if we did not see it always before our eyes.

The Antiquities of every Nation under Heaven are no less sacred than those of the Jews. They are the same thing, as Jacob Bryant and all antiquarians have proved. How other antiquities came to be neglected and disbelieved, while those of the Jews are collected and arranged is an inquiry worthy both of the Antiquarian and Divine. All had originally one language and one religion : this was the religion of Jesus, the Everlasting Gospel. Antiquity preaches the Gospel of Jesus. The reasoning historian, turner and twister of causes and consequences, such as Hume, Gibbon, and Voltaire,—cannot with all his artifice turn and twist one fact or disarrange self evident action and reality. Reasons and opinions concerning acts are not history. Acts themselves alone are history, and these are not the exclusive property of either Hume, Gibbon, or Voltaire, Echard, Rapin, Plutarch, or Herodotus. Tell me the Acts, O Historian, and leave me to reason upon them as I please. Away with your reasoning and your rubbish ! All that is not action is not worth reading. Tell me the What : I do not want you to tell me the Why, and the How. I can find that out myself as well as you can, and I will not be fooled by opinions that you please to impose, to disbelieve what you think improbable or impossible. His opinion who does not see spiritual agency is not worth any man's reading. He who rejects a fact because it is improbable must reject all history and retain doubts only.

It has been said to the Artist,—" Take the Apollo for the model of your Beautiful Man, and the Hercules for your Strong Man and the Dancing Faun for your Ugly Man. Now he comes to his trial. He knows that what he does is not inferior to the grandest Antiques. Superior it cannot be, for human power cannot go beyond either what he does or what they have done ; it is the gift of God : it is inspiration and vision. He had resolved to emulate those previous remains of antiquity. He has done so, and the result you behold. His ideas of strength and beauty have not been greatly different. Poetry as it exists now on earth in the various remains of ancient authors, Music, as it exists in old tunes or melodies, Painting and Sculpture as they exist in the remains of Antiquity and in the works of more modern genius,—each is Inspiration, and cannot be surpassed : it is perfect, and eternal. Milton, Shakespeare, Michael Angelo, Raphael, the finest specimens of Ancient Sculpture and Painting and Architecture, Gothic, Grecian, Hindoo, and Egyptian are the extent of the human mind. The human mind cannot go beyond the gift of God,—the Holy Ghost. To suppose that Art can go beyond the finest specimens of Art now in the world is not knowing what Art is. It is being blind to the gifts of the Spirit.

It will be necessary for the painter to say something concerning his ideas of beauty, strength, and ugliness.

The Beauty that is annexed and appended to folly is a lamentable accident and error of the mortal and perishing life. It does but seldom happen. But with this unnatural mixture the sublime Artist can have nothing to do. It is fit for the burlesque. The Beauty proper for sublime art is lineaments, or forms and features that are capable of being the receptacles of intellect. Accordingly the painter has given, in his Beautiful Man, his own idea of intellectual Beauty. The face and limbs that deviate or altar least from infancy to old age, are the face and limbs of the greatest Beauty and perfection.

The Ugly, likewise, when accompanied and annexed to imbecility and disease is a subject for burlesque, and not for historical grandeur. The Artist has imagined his Ugly Man one approaching to the beast in features and form ; his forehead small, without frontals, his jaws large, his nose high on the ridge, and narrow, his chest, and the stamina of his make, comparatively little, and his joints and his extremities large, his eyes with scarce any whites narrow and cunning, and everything tending toward what is truly Ugly, the incapability of intellect.

The Artist has considered his Strong Man as a receptacle of Wisdom, a sublime energiser. His features and limbs do not spindle out into length without strength, nor are they too large and unwieldy for his brain and bosom. Strength consists in accumulation of power to the principal seat, and from thence a regular gradation and subordination. Strength is compactness, not extent nor bulk.

The Strong Man acts from conscious superiority, and marches on in fearless dependence on the divine decrees, raging with the inspirations of a prophetic mind. The Beautiful Man acts from duty, and anxious solicitude for the fate of those for whom he combats. The Ugly Man acts from love of carnage, and delight in the savage barbarities of war, rushing with sportive precipitation into the very jaws of the affrighted enemy.

The Roman soldiers, rolled together in a heap before them, 'like the rolling thing before the whirlwind' show each a different character and a different expression of fear, or revenge, or envy, or blank horror and amazement, or devout wonder and unresisting awe.

The dead and the dying,—Britons naked mingled with armed Romans, strew the field beneath. Among these the last of the Bards who was capable of attending warlike deeds is seen falling, outstretched among the dead and dying, singing to his harp in the pains of death.

Distant among the mountains are Druid Temples similar to Stonehenge. The sun sets behind the mountains, bloody with the day of battle.

The flush of health in flesh exposed to the open air, nourished by the spirits of forests and floods, in that ancient happy period which history has recorded, cannot be like the sickly daubs of Titian or Rubens. Where will the copier of nature as it now is find a civilised man who is accustomed to go naked? Imagination only can furnish us with colouring appropriate, such as is found in the frescoes of Raphael and Michael Angelo. The disposition of forms always directs colouring in true art. As to a modern man, stripped from his load of clothing, he is like a dead corpse. Hence Rubens, Titian, Coreggio and all of that class are like leather and chalk. Their men are like leather and their women like chalk, for the disposition of their forms will not admit of grand colouring. In Mr. B's Britons the blood is seen to circulate in their limbs: he defies competition in colouring.

No. VI.

" A spirit vaulting from a cloud to turn and wind a fiery Pegasus."—Shakespeare. The Horse of Intellect is leaping from the cliffs of Memory and Reasoning. It is a barren Rock. It is also called the Barren Waste of Lock and Newton.

This picture was done many years ago, and was one of the first Mr. B. ever did in Fresco. Fortunately, or rather, providentially he left it unblotted and unblurred, although molested continually by blotting and blurring demons. But he was also compelled to leave it unfinished, for reasons that will appear in the following.

No. VII.

The Goats,—an experiment picture.

The subject is taken from the Missionary voyage, and varried from the literal fact for the sake of picturesque scenery. The savage girls had dressed themselves with vine leaves, and some goats on board the missionary ship stripped them off presently. This picture was painted at intervals, for experiment with the colours, and is laboured to a superabundant blackness. It has, however, that about it which may be worthy the attention of the Artist and connoisseur for reasons that follow.

No. VIII.

The Spiritual Preceptor—an experiment picture.

This subject is taken from the Visions of Emanuel Swedenborg. (Universal Theology, No. 623) The learned who strive to ascend into heaven by means of learning, appear to children like dead horses, when repelled by the celestial spheres.

The works of this visionary are well worthy the attention of Painters and Poets. They are foundations for grand things. The reason they have not been more attended to is because corporeal demons have gained a predominance. Who the leaders of these are will be shown below. Unworthy Men who gain fame among Men continue to govern mankind after death, and in their spiritual bodies oppose the spirits of those who worthily are famous, and, as Swedenborg observes, by entering into disease and excrement, drunkenness, and concupiscence, they possess themselves of the bodies of mortal men, and shut the doors of mind and thought by placing Learning above Inspiration. O Artists, you may disbelieve all this, but it shall be at your own peril.

No. IX.

Satan calling up his legion, from Milton's Paradise Lost: a composition for a more perfect Picture afterwards executed for a Lady of high rank. An experiment Picture.

This Picture was likewise painted at intervals, for experiment on colours without any oily vehicle. It may be worthy of attention, not only on account of its composition but of the great labour which has been bestowed on it,—that is,— three or four times as much as would have finished a more perfect picture. The labour has destroyed the lineaments. It was, with difficulty, brought back to a certain effect, which it had at first, when all the lineaments were perfect.

These pictures among numerous others painted for experiment were the result of temptations and perturbations, seeking to destroy imaginative power, by means of that infernal machine called Chiaro Oscuro, in the hands of Venetian and Flemish Demons, whose enmity to the Painter himself, and to all Artists who study the Florentine and Roman Schools may be removed by an exhibition and exposure of their vile tricks. They cause that everything in art shall become a Machine. They cause that execution shall all be blocked up with brown shadows. They put the original artist in fear and doubt of his own original conception.

The spirit of Titian was particularly active in raising doubts concerning the possibility of executing without a model; and when once he had raised the doubt, it became easy for him to snatch away the vision time after time, for, when the Artist took his pencil to execute his ideas, his power of imagination weakened so much and darkened, that memory of nature, and of Pictures of the various schools possessed his mind instead of appropriate execution resulting from the inventions,—like walking in another man's style, or speaking, or looking in another man's style and manner, unappropriate and repugnant to your own individual character,—tormenting the true Artist till he leaves the Florentine, and adopts the Venetian practice, or does as Mr. B. has done—has the courage to suffer poverty and disgrace till he ultimately conquers.

Rubens is a most outrageous demon, and by infusing the remembrances of his pictures and style of execution, hinders all power of individual thought, so that the man who is possessed of this demon loses all admiration of any other Artist but Rubens, and those who were his imitators and journeymen. He causes the Florentine and Roman Artist to fear to execute, and though the original conception was all fire and animation he loads it with hellish brownness, and blocks up all its gates of light except one, and that one he closes with iron bars, till the victim is obliged to give up the Florentine and Roman practice and adopt the Venetian and Flemish.

Correggio is a soft and effeminate, and consequently most cruel demon, whose whole delight is to cause endless labour to whoever suffers him to enter his mind. The story that is told in all Lives of the Painters about Correggio being poor and but badly paid for his Pictures is altogether false. He was a petty Prince in Italy, and employed numerous journeymen in manufacturing (as Rubens and Titian did) the pictures that go under his name. The manual labour in these pictures of Correggio is immense, and was paid for originally at the immense prices that those who keep manufactories of art always charge to their employers, while they themselves pay their journeymen little enough. But though Correggio was not poor, he will make any true artist so who permits him to enter his mind, and take possession of his affections. He infuses a love of soft and even tints without boundaries, and of endless reflected lights that confuse one another, and hinder all correct drawing from appearing to be correct; for if one of Raphael's or Michael Angelo's figures was to be traced, and Correggio's reflections and refractions to be added to it, there would soon be an end of proportion and strength, and it would be weak and pappy, and lumbering, and thick-headed like his own works; but then it would have softness and evenness, by a twelve-month's labour where a month with judgement would have finished it better and higher; and the poor wretch who executed it would be the Correggio whom the Life-writers have written of,—a drudge and a miserable man, compelled to softness by poverty. I say again, O Artist! you may disbelieve all this but it shall be at your own Peril.

Note.—These experiment pictures have been bruised and knocked about without mercy to try all experiments.

No. X.

The Bramins.—A Drawing.

The subject is Mr. Wilkin translating the Geeta; an ideal design, suggested by the first publication of that part of the Hindoo Scriptures translated by

Mr. Wilkin. I understand that my Costume is incorrect; but in this I plead the authority of the Ancients who often deviated from the Habits to preserve the Manners, as in the instance of Laocoön, who, though a priest, is represented naked.

No. XI.

The Body of Abel found by Adam and Eve ; Cain who was about to bury it fleeing from the face of his parents.—A Drawing.

No. XII.

The soldiers casting Lots for Christ's garment.—A Drawing.

No. XIII.

Jacob's Ladder.—A Drawing.

No. XIV.

The Angels hovering over the Body of Jesus in the Sepulchre.—A Drawing.

The above four drawings, the Artist wishes were in Fresco on an enlarged scale to ornament the altars of churches, and to make England, like Italy, respected by respectable men of other countries on account of Art. It is not the want of Genius, that can hereafter be laid to our charge. The Artist who has done these Pictures and Drawings will take care of that, Let those who govern the Nation take care of the other. The times require that every one should speak out boldly. England expects that every man, should do his duty in Arts as well as in Arms or in the Senate.

No. XV.

Ruth.—A Drawing.

This design is taken from that most pathetic passage in the Book of Ruth, where Naomi having taken leave of her daughters-in-law, with intent to return to her own country. Ruth cannot leave her, but says, " Whither thou goest I will go, and where thou lodgest I will lodge ; thy people shall be my people and thy God my God ; where thou diest I will die, and there will I be buried. God do so to me and more also if aught but death part thee and me."

The distinction that is made in modern times between a painting and a drawing proceeds from ignorance of art. The merit of a Picture is the same as the merit of a drawing. The dauber daubes his drawings ; and he who draws his drawings draws his Pictures. There is no difference between Raphael's cartoons and his frescoes or Pictures, except that the Frescoes or Pictures are more finished. When Mr. B. formerly painted in oil colours his Pictures were shown to certain painters and connoisseurs who said that they were very admirable drawings on canvas, but not Pictures ; but they said the same of Raphael's Pictures. Mr. B. thought this the greatest of compliments though it was meant otherwise. If losing and obliterating the outline constitutes a Picture Mr. B. will never be so foolish as to do one. Such art of losing the

outlines is the art of Venice and Flanders. It loses all character and leaves
what some people call 'expression'; but this is a false notion of expression.
Expression cannot exist without character as its stamina, and neither character
nor expression can exist without form, and determinate outline. Fresco Painting is susceptible of higher finishing than Drawing on Paper or any other
method of Painting. But he must have a strange organisation of sight who
does not prefer a Drawing on Paper to a Daubing in Oil by the same master,
supposing both to be done with equal care.

The great and golden rule of art as well as of life is this;—that the more distinct, sharp, and wiry the boundary line, the more perfect the work of art,—and
the less keen and sharp, the greater is the evidence of weak imagination,
plagiarism, and bungling. Great inventors in all ages knew this. Protogenes
and Apelles knew each other by this line. Raphael, Michael Angelo, and
Albert Durer are known by this and by this alone. The want of this determinate and bounding form evidences the idea of want in the Artist's mind, and
the pretence of the plagiary in all its branches. How do we distinguish the
oak from the beech, the horse from the ox but by the bounding outline?[*] How
do we distinguish one face or countenance from another but by the bounding
line and its infinite inflexion and movements? What is it that builds a house
and plants a garden but the definite and determinate? What is it that dis-
tinguishes honesty from knavery, but the hard and wiry line of rectitude and
certainty in the actions and intentions? Leave out this line, and you leave out
life itself. All is chaos again, and the line of the Almighty must be drawn out
upon it again before man or beast can exist. Talk no more then of Correggio
or Rembrandt, or any of those plagiaries of Venice or Flanders. They were
but the lame imitators of lines drawn by their predecessors, and their works
prove themselves contemptible disarranged imitations, and blundering mis-
applied copies.

No. XVI.
The Penance of Jane Shaw in St. Paul's Church. — A Drawing.

This Drawing was done above Thirty Years ago, and proves to the Author,
and he thinks will prove to any discerning eye, that the productions of our youth
and those of our maturer age are equal in all essential points. If a man is
master of his profession he cannot be ignorant that he is so, and if he is not
employed by those who pretend to encourage art, he will employ himself, and
laugh in secret at the pretences of the ignorant, while he has every night
dropped into his shoe,—as soon as he puts it off, and puts out the candle, and
gets into bed,—a reward for the labours of the day, such as the world cannot
give,—and patience and time await to give him all that the world can give.

. So ends the famous Descriptive Catalogue. In reading it no one will fail
to see that such names as Titian, Rembrandt, &c., stand partly for the men as
they were in relation to art, but chiefly as those examples which Blake was
shown in their names, stood in relation to *his* art. So considered no part of
these pages is seen to be more true and valuable than the "errors of a wise
man" with which his remarks about "Venetian and Flemish" art are interspersed. The one statement that Rubens, whose weakness, as we all know,

was towards vermillion laid near a grey that had black in it, and a light containing primrose,—covers all things with " hellish brown " is enough to prove that the Rubens who painted in Flanders, and the Rubens who was shown to Blake in London were two separate and widely different artistic facts, unfortunately named here by the same name. This does not account for all Blake's mistakes about colour as related to form, but helps to hint at the origin of some of them.

The greater part of his errors are made by the very process he himself most loudly condemns,—namely, by " generalizing " until truth becomes falsehood. It is, however, an undisputed fact, well worthy of study and by no means easy of explanation, that the noblest and most exalted figures in sacred art were done by men who used hard outlines, while the great masters of the brush left fine records of worldly and courtly dignity side by side with manifest failures to embody convincing or elevating conceptions of religious imaginations or of Biblical characters.

As we read the blatant passages in which Blake,—to use the expressive school-boy phrase, " blows his own trumpet," who is inclined now to be angry with him for doing it ? There are'plenty to-day who, as Mr. Swinburne so finely says, " not for *his* sake, contend to do him honour." But this was not so then. Oppression was not the only thing that made him boastful, though it is, in a sense, mad to be boastful, and " oppression makes the wise man mad." The bitter wrong that underlies all the irritable self-assertion here, and in the so-called " Public address " was this. Blake's art, his talent, his power of pictorial production, which was dearer than life to him, had suffered by oppression. The fact has been noted already, in these volumes and elsewhere, but it could not be too frequently repeated even were it made into a motto and printed at the head of every page, for unless it be remembered, the meaning of every page is incompletely felt.

" PUBLIC ADDRESS."

*** THE following sketch from a prospectus to the engraving of Blake's " Canterbury Pilgrim," is collected from fragmentary notes in the MS. Book. They are here placed in what seems the order in which they were written by the author then. Gilchrist's second volume contains them in a somewhat fanciful sequence. Sentences are dropped and pages transposed without any ascertainable reason. What was, at best, a series of hurried and angry jottings comes forth as a " Public address " in an order which adds to their incoherence, and with a title which their author's MS. does not place at their head. In putting the words " Public address " here the only object is that readers may recognise at a glance what Gilchrist has given under that name. An editorial note at the beginning of the prose selections in Gilchrist's volume, of which this is one, refers to it without giving any hint of the fact that the title is not the author's, and instead of admitting that the text is not the author's either the editor leads the reader astray by saying,—"It has been compiled from a very confused mass of MS. notes . . . . . . As evidence of the writer's many moods these pieces of prose are much best left unmutilated." Not one of the pieces is so left. Even the Descriptive Catalogue is silently deprived of its own preface, and these pages, like the description of the picture called "The last Judgment," are both jumbled and garbled.

For this, when pretence to literal re-production is made,—no pardon can ever be accorded, but it is right to say that even though it has not been quite faithfully fulfilled, the task was not an easy one. Paragraphs intended for a late place in the prospectus,—or *address*, were often written by Blake on early pages of his note-book just as blank space offered itself on turning over the leaves, long after its later pages had been crowded with sentences intended for the opening lines of his manifesto.

The displacements and alterations actually made by the Gilchrist's editor were not due to error thus caused. He divides what is continuous at his own fancy, and makes a new composition of the fragments.

In all else but the claim to accuracy, his editorial note is so admirable, that as a little essay on Blake's art-criticism it deserves to be reprinted, and will no doubt receive that honour many times, as the years go on, at the hands of future editors.

The punctuation here, and elsewhere, is conjectural. Blake's own is on a wrong-headed system which confuses the text. For example, he gives the colon a higher value than the period.

The numbers printed here at the margin indicate the number of the page of the MS. book in which the paragraph printed beside it is to be found. The sequence has not been departed from except when an examination of the MS. gave the impression that the later page was earlier written. Here and there extra sentences written *later* or *sideways* on the margin are indicated. This enables the reader to perceive that Blake's style is not broken to scraps because he was too scatter-brained to write continuously, but because he was here jotting down meditations and recollections for consideration and after-use.

These are notes by Blake for a Prospectus or Advertisement, intended for issue with the Engraving to the Canterbury Pilgrims. (*On P. 57 of the MS. book we learn that in some form this seems to have been printed.*) "This day (*no date*) is published Advertisement to Blake's Canterbury Pilgrims from Chaucer, containing anecdotes of Artists." *Where is it?*

Some erased sentences have been restored for their biographical value,— marked *erased*. What others would have been erased also we cannot tell, since the entire prospectus seems to have vanished as soon as it was published. The present arrangement may stand until the lost print is found. Nothing else can settle the matter.

38

Chaucer's Canterbury Pilgrims,

Being a complete Index of Human Characters as they exist age after age.

The originality of this production makes it necessary to say a few words.

While the works of Pope and Dryden are looked upon as the same art with those of Shakespeare and Milton,—while the works of Strange and Woollett are looked upon as the same art with those of Raphael and Albert Durer, there can be no art in a nation but such as is subservient to the interests of the monopolising trader,* who manufactures art by the hands of ignorant journeymen, till at length Christian charity is held out as a motive to encourage a blockhead, and he is accounted the greatest genius who can sell a good-for-nothing commodity at a great price. Obedience to the will of the monopolist is called Virtue, and the really virtuous, industrious, and independent Barry is driven out to

62 make room for a lot of idle sycophants with whitloes on their fingers.** Englishmen! rouse yourselves from the fatal slumber into which booksellers and trading dealers have thrown you, under the artfully propagated pretence that a translation or a copy of any kind can be as honourable to a nation as an original, belying the English character in that well known saying,—Englishmen improve what others invent. This, even Hogarth's works prove a detestable falsehood. No

63 man can improve an original invention.* Since Hogarth's time we have had very few efforts of originality,** nor can an original invention exist without execution organised and minutely delineated and articulated either by God or man. (*Margin, sideways.*) I do not mean smoothed and niggled, and poco-penned and all the beauties paled out, blurred and spotted out, but drawn with a firm hand at once, with all its ** spots and blemishes, which are beauties,—not faulty,*** like Fuseli, Michael Angelo, Shakespeare, and Milton. I have heard many people say,—"Give me the ideas; it does not matter what words you put them into,"—and others say,—"Give me the design; it is no matter for the execution." These people knew enough of artifice but little of art. Ideas cannot be given but in their minutely appropriate words. Nor can a design be made without its minutely appropriate execution. The unorganised plots of Rubens and Titian are not art nor can their method ever express ideas or imaginations any more than Pope's metaphysical jargon (?) of rhyming. (*later*) Unappropriate execution is the most nauseous of all affectation and foppery.

64 Whoever looks at any of the great and expensive works of engraving which have been published by English traders must feel a loathing and disgust; and, accordingly, most Englishmen have a contempt for art, which is the greatest curse which can fall upon a nation.

The Modern Chalcographic connoisseurs and amateurs admire only the work of the journeyman, picking out whites and blacks in what is called *tints*. They

---

* The words between * and ** erased.
Between * and *** erased.   Between ** and *** erased.

despise drawing, which despises them in return. They see only whether everything is carved down but one spot of light.

Mr. B. submits to a more severe tribunal. He invites the admirers of old English portraits to look at his print.

(*Below,—of another date,—this note intended to hit Rembrandt,—not belonging to this part of the essay.*) He who could represent Christ uniformly like a drayman must have had queer conceptions: consequently his execution must have been queer, and those must be queer fellows who give great sums for such nonsense and think it fine art.

(Upside down,—at foot of P. 64.)

> Great men and fools do often we inspire,
> But the greater fools the greater liar.

65   I do not know whether Homer is a liar, and that there is no such thing as generous contention. I know that all those with whom I have contended in art have striven, not to excel, but to starve me out by calumny and the arts of trading competition.

66   (*Title and verses.*)

67   The English Artist may be assured that he is doing an injury and injustice to his country while he studies and imitates the effects of Nature. England will never rival Italy while we servilely copy what the wise Italians, Raphael and Michael Angelo scorned, as Vasari tells us.

> Call that the public voice which is their error
> Like to a monkey, peeping in a mirror,
> Admires all his colours warm and brown,
> Nor ever once perceives his ugly form.

What kind of intellect must he have who sees only the colours of things and not the forms of things?

Let us teach Buonaparte and whomsoever it may concern that it is not the arts that follow and attend upon Empire, but Empire that attends upon and follows arts.

It is nonsense for noblemen and gentlemen to offer premiums for the encouragement of art when such pictures as these can be done without premiums. Let them encourage what exists already, and not endeavour to counteract by tricks.

Let it no more be said that empires encourage arts, for it is arts that encourage arts. Arts and artists are spiritual and laugh at mortal contingences. (*Here perhaps should be printed the sentence written above about Buonaparte,—ending,* Empire attends upon and follows the arts.) This is their power, to hinder instruction, but not to instruct, just as it is in their power to murder a man but not make a man.

68   No man of sense can think that an imitation of an oleograph is the art of painting, or that such imitation, which anyone can easily perform is worthy of notice, much less that such an act should be the glory and pride of a nation. The Italians laugh at the English connoisseurs, who are most of them such silly fellows as to believe this.

A man sets himself down with colours, and with all the articles of painting He puts a model before him, and he copies that so neat as to make it a deception. Now let any man of sense ask himself one question. Is this art? Can it be worthy of admiration to anybody of understanding? Who could not do this? What man who has eyes and an ordinary share of patience cannot do this neatly? Is this art, or is it glorious to a nation to produce such contemptible copies? Countrymen! countrymen! do not suffer yourselves to be disgraced!

Pp. 69, 70, 71, &c. contain chiefly the account of the picture called the " Last Judgement," with the title, " For the year 1810, Addition to Blake's catalogue of pictures." Probably the sentences about " Premiums," and " such pictures as these," belong to this Addition and not to the Advertisement . . . with anecdotes of artists. On two little clear spaces of P. 72 are found, written sideways, the following two fragments :—

A jockey that is anything of a jockey will never buy a horse by the colour, and a man who has got any brains will never buy a picture by the colour.

When I tell any truth it is not for the sake of convincing those who do not know it, but for the sake of defending those who do.

(In the rest of the book are no more scraps of the Advertisement, we must turn back to the beginning.)

If men of weak capacities have alone the power of execution in art, Mr. Blake has now put to the test. If to invent and to draw well hinders the executive power in art, and his strokes are to be condemned because they are unlike those of artists who are unacquainted with drawing is now to be decided by the public. Mr. Blake's inventive powers and his scientific knowledge of drawing are on all hands acknowledged. It only remains to be certified whether Physiognomic strength and power are to give place to imbecility. *In a work of art it is not fine tints that are required but fine forms. Fine tints without fine forms are always the subterfuge of the blockhead.*

I account it a public duty respectfully to address myself to the Chalcographic Society, and to express to them my opinion, the result of expert practice and experience of many years, that engraving, as an art, is lost to England, owing to an artfully propagated opinion that drawing spoils an engraver. I request the society to inspect my print, of which drawing is the foundation, and, indeed, the superstructure. It is drawing on copper, as painting ought to be drawing on canvas, or any other surface, and nothing else. I request likewise that the society will compare the prints of Bartolozzi, Woollett, Strange, &c., with the old English portraits :—that is, compare the modern art with the art as it existed previous to the entrance of Vandyke and Rubens into the country—since which event engraving is lost—and I am sure the result of the comparison will be that the society must be of my opinion, that engraving, by losing drawing, has lost all character and expression, without which the art is lost.

(No. 19 is the next page which had blank space enough left in 1810 to encourage a continuance of the manifesto,—it continues on that page,—as follows) :—

There is not, because there cannot be any difference between the effect in pictures by Rubens and Rembrandt. When you have seen one of their pictures you have seen all. It is not so with Rafael, Julio Romano, Albert Durer, Michael Angelo. Every picture of theirs has a different and appropriate effect. What

* —— * Later.

man of sense will lay out his money on the life's labour of imbecility and imbecility's journeyman, or think to educate a fool how to build a universe with farthing balls? The contemptible idiots who have been called great men of late years ought to rouse the public indignation of men of sense of all professions.

That vulgar epigram in art, Rembrandt's "Hundred Guelders," has entirely put an end to all genuine and appropriate effect. All, both morning and night, is now a dark cavern. It is the fashion. Yet I do not shrink from comparison in either relief or strength of colour with Rembrandt or Rubens ; on the contrary, I court the comparison and fear not the result. Their effects are in every picture the same. Mine are in every picture different. Rafael, Michael Angelo, Albert Durer, Julio Romano, are accounted ignorant of that epigrammatic wit in art, because they avoid it as a destructive machine, as it is.

I hope my countrymen will excuse me if I tell them a wholesome truth. Most Englishmen when they look at a picture begin immediately searching about for points of light, and clap the picture in a dark corner. This, when done by grand works is like looking for epigrams in Homer.

A point of light is a witticism. Many are destructive of all art. One is an epigram only, and no good work can have them.

Mr. B. repeats here that there is not one character or expression in this print which could be produced with the execution of Titian, Rubens, Correggio, Rembrandt, or any of that class. Character and expression can only be expressed by those who feel them. Even Hogarth's execution cannot be copied or improved. Gentlemen of fortune who give great prices for pictures should consider the following :—

20   Rubens' Luxembourg gallery is confessed on all hands to be the work of a blockhead. It bears this evidence in its face. How can its execution be any other than the work of a blockhead? Bloated gods,—Mercury, Juno, Venus, and the rattletraps of mythology, and the lumber of an awkward French palace are thrown together, around clumsy and ricketty princes and princesses, higledy-piggledy. On the contrary, Julio Romano's "Palace of T." at Mantua is allowed on all hands to be the production of a man of the most profound sense and genius, and yet his execution is pronounced by English connoisseurs, and Reynolds their doll, to be unfit for the study of the painter. Can I speak with too great contempt of such fellows? If all the princes in Europe like Louis XIV. and Charles I. were to patronise such blockheads, I, William Blake, a mental prince, would decollate and hang their souls as guilty of mental high treason.

Who that has eyes cannot see that Rubens and Correggio must have been very weak and vulgar fellows? And are we to imitate their execution! This is what Sir Francis Bacon says,—that a healthy child should be taught and compelled to walk like a cripple, while the cripple must be taught to walk like healthy people. Oh rare wisdom!

21   The wretched state of the arts in this country, originating in the wretched state of political science (which is the science of sciences) demands a firm and determinate conduct on the part of artists to resist the contemptible counter arts, established by such contemptible politicians as Louis XIV., and originally set on foot by Venetian picture-traders, music-traders, and rhyme-traders, to the destruction of all true art as it is this day. An example of these contrary arts is given us

in the characters of Milton and Dryden as they are given in a poem signed with the name of Nat Lee, which perhaps he never wrote, and perhaps he wrote in a paroxysm of insanity, in which it is said that Milton's poem is a rough, unfinished piece, and that Dryden has finished it. Now let Dryden's Fall and Milton's Paradise be read, and I will assert that everybody of understanding must cry out shame on such niggling and poco-pen as Dryden has degraded Milton with. But at the same time I will allow that stupidity will prefer Dryden, because it is rhyme, and monotonous sing-song sing-song from beginning to end. Such are Bartolozzi, Woollett and Strange. To recover art has been the business of my life, to the Florentine original, and if possible to go beyond that original. This I thought the only pursuit worthy of a man. To imitate I abhor. I obstinately adhere to the true style of art such as Michael Angelo, Raphael, and Albert Durer left it,— *the art of invention, not of imitation. Imagination is my World. This world of dross is beneath my notice, and beneath the notice of the Public.** I demand therefore of the amateurs of art the encouragement which is my due. If they continue to refuse, their's is the loss, not mine, and their's is the contempt of posterity. I have enough in the approbation of fellow labourers. This is my glory, and my exceeding great reward. I go on, and nothing can hinder my course.

> And in melodious accents I
> Will sit me down and cry,—I! I!

22

23, 24 (*The Screwmuch lines.*)

The painters of England are unemployed in public works while the sculptors have continual and superabundant employment. Our churches and our abbeys are treasures of their producing for ages back, while painting is excluded. Painting, the principal art, has almost no place among our only public works. Yet it is more adapted to solemn ornament than marble can be, as it is capable of being placed in any height, and, indeed, would make a noble finish placed above the great public monuments in Westminster, St. Paul's, and other cathedrals. To the Society for the Encouragement of Art I address myself with respectful duty, requesting their consideration of my plan as a great public means of advancing fine art in Protestant communities. Monuments to the dead painters by historical and poetical artists like Barry, and Mortimer, (I forbear to name living artists, though equally worthy,) I say, monuments to painters must make England what Italy is; an envied storehouse of intellectual riches.

25 It has been said of late years the English public have no taste for painting. This is a falsehood. The English are as good judges of painting as of poetry, and they prove it by their contempt for great collections of all the rubbish of the Continent brought here by ignorant picture-dealers. An Englishman may well say, "I am no judge of painting" when he is shown these smears and daubs at an immense price and told that such is the art of painting. I say the English public are true encouragers of real art, while they discourage and look with contempt on false art.

---

* to ** erased. The words are valuable as showing the consistency of the author who looked on the Public as being, like himself, truly a portion of the spiritual world, and outside the "world of dross."

26   In a commercial nation impostors are abroad in all professions. These are the
greatest enemies of Genius. * Mr. B. considers it his duty to caution the public
against a certain impostor who * *   In one art, the art of painting, these impostors sedulously propagate an opinion that great inventors cannot execute.
This opinion is as destructive of the true artist as it is false by all experience.
Even Hogarth cannot be either copied or improved.   Can (?) Anglus ever
discern perfection but in the journeyman's labour?

Sideways.   P.S.—I do not believe that this absurd opinion was set on foot till, in my outset into life it was artfully published both in whispers and in print by certain
persons whose robbery from me made it necessary to them that I should be hid
in a corner.   It never was supposed that a copy could be better than an original,
or near so good, till a few years ago it became the interest of certain envious
knaves.   The lavish praise I have received from all quarters for invention and
drawing has generally been accompanied by this: "He can conceive but he
cannot execute."   This absurd assertion has done me, and may still do me the
greatest mischief.   I call for public protection against the villains.   I am, like
others, just equal in invention, and execution of my work.   I, in my own
defence, challenge comparison with the finest engravings, and defy the most
critical judge to make the comparison honestly, asserting in my own defence that
this print is the finest that has been done, or is likely to be done when drawing,
the foundation, is condemned, and absurd nonsense about dots and lozenges
made to occupy the attention to the neglect of all true art.   I defy any man to
cut cleaner strokes than I do, or rougher, when I please, and apart that he who
thinks he can engrave or paint without being a master of drawing is a fool.
Painting is drawing on canvas and engraving is drawing on copper, and nothing
else, and he who draws best must be the best artist, and to this I subscribe my
name as a public duty.   WILLIAM BLAKE.

———

₊ So we come in connected sentences to the end of the manifesto. Valuable
as it is, invaluable as it was when written, it's great purpose, that of vindicating
the value of the characteristics of the imaginative style in art as against the
false idea that smoothness is necessarily "finish," has long ago been fully
served.   Every student now knows only too well that smoothness is often merely
obliteration, and often leaves his own work timidly rough lest it should appear
foolishly smooth.

But in reading the statement that one man cannot take up another man's
beginnings and improve them we are led astray, if we forget that this can only be
true when the continuer is incapable of receiving the true impulse from the work
which he handles.   Should he catch the intention and work forward in the same
spirit, then, supposing his capacities not inferior to those of the "original
inventor" he will do just as well as the inventor himself would were he to
resume labour on a design that he had put aside in past years, and forgotten so
completely, that he had to re-invent whatever of its development is not indicated
in the plan.   But when the continuer is superior to the beginner, then, 'as was
the case when Shakespeare re-wrote old plays for the stage, he will simply put
to the best artistic purpose an opportunity which his predecessors left half used.

But the "advertisement" of the Canterbury Pilgrims did not stop here. The
part written at the end of the MS. book seems to have been its beginning.   Its
end is at the beginning of the book, the author having found that it over-ran

his space, so that he was obliged to turn back. But after he had finished and signed it, and written more than one chance epigram, he seems to have decided to go on with the subject. One isolated *dictum* is to be found on p. 45, twenty pages later than the close of the signed "advertisement."

45   "Let a man who has made a drawing go on, and he will produce a picture, or painting, but if he chooses to have it before he has spoiled it, he will do a better thing."

Then on p. 47 we get at last to what Blake seems to have imagined could be called "anecdotes of artists," which the title of his little pamphlet shows were added to it as one attraction more.

47   They say there is no straight line in nature. This is a lie, like all they say, for there is every line in nature. But I will tell them what there is not in nature. An even tint is not in nature. It produces heaviness. Nature's shadows are ever varying, and a ruled sky that is quite even can never produce a natural sky. The same with every object in a picture. Its spots are its beauties. Now, gentlemen critics, how do you like this? You may rage, but what I say I will prove by such practice, and have already done so, that you will rage to your own distraction. Woollett I knew very intimately by his intimacy with Basire, and I knew him to be one of the most ignorant fellows that I ever knew. A machine is not a man, nor a work; it is destructive of humanity and of art. The word Machination. . . . . .*

Delicate hands and heads will never appear,
While Titian, &c. . . . . as in the Book of Moonlight.

Woollett, I know, did not know how to grind his graver: I know this. He has often proved his ignorance before me at Basire's by laughing at Basire's
48 knife-tools, and ridiculing the form of Basire's graver till Basire was quite dashed and out of conceit with what he himself knew. But his ignorance had a contrary effect upon me. Englishmen have been so used to journeymen's undecided bungling that they cannot bear the firmness of a master's touch.
†Every line is the line of beauty. It is only fumble, and bungle which cannot draw a line. This only is ugliness. But that is not a line which doubts and hesitates in the midst of its course.

9 & 50   *Everlasting Gospel, and the epigram on Fuseli, "The only man I ever knew," &c.*

52   *Everlasting Gospel above. On lower half:*—In this plate Mr. B. has resumed the style with which he set out in life, of which Heath and Stothard were the awkward Imitators at that time. It is the style of Albert Durer and the old engravers, which cannot be imitated by any one who does not understand drawing, and which, according to Heath, Stothard, Flaxman, and even Romney, spoils an engraver; for each of these men has repeatedly asserted this
i, upper absurdity to me in condemnation of my work, and approbation of Heath's lame
part. imitation, Stothard being such a fool as to suppose that his blundering blurs can be made out and delineated by any engraver who knows how to cut dots and lozenges, equally well with those little prints which I engraved after him twenty

* In the MS. the sentence about machination and the quotation from the Book of Moonlight (a lost work of Blake's) are broken as here printed.
† Sideways.

54, upper part.

years ago, by which he got his reputation as a draughtsman. Flaxman cannot deny that one of his very first monuments he did I gratuitously designed for him. How much of his Homer and Dante he will allow to be mine I do not know, as he went far enough off to publish them, even to Italy, but the public will know; and at the same time he was blasting my character to Machlin my employer, as Machlin told me at the time.

53, lower part.

* The manner in which my character has been blasted these thirty years both as an Artist and as a Man may be seen particularly in a Sunday paper called the *Examiner*, published in Beaufort's Buildings,† and the manner in which I have rooted out the nest of villains will be seen in a poem concerning my three years' Herculean labours at Felpham, which I shall soon publish. Secret calumny and open professions of friendship are common enough all the world over, but have never been so good an occasion of poetic imagery. When a base man means to be your enemy, he always begins first with being your friend.‡ We all know that editors of newspapers trouble their heads very little about art and science, and that they are always paid for what they put in on those ungracious subjects.

51, lower part.

Many people are so foolish as to think they can wound M. Fuseli over my shoulder.§ They will find themselves mistaken: they could not wound even Mr. Barry so.

A certain portrait painter said to me in a boasting way: "Since I have practised painting I have lost all idea of drawing." Such a man must know that I looked upon him with contempt. He did not care for this any more than West did, who hesitated and equivocated with me on the same subject, at

55, Everlasting Gospel to end.

which time he asserted that Woollett's prints are superior to Basire's, because they had more labour and care. Now this is contrary to truth. Woollett did not know how to put so much labour into a head or a foot as Basire did. He did not know how to draw the leaf of a tree. All his study was clean strokes and mossy tints. How then should he be able to make use of either labour or care, unless the labour or care of imbecility? The life's labour of mental weakness scarcely equals one hour of the labour of ordinary capacity, like the full gallop of the gouty man to the ordinary walk of youth and health. I allow that there is such a thing as high-finished ignorance, as there may be a fool or a knave in an embroidered coat. But I say that the embroidery of the ignorant finisher is not like a coat made by another, but is an emanation from ignorance itself, and its finding is like its master—the life's labour of five hundred idiots, for he never does the work himself.

What is called the English style of engraving, such as it proceeded from the toilets of Woollett and Strange, for their's were fribble's toilets, can never produce character and expression. I knew the men intimately from their intimacy with Basire, my master, and knew them both to be heavy lumps of

---

* The two upper parts of these pages were written consecutively. The middle was occupied by drawings, and by a late portion of the Everlasting Gospel written *after* the prose. The lower portions were also written consecutively, and now follow.

† Begun in 1808.

‡ Hayley; thus connected by the "living" with Hunt.

§ In the *Examiner* Fuseli's name is coupled with Blake's.

cunning and ignorance, as their works show to all the continent, who laugh at the contemptible pretences of Englishmen to improve art before they even know the first beginnings of art. I hope this print will redeem my country from this coxcomb situation, and show that it is only *some* Englishmen, and not all, who are thus ridiculous in their pretences. Advertisements in the newspapers are no proof of popular approbation, but rather the contrary. A man who pretends to improve fine art does not know what fine art is. Ye English engravers must come down from your high flights. Ye must condescend to study Marc Antonio and Albert Durer. Ye must begin before you attempt to finish or improve; and when you have begun you will know better than to think of improving what cannot be improved.

It is very true what you have said for these thirty years : I am mad, or else you are so. Both of us cannot be in our right senses. Posterity will judge by our works. Woollett's and Strange's works are like those of Titian and Correggio, the life's labour of ignorant journeymen, suited to the purposes of commerce, for commerce cannot endure individual merit ; its insatiable maw must be fed by what all can do equally well ; at least it is so in England as I have found to my cost these forty years. Commerce is so far from being beneficial to arts or empires that it is destructive of both, as all their history shows, for the above reason of individual merit being its great hatred. Empires flourish until they become commercial, and then they are scattered abroad to the four winds.

I do not pretend to paint better than Rafael or Michel Angelo, or Julio Romano, or Albert Durer, but I do pretend to paint finer than Rubens, or Rembrandt, or Titian, or Correggio. I do not pretend to engrave finer than Albert Durer, but I do pretend to engrave finer than Strange, Woollett, Wall, or Bartolozzi, and all because I understood drawing which they understood not.

* Such prints as Woollett and Strange produce will do for those who choose to purchase the life's labour of ignorance and imbecility in preference to the inspired moments of genius and inspiration.

† Woollett's best works were etched by Jack Brown. Woollett etched very ill himself. Strange's prints were, when I knew him, all done by Aliamet and his French journeymen whose names I forget. ‡ The *Cottager's* and *Jocund Peasants*, the *Views in Kew Gardens*, the *Diana* and *Actæon*, and in short, all that are called Woollett's were etched by Jack Browne, and in Woollett's works the etching is all, even though a single leaf of a tree is never correct.

In this manner the English public has been imposed upon, under the impression that engraving and painting are somewhat else besides drawing. Painting is drawing on canvas and engraving is drawing on copper, and nothing else, and he who pretends to be either painter or engraver without drawing is an impostor. We may be clever as pugilists but as artists we are, and have long been, the contempt of the continent. Gravelot once said to my master Basire : " De English may be very clever in deir own opinions, but dey do not draw de draw."

---

* Sideways—later.

† Between lines, written to connect the sideways sentence of 57 with that of 58.

‡ Sideways.

60

* Men think they can copy nature as correctly as I copy imagination. This they will find impossible ; and all the copies or pretended copies of nature, from Rembrandt to Reynolds, prove that nature becomes, to its victim, nothing but blots and blurs. Why are copies of nature incorrect while copies of imagination are correct ? This is manifest to all.

59 again.

† Resentment for personal injuries has had some share in this public address, but love to my art, and zeal for my country a much greater.

---

* At the top of p. 60, apparently continuing what is at the top of p. 59.

† This occupies the lower part of p. 59. It was apparently intended as the last sentence of the pamphlet, and was almost certainly the last written. The corresponding portion of p. 60, that lies opposite as the book opens is occupied with a quotation from *Bell's Weekly Messenger*, dated Aug. 1811. The manifesto *begins* on the next p. 61, over leaf.

ADDITION TO BLAKE'S CATALOGUE OF PICTURES, &c.*

THE Last Judgment is not fable or allegory, but Vision. Fable or allegory is a totally distinct and inferior kind of poetry. Vision, or imagination, is a representation of what actually exists really, and unchangeably. Fable or allegory is formed by the daughters of Memory. Imagination is surrounded by the daughters of Inspiration who in the aggregate are called Jerusalem.

Fable is allegory, but that which is called the Fable is Vision itself.

Fable or allegory is seldom without some vision. Pilgrims' Progress is full of it. The Greek poets the same. But allegory and vision ought to be known as two things, and so called for the sake of eternal life.

(*After a paragraph cut out in the MS. and leaving broken words only,—*)

The (? *Ancients produce fable*) when they assert that Jupiter usurped the throne of his father Saturn and brought on an iron age, and begot on Mnemosyne or Memory the great Muses, which are not Inspiration as the Bible is. Reality was forgot, and the accidents of Time and Space only remembered, and called reality. Such is the mighty difference between allegoric fable and spiritual mystery. Let it be here noted that the Greek Fables originated in Spiritual Mystery and real vision, which are lost and clouded in fable or allegory, while the Hebrew Bible, and Greek Gospel are genuine, preserved by the Saviour's Mercy. The Nature of my work is Visionary or Imagination. It is an endeavour to restore what the Ancients called the golden age.

The Greeks represent Chronos, or Time, as a very aged man. This is fable; but the real vision of Time is an eternal youth. I have, however, somewhat accommodated my figure of time to the common opinion, as I myself am also infected with it, and I see Time aged—alas! too much so.

Allegories are things that relate to moral virtues. Moral virtues do not exist. They are allegories and dissimulations. But Time and Space are real beings. Time is a man. Space is a woman, and her masculine portion is Death.

The Hebrew Bible, and the gospel of Jesus are not allegory but eternal vision, or imagination of all that exists.†

Plato has made Socrates say that poets and prophets do not know or understand what they write or utter. This is a most pernicious falsehood. If they do not, pray is an inferior kind to be called 'Knowing?' Plato confutes himself.

---

* Such is the general title in the MS. Book to all the following.

These first paragraphs are arranged from somewhat disordered notes in the MS. book, which appear to have been intended as an introduction to the description of the composition representing the "Last Judgment." Some occur in the course of the description. They were not sorted out by the author. The places of these in the MS. are indicated in foot-notes.

† Blake inserts at this point, "Note here that Fable or Allegory is seldom without some vision, &c." But it breaks up what little continuity may be found in the subsequent sentences.

The Last Judgment is one of these stupendous visions. I have represented it as I saw it. To different people it appears differently, as everything else does, for though on earth things seem permanent, they are less permanent than a shadow as we all know too well.

In eternity one thing never changes into another thing. Each identity is eternal. Consequently Apuleius' Golden Ass and Ovid's Metamorphoses, and others of the like kind are fable; yet they contain vision in a sublime degree, being derived from real vision in more ancient writings. Lot's wife being changed into a pillar of salt alludes to the mortal body being made a permanent statue, but not changed or transformed into another identity, while it retains its own individuality. A man can never become ass or horse. Some are born with shapes of men who are both. But eternal identity is one thing, and corporeal vegetation is another thing. Changing water into wine by Jesus and into blood by Moses relates to vegetable nature also.

The Nature of visionary fancy or imagination is very little known, and the eternal nature and permanence of its ever existent images is considered less permanent than the things of vegetable and generative nature. Yet the oak dies as well as the lettuce, but its eternal image or individuality never dies but renews by its seed. Just so the imaginative image returns by the seed of contemplative thought. The writings of the Prophets illustrate these conceptions of the visionary fancy, by their various sublime and divine images as seen in the world of vision.

The world of imagination is the world of eternity. It is the divine bosom into which we shall all go after the death of the vegetated body. This world of imagination is infinite and eternal, whereas the world of generation or vegetation is finite and temporal. There exist in that eternal world the eternal realities of everything which we see reflected in this vegetable glass of nature.

All things are comprehended in their eternal forms in the divine body of the Saviour, the true vine of eternity, the Human imagination, who appeared to me as coming to judgment among his Saints and throwing off the temporal that the eternal might be established. Around him are seen the images of existence according to a certain order suited to my imaginative eye,—(*later ; energy.*)

DESCRIPTION OF THE PICTURE.

Jesus, seated between two pillars, Joachim and Boaz, with the word of divine revelation on his knee, and on each side the four and twenty elders sitting in judgment, the heavens opening around him by unfolding the clouds around his throne. The old heavens and the old earth are passing away, and the new heavens and the new earth descending: a sea of fire issues from before the throne. Adam and Eve appear first before the judgment-seat in humiliation; Abel, surrounded by innocents, and Cain, with the flint in his hand with which he slew his brother, falling, with the head downwards. From the cloud on which Eve stands Satan is seen falling headlong, wound round by the tail of the serpent, whose bulk, nailed to the cross round which he wreathes is falling into the abyss. Sin is also represented by a female, bound in one of the serpent's folds, surrounded by her friends. Death is chained to the cross, and Time falls, together with Death, dragged down by a demon crowned with laurel. Another demon with a Key has the charge of Sin, and is dragging her down by the hair. Beside them a figure is seen scaled with iron scales from head to feet, precipitating himself into the abyss, with the sword and balances. He is Og, King of Bashan.

On the right, beneath the cloud on which Abel kneels is Abraham, with Sarah and Isaac, also with Hagar and Ishmael, on the left. Abel kneels on a bloody cloud descriptive of those churches before the flood,—that they were filled with blood and fire and vapour of smoke. Even till Abraham's time the vapour and heat were not extinguished. These states exist now. Man passes on, but states remain for ever. He passes through them like a traveller, who may as well suppose that the places he has passed through exist no more as a man may suppose that the states he has passed through exist no more. Everything is eternal.

Beneath Ishmael is Mahomet, and beneath the falling figure of Cain is Moses, casting his tables of stone into the deeps. It ought to be understood that the persons, Moses and Abraham, are not here meant, but the states signified by those names: the individuals being representatives or visions of those states as they were revealed to mortal man in the series of divine revelations as they are written in the Bible. These various states I have seen in my imagination: when distant they appear as one man; but, as you approach they appear multitudes of nations. Abraham hovers above his posterity which appear as multitudes of children ascending from the earth, surrounded by Stars,—as it was said: "As the stars of heaven for multitude." Jacob and his twelve sons hover beneath the feet of Abraham and receive their children from the earth. I have seen, when at a distance, multitudes of men in harmony appear like a single infant, sometimes in the arms of a female. This represented the Church.

But, to proceed with the description of those on the left hand. Beneath the cloud on which Moses kneels are two figures, a male and a female, chained together by the feet. They represent those who perished by the Flood. Beneath them, a multitude of their associates are seen falling headlong. By the side of them is a mighty fiend with a book in his hand, which is shut. He represents the person named in Isaiah xxii. c., and 20 v. Eliakim, Son of Hilkiah. He drags Satan down headlong. He is crowned with oak. By the side of the scaled figure, representing Og, King of Bashan, is a figure with a basket, emptying out the variety of riches and worldly honours. He is Araunah the Jebusite, master of the threshing floor. Above him are two figures elevated on a cloud representing the Pharisees, who plead their own righteousness before the throne. They are weighed down by two fiends. Beneath the man with the basket are three fiery fiends, with grey beards, and scourges of fire. They represent cruel laws. They scourge a group of figures down into the deeps. Beneath them are various figures in attitudes of contention, representing various states of misery, which, alas, every one is liable to enter into, and against which we should all watch. The ladies will be pleased to see that I have represented the three Furies by three men, and not by three women. It is not because I think the ancients wrong, but they will be pleased to remember that mine is vision, and not fable. The spectator may suppose them clergymen in the pulpit, scourging sin instead of forgiving it.

The earth beneath these falling figures is rocky and burning, and seems as if convulsed by earthquake. A great city, on fire, is seen in the distance. The (?) armies are fleeing upon the mountains. On the foreground Hell is opened, and many figures are descending into it, down stone steps, and beside a gate, beneath a rock, where sin and death are to be closed eternally by that fiend who carries the key in one hand and drags them down with the other. On the rock, and above the gate, a fiend with wings urges the wicked onward with fiery darts. He is Hazael the Syrian, who drives abroad all those who rebel against their Saviour. Beneath the steps is Babylon, represented by a King, crowned, grasping his sword and sceptre. He is just awakened out of his grave. Around him are other kingdoms arising to judgment, represented in this picture by single persons according to the descriptions in the Prophets. The figure dragging up a woman by the hair represents the Inquisition, as do those contending on the sides of the pit, and in particular, the man strangling a woman represents a cruel church.

Two persons, one in purple, the other in scarlet, are descending down the steps into the pit. These are Caiaphas and Pilate, two states where all those reside who calumniate and murder under pretence of holiness and justice. Caiaphas has a blue flame like a mitre on his head. Pilate has bloody hands that can never be cleansed. The females behind them represent the females belonging to such states, who are under perpetual terrors, and vain dreams, plots, and secret deceit. Those figures that descend into the flames before Caiaphas and Pilate are Judas and those of his class. Alutophil is here, with the cord in his hand.*

Between the feet of Adam and Eve appears a fiery gulph descending from the sea of fire before the throne. In this cataract four angels descend headlong with four trumpets to awake the dead. Beneath these is the seat of the harlot named Mystery in the Revelations. She is seized by two beings, each with three heads. They represent vegetative existence. As it is written in the Revelations they strip her naked and burn her with fire. It represents the eternal consumption of vegetable life and death with its lusts. The wreathed torches in their hands represent eternal fire, which is the fire of generation or vegetation: it is an eternal consummation.

Those who are blessed with imaginative vision see this eternal female, and tremble at what others fear not, while they despise and laugh at what others fear. Beneath her feet is a flaming cavern, in which are seen her kings and councillors, and warriors, descending in flames, lamenting and looking on her in astonishment and terror, and Hell is opened beneath her seat; on the left hand the great Red Dragon with seven heads and horns. He has Satan's book of accusations, lying on the rock, opened before him. He is bound in chains by two strong demons. They are Gog, and Magog, who have been compelled to subdue their master (Ezekiel xxxviii. c. 8 v.) with their hammer and tongs about to new-create the seven-headed kingdoms. The graves beneath are opened and the dead awake and obey the call of the trumpet. Those on the right hand awake in joy, and those on the left in horror. Beneath the Dragon's cavern a skeleton begins to re-animate, starting into life at the trumpet's sound,

---

* Here, in the original, follows the paragraph beginning " In eternity one thing never changes into another, consequently Apuleius' Golden Ass," &c., and ending —" changing water into wine by Jesus, and into blood by Moses relates to vegetable nature also." It interrupts the narrative and was probably not intended to be printed where it is written.—ED.

while the wicked contend with each other on the brink of perdition. On the right a youthful couple are awaked by their children: an aged patriarch is awaked by his aged wife. * He is Albion our Ancestor, patriarch of the Atlantic Continent whose history preceeded that of the Hebrews, and in whose sleep and chaos, creations began. The good woman is Britannica, the wife of Albion, Jerusalem is their daughter.* Little infants creep out of the flowery mould into the green fields of the blessed, who, in various joyful companies embrace and ascend to meet eternity.

The persons who ascend to meet the Lord, coming in the clouds with power and great glory, are representatives of those states described in the Bible under the names of the Fathers before and after the flood. Noah is seen in the midst of these, canopied by a rainbow; on his right hand Shem; on his left Japhet. These three persons represent Poetry, Painting, and Music,—the three powers in man of conversing with Paradise which the flood did not sweep away. Above Noah is the Church Universal represented by a woman surrounded by infants. There is such a state in eternity: it is composed of the innocent civilized heathen, and the uncivilized savage who, having not the law, do by nature the things contained in the law. This state appears like a female crowned with stars driven into the wilderness. She has the moon under her feet. The aged figure with wings, having a writing tablet, and taking account of the numbers who arise is that Angel of the Divine Presence mentioned in Exodus xiv. c, 10 v., and in other places. The angel is frequently called by the name of Jehovah Elohim. †The I am, of the oaks of Albion.†

Around Noah and beneath him are various figures risen into the air. Among these are three females, representing those who are not of the dead but who are found alive at the Last Judgment. They appear to be innocently gay and thoughtless, not being among the condemned, because ignorant of crime in a corrupted age. The Virgin Mary was of this class. A mother meets her numerous family in the arms of their father. These are representations of the Greek learned and wise, and also of those other nations such as Egypt and Babylon in which were multitudes who shall meet the Lord coming in the clouds.

The children of Abraham, or Hebrew Church, are represented as a stream of figures on which are seen stars somewhat like the Milky Way. They ascend from the earth, while figures kneel, embracing above the graves, and represent religion, or civilised life, such as it is in the Christian Church which is the offspring of the Hebrew. Just above the graves and above the spot where the infants creep out of the ground stand two,—a man and a woman. These are the primitive Christians. The two figures in purifying flames by the side of the Dragon's cavern, represent the latter state of the church when on the verge of perdition, yet protected by a flaming sword. Multitudes are seen ascending from the green fields of the blessed in which a Gothic Church is representative

---

* The words between the asterisks were added later by Blake. At the time this description was written, 1810, there was no intention to mention Albion. This seems to suggest that "Jerusalem" was still in progress, probably but little of it belongs to 1804. This also dates the substitution of the word "Albion," for "Man" or "Fallen Man" in the MS. of Vala.

† Once more, a later insertion of Blake's.

of true art, (called 'Gothic' in all ages by those who follow the fashion, as that is called which is without form or fashion.) By the right hand of Noah, a woman with children represents the state called Saban the Syrian. It is the remains of civilization in the state from which Adam was taken. Also on the right hand of Noah a female descends to meet her lover or husband, representative of that love called friendship which looks for no other heaven than the beloved, and in him sees all reflected as in a glass of eternal diamond.

On the right hand of these rise the diffident and humble, and on their left a solitary woman with her infant. These are caught up by three aged men who appear as suddenly emerging from the blue sky for their help. These three aged men represent divine providence as opposed to and distinct from divine vengeance,—represented by three aged men, on the side of the picture among the wicked, with scourges of fire.*

Above the head of Noah is Seth. This state called Seth is in a higher state of happiness than Noah, being nearer the state of innocence. Beneath the feet of Seth two figures represent the two seasons of Spring and Autumn, while beneath the feet of Noah four seasons represent the changed state made by the flood.†

By the side of Seth is Elijah. He comprehends all the prophetic characters. He is seen in his fiery chariot bowing before the throne of the Saviour. In like manner the figures of Seth and his wife comprehend the Fathers before the flood and their generations. When seen remote they appear as one man. A little below Seth, on his right, are two figures, a male and a female, with numerous children. These represent those who were not in the line of the Church and yet were saved from among the antediluvians who perished. Between Seth and these a female figure represents the solitary state of those who, previous to the flood, walked with God.

All these rise toward the opening cloud before the throne, led onward by triumphant groups of infants. Between Seth and Elijah three female figures crowned with garlands represent learning and science which accompanied Adam out of Eden.

The cloud that opens, rolling apart from before the throne, and before the new heaven and the new earth is composed of various groups of figures, particularly the four living creatures mentioned in Revelations as surrounding the throne. These I suppose to have the chief agency in removing the old heaven and old earth to make way for the new heaven and the new earth, to descend from the throne of God and of the Lamb. That living creature to the left of the throne gives to the seven angels the seven phials of the wrath of God, with which they, hovering over the deeps beneath, pour out upon the wicked their plagues. The other living creatures are descending with a shout, and with the sound of the trumpet, and directing the combats in the upper elements. In the two

---

* Here follows in the MS. the paragraph beginning "If the spectator could enter into these images——" and ending,—"an insignificant blur or mark." It has no place in the description which is resumed after it as though it had not been written.

† The words "the changed state produced by the flood" replace in the original the words "our present state of existence," erased.

corners of the picture, on the left hand, Apollyon is foiled before the sword of Michael, and on the right, the two witnesses are subduing their enemies.

On the cloud are opened the books of remembrance of life and of death. Before that of life, on the right, some figures bow in lamentation. Before that of death, on the left, the Pharisees are pleading their own righteousness. The one shines with beams of light, the other utters lightenings and tempests.*

Around the throne heaven is opened, and the nature of eternal things displayed, all springing from the Divine Humanity. All beams from him. He is the bread and the wine. He is the water of Life. Accordingly on each side of the opening heaven appears an Apostle, that on the right represents Baptism. That on the left represents the Lord's Supper.†

Over the head of the Saviour and Redeemer, the Holy Spirit, like a dove, is surrounded by a blue heaven in which are the two cherubim that bowed over the ark, for here the temple is open to heaven and the ark of the covenants is a dove of peace. The curtains are drawn apart, Christ having rent the veil. The candlestick and the table of show-bread appear on each side. A glorification of angels with harps, surrounds the dove.

The Temple stands on the mount of God. From it flows on each side a river of life, on whose banks grows the Tree of Life, among whose branches, temples and pinnacles, tents and pavilions, gardens and groves, display Paradise with its inhabitants walking up and down in conversations concerning mental delights. *Here they are no longer talking of what is good and evil, of what is right or wrong, and puzzling themselves in Satan's Labyrinth, but are conversing with eternal realities as they exist in the human imagination.‡

Jesus is surrounded by beams of glory in which are seen all around him infants emanating from them. These represent the eternal births of intellect from the Divine Humanity. A rainbow surrounds the throne and the glory, in which youthful nuptials receive the infants in their hands. The Eternity woman is the emanation of man. She has no will of her own. There is no such thing in eternity as a female will.

On the side next Baptism are seen those called in the Bible, Nursing Fathers and Nursing Mothers. They represent Education. On the side next the Lord's Supper, the Holy Family, consisting of Mary, Joseph, John the Baptist, Zacharias, and Elizabeth receiving the bread and wine among other spirits of the Just made perfect. Beneath these a cloud of women and children are taken up, fleeing from the rolling cloud which separates the wicked from the seats of bliss. They represent those who, though willing, were too weak to reject error without the assistance and countenance of those already in the truth, for a man

* Here follows the paragraph beginning with the words "A last Judgment is necessary because fools flourish" which were added later by Blake to the MS., and ending—" the purpose of hindering them from oppressing the good."

† After the paragraph ending—" the Lord's Supper" comes the paragraph beginning,—" All life consists of these two,—throwing off error, and receiving truth,—and ending, "a Last Judgment passes upon that individual."

‡ The words between asterisks were added here later by Blake, and were followed by the paragraph beginning, "We are in a world of generation and death"—and ending—" Venetian painters who will be cast off and lost from art."

can only reject error by the advice of a friend or by the immediate inspiration of God. It is for this reason, among others, that I have put the left hand of the throne, for it appears so at the Last Judgment for a protection.

END OF THE DESCRIPTION OF THE PICTURE.

*** The following paragraphs appear to have been intended as a sequel to the description. Those whose places are not indicated in foot-notes above, come all together at the end. They chiefly unite the idea of Imagination as the Saviour with art, considered as a service and vision as a manifestation of Him.

BLAKE'S SEQUEL TO HIS DESCRIPTION OF THE PICTURE OF THE LAST JUDGMENT.

If the spectator could enter into these images in his imagination, approaching them on the fiery chariot of his contemplative thought,—if he could enter into Noah's rainbow, could make a friend and companion of one of these images of wonder, which always entreat him to leave mortal things, (as he must know) then would he arise from the grave, then would he meet the Lord in the air, and then he would be happy. General knowledge is remote knowledge. It is in particulars that wisdom consists and happiness too. Both in art and in life, general masses are as much art as a pasteboard man is human. Every man has eyes, nose, and mouth. This every idiot knows. But he who enters into and discriminates most minutely the manners and intentions, the characters in all their branches, is the alone wise or sensible man, and on this discrimination all art is founded. I entreat, then, that the spectator will attend to the hands and feet, to the lineaments of the countenance. They are all descriptive of character, and not a line is drawn without intention, and that most discriminate and particular. As poetry admits not a letter that is insignificant, so painting admits not a grain of sand, or a blade of grass insignificant,—much less an insignificant blur or mark.

A Last Judgment is necessary because fools flourish. Nations flourish under wise rulers and are depressed under foolish rulers. It is the same with individuals as with nations. Works of art can only be produced in perfection where the man is either in affluence or above the care of it. Poverty is the fool's rod which at last is turned on his own back. That is a Last Judgment when men of real art govern and pretenders fall. Some people, and not a few artists, have asserted that the painter of this picture would not have done so well if he had been properly encouraged. Let those who think so reflect on the state of nations under poverty and their incapability of art. Though art is above either, the argument is better for affluence than poverty, and though he would not have been a greater artist he would have produced greater works of art in proportion to his means. A Last Judgment is not for the purpose of making bad men better, but of hindering them from oppressing the good.*

† All Life consists of these two, throwing off error, and knaves from our company continually, and receiving truth, or wise men, into our company

---

* This paragraph was written later,—probably 1812, but meant for insertion here.

† "These two" actions correspond with the Sacraments of Baptism, and the Lord's Supper respectively.

continually. He who is out of the church and opposes it is no less an agent of religion than he who is in it. No man can embrace true art until he has explored and cast out false art, such is the nature of mortal things, or he will be himself cast out by those who have already embraced true art. Thus my picture is a history of art and science, the foundation of Society, which is humanity itself. What are the gifts of the spirit but mental gifts? When any individual rejects error and embraces truth, a last Judgment passes upon that individual.

* We are in a world of generation and death, and this world we must cast off if we would be painters (sic) such as Raphael, Michael Angelo, and the ancient sculptors. If we do not cast off this world we shall be only Venetian painters who will be cast off and lost from art.

The painter hopes that his friends Amytus, Melitus, and Sycon † will perceive that they are not now in ancient Greece ; and though they can use the poison of calumny the English public will be convinced that such a picture as this could never be painted by a madman, or one in a state of outrageous manners, as these bad men both print and publish by all the means in their power. The painter begs public protection and all will be well.

(Here followed a paragraph through which Blake seems to have drawn his pen. It is found in the chapter on the MS. Book, Vol. I., p. 332.)

Men are admitted into heaven not because they have curbed and governed their passions, or have no passions, but because they have cultivated their understandings. The treasures of heaven are not negations of passion, but realities of intellect, from which the passions emanate, uncurbed in their eternal glory. The fool shall not enter into heaven, let him be ever so holy. Holiness is not the price of entrance into heaven. Those who are cast out are all those who, having no passions of their own, because no intellect, have spent their lives in curbing and governing other people's by the various arts of poverty and cruelty of all kinds. The modern church crucifies Christ with the head downwards. Woe, woe, woe to you hypocrites! Even murder, which the courts of justice, more merciful than the church, is not done in passion but in cold blooded design and intention.‡

Many suppose that before the Creation all was solitude and chaos. This is the most pernicious idea that can enter the mind, as it takes away all sublimity from the Bible and limits all existence to creation and chaos, —to the time and space fixed by the corporeal and vegetated eye, and leaves the man who entertains such an idea the habitation of unbelieving demons. Eternity exists, and all things in eternity, independent of creation which was an act of mercy. I have represented these who are in eternity by some in a cloud, within the rainbow that surrounds the throne. They merely appear as in a cloud when anything of creation, redemption, or judgement is the subject of contemplation, though their whole contemplation is concerning these things. The reason they so appear is

---

* A sentence added later. ? 1812.

† ? Flaxman, Hayley, and Cromek, "in disguise," the late date makes it probable. It also dates and explains p. 93 of "Jerusalem."

‡ This use of the word "murder" in spiritual sense should have been noted in the course of Vol. I., Chapter vii.

the humiliation of the reasoning and doubting selfhood and the giving up all to inspiration. By this it will be seen that I do not consider either the just or the wicked to be in a supreme state, but to be every one of them states of the sleep which the soul may fall into in its deadly dreams of good and evil when it leaves Paradise following the serpent.

Many persons, such as Paine and Voltaire, with some of the ancient Greeks, say :—" We will not converse concerning good and evil : we will live in Paradise and Liberty." You may do so in spirit, but not in the mortal body as you pretend, until after a last Judgement. For in Paradise they have no corporeal and mortal body. *That* originated with the fall and was called Death, and cannot be removed but by a Last Judgment. While we are in the world of mortality we must suffer The whole Creation groans to be delivered.

There will always be as many hypocrites born as honest men, and they will always have superior power in mortal things. You cannot have liberty in this world without what you call* moral virtue, and you cannot have moral virtue without the subjection of that half of the human race who hate what you call moral virtue.

The nature of hatred, and envy, and of all the mischiefs in the world is here depicted. No one envies or hates one of his own party. Even the devils love one another in their own way. They torment one another for other reasons than hate or envy : These are only employed against the just. Neither can Seth envy Noah, or Elijah envy Abraham. But they may both of them envy the success of Satan, or Og, or Moloch. The horse never envies the peacock, nor the sheep the goat : but they envy a rival in life and existence, whose ways and means exceed their own. Let him be of what class of animals he will, a dog will envy a cat who is pampered at the expense of his comfort, as I have often seen. The Bible never tells us that the devils torment one another through envy. It is through this that they torment the just. But for what do they torment one another? I answer: For the coercive laws of hell,—moral hypocrisy. They torment a hypocrite when he is discovered : they punish a failure in the tormentor who has suffered the subject of his torture to escape. In Hell all is self-righteousness. There is no such thing there as forgiveness of sins. He who does forgive sin is crucified as an abettor of criminals, and he who performs works of mercy in any shape whatever is punished, and if possible destroyed,—not through envy, or hatred, or malice, but through self-righteousness that thinks it does God service, which God is Satan. They do not envy one another. They contemn or despise one another. Forgiveness of sin is only at the judgement-seat of Jesus the Saviour where the accuser is cast out not because he sins, but because he torments the just, and makes them do what he condemns as sin, and what he knows is opposite to their own identity.

It is not because angels are holier than men or devils that makes them angels, but because they do not expect holiness from one another, but from God only.†

The player is a liar when he says " Angels are happier than men because they are better." Angels are happier than men or devils because they are not always prying after good and evil in one another, and eating the tree of knowledge for Satan's gratification.

---

* The words " what you call " are later in date.

† The difference between Blake's conception of an angel in 1789 and 1810 is worth noting. The progress in nobility of mind, it shows, is peculiarly unlike " a madman, or one in a state of outrageous manners."

The Last Judgment is an overwhelming of bad art and science. Mental things are alone real. What is called corporeal, nobody knows of. Its dwelling place is a fallacy, and its existence an imposture. Where is the existence out of mind, or thought? Where is it but in the mind of a fool? Some people flatter themselves that there will be no Last Judgment, and that bad art will be adopted and mixed with good art,—that error, or experiment will make a part of truth, and they boast that it is its foundation. These people flatter themselves. I will not flatter them. Error is created. Truth is eternal. Error, or creation will be burned up, and then, and not till then, truth or eternity will appear. It is burned up the moment men cease to behold it. I assert for myself that I do not behold the outward creation, and that to me it is hindrance, and not action. It is as the dirt upon my feet,—no part of me.*

"What," it will be questioned, "when the sun rises do you not see a round disk of fire something like a guinea? Oh! no! no! I see an innumerable company of the heavenly host crying,—'Holy, holy, holy, is the Lord God Almighty!'" I question not my corporeal eye any more than I would question a window concerning a sight. I look through it and not with it.

The Last Judgment (will be) when all those are cast away who trouble religion with questioning concerning good and evil, or eating of the tree of those knowledges or reasonings which hinder the vision of God, turning all into a consuming fire. When imagination, art, and science, and all intellectual gifts, all the gifts of the Holy Ghost are looked upon as of no use, and only contention remains to man, then the Last Judgment begins, and its vision is seen by every eye according to the situation which he holds.

---

* See Vol. I., p. 231.

———————

₊ The following references will enable the reader to trace the stories of the Four Zoas through the different books. The sets are headed here by " Vala," as the most complete. It is the last in the arrangement of the books in Vol. III. simply for the convenience of separating the printed and lithographic pages as much as possible. In period of composition and in scheme it is wider than either " Jerusalem " or " Milton," and may be said to enclose them.

———————

SOME REFERENCES.

URIZEN IN "VALA."

NIGHT I.

L. 238.—Fallen Man rests. Urizen sleeps in porch.

L. 278.—He hangs his lamps in Human brain.

L. 282.—Vala calls him to descend.

Ll. 290 to 322.—He descends (else Man were murdered by Luvah) gloomy, indignant, claiming to be God. Smiles on Los,—gives Luvah into his hands. Los competing with him, he claims to be "God the destroyer." The Spectre is the Man. Sleeps at night like a bird in the shell.

L. 426.—Perverse rolled wheels of Urizen and Luvah, downwards and outwards, in wars of death. Compare "Jerusalem," page 43, lines 1 to 5, and 41 to 45.

L. 439.—They contend round the holy Tent.

Ll. 446 to 462.—They awoke, while Albion wept and his affections slept. They conferred. Urizen said he would go to North. Sent Luvah South with half the tents. Would lay sceptre on Jerusalem in the brain. Has bought and sold each tenth man.

L. 475.—Luvah having replied that he would not obey but would smite Albion, then fight Urizen. Urizen darkened him, brooding death to him.

L. 495.—Then in general darkness Urizen commanded the departure of his armies to North. They go, leaving the fight and the rage of Luvah. They fall into unknown space. Compare "Jerusalem," page 18, line 45.

NIGHT II.

Ll. 1 to 8.—Albion, on the couch of death, called Urizen, bid him take the sceptre, but pity the youth of Luvah.

Ll. 9 to 33.—Urizen rose like a star. He strode above in fear. Stood in human brain. Horror of death shot through feet. Ordered Luvah and Vala, shrinking. He ordered the bands of Heaven to build him the Mundane Shell. They do so. They make instruments, compass, plough, &c. The lions of Urizen stand round anvil. They petrify human imagination into rock and sand. Compare "Jerusalem," page 23, lines 10 and 58; page 9, lines 49 and 66; page 4, lines 5 and 67; page 12.

L. 60.—The building on Salisbury Plain. Compare "Jerusalem," page 66, line 4.

L. 69.—The furnaces were in Ulro. Urizen's lions stood in human forms.

L. 72.—Sees Luvah in furnaces to avert his own despair. Compare "Jerusalem," page 7, line 32.

L. 101.—Urizen, who was Faith and Certainty (when he was in the South), is changed to doubt.

L. 115.—Urizen held the plough of Ages—(the sun)—dragged by bulls of Luvah (as the sun is every morning).

Ll. 162 to 176.—Urizen's building. Square. Twelve halls. Three domes. Compare "Jerusalem," page 58, line 21.

Ll. 177 to 206.—Ahania and Urizen.

Ll. 240 to 258.—The Mundane Shell, whose building was permitted lest man should fall into Eternal Death.

L. 280.—To plant divisions in the soul of Urizen and Ahania, and conduct the voice of Enion to Ahania's pillow, Los and Enitharmon go down.

L. 320.—Urizen saw Los throw his arms around Ahania's image.

L. 376.—That Ahania's spirit might be drawn down to Enion's vortex, Enion was driven into the deathful infinite by Los.

L. 411.—Ahania, at the sound of Los's lamentation made while Los slept on his couch, saw Enion in the void, and never could rest again on her pillow.

NIGHT III.

Ll. 1 to 11.—Urizen protested with by Ahania for thinking of the future.

Ll. 12 to 23.—Urizen foretells birth of Los, and of Luvah, as death in Loins of Los, and Vala in womb of Enitharmon.

Ll. 26 to 44.—Urizen protested with by Ahania for giving steeds of light to Luvah. Bidden resume light. Is told that while he slumbers and Albion is smitten, Ahania sees.

Ll. 46 to 106.—Ahania's vision in slumbers of Urizen. (Compare "Jerusalem," page 29, from line 28.) Urizen, to vindicate his Godhead, casts out Ahania. She fell. His sons fled to east and west, and left north and south.

L. 153.—Urizen rushed down with his hosts.

L. 160.—Of his broken pieces Tharmas emerged.

NIGHT IV.

L. 24.—Urizen and Luvah cursed by Tharmas.

L. 37.—Urizen was our God, says Los. He is fallen. I am God.

L. 112.—Tharmas refers to Urizen giving the horses of light to Luvah.

L. 128.—Tharmas refers to fall of Urizen.

L. 140.—Tharmas refers to ambition of Urizen. He bids Los rebuild the furnaces.

L. 160.—The ruins of Urizen seen by Los.

Ll. 164 to 245.—The furnaces of Urizen rebuilt by Los, and the mills. The chain of sorrow and love surrounds Enitharmon, and makes Urizen groan. Los pours molten iron round Enitharmon and Urizen. Urizen is bound into organs as described in book of Urizen, during seven ages.

L. 285.—He became enslaved Humanity, and so did Los by sympathy.

L. 292.—Urizen's hurtling bones infect Los.

NIGHT V.

L. 43.—Urizen darkens Luvah who casts Urizen's spear. Compare "Night" I, line 415.

L. 107.—The snows of Urizen (now cold in science and doubt).

L. 185.—Urizen trembles and shudders in the (northern) dens of Urthona to hear the howls of Orc.

Ll. 190 to 238.—He laments on his different state now (that he is cold doubt), recalling what he was (when he was warm faith) before he gave faith up to Love. He will arise and explore his dens.

NIGHT VI.

Ll. 1 to 45.—Urizen rises, leaning on spear, and explores. He meets his three daughters. He laments and curses sons and daughters. Urizen, surrounded by waves of Tharmas, froze them.

Ll. 46 to 136.—Urizen fought with Tharmas, left him, and journeyed among monsters once his children.

L. 137.—He passed thus by West, South, and goes East; but all is in the North.

Ll. 141 to 146.—The East is a void. He goes into it by falling.

L. 220.—After many adventures he tries to create a new world and bind futurity in a chain.

L. 229.—Having fixed the sciences and lamented selfishly, he is covered with a white woof.

L. 250.—The web was rent by Torment.

L. 251.—Urizen wandered off in sorrow.

L. 258.—Urizen fell into the West.

L. 269.—His seat in Eternity is South.

L. 280.—He goes to the peaked rock of Urthona.

L. 305.—His sons rise from Urthona's cliffs.

NIGHT VII.

Ll. 5 to 170.—Urizen goes to Orc. They wrangle long. The serpent and the tree of mystery.

L. 242.—Urizen as the son of Vala described by Enitharmon.

L. 257.—His growing up and his struggles with Luvah.

L. 484.—Urizen's spectre drawn by Los from ranks of war, leaving spectrous form. Tiriel is divided and became Palamabron, and Urizen became Rintrah.

L. 490.—Urizen, Los's enemy, was thus in his hands.

L. 495.—Urizen sat on his rock, and, seeing the shadow (spectre of Urthona) brooding, triumphed and said that the time of prophecy was over, and he should rule all.

L. 509.—Urizen built his temple in form of the Human Heart. He put in the Sun. He ordained priests.

L. 609.—Urizen, wet, vibrated torrent on torrent.

L. 620.—The arts of Urizen were pity and affection.

L. 623.—Vala becomes Urizen's harlot.

L. 655.—Urizen's sons left plough, harrow, and loom. (Compare " Jerusalem," page 65, line 12.)

L. 685.—Urizen's bow to be brought by Vala.

NIGHT VIII.

L. 226.—Urizen's laws irrigate the roots of the tree of Mystery with tears of victims.

L. 367.—Urizen tempted away children of Los by his arts.

L. 380.—The enormous worlds roll in Urizen's power.

L. 406.—Rahab went to Urizen in pride.

L. 414 to 454.—Urizen sat, stonied, in terror of eternal death. He lost the form of Man and fell into a dragon. He descends weeping.

L. 498.—Urizen is sought in vain by Ahania—that is, the Urizen of the South. She describes Mortality.

L. 571.—Where Urizen is (during mortality, or un-improved knowledge, see l. 545), is told by Enion in reply.

NIGHT IX.

L. 33.—The books of Urizen burned at the Last Judgment.

L. 81.—Flames cut off tyranny from the earth round the dragon form of Urizen. In the North there is a rock forsaken where Urizen gave the horses of light into the hands of Luvah.

L. 134.—Eternal Man calls Urizen.

L. 138.—Urizen's dragon form (death) bidden to lie down while he rises in his true form.

L. 161.—Urizen weeps to put off the dragon and put on the human form.

L. 186.—Urizen decides to no longer think of Futurity or act as a restrainer. He casts off his snow and rises exulting into the heavens.

L. 197.—At his feet Ahania falls down dead with joy.

L. 199.—He drops a tear.

L. 200.—The three daughters of Urizen guard Ahania's death couch.

L. 203.—Eternal Man prophecies to Urizen.

L. 224.—Urizen confesses error.

L. 284.—Urizen arose with the Eternal Man from the rock.

L. 288.—The sons of Urizen seized the plough. They level fortifications and destroy implements of destruction.

L. 307.—Urizen's limbs shine with ardour. He laid his hand on the plough.

L. 312.—He commanded and they brought the seed of men. He sowed.

L. 326.—All the while the flames of Orc follow Urizen.

L. 336.—His work done, Urizen reposes happily.

L. 343.—Ahania having risen again from death, Urizen rejoices with her.

URIZEN IN "JERUSALEM."

P. 7, l. 32.—He beholds Luvah shut by Vala in furnaces, and seeks by iron power to avert his own despair.

P. 16, l. 31.—The counties of England fled out at Jerusalem's gates from the conflict of Urizen and Luvah.

P. 31, l. 57.—Vala complains that Urizen is the champion of Albion, and that they will slay her Luvah.

P. 36, l. 29.—The Zoas clouded rage. Urizen assumes the East.

P. 43, l. 2.—The Zoas prevent Albion walking about in the four complexions. Urizen does so by being cold and scientific.

P. 58, l. 21.—Los seeks to create a world of generation from the mathematic world of death. Urizen directs the awful building, a temple, in form of the human heart.

P. 58, l. 44.—It is described up to line 44, which sums it up as the ancient world of Urizen in the Satanic void.

P. 59, l. 11.—Four chaotic universes—Urizen's to South.

L. 15.—When Urizen's South world was assumed by Luvah, Albion was slain.

P. 63, l. 4.—Urizen is named as one of the Living Creatures, the cherubim of Albion, who tremble before the spectre, Los, in the starry harness of the plough of Nations.

P. 65, l. 11.—Passage from Vala. The sons of Urizen leave the plough and forge the sword when Albion sounds clarion in East, and Luvah is killed, bound round with vegetation for 6000 years.

L. 44.—Before the battle the sons used to rise to Urizen's harps.

L. 46.—Vala to bring the bow of Urizen and arrows of desire.

L. 47.—The golden horses of Urizen rage, compelled to the chariot of Love.

P. 66, l. 4.—The building (see above, p. 58, l. 21) was on Salisbury Plain. It is more described.

P. 74, l. 1.—The Zoas clouded rage. Urizen stood by Albion with Theotormon, &c., who are Verulam, &c.

P. 74, l. 4.—The Zoas named.

P. 88, l. 48.—In Entuthon of Urizen, as well as in Udan Adan and Golgonooza, Los stood dividing the Space of Love with brazen compasses, while the Spectre joyed, eyeing Enitharmon.

P. 96, l. 41.—Urizen and other Zoas rose into Albion's bosom when the heavens burned.

P. 97.—At the word of the Universal Father, bright beaming Urizen laid his hand on the South and took a bow of gold.

URIZEN IN "MILTON."

In extra page 8, Urizen is known to be Satan drawn down by Orc and the shadowy female into generation.

P. 16, l. 36.—He beheld "Milton."

In extra page, called "17," he, in the last line, emerged from his rocky form and from his snows.

P. 17, ll. 1 to 14.—He met Milton, turned the clay in which Milton walked to marble, so that his feet bled; then he rose and met him by the streams of Arnon and strove with him there. He poured freezing water on Milton's brow. Milton took red clay of Succoth, and, beginning at his feet, filled up his furrows of many years, creating new flesh, and giving him Human form in the Valley of Beth Peor.

L. 26.—The strife was for many periods. Rahab beheld it from Mount Carmel.

P. 18, l. 8.—Milton stood silent, forming Urizen.

P. 24, l. 2.—Urizen finished in howling woe the Seat of Satan, of which Luvah laid the foundation.

P. 24, ll. 45 and 49.— Satan's seat is the False Tongue. The sense of Touch. It is a region where, among others, the sons of Urizen labour.

P. 34, l. 36.—The South was originally the glorious world of Urizen, before all the Zoas fell to the centre in ruin when Luvah assumed this world.

P. 34, l. 43.—Southward, and by the East in the breach of Milton's descent, the Sons of Ololon stood in a dark land of death, pitying and gentle to awaken Urizen.

P. 39, l. 4.—Urizen, from his mantle of years, wove the forty-eight starry Regions, or Cities of the Levites, into sexes.

P. 40, l. 53.—In the strife among the brooks of Arnon with Milton's spirit, Urizen fainted in terror.

P. 42, l. 6.—This, and the strife with all the Zoas, is beheld by Blake.

URIZEN IN "THE SONG OF LIBERTY."

Para. 14.—Urizen as a hoary element is awoke by the fall of Orc.

Para. 15.—He rushes down.

Para. 16.—He falls on Urthona's dens.

Para. 18.—He promulgates his ten commands in the deep.

URIZEN IN "AMERICA."

P. 3.—As the Guardian Prince of Albion, Urizen burns at night in his tent— in his mind's eye.

P. 5.—As Albion's Angel he sees Orc as a serpent.

P. 7.—He rebukes Orc.

P. 8.—Orc tells him (without knowing him) of his own perversion of joy into commands.

P. 9.—Urizen replies to Orc, indignant and weeping.

P. 13.—He burned in the Eastern sky, spreading his wings.

P. 15.—But the streaks of red (sunrise) were like a pestilence on his limbs. He was consumed in fires of enthusiasm lit by Orc.

URIZEN IN "EUROPE."

L. 45.—Urizen, unloosed from chains, glows in the North.

L. 96.—As Albion's angels he falls smitten with his own plagues.

L. 106.—He seeks his ancient temple, serpent-formed.

L. 109.—He goes along the infinite shores of Thames to golden Verulam. The formation of his Temple is explained.

L. 130.—He arrived at the Southern Porch, at the stone of night (the mortal eye). It is now sunk beneath the attractive North.

L. 135.—As Albion's Angel he rises on the stone of Night.

L. 136.—As Albion's Angel he sees his full form, as Urizen, with his books. He is reading the brazen book of the heart. (That is "assuming the cast.")

L. 144.—He feeds his soul with pity.

L. 146.—As aged ignorance he, with the voice of the Angel, preaches, canting.

L. 160.—As a judge he flies from Westminster, where Orc is heard as in America.

L. 172.—Orc fires roll between Urizen's clouds.

L. 180.—Urizen as Newton blows his trumpet. The Angelic hosts fall.

LUVAH IN "VALA."

NIGHT I.

L. 239.—Urizen slept in the porch. Luvah and Vala fly up from the heart to the brain.

L. 241.—Luvah seized the horses of light, and arose into the chariot of day.

L. 261. - Luvah was lost in bloody beams of Enitharmon's false morning.

L. 274.—Los sees the invisible knife descend into the gardens of Vala, and Luvah walking on the winds.

L. 288.—Luvah and Vala shuddered in their orb of blood at the Image of Eternal Death.

L. 291.—Luvah must have murdered Albion if Urizen had not descended.

L. 298.—Urizen gave Luvah and Vala into the hands of Los, to make him punish them.

L. 331.—Los, having resisted the command and having struck down Enitharmon, feels love and pity arise in his veins. Luvah and Vala should have been in them, but they had ascended into the sky, and remained forsaken there.

L. 336.—Eternity or the Saviour put on Luvah's robes of blood.

L. 426.—Urizen's and Luvah's wheels revolved perverse, downwards and outwards, in wars of Eternal Death.

L. 439.—Luvah's war related by messengers from Beulah.

L. 446.—Urizen and Luvah awake while Albion's family sleep. They confer. Urizen will go North; Luvah, South. They will share all command over every other power.

L. 463.—Luvah refuses Urizen's dictation, claiming to be more than his equal.

L. 475.—Urizen having brooded death to Luvah, Luvah poured the lances of Urizen on him. Discord began, and cries and yells shook the wide firmament.

L. 498. - Urizen's sons suddenly all retreat to the North, leaving the rage of Luvah to pour its fury on himself and on Albion.

L. 500.—All fall together.

NIGHT II.

L. 7.—Albion bids Urizen pity the youth of Luvah.

L. 20.—Luvah and Vala, trembling, beheld the great Work-Master.

L. 70.—Luvah was cast into the furnaces of affliction and sealed ("Jerusalem," p. 7, l. 32).

L. 78. - Luvah's voice from the furnaces tells how Vala grew up till she became a dragon.

L. 100.—He suffers because he was Love, and Hatred awakes in him.

L. 105.—Luvah weeps for Urizen's ambition, patient in afflictions, reasoning from the loins in unreal forms of Ulro's night.

L. 109.—Luvah was melted. Vala fell, a heap of ashes.

L. 114.—The bulls of Luvah dragged Urizen's plough.

L 209.—Los and Enitharmon went down to see the woes of Vala and Luvah.

L. 225.—Only Luvah's feet are seen by the shadow of labouring Vala.

L. 239.—The Divine Vision appeared in Luvah's robes of blood.

L. 255.—This was done when Luvah fell, lest the state called Luvah should cease.

NIGHT III.

L. 22.—Luvah in the loins of Los, a dark and furious death.

L. 31.—Ahania asks Urizen why he listened to the voice of Luvah, to give him the steeds of light that no longer obey him.

L. 48.—Luvah hid Los and Enitharmon, and dwelt in Albion's cloud.

L. 53.—Luvah absorbs the Man, who falls trembling before him.

L. 59.—Though Luvah is Man's shadow.

L. 69.—Luvah descends from the cloud as the Son of Man.

L. 79.—He strives to gain dominion over Albion.

L. 83.—He is put forth from Albion's presence.

L. 85.—He is bidden die for Vala.

L. 94.—Luvah and Vala went down the Human Heart, whose blood foamed high.

L. 100.—Luvah fell from Vala as far as the East and West.

L. 129.—Luvah strives in Non-Entity, scorned by Vala, age after age wandering.

NIGHT IV.

L. 24.—Tharmas invokes the all-powerful curse of an honest man on Urizen and Luvah.

L. 112.—When Urizen gave the horses of light to Luvah, Urthona and Tharmas were still friends and companions.

L. 129.—Luvah is now hidden in elemental forms of life and death.

L. 139.—Enion is divided and vanished from Tharmas like Luvah and Vala.

L. 141.—Tharmas reproaches Luvah with ambition.

L. 240.—The council of God watched the body of Man, clothed in Luvah's robes of blood—the body to which Los bound Urizen in seven ages.

L. 256.—The feminine affections or Muses could not otherwise look on the imagination. The daughters of Beulah could not behold the Saviour.

NIGHT V.

L. 42.—As soon as Orc was born the Demons of the deep cried out that Luvah, King of Love, had become King of rage and death.

L. 43.—Urizen cast darkness round Luvah, who poured the spears of Urizen round the eternal tent. Discord began, &c. (identical line from Night I., line 475). Orc's birth and story follow. Luvah is now Orc.

L. 226.—Urizen, speaking from Urthona's dens, tells how he seized Luvah and Vala as they fell.

NIGHT VI.

L. 33.—The daughters of Luvah envied the light of the daughters of Urizen.

L. 88.—Urizen was scared at the sight of the ruined spirits, once his children and Luvah's.

L. 146.—For it was in the vacuity of Luvah's empty world that Urizen fell.

L. 228.—When the sciences were fixed Urizen gained a new dominion over his children and Luvah's.

L. 270.—In Eternal times the seat of Luvah is in the East.

NIGHT VII.

L. 16.—The bulls of Luvah bellow round Orc, whose debate with Urizen follows.

L. 151.—Urizen is certain that Orc is Luvah. He begins to organize a serpent body (Luvah falls from Vala as far as East and West).

L. 246.—Albion saw his wife assume a double form after the birth of Urizen, and called the enormity Luvah and Vala.

L. 253.—Luvah conferred with Urizen to bind Albion and enslave his children.

L. 261.—He enslaved them to vegetative forms, assuming Albion's place and smiting him.

L. 272.—The Spectre of Urthona remembers the days when Luvah was sweet and melodious with Tharmas and himself.

L. 410.—Los bids the Spectre of Urthona turn his eyes inward and behold the Lamb of God in Luvah's robes of blood.

L. 652.—The death of Luvah voted : he is to be nailed to a tree for six thousand years. (" Jerusalem," p. 65, l. 9.)

L. 696.—Orc rent Vala. His human form consumed, he remained only a serpent round the tree of Mystery.

L. 757.—Vala went forth and heard sweet voices on the waters like the voice of Luvah.

NIGHT VIII.

L. 58.—Urizen saw the Lamb of God in Luvah's robes of blood.

L. 60.—He saw a new Luvah, or Orc, opposite to him, a serpent form.

L. 82.—The Shadowy Female (fallen Vala) mingles in the tree with Orc (fallen Luvah).

L. 109.—They become a dark hermaphrodite—the battle taking a form that Urizen intended not.

L. 154.—The Shadowy Female says that if her eyes might but behold Luvah, she would deliver the Sons of God from bondage to lower forms.

L. 171.—Mingling of Urizen and Luvah by Urizen spreading himself in deceitful religions through all the branches of the tree of Mystery in the power of Orc.

L. 245.—The hermaphroditic form, previously called " Luvah and Vala," was seen.

L. 243.—The satanic Luvah burst from it, hiding Vala in himself.

L. 259.—The Lamb of God put on Luvah's robes of blood that Mystery might be put off.

L. 275.—Mystery was the vegetative Vala created by Satan.

L. 376.—When Luvah, in Orc, became a serpent, he descended into the state called Satan. Satan's story from "Milton" related.

L. 454.—Orc in wrath and fury has risen into the heavens.

NIGHT IX.

L. 93.—A horrible rock in the North was forsaken when Urizen gave the horses of light into Luvah's hands.

L. 141.—The eternal man wrathfully bid Luvah rage in the dark deeps even to consummation.

L. 150.—His anger against Urizen was greater than against Luvah.

L. 178.—Urizen has no joy; he complains that he has given it all to Luvah and Vala.

L. 183.—But in future Orc may rage unchecked.

L. 354.—And now fierce Orc had quite consumed himself in mental flames.

L. 359.—The Regenerate Man made Luvah and Vala his servants.

L. 371.—Luvah and Vala descended and entered the gate of dark Urthona.

L. 381.—In bright clouds over Vala's head Luvah hovered invisible.

L. 382.—They renewed their golden age.

L. 384.—Luvah bid Vala arise from the grass and the dew.

L. 446.—Luvah placed Vala in a green and pleasant land.

L. 455.—Luvah gave her a house.

L. 460.—Vala dreamed of Luvah, and delighted in her house.

L. 554.—The sleepers in Beulah were entertained with visions now described, when Luvah and Vala were closed up in their world of shadowy forms.

L. 584.—The flames of Luvah and Vala served wine all day and night to the Regenerated Man who sat at feast.

L. 615.—The same line repeated.

L. 688.—The eternal man told Luvah that the vintage was ripe.

L. 695.—The shepherds shout for Luvah.

L. 696.—The bulls of Luvah are to tread the corn.

L. 704.—Attempting to be more than man we become less, said Luvah.

L. 705.—He arose from the bright feast.

L. 706.—His crown of thorns fell from his head.

L. 711.—He stood before the wine-press.

L. 715.—His villages rose and sang.

L. 718.—The legion of Mystery fell into his wine-press.

L. 723.—Odours arose that sang, saying, "Terrible wine-presses of Luvah, O caverns of the grave!"

L. 738.—The sons and daughters of Luvah tread the grapes.

L. 781.—Luvah was exhausted and filled with new wine.

L. 786.—He was laid on the floor for dying.

L. 790.—Luvah and Vala and their children awoke, and re-ascended to the eternal man.

LUVAH IN "JERUSALEM."

P. 7, l. 30.—Luvah was cast into the furnaces and sealed, and Vala fed the furnaces.

L. 39.—He howled in the furnaces, preparing Albion's spectre to reign over Los.

P. 16, l. 31.—The counties of England fled from the contest of Luvah and Urizen.

P. 21, l. 16.—The spiritual forms of Gwendolen and Ragan without a veil wither in Luvah's sepulchre.

L. 31.—Hand drives Albion's daughters with stripes through Babylon, because they taught Luvah to rise into Albion's clouded heavens.

P. 22, l. 31.—Albion sees his spectre in Luvah, whom he slew.

P. 24, l. 51.—Albion laments that he can no more behold the Lamb of God, who is closed in Luvah's sepulchre.

L. 52.—Albion asks why Luvah, the gentlest, mildest Zoa, should smite him.

L. 57.—He sees the Lamb, who was closed in Luvah's sepulchre, and who looks mercifully on him.

P. 25, l. 6.—As the sons of Albion have done to Luvah they have, in him, done to the Lamb.

L. 27, stanza 10.—As Satan Luvah tears forth from Albion's loins (compare p. 47, l. 3).

P. 29, l. 56.—Luvah descends from the cloud of Albion's wearied intellectual shadow.

L. 61.—He strives to gain dominion over Albion.

L. 64.—His smitings are boils on Albion.

L. 73.—Luvah and Vala went down the Human Heart as the blood foamed high.

L. 79.—Luvah fell from Vala's bosom to the East and West.

P. 30, l. 39.—Luvah draws the curtains round Albion, who has entered Vala's bosom in the loins—the place of the Last Judgment.

P. 31, l. 24.—Luvah built the Tower of London in Jerusalem's Eastern Gate.

L. 50.—Vala says that Luvah gave her to Albion.

L. 55.—The strife of Albion and Luvah is great in the East.

L. 57.—Luvah will be slain by Albion and Urizen, his champion.

P. 33, l. 41.—Vala says she emanated from Luvah over the towers of Jerusalem.

P. 34, l. 46.—The daughters of Albion divided Luvah into three bodies.

P. 36, l. 29.—Luvah assumes the South.

P. 41, l. 13.—The first spectre to assimilate with Luvah in Albion's mountains was Bath.

P. 43, l. 2.—Luvah, pitying and weeping.

P. 47, l. 3.—Luvah came forth from Albion's loins in fibrous veins.

L. 13.—Luvah mingles with sons of Albion,—victim and punisher,—cries are heard.

P. 49, l. 68.—Luvah is named Satan, because he has entered that state.

P. 54, l. 11.—Albion broods revenge, seeing Luvah assimilate with his sons, bound in bonds of spiritual hate from which springs sexual love as iron chains.

P. 58.—Albion's spectre is death. Luvah's, generation. Their mingling is Hermaphroditic. Death is masculine. Generation feminine. Los creates generation from death.

P. 59, l. 12.—Luvah is a chaotic universe to the East.

L. 15.—When Luvah assumed the South, all the Zoas fell to the centre.

P. 60, l. 2.—Albion's spectre, who is Luvah, terrified Los, while still unformed, and merely bloody veins.

P. 62, l. 20.—Jesus said, Luvah and Vala must be created, and not left in the gnawing grave.

P. 65, l. 3.—Los will attempt to decide two worlds for Salvation, Mercy, and Justice, and to cast Luvah into the Justice or wrath, and Albion into the Mercy, or pity.

L. 9.—In the depths of Albion's bosom, the Eastern heaven, the death of Luvah is voted. A death of six thousand years, bound round with vegetation. So he is nailed to Albion's tree in Bath.

L. 29.—The song, addressed to Vala, sung by Albion's sons round Luvah's stone of trial.

L. 74.—While they rejoice over Luvah and Vala their victim, the sons of Albion, suddenly become what they behold.

L. 78.—They turn their iron necks towards Luvah.

P. 66, l. 15.—Luvah is France, the victim of the sons of Albion.

P. 73, l. 22.—Where Luvah's world of opaqueness grew to a period it became a limit called Satan, rocky, formless. Here Los, as one of the Elohim, opened his furnaces.

P. 74.—Luvah in list of Zoas, and equivalent names.

P. 75, l. 26.—The Twenty-seven Heavens are formed by Los within the Mundane Shell to bring the prisoners of death, Luvah and Albion, into life eternal.

P. 80, l. 17.—Vala says Luvah ordered her to murder Albion in unreviving death. But Albion conquered Luvah and slew him.

L. 22.—Luvah had prepared the knife and given it to Vala.

L. 29.—When Luvah was slain, Vala embalmed Albion's body in moral laws, for their spectres being mingled, what happened to one happened to the other. The fear was lest Albion's spectre should arise and murder Luvah in unreviving death. Her moral laws are odours of jealous stupefaction. She prays that the Lamb of God may come to her in Luvah's tents, and not seek to revive her embalmed dead.

L. 82.—In Luvah's wine-press cups of silver are filled with the groans and sobs that are the win of lovers.

P. 82, l. 83.—In this wine-press the Worm is formed into a form of love.

P. 83, l. 11.—A form for Luvah and a form for Vala is determined by Hants, Devon and Wilts, on the Thames—a form of vegetation nailed to the tree of Mystery.

P. 90, l. 17.—The twelve sons of Albion drank and imbibed the Life and eternal form of Luvah.

L. 26.—Hand, in cruel pride, commingling with Luvah, cut Reuben from Surrey.

L. 43.—The sons, commingling with Luvah, become one great Satan.

P. 95, l. 17.—Albion, regenerated and arisen, compelled Luvah to his loom.

P. 96, l. 41.—Luvah, with other Zoas, arose into Albion's bosom.

P. 97, l. 9.—Luvah stretched his hand to the East and took a silver bow, to shoot the arrows of love.

LUVAH IN "MILTON."

P. 11, l. 8.—Leutha and Satan are together the spectre of Luvah. (Leutha is a portion of Vala, that which Satan hid.) ("Vala" VIII. 248. In Night VIII. also the myth of the Bard's song in Milton is explained—from l. 376, onwards.)

P. 17, l. 17.—Luvah's place is in the East.

L. 19.—All fell when he assumed the South.

P. 19, l. 20.—Luvah's Bulls each morning drag the sulphur sun out of the deep.

P. 24, l. 2.—Luvah laid the foundation of Los' wine-press. Urizen finished it.

L. 3.—Luvah's sons tread the grapes. They are red. ("Vala" IX. 738.) The wine-press is war. The human forms of insects dance round it.

L. 35.—The joys of Luvah's daughters are cruel.

L. 41.—His songs lure youth to death.

P. 25, l. 1.—His sons shout at the wine-press as Los descended.

P. 34, l. 37.—Luvah was in the East.

L. 38.—When he assumed the South all fell to the centre.

P. 35, l. 59.—Luvah slept by the lark's nest, and here is his empty tomb.

P. 37, l. 45.—The covering cherub, or Twenty-seven heavens, is the spectre of Albion which the spectre of Luvah inhabits, and is the Newtonian Voids between the Atoms.

THARMAS IN "VALA."

NIGHT I.

L. 20.—Begin with Tharmas, parent power, darkening in the West.

L. 21.—He cries out to Enion that his emanations are lost (as he darkens), and he and they are victims to the living. (Compare "Jerusalem," p. 43, l. 3.) Enitharmon is in his bosom. He pities but does not love her. He will build Enion a labyrinth.

L. 30.—Enion says that love is lost (as his emanations); terror and duty are left. She wishes to be hid. She has seen sin in his secret soul.

L. 40.—Trembling and pale, sat Tharmas, weeping into his cloud. He confesses his sins. He cannot look on them or he will kill himself in despair.

L. 58.—Enion drew the spectre forth from Tharmas in her loom.

L. 70.—For three days and nights, rearing up his form on the rocks, he was exalted in pride. He found Enion hidden in a cave.

L. 78.—She did not know what she was, being separate now, and called to him.

L. 82.—She having waited for three days, on the seventh the spectre stood before her manifest. He scorned, but loved her.

L. 86.—He threatened to smite her with his tongue.

L. 98.—She says that he, the spectre, is the wrath of Tharmas embodied with deceit.

L. 106.—She wove him a tabernacle of delight. He groaned. Then stretching forth his hand, turned round the circle of Destiny, and bid her return when the day of clouds was over.

L. 111.—So saying he sank down in the sea, a pale, white corpse, his spectre issuing from his feet in flames.

L. 134.—She finds that his emanations were her children's souls, and that in weaving him into her loom she has murdered them.   She hardly knows him.

L. 141.—The spectre said she had sinfully darkened his world, and now he will hold her with jealousy, a prisoner.

L. 147.—They contended in his caves.

L. 149.—They mingled and became half woman, half serpent.

L. 159.—Presently she brought forth two infants ; Los and Enitharmon.

L. 209.—The daughters of Beulah give a form of vegetation to spectres, but the spectre of Tharmas is Eternal Death.   They pray for help, and close the gate of the tongue.

L. 456.—The clouds of Tharmas and Urthona can, even in the zenith, enclose half the tents of men.

L. 484.—Tharmas, pitying, took in a portion of Los's life that fled from his bosom in fear.   It is Enitharmon.   Enion murdered her and hid her in her bosom.   (Enitharmon was vegetated, and born to be the mortal wife of Los ; his emanation yet his wife till the sleep of death is passed.)

L. 500.—All the Zoas fell.

NIGHT II.

L. 248.—Many a window from the Mundane Shell looked into the world of Tharmas.

L. 315.—Memory wishes to repose among the flocks of Tharmas.

NIGHT III.

L. 161.—Tharmas reared up his hands from amidst the ruins of fallen Luvah —Urizen.   He cried, "Fury in my limbs!" &c.

L. 169.—He declares himself a fool to have lost his sweetest bliss, and calls for Enion.

L. 176.—But, the bonds of Destiny being broken, he began to hate Enion, who laments, as Ahania did when Urizen had cast her out.

L. 195.—Tharmas, looking on her, becomes what he beholds, and her grief is added to his rage.   His love and hope are ended.   She vanishes.

NIGHT IV.

L. 1.—Tharmas rode on the dark abyss, from which Los and Enitharmon emerged.   He yearned over them.

L. 7.—He asked Enion why he felt such love.

L. 25.—Having cursed Urizen and Luvah, he bids Los rebuild the universe beneath his power.

L. 33.—Los refused with indignation.   He claims to be all-powerful.

L. 43.—Doubting stood Tharmas.

L. 55.—Presently he took her away in a broad wave far West, embalming her bleeding wound.   Los howled at the separation.   He fell on the shore, a Spectre of Urthona, jealous of Enitharmon.

L. 78.—The Spectre tells that Tharmas once fled from the battle like the raven of dawn.

L. 106.—He tells that he beheld Tharmas rotting on the rocks and protected him, a ghastly corpse, from the vultures.

L. 110.—Tharmas recognizes him.   They had been friends before Urizen and Luvah changed.   He returns Enitharmon to Los, or rather to the Spectre, and bids him take her for reward and bind the real useful Los, lest he rise again from death (his fall was death).

L. 128.—The spectre seeing Enitharmon dying at his feet, Tharmas stood before Los and said, "Now all comes into the power of Tharmas."

L. 135.—He says that the eternal form of Los shall never renew. "My uncertain prevails against thee." He bids Los rebuild the furnaces, choose life and not struggle against him.

L. 156.—So saying, Tharmas removed his waters all away from Los, who in the void beheld the ruins of Urizen, rebuilt his furnaces, and bound Urizen's changes.

NIGHT V.

L. 76.—Los built Golgonooza on the lake of Udan Adan, and built Laban on the Limit of translucence. Tharmas laid the foundation stone. Los finished it in howling woe.

L. 107.—The fires of Orc warred with the waves of Tharmas and the snows of Urizen.

NIGHT VI.

L. 43.—That the daughters of Luvah may curse Tharmas, and Los his adopted son, Urizen resolves to give them conceit, repentance, and obstinacy, as cords, whips, and food. So said Urizen, cursing his own and Luvah's daughters.

L. 47.—Tharmas heard screams and the curse, and came riding furious, but his waves were frozen.

L. 54.—Urizen, who had frozen his waves, stole over them. Tharmas fled from him, but fought, flying.

L. 63.—He suggested to Urizen that Urizen should withhold all light from him while he withheld all food from Urizen, so that they might both die.

L. 77.—Urizen silently passed him, making his way towards Urthona's world.

L. 261.—Northwards was Urthona's throne, black, solid. The East, into which Urizen fell, was void, but Tharmas rolled his waves in ceaseless eddies through the caverns of fire, air, and earth, seeking in vain for Enion's limbs.

L. 270.—But in Eternal Times Tharmas is in the West.

L. 292.—Tharmas stayed his flight beside the Spectre of Urthona.

NIGHT VII.

L. 1.—Then Urizen arose, the Spectre fled and Tharmas fled.

L. 272.—The Spectre recalls eternal times with Tharmas mild.

L. 476.—Orc revived in his younger brothers (the unvegetated sons) whom Los loved. Los refused to vegetate them (to sacrifice their infant limbs) for Enitharmon's smiles prevailed over self-protection. (Their children were a source of danger to them.)

L. 480.—This produced hopes of Enion's return in Tharmas.

L. 711.—The shadowy female, who is the form of life, strove to stay Tharmas in his flight that Urizen might live. Tharmas said, "Art thou Enion? Is the shadow of hope returned?"

L. 714.—She answered that she was Vala.

L. 716.—Tharmas told of his old happy life with Enion, his garden, whom he watered.

L. 741.—He tells Vala that her sins have lost him heaven and bliss, that, she is his curse, and that till he can bring love into the light he never will depart from his great wrath.

NIGHT VIII.

L. 33.—Los received the vegetating dead from out of the war of Urizen and Tharmas.

L. 51.—They descended from this war and from the shadowy female clouds.

L. 430.—When Urizen had become a dragon he saw Tharmas with envy.

L. 460.—But Tharmas and Urthona felt the stony stupor rise into their limits. Tharmas became like a rolling pillar of sand.

L. 470.—Tharmas gave his power to Los.

L. 478.—Orc having bound all living things by means of the nameless shadowy female, Tharmas rode furious through the afflicted worlds, seeking for Enion.

NIGHT IX.

L. 183.—Urizen no longer curbs the rage of Tharmas.

L. 479.—The regenerate Vala having bathed in a river, her eyes were opened to the world of waters, and she saw Tharmas sitting on the rocks.

L. 480.—He stroked the water from his beard, said he had calmed his rage, and prayed for Enion.

L. 493.—Vala, in pity, called for Enion for him.

L. 502.—Presently, returned to her house, she saw two little children under the trees, and knew that they were Tharmas and Enion.

L. 548.—They stayed in eternal childhood among Vala's flocks.

L. 551.—They are the shadows of Tharmas and Enion in Vala's world.

L. 589.—Enion arose in the morning, after a whirlwind had risen from the centre, with a shriek and a rattling of bones.

L. 608.—Joy thrilled through the form Tharmas, humanizing. Mild he embraced her whom he sought.

L. 649.—The time of harvest came. Tharmas took the winnowing fan.

L. 651.—The nations were tossed like chaff into his sea.

L. 679.—Whilst the flail of Urizen and the fan of Tharmas sound loud, all the slaves in the world sing a new song.

L. 768.—The Eternal Man bid Tharmas and Urthona arise from the feast.

L. 770.—Urthona, limping from his fall, on Tharmas leaned. Tharmas took his shepherd's crook.

L. 780.—Tharmas went down to the wine-press and beheld the sons and daughters of Luvah quite exhausted.

L. 786.—The sons of Tharmas and Urthona put Luvah on the ground for dying.

L. 804.—Tharmas takes the storms in his hands and turns the whirlwinds loose on the mills of Urthona. Stern philosophy and bitter knowledge come as bread from the corn of those mills.

L. 816.—Tharmas sifts the corn.

L. 832.—When the sun left his blackness and found a fresher morning, Tharmas brought his flocks upon the hills and in the vales around the Eternal Man's bright tent. The little children play among the flocks.

THARMAS IN "JERUSALEM."

P. 14, l. 4.—Tharmas the vegetated tongue,—even the devouring tongue. A threefold region: a false brain, a false heart, and false bowels, altogether composing the false tongue, beneath Beulah as a watery flame revolving every way, and as dark roots and stems, a forest of affliction growing, in seas of sorrow.

P. 43, l. 3.—Tharmas indolent and sullen.

When America was closed, Tharmas was dashed on the rocks of the Victims in Mexico.

P. 59, l. 12.—Tharmas is a chaotic Universe to the West.

P. 63, l. 5.—Luvah slew Tharmas, Angel of the Tongue.

P. 74, l. 4.—Tharmas corresponds to Theotormon.

P. 83, l. 5.—Los calls on Enion and Tharmas not to absorb him in dire grief.

P. 95, l. 16.—Tharmas is "compelled to his sheepfold" by the Regenerate Albion.

P. 96, l. 41.—He arose into Albion's bosom.

P. 97, l. 10.—Westward he took a bow of brass.

THARMAS IN "MILTON."

P. 3, l. 10.—Jesus became the prey of Tharmas as False Tongue. (Compare Theotormon in Asia, giving the Gospel of sorrow, and Albion worshipping a watery vision—the mixture of Tharmas, Urizen, and Luvah—in "Jerusalem" and "Vala.")

P. 17, l. 17.—Tharmas is a chaotic universe to the West.

P. 23, l. 48.—Tharmas founded Bowlahoola, named Law by mortals,—before Laban in the City of Golgonooza, named Art and Manufacture, because of Satan. Here Los's anvils stand, and his furnaces rage. Bowlahoola is the stomach in every individual man.

P. 34, l. 37.—Tharmas, to the west, an intersecting globe.

P. 42, l. 6.—Ololon beholds Tharmas.

URTHONA AND LOS IN "VALA."

NIGHT I.

L. 11.—Los was the fourth immortal starry one,—Urthona was his name.

L. 159.—Los and Enitharmon born of Enion and Tharmas as two little infants.

L. 213.—They lived nine times and wandered nine spaces.

L. 217.—Alternate love and hate, his breast; hers, scorn and jealousy.

L. 225.—They wandered in the world of Tharmas.

L. 237.—Enitharmon sings a song of death—or of Vala—to Los. She tells of Albion's fall.

L. 255.—Los smote her on the earth.

L. 257.—He will not die, though she sings her song of death. He tells of Albion also, and of redemption.

L. 281.—She called for Urizen to descend and help her.

L. 286.—Night darkened as she spoke.

L. 290.—The wandering man bow'd his faint head as Urizen descended.

L. 293.—Urizen said gloomily, " Now I am God from Eternity to Eternity."

L. 294.—Los sat sullen, plotting revenge.

L. 298.—Urizen gave Luvah, the murderer, into the hands of Los, bidding him not pity Vala, and take the stars for servants if he would obey.

L. 305.—Los will not obey, but with contrary acts will strive for mastery.

L. 315.—Urizen having repeated his claim to authority ended by telling Los that all of Man but his Spectre is delusion and fancy.

L. 323.—Los saw the wound of his blow. He wept. He embraced Enitharmon to heal the wound.

L. 327.—They eat the fleshy bread, they drank the nervous wine. They forsook Luvah and Vala, leaving them on high, in jealousy.

L. 335.—They saw the Incarnation.

L. 346.—Los and Enitharmon sat in discontent and scorn. Their nuptial song follows.

L. 478.—Urthona stood by his anvil with a mass of iron prepared for spades and coulters,—a portion of his life divided. Tharmas took her in. His spectre fled to Enion, and his body fell endlong a raging serpent.

NIGHT II.

L. 207.—Los joyed and Enitharmon laughed at the woes of Urizen and Luvah, and Vala and Ahania. They went down to see them.

L. 277.—They were driven down by their desires to plant divisions in the soul of Urizen and Ahania.

L. 286.—Los and Enitharmon walked forth on the dewy earth.

L. 293.—Los said the lily and rose, and all the garden mock at him for his solitude. Enitharmon refuses him.

L. 306.—She answers that she is secure now from his smitings.

L. 310.—Los says that he fades, dissolved in raptured trance.

L. 318.—Enitharmon says that he winds his arms round Ahania's image. She says Urizen calls her. She vanishes, leaving a corpse in the arms of Los.

L. 327.—Los says that he will, in jealousy and revenge, enter the bosom of Urizen, so that she shall still be in his arms.

L. 330.—Los languished and fell dead.

L. 333.—Enitharmon, returning, sang and revived him to life.

L. 335.—Enitharmon's song.

L. 375.—Thus Los lived, driving Enion far away that he might draw Ahania's spirit into her vortex.

NIGHT III.

L. 20.—Vala shall become a worm in Enitharmon's womb.

L. 22.—Luvah in the loins of Los shall be a dark and furious death.

NIGHT IV.

L. 2.—Tharmas saw Los and Enitharmon emerge from the abyss.

L. 25.—Tharmas bids Los rebuild the universe of death and decay, and Enitharmon to weave soft delusive forms of man for his comfort.

L. 33.—Los answered in furious pride. He refuses to obey.

L. 40.—He claims to be now God over all. He was Urthona, keeper of the gates of Heaven, but now is all-powerful Los, and Urthona is but his shadow.

L. 46.—Tharmas hesitated whether he should destroy Los.

L. 47.—Los stood in scorn, sparks issuing from his hair. Enitharmon shrieked out that her world (built by Urizen) might be saved.

L. 55.—Tharmas, in a cold wane, raped Enitharmon away from Los.

L. 59.—The fibres where she joined to his side were rent.

L. 64.—He, having fallen on rocks, became a blue and leaden spectre.

L. 75.—It was the spectre of Urthona. He saw Enitharmon and writhed.

L. 78.—He spoke to Tharmas of olden days and told of the birth of Enitharmon as globe of blood from his side.

L. 103.—As Urthona he issued from the nostrils of Enion.

L. 110.—Tharmas bids the shadow bind the fallen Los and take Enitharmon for his reward.

L. 123.- Groaning the Terror (the spectre of Urthona, the shadow) rose and drove his rocks on the tide till a world rose, dark, dreadful, and Enitharmon lay at his feet.

L. 126.—The dolorous shadow joyed.

L. 156.—Tharmas, having uttered a claim to be God over all, departed with his waters, and left a void round Los.

L. 160.—Los beheld the ruins of Urizen beneath, a horrible chaos of whirling rocks.

L. 164.—Then he seized on the round furnaces of Urizen and built them anew.

L. 198.—Then followed the binding of Urizen, as in " Book of Urizen."

L. 264.—The corse of Man lay on the rock. (This is Urizen after binding.) The sea of Time and Space (or Los and Enitharmon) beat round. Man's limbs vegetated as a polypus.

L. 275.—The limits having been found, Los felt the limit and saw the finger of God touch his seventh furnace.

L. 279.—In terror Los shrank from his task. He beheld Urizen, and became what he beheld.

NIGHT V.

L. 1.—Infected, mad, Los danced on his mountains high.

L. 4.—Beside his anvil he danced with the hammer of Urthona.

L. 5.—Enitharmon's limbs froze on the earth.

L. 14.—They shrunk as far as zenith from Nadir.

L. 16.—They left Urizen bound in chains of Intellect among the furnaces.

L. 37.—Enitharmon groaned till Orc was born.

L. 42.—Then Luvah, King of Love, became King of Rage and Death.

L. 66.—The demons sang round Orc and Enitharmon. Los seized Orc and took him down into the deeps.

L. 70.—Enitharmon nursed him in darkness.

L. 75.—And Los, now fearing eternal death and extinction, built Golgonooza.

L. 80.—Los saw Orc, now fourteen years old, embracing Enitharmon and plotting his death.

L. 83.—The girdle grew round his breast again and again, till it became the chain of jealousy.

L. 103.—With this chain obdurate Los bound down his loved joy.

L. 110.—Los folded Enitharmon in a cold cloud.

L. 112.—He saw the spectre change over Orc, concentred into love of parent, storgeous appetite, craving.

L. 114.—Orc described at length.

L. 143.—When Los and Enitharmon returned to Golgonooza they repented that they had bound Orc.

L. 149.—Starting at midnight they travelled nine days through Entuthon Benython.

L. 155.—But when they came to the rock they found Orc rooted there.

L. 172.—They could not release him, and fell fainting at his side.

L. 173.—Urthona's spectre revived them, rubbing their temples with herbs of the pit.

L. 176.—On the way home Vala began to re-animate in Enitharmon's breasts, whose gates broke.

NIGHT VI.

L. 78.—Urizen, wandering, went towards the world of Urthona.

L. 82.—To create a world for Los he mingled howlings and horrors of mountain and abyss (desires and thoughts of nature).

L. 83.—Los brooded with delight on the darkness, nor saw Urizen's globe of fire.

L. 270.—In eternal times Urthona is in the North.

L. 280.—From Urthona's peaked rock, Urizen saw the world of Los.

L. 287.—The shadow of Urthona, in scales of iron, stopped his way.

L. 304.—Four sons of Urizen, arriving from the cliffs of Urthona, led Urthona's squadrons. Urizen fled from them.

L. 314.—They weave a dire web, and prepare Urthona's path before him.

NIGHT VII.

L. 2.—When Urizen and Tharmas fled, the spectre fled and hid beneath a rock.

L. 166.—Urizen having long striven with Orc, cold against heat, at last gave him a serpent form, nor knew the dread result. Then Los sat in showers of Urizen watching cold Enitharmon.

L. 167.—His broodings rushing down produce eggs which burst forth in the winds of the tree of Mystery. Urizen traced his verses, and the shadow of Enitharmon, who lay on the knees of Los, was drawn down to the roots of the tree and wept o'er Orc.

L. 180.—Presently Los, looking on her till he felt her pale disease, lamented jealously.

L. 207.—Enitharmon did not hear him. Her shadow still descended down the tree.

L. 215.—The spectre of Urthona saw it.

L. 220.—He wooed Enitharmon.

L. 228.—The shadow of Enitharmon told him secrets of Eternity unheard before.

L. 265.—The spectre answers, doing the same.

L. 306.—He ends by telling her that he is the spectre of the living.

L. 309.—She wept, and embraced her once loved lord, now but a shade, herself also a shade.

L. 323.—The shadow of Enitharmon, having burst the gates of her heart, brought forth Orc.

L. 332.—The spectre, having given her charge over, Orc entered the bosom of Los.

L. 335.—Los first embraced the spectre as a brother. (Compare " Milton.")

L. 365.—The spectre having conferred with Los and convinced him that he was not a brother but his real self, Los resolved to quell his fury and teach peace to revenge and repentance to cruelty.

L. 373.—Los and the spectre built Golgonooza.

L. 389.—Enitharmon having eaten of the fruit of the tree of Mystery and learned that life lived on death, made Los eat of the same fruit.

L. 390.—He did so, and sat down in despair.

L. 450.—After much further conference they agree to create forms to be ransoms for their souls, and do so.

L. 470.—They had new children ; first Rintrah and Palamabron, in whom Orc revived.

L. 476.—Los loved them, and refused to sacrifice their infant limbs to self-preservation.

L. 490.—He even beheld Urizen, as an infant breathed from Enitharmon, and not as his enemy.

· L. 495.—But Urizen attempted to gain universal dominion.

L. 527.—Therefore Los reared up his mighty stature.

L. 560.—Los was given over to war.

L. 519.—Enitharmon stretched on the earth feared him, and feared that unless he kept light on his watch-tower he would be slain.

L. 610.—Then in the caverns of the grave, the nameless shadowy female who had broken Enitharmon's heart, and who was Vala, stood before Orc.

L. 619.—Orc rolled his flames on the clouds of Urthona.

L. 652.—They vote the death of Luvah, and nail him to the tree.

NIGHT VIII.

L. 20.—Then Los beheld the Divine Vision, through the broken gates of Enitharmon's heart.

L. 29.—Enitharmon sighed forth spectres on the winds of Golgonooza, and Los stood at the gate of pity receiving them.

L. 35.—Enitharmon built the looms of Cathedron in the gate.

L. 55.—And some were woven single, some double, some threefold, in merciful pity and compassion.

L. 179.—Enitharmon wove in tears bodies of the spectres, calling them her beloved sons and daughters.

L. 183.—Los employed the sons in his furnaces.

L. 187.—Until a perfected Universal female form appeared, and they called it Jerusalem the Holy.

L. 255.—Pitying, the Lamb of God descended through Jerusalem's gates to put off Mystery.

L. 275.—Mystery was Vala, created by the synagogue of Satan. She is also Rahab and Tirzah, and the Shadowy Female.

L. 293.—Her song of delight over sufferings of the human form when fastened to the flesh is heard.

L. 317.—The Lamb of God descended through the nether portions of Luvah, bearing this suffering.

L. 320.—They nailed him on the tree of Mystery.

L. 332.—Los took the body down from the cross, weeping.

L. 345.—Los was the shadowy prophet who fell from his station in the eternal bosom and divided a multitude. (Compare Night I. l. 17.)

L. 350.—He repeats to Rahab his generations.

L. 362.—He tells her the story of Satan and Palamabron, as in the book of " Milton."

L. 373.—He explains Satan to her.

L. 403.—He finally bids her set Jerusalem free.

L. 405.—But she departed from him in pride and revenge.

L. 460.—All the Zoas fell into stony stupor. Urthona shot forth a fibrous form.

L. 470.—Urthona gave his strength to Los.

L. 474.—For the Nameless Shadow bound all things in a living death, that mortality might be put off by the Saviour.

L. 575.—Ahania having sung a song of the sorrow of the world and mortality, Los heard and wept.

L. 577.—Los and Enitharmon took the body of the Lamb from the cross and placed it in a sepulchre he had hewn for himself, and Jerusalem wept over the body two thousand years.

NIGHT IX.

L. 1.—And Los and Enitharmon builded Jerusalem, weeping over the sepulchre.

L. 5.—Terrified at Non-Existence, Los tore down the sun and moon, cracking the heavens across. Then the fires of Eternity fell and the dead awoke to judgment.

L. 786.—Then, the Eternal Man having awoke and feasted with the four Zoas, Urthona rose from the feast, as did the others and the four females.

L. 796.—Los, who is Urthona, took the corn out of the stores of Urizen and ground it in his mills.

L. 817.—He made the bread of ages—the bread of knowledge—and took his repose in winter in the night of Time.

L. 834.—His hammer sounds in the deep caves beneath.

L. 843.—He arose in strength, no longer divided from Enitharmon, no longer the spectre of Los. He forms the golden armour of science for intellectual war.

URTHONA AND LOS IN "JERUSALEM."

P. 5, l. 28.—The sons of Albion revolve on the furnaces of Los to destroy them.

L. 49.—Jerusalem is drawn by maternal anguish out of the furnaces of Los.

L. 50.—Los heard her lament. His tears fell. His emanation divided in twain, Eastward toward the wheels (or systems) of Albion's sons (or reasonings), but Westward a black horror.

P. 6, l. 1.—The wheels drive his spectre to divide from his back. It cursed him for his friendship to Albion.

L. 8.—Los raged and stamped the earth, but still his spectre divided and sought to destroy his Human (or imaginative) perfection.

P. 7, l. 9.—The spectre told him that sympathy was a mistake, imagination a delusion, and love a sin. It relates much of the myth in symbolic terms.

L. 51.—Los prophesied, though he was divided. He prayed for help to the Lamb of God.

P. 8, l. 20.—While Los spoke the spectre fell shuddering before him.

L. 30.—Los said that the spectre was his own pride and self-righteousness.

P. 9, l. 32.—He bid the spectre arise and work with him at the furnaces.

P. 10, l. 17.—Los to resist the evil actions of the Reasoning power on the mind stands in London building Golzonooza (the City of Art).

L. 20.—Los must create a system or be enslaved by another man's.

L. 21.—He will not reason or compare, his business is to create.

L. 32.—He calls his spectre "Spectre of Urthona," and forbids it to destroy his children.

L. 61.—The spectre having rebuked Los and pitied himself for his mortality, Los wipes his tears, and compels him to work, but can give him no comfort.

P. 11, l. 11.—All the children of Los came forth from the furnaces in the spaces of Erin for Jerusalem's sake.

L. 13.—They wept with joy together, but Los was built in from Eternity in Albion's cliffs.

P. 12, l. 5.—Los beholds Albion dead and his own emanation dividing.

L. 13.—He sees the reason of the creation of this world of mortality, giving a body to falsehood that it may be cut off for ever.

L. 24.—And Los and his sons built Golgonooza.

L. 44.—While Jerusalem wanders outside his gates among the dark Satanic wheels.

L. 45.—The fourfold divisions of the sons of Los and of Golgonooza.

P. 13, l. 25.—In the midst of the city is Laban, and a moat of fire surrounds Laban, Los's palace and Cathedron's looms.

L. 55.—Los walks round the walls night and day.

P. 14, l. 9.—Los views not only the Zoas but the four females.

L. 13.—Enitharmon is the vegetated mortal wife of Los ; his emanation, yet his wife till the sleep of death is past.

L. 16.—Los beheld his translucent sons and daughters and the four points.

L. 32.—And he beheld Jerusalem.

P. 15, l. 21.—Blake sees in deadly fear Los in London raging round his anvil, forming an axe of gold, cutting the fibres of Albion's sons from his hills that they may roll apart over the nations.

L. 34.—Albion sat on a rock in the valley of Hinnom among the furnaces of Los.

P. 16, l. 28.—Here Los fixed down the counties of England, Scotland, Wales, and Ireland.

L. 60.—Entuthon's halls were builded by Los and his children.

L. 62.—All things on earth are seen in the bright sculptures of Los's halls.

P. 17, l. 1.—The spectre divides and Los compels it to divide, to follow the daughters of Albion as the hound follows the scent.

L. 6.—But Los bends his fury against Albion's sons.

L. 10.—The daughters woo Los. He shows them his spectre. They flee.

L. 16.—Los compels his spectre to work lest it should devour Enitharmon.

L. 48.—Los having explained to himself the philosophy of love, negation, and organization, Enitharmon heard and was comforted but still divided.

L. 55.—The trembling globe shot forth self-living and Los howled over it.

L. 59.—He sent his spectre to Schofield.

P. 19, l. 33.—Los was roofed in from Eternity in Albion's cliffs.

L. 38.—Los, the strong guard of Albion, walked round beneath the moon.

P. 30, l. 1.—The story of Albion, Vala, and Jerusalem having been continued up to the incident of Albion and Luvah's attempt to gain dominion over him; the two who perceive this and bring an account of it are here said to be the emanation of Los and his spectre.

L. 4.—The spectre here is named Urthona.

P. 11.—The sons of Eden praise Urthona's spectre in songs, because he kept the Divine vision in time of trouble.

L. 16.—The two wept and trembled, and Los put out his hand and took them into his bosom.

L. 18.—Albion shrunk from Los's bosom, rending the fibres of brotherhood, and in feminine allegories enclosing Los.

L. 19.—But the Divine vision appeared with Los, following Albion into his central void among his oaks.

L. 20.—Los prayed.

L. 40.—And the end of his prayer was that the Veil might be rent.

P. 31, l. 3.—Albion having covered his Western heaven with clouds, Los took a globe of fire and searched his interiors. He sought to persuade Albion not to take vengeance.

L. 43.—At length, on London stone, Los sat, and heard Jerusalem's voice.

L. 50.—And Vala.

P. 32, l. 3.—Los trembled, and was astonished at the vision of Albion with his points reversed inwards.

L. 6.—He saw his furnaces in ruins. Los is the Demon of the Furnaces.

P. 33, l. 17.—The contentions of Vala and Albion are continued. Los heard them. He opened his furnaces before Vala.

L. 24.—He heard the shriek of childbirth, and prophesies with regard to the sexes.

L 41.—He spoke, standing on Mame Tor.

L. 51.—He bids man, as a worm of sixty winters, consider sexual organization and hide himself in the dust.

P. 35, l. 9.—Los prophecies of death and salvation, and the delivery of individuals from the blame of states.

L. 17.—He speaks from the furnaces, descending into Non-Entity.

P. 36, l. 3.—Sixty winters Los raged in the divisions of Reuben.

L. 11.—Reuben stood before Los's furnaces in a horrible dreamful slumber.

L. 21.—Jerusalem trembled, seeing her children driven by Los's hammer in visions of Beulah on the edge of Non-Entity.

L. 40.—The sea poured in amain upon the sons of Albion as Los bended the senses of Reuben.

P. 37, l. 1.—Los felt his spectre arising, and called to Albion to arouse himself.

P. 38, l. 55.—The gate of Los is described.

P. 39, l. 11.—Albion fled through the gate of Los, going to Eternal death.

L. 7.—The fourth Region of Humanity is named Urthona.

L. 9.—Urthona here is named Los.

L. 12.—Los was the friend of Albion.

L. 25.—The soul of Los was rent. He questioned of atonement.

P. 40, l. 1.—Los shuddered, beholding Albion's disease.

L. 52.—Submitting to be called a son of Los, Winchester devoted himself for Albion.

L. 59.—Los built the stubborn structure of the English language lest Albion should be a dumb despair.

P. 42, l. 2.—Los opened the furnaces before Albion.

L. 5.—Los must have died, but the Divine Vision saved him.

L. 9.—Albion called Los a deceitful friend.

L. 19.—Los answered, "Righteousness and Justice I give thee."

L. 45.—He ended, "Thy selfhood is for ever accursed from the Divine Presence."

L. 46.—So Los spoke, then turned his face and wept for Albion.

L. 55.—Albion having sent Hand and Hyle against Los, he stood at his furnaces awaiting the fury of the Dead, who bid him to build Babylon, city of moral law, not Golgonooza, city of art.

L. 77.—Los drew his seven Furnaces that thundered loud around Albion's cliffs, and as Albion built his frozen altars Los built the Mundane Shell.

L. 81.—This is the Net and Veil of Vala among the souls of the dead.

P. 43, l. 3.—Urthona, doubting and despairing—such was his poisonous wheel.

L. 12.—Then Los grew furious, and said, "Why stand we here trembling around, calling on God for help, and not on ourselves, in whom God dwells?" He then prophesied of art, truth, and demonstration. He asked if they meant to take greater vengeance in their sepulchre. (Compare "Everlasting Gospel.")

P. 44, l. 1.—Having heard Los in paleness, they arose, and bore Albion back through the gate.

L. 31.—Los was named Elijah, the spirit of prophecy, by Albion's friends, who conjured him in the name of the Highest to watch over them till Jesus should appear.

L. 32.—Stricken with Albion's disease, they become what they behold among the furnaces of Los.

P. 46, l. 5.—Lincoln, Durham, Carlisle, Counsellors of Los.

L. 6.—Ely, scribe of Los.

L. 20.—The furnaces of Los rage.

P. 47, l. 2.—Where the Thames shudders, and Los's furnaces stand in Albion's loins, Luvah tore forth.

P. 53, l. 1.—Los, who is the Vehicular Form of Strong Urthona, wept over Albion.

L. 4.—The roots of Albion's tree entered the soul of Los. He sat before his furnaces in sackcloth. The roots in gnawing pain divided him from his Emanation, enclosed all his children time after time, condensing them into Nations, Peoples, and Tongues.

L. 10.—The furnaces, sevenfold, each within the other, are incomprehensible to vegetated mortal eyes and single vision.

L. 12.—The Bellows are the Animal Lungs, the Hammer the Animal Heart.

L. 13.—The Furnaces the Stomach for digestion, terrible their fury, like seven burning heavens ranged from South to North.

L. 15.—Here on the banks of the Thames Los built Golgonooza.

P. 56, l. 1.—Los chaunts a song in the valley of Middlesex, asking what man may be and what woman. He asks what became of that which they have onwoven with such tears and care—the essence of manhood.

L. 26.—It has come as a mere physical appetite at the gates of the body, symbolized always as the dog at the wintry door.

L. 28.—Its likeness was a worm, its feminine dwelling-place a clod.

L. 35.—And Los defies the semblance of ignominy in the masculine impulse, though it has seemingly fallen to be subservient to the powers and the instruments that should be its servants,—or, as in next page, l. 14, the plough has gone over Albion, and mind is buried in sense, the living ploughed in among the dead.

L. 38.—The flesh answers that it cannot live without experience, and that in the perceptions of the senses it looks upon the veil that hides the perceptions of the Imagination of God.

L. 43.—Los utters the great cry of life,—Why has matter a will? Why is there another personality in the universe different from that of mind? Why did Paul create a female will? Paul is equivalent to Urizen in the quaternary Paul, Constantine, Charlemagne, Luther. His creation of a female will is equivalent for Urizen giving the horses of light to Luvah.

P. 58, l. 16.—Los fixes the mental spectrous male and female as Rational Philosophy and Mathematic Demonstration (male), and Pleasure and Affection (female), that they may war on one another; for the commingling of Albion's and Luvah's spectre was Hermaphroditic.

L. 31.—Hyle and Schofield, the worm in the infant, motherhood ("I have said to the worm, 'Thou art my mother'"), and the passionate egotistic natural love in man (Schofield is bound in iron armour) arch over the moon, the feminine place of tender dreams. Los fixes them there.

P. 58, l. 42.—Six nations, pillars of Los's halls. Britain his forge. America, North and South, his bath of living waters. The Veil having begun to vegetate, Los formed gates between weeping and suffering, so that presently the veil became the Mundane Shell, place of Redemption and of awakening again into eternity.

L. 11.—Urthona, to the North, a Universe that remained chaotic.

L. 21.—When all fell towards the centre, in the midst of the ruins was the universe of Los and Enitharmon.

L. 22.—Cathedron's looms are in the West of the North; Los's furnaces in the South of the North.

L. 26.—The daughters of Los work sorrowing at the looms.

P. 60, l. 2.—Los sits terrified, beholding Albion's spectre, who is Luvah.

P. 62, l. 35.—Los beheld the Divine Vision among the furnaces. But he wept, and often despaired, because the Vision was closed in clouds, and his emanation and his children parted from him.

P. 63, l. 4.—Urthona's name mentioned as one of the four Cherubim of Albion.

L. 26.—Los tells the literalist—the "stupid druid"—that unless a body that is chaste can be woven over an unchaste mind, the body, called "the female," cannot be chaste. Forgiveness of sin is therefore necessary.

L. 31.—When, he cries, will Jehovah give us victims from his flocks and herds ; when shall the lower states of mind be sacrificed rather than the higher be forbidden, and art enslaved because there is evil elsewhere?

L. 35.—Los did not always know what was done, in what region of vision to place his prophecy. The fragmentary nature of the page and the apparent loss of a paragraph makes this passage, though clear in meaning, obscure in the question what is its reference,—what murder is spoken of.

P. 64, l. 6.—Los perceived all the daughters of Albion as one,—Vala.

L. 17.—Wherefore art thou living, cried Los, and man cannot live in thy presence?

P. 66, l. 16.—Los beholds in terror the sacrifices of the daughters of Albion's victims.

P. 69, l. 6.—The Polypus, the cancer, of roots of reasoning, doubt, despair and death, an enormous form at variance with itself stood envying. It is driven out by Los time after time from Albion's cliffs.

L. 30.—No one can consummate bliss in Los's world without becoming a generated mortal, a vegetating death.

P. 71, l. 55.—But now Albion is darkened and Jerusalem lies in ruins, above the mountains of Albion, above the head of Los.

L. 56.—Los shouted with ceaseless shoutings for aid Divine, but did not speak to Albion, lest Albion should turn his back on the Divine Vision.

L. 63.—The children of Los wept round him seven days of eternity.

P. 72, l. 8.—Los, for Jerusalem's sake, turned the four gates of Albion over the twelve, four-square, and called them the gates of Jerusalem.

L. 12.—Four sons, Rintrah and Palamabron and Theotormon and Bromion, remained with Los to guard the four walls of Jerusalem.

L. 45.—The four gates of Los surround the universe,—they are described.

P. 73, l. 2 —Los's furnaces howl loud, self-moving, lamenting.

L. 24.—Los, who is of the Elohim, fixes the sexual.

L. 32.—He demolishes Natural Religion's holiness time after time.

L. 44.—The spectres of the dead howl round the porches of Los.

P. 74, l. 4.—Urthona's name given in its place as last of the quaternary.

L. 29.—Hyle roofed Los in Albion's cliffs by the affections rent asunder and opposed to thought.

P. 75, l. 7.—Los in six thousand years walks up and down continually, that not one moment of time be lost, and every revolution of space he makes permanent in Bowlahoola and Cathedron.

L. 23.—The Twenty-seven Heavens are formed by Los within the Mundane Shell.

P. 78, l. 3.—Los walks round breaking the rocky spectres with his hammer.

L. 10.—He laments, viewing Jerusalem in sackcloth.

P. 80, l. 41.—Los saw, terrified, the spindle in Vala's hand turning as she sang, with blood and fire, and the cloud of Rahab vibrating with the daughters of Albion.

P. 82, l. 22.—Guendolen tells what she heard Enitharmon say to Los.

L. 55.—Los sees the envious blight of Cambel envying Guendolen above his seventh furnace.

L. 62.—She laboured to form the mighty form of Hand according to her will in Los's furnace.

L. 72.—Guendolen, also in the eddying wind of Los's bellows, began her dolorous task of love.

L. 77.—They began to give their souls away in the furnaces of affliction.

L. 78.—Los saw and was comforted.

L. 79.—He said, " I know I am Urthona, keeper of the Gates of Heaven."

P. 83, l. 66.—Los, having spoken at great length to Albion and to the daughters of Beulah, saw his emanation, a faint rainbow before him waving in the awful gloom of London.

L. 75.—Then he arose from his watch, put on his golden sandals, and went down from Golgonooza, and heard the voice of Albion's daughters on Euphrates, that is, on Thames.

P. 84, l. 6.—The furnaces of Los are built where Jerusalem lies in ruins.

L. 22.—The daughters call to Los to help to divide them from the terrors of the sons.

P. 85, l. 3.—Los smiled, and brought Reuben from his wanderings into Canaan, or Divine Analogy.

L. 14.—Los replies upon his watch. All listen.

L. 22.—He sings to Jerusalem, urging her not to build an earthly kingdom in pride, or to dwell with Babylon, but to come forth.

P. 86, l. 33.—As he sings his sons labour in thunders, and his daughters spin fibres of love for Jerusalem.

L. 48.—So dread is Los's fury that none dare approach him without becoming his children in the furnaces of affliction.

L. 50.—Enitharmon, like a faint rainbow, waved before him.

L. 57.—She separated, and stood before him, a female, weeping.

L. 61.—Two wills they had, two intellects, and not as in time of old.

L. 62.—Silent they wandered, hand in hand, like two infants, away from Enion.

P. 87, l. 3.—Los spoke his love to Enitharmon.

L. 12.—She replied that she would do her will, not his, and that he is Albion's victim.

P. 88, l. 1.—Los and Enitharmon dispute on man and woman.

L. 55.—The four Zoas, in all their faded majesty, burst out in fury.

P. 90, l. 28.—Los speaks of the individual and the universal in the spirit of prophecy.

L. 57.—And he demonstrates with the blows of his hammer. He works for Albion against Natural Religion, or the worship of the Maternal Humanity.

P. 91, l. 1.—He tells of forgiveness, of friends and enemies, of general forms and minute particulars.

L. 31.—The spectre builds stupendous forms, repeating the smaragdine table of Hermes to draw Los down.

L. 52.—But Los altered his spectre till he had completely divided him into a separate space.

L. 55.—He upholds wisdom as more important than holiness.

P. 92, l. 7.—Los describes the creation of Albion fourfold.

L. 13.—Enitharmon having lamented that she would vanish at the close of the song, Los tells her that sexes must vanish and cease when Albion arises from his sleep.

P. 95, l. 15.—Albion having arisen, beheld Urthona, mighty, labouring at his anvil in the great spectre Los.

·L. 19.—Therefore the sons of Eden praise Urthona's spectre in songs, because he kept the Divine vision in time of trouble.

P. 96, l. 7.—Albion sees the Divine similitude in the appearance of Los.

L. 22.—He tells Los that he sees him so.

L. 32.—Self was lost in the contemplation of faith and wonder at Los's sublime honour.

L. 41.—Urthona and the other Zoas arose into Albion's bosom.

P. 97, l. 11.—Urthona, Northwards, took a bow of iron.

URTHONA AND LOS IN "MILTON."

P. 3, l. 26.—The hammer of Los creates from Golgonooza three classes of men.

P. 4, l. 20.—The loom of Enitharmon, weaving the web of life out of the ashes of the dead by fibres of soft affections, weaves these three classes.

P. 5, l. 2.—The Classes are the Elect, the Redeemed, the Reprobate.

L. 5.—Satan, of the elect, made tyrannical attempts on Los with endearing love.

L. 7.—He entreated Los to give him Palamabron's station.

L. 11.—Los gave to him the harrow of the Almighty. Palamabron feared to be angry lest Los should believe, not him, but mild Satan.

L. 32.—The horses of the harrow having been maddened, Palamabron, regretting that he had not told Los all his heart, called, and Los and Satan came before him.

L. 36.—Los trembled as Satan, with mild tears, laid on Palamabron the blame of his own faults.

L. 37.—Though he was the Prophet of Eternity, Los almost believed Satan.

L. 42.—He bid each keep his own station thenceforth.

P. 6, l. 7.—Satan having returned to his mills, Los saw the servants drunk with Palamabron's wine and songs.

L. 11.—He took off his left sandal, placing it on his head, in sign of mourning.

L. 16.—He bid each resume his labour, marking that day as a mournful day.

L. 45.—After a great struggle, in which all the four ungenerate sons of Los took part on different sides, Los hid Thulloh (the friend of Satan) from Enitharmon, and then buried him, weeping.

P. 7, l. 12.—Then after Palamabron had argued his case in a great assembly, Los, in his rage, rent up nations, and displaced continents, but closed up Enitharmon from the sight of all these things.

P. 9, l. 3.—He hid her on the Thames.

P. 16, l. 31.—When Los, the Vehicular Terror, saw Milton come, Enitharmon cried out that he would unloose Satan upon Albion.

L. 35.—Therefore Los shot out fibres from his limbs to oppose the journey of Milton.

P. 17, l. 16.—Urthona's Universe among the Zoas is to the North.

L. 25.—In the midst of the four is built the Universe of Los and Enitharmon.

L. 17.—The fires of youth (Orc) were bound in chains by Los and Enitharmon.

P. 18, l. 21.—The spectrous body of Milton redounded from Blake's left foot into Los's mundane space.

L. 49.—Milton, and the Seven eyes of God, pass through Los's three gates, and join the watchers in the Ulro.

L. 51.—Los saw them and wept.

L. 57.—But he recollected a prophecy that Milton should ascend from Felpham, and set free Orc from his chain of jealousy.

P. 19, l. 1.—He started at the thought, and went down into Udan Adan.

L. 35.—Los heard the multitude of Ololon lamenting that they had driven Milton down into the Ulro. He heard them call the Divine family in prayer. He saw the cloud of Milton over Europe.

P. 20, l. 4.—While Los heard, and while Blake bound the world on his foot to walk through Eternity, Los descended behind him, kissed him, wished him health, bound on the same sandal, and became one man with him.

L. 15.—Thus Blake became the Shadowy Prophet, who (as told in "Vala," VIII., 345) six thousand years ago fell from his station, and now returns.

L. 16.—So spoke Los.

P. 22, l. 31.—And having met Rintrah and Palamabron and conferred with them, explained that he had embraced and become one with Milton, the "falling death," and man lives not by wrath but by mercy.

P. 22, l. 44.—But when Los had spoken at length to them, Rintrah and Palamabron left him unconvinced. They saw that wrath now swayed him, and now pity absorbed him. So it would always be.

L. 51.—Los's anvils stand in Bowlahoola—explanations and other symbols are given.

L. 68.—Los is by mortals named Time; Enitharmon is named Space.

L. 74.—All the gods of the kingdoms of earth labour in Los's halls.

L. 75.—Everyone is a fallen son of the Spirit of Prophecy.

L. 76.—He is the fourth Zoa that stood around the throne Divine.

P. 24, l. 1.—The wine-press of Los (or Luvah and Urizen) is Eastward; its description and explanation as in "Vala," IX., 730.

P. 25, l. 16.—Los refused to allow righteousness to be preached and the sinner punished with death till all the earth was harvested.

L. 17.—Los called his fellow labourers to the great vintage and harvest, that in the end they might rush forward to supper of the Lamb and his bride and the awakening of Albion, their ancient friend.

P. 26, l. 1.—The constellations are sons of Los and labourers.

L. 10.—So are the flies, the trees, the brooks, the meadows.

L. 16.—On the right hand of Los wail the souls descending to the body.

L. 17.—Those delivered from the body, on the left hand.

L. 23.—The labours of the sons of Los, and the meaning of the term souls, are there explained. The explanation continues to the end of page 28.

L. 25.—The strife of the elements, or fallen Zoas, is corporeal and not mental as the wars of Eternity. They strive in Los's halls.

P. 34, l. 35.—Urthona's universe is to the North of that of Los.

P. 35, l. 27.—Ololon scanned all the couches of the dead—even of Los and

Enitharmon. The gate of Los where the lark mounts, and the moment that Satan cannot find, are described.

P. 36, l. 21.—When Los joined with Blake he took him to Felpham that he might see all these visions.

P. 37, l. 56.—The Mundane Shell explained. The fires of Los rage in the remotest bottoms of the c´ us so that none can pass otherwise than by descending to Los, to Bowlahoola, Allamanda, and Entuthon Benython.

P. 40, l. 12.—The lake into which the spectre should be cast is that of Los, which even burneth with fire

L. 52.—Los, as the strong guard of Albion, walks round beneath the moon.

P. 42, l. 6.—Los was beheld by Ololon.

P. 44, l. 31.—As the Lark mounted, Los and Enitharmon rose over the hills of Surrey.

L. 34.—Los listens to the cry of the poor man, his cloud low bent over London in anger.

END OF VOL. II.

www.ingramcontent.com/pod-product-compliance
Lightning Source LLC
Chambersburg PA
CBHW032301280326
41932CB00009B/655